Origins of
Individual Differences in Infancy

The Colorado Adoption Project

DEVELOPMENTAL PSYCHOLOGY SERIES

SERIES EDITOR

Harry Beilin

Developmental Psychology Program
City University of New York Graduate School
New York, New York

In Preparation

ROBERT L. LEAHY. *The Development of the Self*

KATHERINE NELSON. *Making Sense: The Acquisition of Shared Meaning*

PIERRE M. VAN HIELE. *Structure and Insight*

Published

ROBERT PLOMIN AND JOHN C. DEFRIES. *Origins of Individual Differences in Infancy: The Colorado Adoption Project*

STEVEN R. YUSSEN. (Editor). *The Growth of Reflection in Children*

ROBBIE CASE. *Intellectual Development: Birth to Adulthood*

J. BARRY GHOLSON AND TED R. L. ROSENTHAL. (Editors). *Applications of Cognitive-Developmental Theory*

ALLEN W. GOTTFRIED. (Editor). *Home Environment and Early Cognitive Development: Longitudinal Research*

EUGENE S. GOLLIN. (Editor). *Malformations of Development: Biological and Psychological Sources and Consequences*

DAVID MAGNUSSON AND VERNON L. ALLEN. (Editors). *Human Development: An Interactional Perspective*

DIANE L. BRIDGEMAN. (Editor). *The Nature of Prosocial Development: Interdisciplinary Theories and Strategies*

ROBERT L. LEAHY. (Editor). *The Child's Construction of Social Inequality*

RICHARD LESH AND MARSHA LANDAU. (Editors). *Acquisition of Mathematics Concepts and Processes*

The list of titles in this series continues on the last page of this volume.

Origins of
Individual Differences in Infancy

The Colorado Adoption Project

Robert Plomin
John C. DeFries

Institute for Behavioral Genetics
University of Colorado
Boulder, Colorado

With a foreword by Jerome Kagan
Harvard University

1985

ACADEMIC PRESS, INC.

(Harcourt Brace Jovanovich, Publishers)

Orlando   San Diego   New York   London
Toronto   Montreal   Sydney   Tokyo

Quotations that refer to Hoopes, 1982, in various places throughout Chapter 14 of this book are reproduced by permission of the Child Welfare League of America, Inc. from *Prediction in Child Development: A Longitudinal Study of Adoptive and Nonadoptive Families,* by J. L. Hoopes. Copyright 1982 by the Child Welfare League of America, Inc.

Quoted material from J. C. DeFries, "Commentary on L. L. Cavalli-Sforza, 'Quantitative genetic perspectives: Implications for human development,' " in *Developmental Human Behavior Genetics* (pp. 147-148), edited by K. W. Schaie, V. E. Anderson, G. E. McClearn, and J. Money (Lexington, Mass.: Lexington Books, D. C. Heath and Company, copyright 1975, D. C. Heath and Company) is reprinted by permission of the publisher.

Quoted material from L. Kamin, "Studies of adopted children," in *The Intelligence Controversy: H. J. Eysenck versus Leon Kamin* (copyright 1981 Multimedia Publications (U.K.) Ltd., Personality Investigations, Publications and Services, Ltd. and Leon Kamin) is reproduced by permission of John Wiley & Sons, Inc.

Quoted material from Kadushin, 1978, is reprinted by permission of the National Association of Social Workers from *Social Service Research: Reviews of Studies*, edited by H. S. Maas, 1978, New York: National Association of Social Workers. Copyright 1978 by the National Association of Social Workers.

ACADEMIC PRESS, INC.
Orlando, Florida 32887

United Kingdom Edition published by
ACADEMIC PRESS INC. (LONDON) LTD.
24–28 Oval Road, London NW1 7DX

Library of Congress Cataloging in Publication Data

Plomin, Robert, Date
   Origins of individual differences in infancy.

   Includes index.
   1. Individuality in children. 2. Infant psychology.
3. Nature and nurture. 4. Children, Adopted--Psychology.
I. DeFries, J. C., Date 1985. II. Title.
BF720.I55P56   1985   155.4'22   84-18570
ISBN 0-12-558280-3 (alk. paper)

PRINTED IN THE UNITED STATES OF AMERICA

85 86 87 88   9 8 7 6 5 4 3 2 1

Contents

Foreword

A major disadvantage of young disciplines is the difficulty in deciding whether ambiguous affirmation of strong hypotheses is due to faulty theory or insufficiently sensitive methods. Theorists favorable to predictions from psychoanalytic theory often reject, on reasonable grounds, the empirical refutations of libido theory by claiming unduly crude methods. By contrast, Lashley's hypothesis of equipotentiality could be securely put to rest when procedures to study the central nervous system became more powerful.

The stunning advances in human biology and psychology over the last decade have brought the two disciplines closer than they have been since the two decades after Darwin's revolutionary book, and behavioral genetics is one of the sturdy connecting strands. In sharp contrast to the period just after World War II when I was sitting in graduate seminars, the current generation of psychologists is friendlier to the reasonable notion that some of the theoretically important psychological qualities that differentiate children and adults are under the influence of genetic variation. The task before us is to detect those qualities in their least disguised form and to quantify the complementary influences of biological and experiential factors—no easy assignment.

This effort is especially frustrating because most of the procedures that have attained a semblance of community consensus measure relatively gross psychological characteristics, with names like intelligence, extraversion, and emotionality. None of these categories specifies time, place, or target, and each implies that the individual variation in these characteristics is preserved across extremely varied contexts. But standardized measures of more delineated qualities are not available, and the few procedures that have attained some popularity appear to be of limited power. Under these conditions, what should two of the country's leading behavioral geneticists do? A reasonable response is similar to the answer that the Swedish novelist Lagerqvist ascribed to God when a group of dead people asked Him why He made life so difficult. "I did the best I could," was God's reply.

This ambitious, technically competent, and clearly written summary of the Colorado Adoption Project clarifies many questions surrounding genetic and environmental influences on an infant's psychological characteristics by comparing the resemblance between the characteristics of children at 1 and 2 years of age and what appear to be similar dispositions in the biological and adoptive parents. It is the most extensive investigation of the degree of resemblance between infants and their biological and adoptive parents ever implemented. For this reason alone, the authors deserve our gratitude. Empirical projects of this magnitude usually facilitate progress in young sciences, for when a corpus of information is large and the analyses elegant, a careful reader gains access to evidence that permits an adjustment of a priori probabilities. Here is a sampler of four.

One of the most important findings is that the influence of environmental experiences on psychological differentiation increases between the first and the second birthday, supporting the growing conviction that the first year is under strong maturational control. Further, during the second year, differences in language ability seem to be more closely related to environmental experiences than differences in competences that are less dependent on verbal skill. And with the exception of a slight verbal precocity among girls, the research affirms the work of others in indicating minimal sex differences during infancy. Finally, of great practical significance is the fact that differences between adopted and nonadopted infants are absent or trivial, implying that early adoption is not a traumatic event for most children.

But the yield from this project also allows investigators to judge the utility of some popular instruments that are used in this domain of inquiry. Validity judgments cannot be made on the abstract meaning of propositions like, "Intelligence in infants is an inherited quality," but rather on the particular referential or evidential sources that give empirical meaning to the abstract propositions. Thus, one is always evaluating a conclusion with regard to its evidential origins. This principle, which was an effective monitor of generalizations in the 1950s, is often ignored by the new generation of social scientists, some of whom may have assumed that the component of operationism in the philosophy of logical empiricism is without any value simply because the other tenets, especially parsimony and verifiability, have proven to be obstructive of progress. A significant contribution of this report is its critical evaluation of some widely used measurement strategies in contemporary psychology. Because the sample was large and geographically scattered, it was necessary to administer self-report instruments to evaluate the child's temperament and the parents' personality, and to use the HOME scale as an index of variation in familial environments. Thus, when the authors, in summarizing the corpus of data, write that "Individual differences in infancy are neither predictable from parental or environmental measures nor predictive of individual differences among children or adults," they can be interpreted as proposing a partial indictment of the procedures used.

One of the most surprising results is the absence of commanding evidence for effects of either genetic contributions, environmental experiences, or gene–environment interaction on the standard indexes of intelligence. Most of the variance in the young child's Bayley scores at 1 and 2 years of age (70%) cannot be accounted for either by variation in the biological parents' IQ or by those aspects of the environment that are measured by the HOME scale. I suspect this fact is due, in part, to the inability of the HOME scale to provide a sensitive index of the variation in stimulation in middle-class homes. A similar conclusion holds for many of the temperamental dispositions. Similarly, the absence of evidence for a strong genetic contribution to the child's sociability, emotionality, and irritability is inconsistent with other work (some by Robert Plomin) that discovered genetic contribution to a fearful versus a social approach to strangers when behavioral observations, rather than parental report, were quantified.

Because these summarizing inferences are apt to violate the expectations of many readers, I believe the data can be viewed as an evaluation of the validity of these particular sources of evidence in relation to the questions posed in this inquiry. Parental descriptions of their own salient personality qualities, or the qualities of their infants, do not share a great deal of communality with measures based on direct behavioral observations, the reports of knowledgeable others, or indirect probes. Although the subjectively derived evaluations have a meaning, it appears to be a special one that is different from the meaning of information gathered in the more objective mode. Younger scholars should not ignore these singularly significant results as they prepare the next productive attack on the same problems.

This is a rich bounty for one project: an affirmation of ideas about sex differences, a note of reassurance for future adoptive parents, and a warning regarding certain methods. And the project goes on. Although this report focuses on the infant, these same children are being evaluated at 3, 4, and 7 years of age, and the authors plan to assess these children with the same battery that was administered to their biological parents 16 years earlier. Robert and John—well done!

Jerome Kagan
Harvard University

Preface

Nature and nurture in infancy are the dual themes of this first comprehensive report of results of the decade-long Colorado Adoption Project (CAP), a prospective, longitudinal adoption study. The results presented in this book derive from analyses of data on 182 adopted infants and 165 nonadopted infants who were tested at both 12 and 24 months of age and whose parents (biological as well as adoptive parents of the adopted infants) were also tested. The infants and their parents were assessed for diverse psychological characters such as general and specific cognitive abilities, language, temperament, and behavioral problems. Some of the most exciting results emerge from analyses based on measures of the adoptive and nonadoptive home environments. This multivariate approach to the study of individual differences in infancy should make the CAP findings of interest to any student of human development, including researchers, educators, and parents. Although the presentation requires some knowledge of elementary statistics, we have attempted to write about the CAP results at a level that will make them accessible to the broadest possible audience.

Our basic science question, the genetic and environmental origins of individual differences in infancy, is an applied question for the nearly 1000 adoptive and nonadoptive parents participating in the CAP. We are deeply grateful for their cooperation and encouragement. The parents in each family traveled to Boulder or Denver to complete a gruelling 3-hour battery of tests and welcomed us into their homes for a 3-hour visit when their child was 12 months old and again at 24 months. The families began participating in 1976, and nearly all of them continue to participate in the ongoing longitudinal project.

As described in the first chapter, the study was made possible by the enthusiastic support of two adoption agency administrators and their agencies: John Califf of Lutheran Social Services of Colorado and Dolores Schmidt of Denver Catholic Community Services. We worked with these two people for over a year to solve ethical and procedural problems involved in testing biological parents who relinquish their newborns for adoption while preserving their anonymity and in contacting and testing the adoptive parents of these children. In the ensuing years, the conscientious dedication of these individuals and their assistants has been responsible for the high participation rates of the biological and adoptive parents and for the avoidance of any mishaps. Our collaboration with them has been delightful since its inception in 1974, long before we obtained grant support for the CAP; in fact, they played an instrumental role in obtaining support for the project by convincing a site visit team that the research was feasible.

The nonadoptive families in the CAP are matched to the adoptive families with respect to characteristics described in Chapter 3. We are grateful to several Colorado hospitals that made their files available to us so that we could screen birth records for families that might meet our selection criteria, informed the families about the project, and encouraged the parents' participation. These hospitals are Boulder Community Hospital, Aurora Community Hospital, McKee Medical Center in Loveland, and Weld County Hospital in Greeley. We especially appreciate the help of Pete Bukowich, Director of Medical Records of Boulder Community Hospital, who was enthusiastic about our research from the start and made it easy for us to gain support from the other hospitals.

We are extremely grateful to the National Institute of Child Health and Human Development for continuous support of the CAP by a research grant (HD-10333) that was first awarded in 1977 and was renewed in 1982. Funding for the CAP began in 1976 with awards from the University of Colorado Biomedical Research Support Grant and the National Institute of Mental Health (MH-28076). The W. T. Grant Foundation gave support to the project in 1977. In 1978 and 1982, the National Science Foundation awarded grants (BNS-7826204 and BNS-8200310) that enabled us to collect videotape recordings of mother–infant interaction at 1, 2, and 3 years of age. Finally, the Spencer Foundation provided support since 1982 for the purpose of testing the remaining CAP infants, especially the younger adopted and nonadopted siblings of the probands, at 5 and 7 months of age on a measure of novelty preference. We appreciate the willingness of these agencies to cosponsor this large-scale, longitudinal project.

We were most fortunate in having an excellent team of professional testers and other staff members working on the project. The majority of the testing of biological parents was conducted by Judy Fredericks, a social worker employed at the adoption agencies. Our real heroines are the full-time testers—Judy Arneson, Marilyn Fitzsimmons, Debra Hutchinson, Diane Perry, Martha Ramos, and Elizabeth Rice—who traveled day after day to the homes of the CAP families. Two postdoctoral researchers, Sandra Singer and Karen Hardy-Brown, helped coordinate the project. Allan Kuse originally organized data management procedures; these were refined by Robin Corley, who also developed an efficient ''front-end'' program for retrieving information from the extensive data tapes of the CAP. Other staff members over the years included Joseph Gregg, Karen Jax, Bernice Moon, Margaret Nettles, Cathie Radin, Christy Ross, and Anne Weiher.

Graduate students of the Institute for Behavioral Genetics made major contributions to the project in every phase from planning to publishing. Three students conducted their dissertation research using data from the CAP: Laura Baker, who is now an assistant professor of psychology at the University of Southern California; Karen Hardy-Brown, who continues to work on CAP analyses of communicative behavior; and Hsiu-Zu Ho, who is an assistant professor of psychology at the University of California, Santa Barbara. CAP data were used in research for the M.A. degree in psychology by Denise Daniels, Treva Rice, and Lee Thompson. Other graduate students who contributed to the CAP are Connie Eppich, John Greenhalgh, and Tee Roberts.

The Institute for Behavioral Genetics is a most congenial and efficient host for this long-term, large-scale project, providing backup continuity for the project in terms of personnel and funds to cover the innumerable hidden costs involved in such research. In particular we single out Rebecca Miles, who provided excellent editorial advice. We are also grateful to Agnes Conley for typing the manuscript.

We gratefully acknowledge the advice given us by various people, including the many anonymous reviewers of our numerous grant applications. We especially profited from the wisdom of one of our colleagues at the Institute for Behavioral Genetics, Steven Vandenberg, who initiated the longitudinal Louisville Twin Study and conducted several other large-scale human behavioral genetic studies. We extended our analytic capabilities by collaboration with David Fulker, beginning several years before he became a faculty member of the Institute. Our interaction with members of the MacArthur Research Network on the Transition from Infancy to Early Childhood helped us in our thinking about this book, especially our collaboration with Judy Dunn of Cambridge University, who spent a sabbatical year with us at the Institute. Finally, we profited from the advice of the following colleagues and friends: Joseph Fagan, Leonard Heston, John Loehlin, Robert McCall, William Meredith, Sandra Scarr, and Morton Weir.

1

Individual Differences

Behavioral individuality during infancy—its description, correlates, and causes—is the focus of this book. In 1975, we initiated the Colorado Adoption Project (CAP) by testing biological parents who planned to relinquish their infants for adoption, and we have subsequently completed over 1000 visits to the homes of adopted and matched nonadopted infants at 1, 2, 3, and 4 years of age. The magnitude of this study reflects our perception of the need for large-scale, longitudinal studies of individual differences and our commitment to the belief that the adoption design is the most powerful methodology available to study the origin of individual differences. Before describing the CAP design and its results, the twin themes of this book—individuality and behavioral genetics—are briefly discussed.

Individuality and Universality

Individuality refers to differences among individuals in a population. We are interested in searching for the correlates and causes of such variability, and we find behavioral genetic methodologies to be particularly useful in this quest. Universality, in contrast, designates a profoundly different approach, one that assumes invariance within the human species or at least emphasizes the modal, normative behavior of the species. McCall (1981) discussed a similar distinction using the terms *individual differences* and *developmental function*. Individuality and universality are different perspectives; perspectives are neither right nor wrong, only useful or not useful for a particular purpose. However, it is critical that the gulf between these two approaches be appreciated. The two perspectives differ in their focus and in their level of analysis.

1

Description

Some developmentalists focus on the average behavior of a species. Such modal descriptions approach universality only when we move back far enough so that individual features begin to blur. For example, nearly all humans learn to walk and talk, and we can describe the usual developmental sequence in which components of these behaviors appear in infancy. From this distance, individual differences in walking and talking within the human species are by no means eye-catching.

We could move even farther back and consider pan-primate trends such as bipedalism or frontal vision, in which differences within the primate order blur. An even grander view could lose sight of differences between orders in the coalescence of mammalian trends such as the carefully choreographed set of attachment behaviors characteristic of mammalian caregivers and their altricial young. However, most developmentalists prefer to be back just far enough to see modal patterns of development for *Homo sapiens*.

Considering the difficulty of describing modal patterns of development in infancy, it is not surprising that most developmentalists do not study individual differences. However, individuality is apparent even for such highly canalized behaviors as walking and talking. In infancy, variability in the rate of motor and language development is conspicuous, especially to new parents who worry about their infant's development in relation to the modal information provided in the baby books. The range of variability in developmental rates has been documented by Bayley (1969), whose standardization sample for the Scales of Infant Development provides norms quite different from the highly cited norms of Shirley (1933). Table 1.1 lists the average age and the range of variability for components of walking and talking. The table shows that the normal range surrounding most motoric and language milestones during the first year of life increases with age. As a rough rule of thumb, particularly for language development, the range in months is about the same as the mean age. For example, 7 months is the average age at which infants vocalize four different syllables; the range is also 7 months (5–12 months). The age range for motor development is somewhat less than the average age.

After infancy, even highly canalized behaviors such as walking and talking show differences in outcome levels if we zoom in with our observational lens to a distance that brings individual differences into focus. Variability in motoric development leads to marked individual differences in running speed, agility, and strength. Similarly, the developmental course of language leads to considerable variability in vocabulary, verbal fluency, and ability to learn a second language. For behaviors less highly canalized than walking and talking, such as stylistic aspects of behavior often included under the rubric of temperament, individual differences abound and it is difficult even to speak of modal developmental patterns. Of course, both means and variances are appropriate descriptive statistics. However, as discussed later, we believe that a powerful science of behavioral development needs to explain not only average developmental functions but also the variations on these themes.

TABLE 1.1

Means and Variability for Measures of Motor and Language Development[a]

Measure	$\overline{X}$	Range
Motor development		
Crawling movements (when placed on stomach on firm surface, child makes alternating crawling movements with legs)	1 week	3 days– 3 months
Sits with support	2 months	1–5 months
Pulls to sitting position	5 months	4–8 months
Stands up by furniture	9 months	6–12 months
Walks alone (at least three steps)	12 months	9–17 months
Walks sideways	14 months	10–20 months
Language development		
Response to voice	3 weeks	1–8 weeks
Expressive vocalizations	4½ months	3–8 months
Vocalizes four different syllables	7 months	5–12 months
Responds to verbal request	9 months	6–14 months
Imitates words	12½ months	9–18 months
Says two words	14 months	10–23 months

[a]Adapted from the Bayley Scales of Infant Development (Bayley, 1969).

Causes and Correlates

When we search for causal processes of development, the gulf between the two perspectives widens. This chasm is not easily recognized in the developmental literature, because causes of modal development are frequently assumed to be causes of the development of individuality as well. For example, the mainstay of analyses of causes of universal or modal development is the deprivation experiment, such as Harlow's "mother love" studies (Harlow & Harlow, 1962). Rhesus monkeys deprived of social contact for varying lengths of time manifest abnormal social development. By reinstating the various aspects of the normal rhesus environment, it is possible to determine which environmental factors are critical for normal social development. For example, one surprising result is that isolation with mothers but without peers results in some developmental deficits; however, isolation with peers but without mothers is sufficient for normal development.

Leaving aside difficult issues such as what the deprived animal is deprived of, a major problem with deprivation experiments is that they deprive animals of some aspect of the species' evolutionarily expected environment. That is, development has evolved in the context of environmental conditions usually encountered by a species; changing these conditions can change the course of development. When isolation is complete and lasts for the first year of life, rhesus monkeys show persistent social impairment. In the real world, of course, infant monkeys would not survive in isolation.

Understanding indispensable conditions of development is certainly a laudable goal. Interest in deprivation studies, however, sometimes stems from the mistaken belief that results of such studies are relevant to the study of individual differences within the human species. If deprivation experiments show that social stimulation is necessary for normal development, then does it not follow that differences in social stimulation experienced by infants in the world outside the laboratory are related to developmental differences? The answer is emphatically no: The causes of modal species' development bear no necessary relationship to the causes of individual differences within the species. Total isolation is not part of the continuum of social environments faced by human infants. There is no a priori reason to expect that, given the modicum of social interaction necessary for the survival of an infant, experiential differences within the "normal" range differentially affect development. Although experiential differences within the evolutionarily expected environment may indeed have an effect, the point here is that knowledge of the causes of modal development helps us little in understanding the etiology of individuality.

The converse also holds: The causes of individual differences within species bear no necessary relationship to the causes of modal species' differences. There are fewer examples of errors made in this direction, although research on language acquisition can be used to illustrate the principle. A universals perspective has dominated the field of language, largely because of Chomsky's theory, which posits an innate language construct tuned to the structure of language (Chomsky, 1957, 1980). Researchers attempting to disprove Chomsky's theory have demonstrated that individual differences in infants' rates of language acquisition are related to differences in the infants' language-learning environments. However, these results have no bearing on the issue of the origin of our species' universal propensity to use language (Hardy-Brown, 1983). As a specific example, consider the finding that individual differences in infants communicative competence are related to mothers' contingent vocalizations (Hardy-Brown, Plomin, & DeFries, 1981). This finding does not imply that contingent vocal responding is necessary for the modal development of human language. If a deprivation experiment were conducted and aspects of the language-learning environment were added one by one to a noiseless condition, the results would not tell us anything about the effects of contingent vocal responding on normal human language.

In summary, the perspectives of individuality and universality are different both in their description of behavioral development and in their search for causal factors.

Cultural Differences

Although anthropologists are beginning to consider variability within cultures, the modal behavior of a culture has been the principal target of cross-cultural research. One of the reasons why anthropologists often disagree so sharply on cultural descriptions may be that individual variability within the culture makes it difficult to characterize a modal cultural type. An example is Freeman's (1983) detailed critique of Margaret Mead's famous work, *Coming of Age in Samoa*. Freeman reverses nearly all of Mead's interpretations and builds a case that Franz Boas, Mead's mentor, wanted to find an example of a culture that showed a markedly different reaction to adolescence as ammunition in his fight against genetic determinism in the 1920s. Freeman uses Mead's own data to show variability within the Samoan culture. Of the 25 girls interviewed by Mead, data for 4 girls who did not fit the tranquil picture she described for Samoan adolescence were relegated to a separate chapter and did not enter into her conclusions. However, Freeman shows that the delinquent acts of these 4 girls, when tallied with those of the other 21 girls, yielded a rate of juvenile delinquency that was 10 times the recent rate in England.

Our prediction is that variability within cultures is vastly greater than average variability among cultures. However, it is critical to recognize that the causes of average differences between groups are not necessarily related to the causes of individual differences within groups. That is, even if the presumed sexual freedom of the Samoans led to a tranquil adolescence as Mead suggested, we could not conclude that individual differences in adolescent reactions within our culture are related, for example, to the sexual permissiveness of parents. Moreover, Boas' use of the Samoan data to argue that nurture dominates nature in development is a fundamentally flawed argument. Even if the Samoans had been, on the average, as different from other cultural groups as Mead suggested, we could not safely assume that the average difference between cultures is environmental in origin, because isolated groups differ genetically as well as environmentally. On the other side of the argument, finding universals of development across cultures—grist for the mill of sociobiology—does not prove that nature dominates nurture, because universal environmental contingencies could shape all cultures to produce similar results.

Average Group Differences

Not all developmental research falls squarely in the camp of individuality or of universality. Indeed, most appears to lie in the middle in the sense that it focuses on average group differences within a species rather than on individual differences or species universals. Conceptually, however, research on average group differences lies closer to the perspective of universality than to that of individuality. For example, developmental research frequently compares average differences between younger and older groups of children. The goal of research of this type is nearly always the description of universal processes of development. Individual differences within the age-groups are usually treated as error.

Another class of studies of average group differences appears at first glance to be truly intermediate to the individuality and universality perspectives. For example, many developmental studies describe and attempt to explain average differences between boys and girls. In fact, such studies also are more aligned in spirit with the universals perspective. In studies of average differences between the sexes, the goal is often to describe and explain male and female variations on the universal theme of development. If such studies were attuned to individual differences, it would quickly be realized that average differences between the sexes typically account for a trivial amount of individual variability. For example, one of the best documented gender differences in the cognitive realm is the superiority of females on tests of verbal ability (Maccoby & Jacklin, 1974). However, this average difference between the sexes accounts for only about one percent of the variance in verbal ability (Plomin & Foch, 1981). In other words, if all we know about individuals is their gender, we know next to nothing about their verbal ability. Furthermore, if an average difference between groups accounts for only one percent of the variance, attempts to replicate the finding will often fail unless the sample sizes are large. This problem is magnified considerably when attempts are made to partition this variance into causal factors.

Average group differences are occasionally mentioned in this report. For example, we consider average scores for boys and girls, 1- and 2-year-olds, and adopted and nonadopted children. However, discussions of average group differences are always put in the context of individual variability.

The Importance of Individual Differences

Earlier we stated that individuality and universality are perspectives and, as such, cannot be right or wrong; they are only more or less useful for a particular purpose. Because the perspective of the CAP—indeed, its raison d'etre—is the study of individual differences, a few words in defense of the study of individuality are warranted. An apologia for studying developmental individuality, the "very standard deviation" (Levine, Carey, Crocker, & Gross, 1983), may be especially necessary, given that the mainstream of developmental research employs the universals perspective.

In terms of application, the perspective of individuality is crucial because questions of societal relevance usually involve individual differences. For example, the interesting question of why humans are natural language users has less social significance than asking why some children are language delayed, why some are reading disabled, and why some have a propensity to acquire vocabulary easily and to use words fluently. As mentioned earlier, it cannot be assumed that average differences between groups yield answers of relevance to these individual-differences questions.

Although the societal importance of individual differences is generally recognized, the value of an individual-differences approach for testing theories is not often considered. This approach can be used as a crucible for testing theories by asking how well a theory holds up across individuals. For example, the demonstration that, on the average, 14-month-olds say two words and 20-month-olds use two-word sentences does not lead very far. When we focus on the average 14-month-old and the average 20-month-old, we effectively have only two data points. If we show that, on the average, parents of 20-month-olds use lengthier utterances than parents of 14-month-olds, we can do little more than ask whether this mean difference accounts for a significant amount of variance among individuals. Significant mean differences usually explain only a small portion of the variance. We cannot assume that the relationship is causal. It is particularly difficult to make progress in understanding etiologies of developmental phoenomena with a universals perspective. For example, as mentioned earlier, the results of experimental interventions such as enrichment and deprivation, although important in pointing to what can affect the development of a character, do not tell us much about what does affect the development of the character in the world outside the laboratory (McCall, 1977).

In contrast, an individual-differences perspective permits study of the strength of a relationship between parental language and infant language across individuals. Although demands on data for individual differences analyses are much more stringent in terms of sample size and psychometric properties such as reliability, collecting data that can stand up to individual differences analyses opens the door to powerful analytical techniques such as causal modeling and quantitative genetics. This leads us to believe that questions posed in terms of individual differences are more likely to receive answers than are questions concerning normative development. Furthermore, it should be noted that data collected for the purpose of conducting individual-differences analyses are just as useful for studying normative questions; indeed, such data are especially useful because they usually involve large, representative samples. However, data collected solely for the purpose of studying normative issues are not often applicable to the study of individual differences.

Finally, the study of individual differences is warranted because, like our Colorado mountains, they are there. In the case of individual differences in behavioral development, they are there as impressively as the Rockies. Thus, any developmental theory must be able to account for such variance. As discussed in the following chapter, it is our conviction that behavioral genetics provides a particularly powerful methodology for studying the etiology of individual differences in development.

2

Behavioral Genetics

The environmentalism that prevailed through the 1960s has given way to a more balanced view that recognizes genetic as well as environmental influences on development. The reticence to accept genetic influence was in part due to misunderstandings about the ways in which genes influence development and the implications of discovering genetic efforts. In this chapter, we discuss these issues and describe the methods used in human behavioral-genetic research.

How Genes Affect Behavior

Most developmentalists understand at least the general idea that genes consist of DNA and that they code for amino acid sequences of protein. Also, nearly everyone notices behavioral differences among children. However, the relationship between DNA and behavior—how genetic variability is related to behavioral variability—is often misunderstood. This confusion is not surprising in view of the fact that gene–behavior pathways have been worked out in only a very few cases, usually involving simple behaviors and simple physiological systems. However, even if we do not know the specifics of gene–behavior pathways, we do know the general ways in which genes come to have an effect on behavior. For example, research in behavioral genetics during the 1960s and 1970s indicates that the effects of genes on behavior are often pleiotropic; behavioral characters are often polygenic; and gene differences often cause behavioral differences among individuals within populations.

Pleiotropic Effects

The essence of DNA is its triplet code for specifying amino acid sequences in protein. A sequence of three nucleotide base pairs of DNA codes for 1 of 20 amino acids. The DNA is first transcribed by RNA, which proceeds to the ribosomes outside the nucleus of the cell. The order of the triplets of RNA then directs the sequence in which amino acids are linked to form polypeptides, the primary constituents of enzymes and other proteins such as neurotransmitters and hormones. The 3 billion base pairs of DNA also code for polypeptides that regulate other genes by starting or stopping their transcription, directing the processing of their nuclear RNA, and changing their position (transposable elements). Thus, the effect of genes on behavior is indirect. They produce and regulate the production of polypeptides that, in turn, interact with existing anatomical and physiological systems.

Natural selection does not occur for major gene–behavior pathways through its effect on simple physiological connections. Selection operates on whole organisms in all their behaving complexity. It is now generally recognized among evolutionary biologists that the behavior of an organism is the leading edge of evolution. If certain behavioral differences among individuals are related to their reproductive fitness, natural selection will exert its slow but inexorable "multiple discriminant analysis," winnowing genetic variations that make a difference.

Often genes seem far removed from their most obvious site of action. Artificial selection demonstrates this point readily because it is so simple and severe, selecting for a single character without regard to balancing other characters to maintain the overall reproductive fitness of the organism. For example, in the longest systematic mammalian selection study, the target for selection was activity of mice in an open-field arena (DeFries, Gervais, & Thomas, 1978). After 30 generations of selection for high and low activity, there is no overlap in the distributions of activity scores for high- and low-active lines. The high-active mice now run the equivalent total distance of the length of a football field in 6 min. Although this difference in open-field activity is apparently due to many genes with relatively small effects, one gene has a major influence. There are almost no albino mice in the high-active lines, whereas the low-active lines are completely albino. Why should the single gene that governs coat color also affect activity in the open field? The answer is that albinism is due to the absence of melanin, the coloring pigmentation of the skin and the eye. Lack of pigmentation makes the eye more sensitive to light so that the open field, with its usual bright lighting, is more stressful to the photophobic albino mice. When visual stimulation is reduced by the use of red light, there is no difference in open-field behavior between albino and pigmented mice of otherwise similar genetic backgrounds (DeFries, Hegmann, & Weir, 1966). Thus, a gene that most obviously influences coat and eye color also has effects on a seemingly unrelated behavior such as activity in an open-field arena. These manifold effects of genes are called *pleiotropic*. The point is that all genes may have pleiotropic behavioral effects.

Polygenic Effects

Because we have all learned about Gregor Mendel and his pea plants, we tend to think about genetic influence as the simple effect of a single gene on a single, clear-cut observable trait—as in the case of the gene found to be responsible for producing wrinkled rather than smooth peas. We also learn about single-gene mutations, such as those responsible for sickle-cell anemia or PKU, that have such dramatic effects in humans. However, most genetic influences are far less dramatic. In fact, it is likely that genetic influences on development involve the cumulative effects of many genes.

In the early part of this century, a debate raged among biologists as to the generality of the laws of heredity discovered by Mendel in the mid-nineteenth century and rediscovered in several laboratories at the turn of the century. One group, the biometricians, argued that Mendel's laws cannot be general, because most characters display smooth normal distributions rather than qualitatively distinct phenotypes such as those studied by Mendel. The multiple-factor theory of Nilson-Ehle (1908) and Emerson and East (1913) resolved the controversy by showing that if many genes affected a character, the result would be a normal distribution even though each gene operated exactly as Mendel hypothesized.

Empirically, no single major gene has been demonstrated to be responsible for any complex behavior. This statement would seem to contradict the apparent discoveries of major single-gene effects frequently touted for the psychoses and for spatial ability (e.g., Stafford, 1961). However, the history of these discoveries indicates that they are likely to be short-lived, usually lasting only until the next study fails to replicate the finding. (See Corley, DeFries, Kuse, & Vandenberg, 1980, in the case of spatial ability.)

One might nevertheless counter that many single-gene mutations have been clearly shown to affect behavior. For example, over a hundred single-gene mutations affect IQ (McKusick, 1981). However, these mutations are rare and affect so few individuals that they have a negligible impact on the variance of the trait in the population even though their impact can be considerable for afflicted individuals. Untreated PKU, for example, has a dramatic effect on IQ; however, only about 1 in 20,000 individuals is homozygous for the recessive allele that leads to PKU. Other mutations are equally or even more rare and, taken together, hardly create a bump on the normal distribution of IQ.

Mutation studies should be viewed as examples of how a single gene can seriously disrupt behavioral development, just as deprivation studies demonstrate the power of environmental "mutations" to alter the course of development. By no means do they suggest that a single gene is responsible for the behavior. If we think of behavior as a finely tuned automobile with thousands of parts required to make it run properly, malfunctioning of any one of the parts could stop the automobile, but this would not mean that the faulty part was solely responsible for the automobile's operation. A good behavioral example is the work done in the past few years on the behavior of bacteria. Bacteria do behave, moving toward or away from many kinds of chemicals by rotating their four to eight propeller-like flagella. Rapid advances have been made in isolating the genes and the proteins responsible for various components of this behavior (Adler, 1976; Parkinson, 1977). One clear message from this research is that many genes are involved in even the simplest behaviors. For example, at least 20 different genes have been isolated that affect the recognition of a chemical stimulus—bacteria do this by means of genes that produce proteins that bind with particular substances. The point is that, even though a mutation of any one of these genes can seriously disrupt the behavior of bacteria, normal behavior is influenced by many genes. If many genes affect recognition of a few chemical stimuli in bacteria, it seems safe to assume that polygenic influences predominate in human development. It is for this reason that the following discussion emphasizes quantitative genetics in contrast to molecular, single-gene, or chromosomal analyses. Advances in molecular genetics during the 1970s (e.g., Housman & Gusella, 1980) hold great promise for one day directly assessing genetic variability among individuals and relating such genetic variation to observed differences in behavior. Similarly promising are new developments in the analyses of chromosomal anomalies such as new banding techniques to identify small fragments of chromosomes (Sanchez & Yunis, 1977) and identification of "fragile" sites on chromosomes (e.g., Turner & Opitz, 1980). Nevertheless, for the foreseeable future, investigations of complex, polygenically and multifactorially determined psychological characteristics will require the indirect methods of quantitative genetics.

Population Parameters

Quantitative behavioral genetics focuses on the description of individual differences in a population and the extent to which genetic differences among individuals account for these observed differences. It does not address universals, either genetic or environmental. For example, for fruit flies, mice, and men, at least half of all expressed DNA is nonvarying within the species. As a matter of fact, a surprising amount of genetic material is constant across species within an order; chimps and humans are about 50% similar genetically (Plomin & Kuse, 1979). However, questions concerning such genetic constants, either across or within species, are not addressed by quantitative genetic methods, which are relevant only to the study of individual differences within a population.

As obvious as this point might seem, it is a frequent source of misunderstanding. One still reads that it makes no sense to attempt to untangle genetic and environmental influences in development, because they interact; that is, both genes and environment are prerequisites for behavioral development. Although it is certainly true that no behavior will occur unless there is both an environment and an organism, this truism misses the point that behavioral-genetic methods are not applicable to the behavior of single individuals. They investigate the genetic and environmental causes of observed differences among individuals in a population. Just as psychologists have always asked whether variation in experience is related to variation in behavior, we can also ask about the extent to which genetic variation is related to behavioral variability.

This exclusive focus on variability might at first appear to be limiting; however, most of the societally important questions asked by psychologists involve individual differences rather than universals. Some areas of psychology, such as psycholinguistics, have traditionally focused on universals more than on individual differences; for this reason, these areas are slower to accept behavioral genetics, although even they are changing (Hardy-Brown, 1983). This is less of a problem with respect to personality and mental development. Although some personality research areas (e.g., attachment) have traditionally been viewed from a universals perspective, personality has been the stronghold over the years for the study of individual differences. Similarly, although theories such as Piaget's emphasize normative development, the psychometric tradition has continued to promote the study of individual differences in the development of cognition.

A related issue is that behavioral-genetic methods are used to study individual differences in a particular population with that population's mix of genetic and environmental influences at the time. Genetic and environmental sources of variance could differ in different populations, as they could in the same population at different times. Behavioral genetics has been criticized because it does not consider all possible combinations of genetic and environmental sources of variance (e.g., Feldman & Lewontin, 1975)· however, the subset of genetic and environmental influences present in our population at any given time is by no means a trivial subset. The fact that genetic and environmental population parameter estimates— just as any other descriptive statistics, such as means and variances—change as the population changes is a strength not a weakness.

Because quantitative behavioral genetics is descriptive, it considers "what is" in a population rather than "what could be" or "what should be." That is, when behavioral-genetic research points to genetic influence for a particular behavior, it only means that, given the genetic and environmental influences impinging upon that population at that time, genetic differences among individuals account for some observed differences in behavior. It does not mean that this is the natural order of things, nor does it mean that environmental influences cannot make a difference. Even if genetic variance were found to account for all the observed variance for a particular behavior (no example even comes close to this condition), a novel environmental influence could nonetheless substantially alter the behavior. Despite the fact that behavioral genetics describes what is rather than what could be, these two purposes should be viewed as complementary. If one wanted to change behavior, a first step would be to examine existing sources of variability. For example, an environmental factor such as a particular parenting technique would not be a wise choice for intervention if it already is varying widely in the population and yet is not related to variation in the target behavior of children. Moreover, it is our belief that more sophisticated approaches to the study of the environment will take advantage of our knowledge about genetic variation.

Implications of Genetic Effects

Misconceptions concerning the operation of genes are partly responsible for misunderstandings about the implications of genetic effects on behavior. Both have slowed the acceptance of behavioral genetics into the mainstream of psychology. Much of this concern has surfaced in the field of IQ; perhaps other fields can avoid the same battles.

Worries about the implications of finding genetic effects on behavioral development are groundless because such findings do not imply immutability, absence of developmental change, or lack of environmental influence. Most importantly, demonstrations of genetic influence carry no implications as to social action.

Mutability

One implicit misunderstanding is that genes connote destiny, that they are immutable forces determining behavior. The main point of the previous section is that genes do not influence behavior in this deterministic way. Because of the complexities of pleiotropic, polygenic effects, genetic influences are indeed just influences—propensities, or tendencies, that nudge development in one direction rather than another. Moreover, genetic variation does not refer to an individual but rather to an average effect of genetic influences in a population. One person might differ from the population average primarily for genetic reasons, another primarily for environmental reasons. Changing environmental contingencies in the population could alter the proportion of genetic and environmental variances, but only by means of their effects upon individuals.

Developmental Change

A major reason for the previous lack of interest in genetics among developmentalists is that a genetic effect tends to be thought of as synonymous with static, unchanging development. An implicit assumption is that genetic influences are locked at full throttle at the moment of conception. On the contrary, however, developmental genetics focuses on the role of genes in the regulation of developmental change. Genes are just as likely to be sources of change as they are of continuity, and exploration of these effects is at the heart of the new interdisciplinary field of developmental behavioral genetics (Plomin, 1983b).

Environmental Influence

Somewhat surprisingly perhaps, behavioral genetics provides some of the best evidence for the importance of environmental influences in development. Behavioral-genetic theory and methodology provide a balanced approach that considers environmental as well as genetic influences, rather than assuming that one or the other class of influence is omnipotent. Moreover, an understanding of genetic influence is likely to provide the best leads for elucidating environmental influences, an important topic discussed at length later in this chapter.

Social Action

The deepest fears about finding genetic influences on behavior lie with the specter of political misuse of the information. These fears often stem from unexamined assumptions that genetic effects are immutable and that nothing can be done about them. As an antidote to this prevailing view, we would suggest that the more that is known about a condition (both genetically and environmentally), the more likely that it can be successfully treated. PKU is the classic model. Prior to the discovery of this recessive, single-gene metabolic defect, these individuals represented about one percent of the institutionalized mentally retarded population. Identification of the unique etiology of this small subgroup led to the discovery of a rational intervention, an environmental dietary regimen that limits the intake of phenylalanine so that the deficiencies in activity of the enzyme phenylalanine hydroxylase do not lead to high levels of phenylalanine, damaging to the developing brain. Discovering a genetic phenomenon thus led to one of the most powerful, known environmental interventions for mental retardation. It did not lead to the eugenic programs that those who fear genetics might predict.

In general, finding genetic influences upon behavior is compatible with a wide range of social action, including no action at all. Policy decisions involve value judgements, and, in general, it is our belief that wiser decisions can be made with knowledge rather than without it. Considering genetic variance can be enlightening. For example, finding a relationship between a parental behavior and children's personality could suggest intervention if it appeared that the relationship were environmental. Children's shyness, for instance, might be related to the fact that their parents do not expose them to many social situations. Given this relationship, one might take the next step and suggest that parents expose their children to more social encounters in order to ward off shyness. However, a genetic explanation looms large if parents who choose not to socialize are simply more shy than other parents. Thus, shy parents could have children who are shy for hereditary, not environmental, reasons; the ostensibly environmental relationship could in fact merely reflect such genetic differences among families. As convoluted as this might sound reading it for the first time, one of the most important results of the CAP analyses is the evidence they provide for genetic mediation of ostensibly environmental relationships.

When all is said and done, an overriding concern about behavioral genetics is that it appears to go against our basic democratic principles. Are not all men created equal? Our founding fathers were not so naive as to think that all men are inherently identical. Even in the seventeenth century, the English philosopher, John Locke, whose treatise *Of Civil Government* played a key role in the American revolution and in educational thought, had a more balanced view of the nature–nurture question than is usually recognized. By equality of men, Locke clearly refers to political equality, not to an absence of individual differences (Loehlin, 1983). Everyone should be equal in opportunity and before the law. In a democracy, we do not treat people equally because they are identical; there would be little need for principles of equality if that were true. The essence of democracy is to treat people equally in spite of their differences.

Major Methods of Behavioral Genetics

In this section we briefly describe the methods used in human behavioral genetics for the purpose of ascribing phenotypic variation to genetic and environmental components of variance. Our goal here is to present the background needed to interpret the data presented later. It is neither possible nor necessary to give a full exposition of behavioral genetics and its theoretical quantitative genetic background—for details, several behavioral-genetics texts are available (e.g., Dixon & Johnson, 1980; Fuller & Thompson, 1978; Plomin, DeFries, & McClearn, 1980; Vale, 1980).

Family Method

The basic methods of human behavioral genetics are family, twin, and adoption studies. Family studies compare genetically related individuals in order to examine the sine qua non of genetic influence: familial resemblance. Of course, familial resemblance does not prove genetic influence because resemblance among family members could be mediated environmentally as well as genetically.

Twin Method

The field of behavioral genetics is in the odd position of having more data on twins than on other kinds of relatives. This is due to the ease with which the twin design can be used as a sieve to screen traits for genetic influence. The twin method was first proposed a century ago by Francis Galton, the father of human behavioral genetics. The method can be viewed as a natural experiment in which pairs of individuals in one group (identical twins) are identical genetically and pairs in the other group (fraternal twins) are only half as similar genetically. If heredity influences a character, then identical twins should be more similar for the character than are fraternal twins. If, on the other hand, heredity is unimportant, then the twofold greater genetic similarity of identical twins should not make them more similar than fraternal twins. Quantitative estimates of the proportion of observed variance that can be explained by genetic variability can be derived from the differences in correlations between members of identical and fraternal twin pairs.

Factors that can affect this estimate of genetic influence include assortative mating, nonadditive genetic variance, and unequal environments for the two types of twins. Assortative mating is the tendency for like to mate with like. (Birds of a feather do appear to flock together; research has provided no support for the alternative adage that opposites attract.) Assortative mating increases the genetic similarity of fraternal twins because their parents are genetically more similar than usual with respect to genes that affect the characters for which the parents have mated selectively. It cannot increase identical twin correlations, however, because identical twins are already genetically identical. Thus, assortative mating reduces the difference between identical and fraternal twin correlations and in this way underestimates the importance of genetic influence.

A counterbalancing effect is nonadditive genetic variance. When we say that first-degree relatives are 50% similar genetically, we are referring only to one type of genetic variance. Genetic variance can be divided into additive and nonadditive components. Additive genetic variance includes those genetic effects that add up linearly according to gene dose, for the two alleles at a locus as well as across loci for polygenic traits. That is, if a particular allele affects a character, it will have that same average effect regardless of the individual's other alleles. Because of this, additive gene effects "breed true" in that first-degree relatives will resemble each other to the extent that genetic variance is additive. The rest of the genetic variance is nonadditive. A familiar example of a nonadditive effect is the dominance of one allele over another. The distinction between additive and nonadditive genetic variance is useful because, although the covariance of first-degree relatives contains half of the additive genetic variance affecting a character, it can be shown that parents and offspring share no dominance genetic variance and siblings share only a small fraction. Thus, to the extent that genetic factors operate in a nonadditive manner, heredity will contribute more to differences than to similarities among family members with the exception of identical twins, who are identical for all genes and thus completely share all genetic effects whether additive or nonadditive. Specifically in terms of the twin method, nonadditive genetic variance will lead to overestimates of genetic influence because it increases the difference between identical and fraternal twin correlations by lowering the latter while leaving the former unaltered. However, because assortative mating and nonadditive genetic influence have counterbalancing effects, it is assumed that the usual formula for estimating genetic influence—doubling the difference between correlations for identical and fraternal twins—provides a reasonable first approximation.

The twin method assumes that the environmental similarity experienced by pairs of identical twins and pairs of fraternal twins is roughly the same. This is the so-called equal environments assumption. If it is not a reasonable assumption, then the difference between identical and fraternal twin correlations could represent environmental as well as genetic differences. On the face of it, the assumption does seem reasonable because both types of twins share the same womb, are reared in the same family, and are the same age (and usually the same sex, given that only same-sex fraternal twins are usually used for comparisons with identical twins, who are always the same sex).

Although the possible falsity of the equal environments assumption is frequently used to argue against the twin method, there is surprisingly little research on the topic. In general, identical twins do not appear to be treated much more similarly than fraternal twins. Even though identical twins are slightly more similar than fraternal twins on a few environmental measures, these experiential differences do not make a difference in their behavior (Plomin et al., 1980).

Although we conclude that the twin method is a useful tool in the armamentarium of human behavioral genetics, the strongest evidence for genetic influence will come from the convergence of results from family, twin, and adoption studies. We now briefly describe the most powerful human behavioral-genetic methodology, the adoption design.

Adoption Studies

In any experimental design, we try to study one factor while either holding others constant or randomizing their effects. The adoption design randomizes family environment while studying the effects of heredity when analyses focus on genetically related individuals reared in unrelated environments. On the other side of the coin, the adoption design randomizes heredity while studying family environmental influences when it is used to examine genetically unrelated individuals in the same family. In this way, adoption studies disentangle hereditary and environmental influences that are interwoven when family members share both heredity and family environment.

The adoption design is generally considered to be the most powerful method in human behavioral genetics. For example, the eminent human geneticist L. L. Cavalli-Sforza (1975), stated in an overview entitled *Quantitative Genetic Perspectives: Implications for Human Development:*

> One of the conclusions from this research has already been stated a number of times. It is that there is no way to distinguish between cultural and biological transmission unless one can study adoptions and test the similarity with *both* biological *and* adoptive relatives. . . . In the absence of adoption studies, there is no hope of distinguishing rigorously whether standard measurements of inheritance, that is similarities between relatives (of any kind), are due to genetic determination of the trait differences, or to sociocultural inheritance (more generally, phenotypic transmission), or to a mixture of the two because correlations between relatives are similar in both models. (p. 134)

Moreover, even the most vociferous critics of behavioral genetics acknowledge the power of the adoption design. For example, Lewontin (1975) has said:

> All of the difficulties discussed above arise because both environmental and genetic theories predict qualitatively the same results, a decreasing similarity with decreasing relationship. The way to get around this problem is to break the connection between genetic relationship and

environmental relationship. In experimental plants and animals this is done by randomizing relatives over environment. In the human species, *this means adoption studies*. (p. 391)

Kamin (1981) similarly has endorsed the power of the adoption design:

> The fact that parents and children resemble each other in IQ does not in itself tell us anything about the relative importance of heredity and environment. The problem, of course, is that parents provide their children both with genes and with environment. The high-IQ parent is likely to provide his or her child with intellectual stimulation in the home, and is likely to stress the importance of doing good school work. The same parent has transmitted his or her genes to the child. There is no way, in ordinary families, of separating the effects of genes from those of environment. The great virtue of studies of adoptive families is that, in theory at least, they allow us to separate genetic from environmental transmission. The adoptive parent provides his or her child with environment but not with genes. Thus the IQ correlation between adopted child and adoptive parent is of considerable theoretical interest—particularly when it is compared to other relevant IQ correlations. (p. 114)

Although the adoption design has not been subjected to as much criticism as the twin method, it involves two assumptions, representativeness and absence of selective placement, that may be questioned. Representativeness, of course, is just as much an issue for family and twin studies—indeed for all science—as it is for adoption studies. Adoptive families usually are not completely representative of the population. They frequently are above average in IQ-related characteristics such as education and income. However, the real issue for behavioral-genetic analysis is variance, and there usually is some restriction of variance in adoption studies. Nonetheless, this is not as serious a problem as one might expect at first glance. If biological and adoptive relationships are similarly restricted, the restriction of variance is not likely to affect estimates of the relative influence of genetic variance on phenotypic variability.

The other issue is selective placement, which involves the matching of characteristics of genetic and adoptive relatives. Most often, this means that adoption agencies match adoptive parents to the biological parents of adoptees. Older adoption studies of IQ typically showed some selective placement. The effect of selective placement is to raise estimates of genetic influence and estimates of the influence of family environment; thus, it may not distort the relative influences of genes and family environment (DeFries & Plomin, 1978).

In addition to separating the relative contributions of hereditary and family environmental influences to correlations among family members, adoption studies are useful for studying environmental influences unconfounded by heredity. Studies that attempt to find relationships between parenting measures and children's behavior in nonadoptive families run the risk of confounding hereditary and environmental relationships. For example, as mentioned earlier, social interactions in a family might be shown to be related to infant sociability; however, social interactions could be a function of parental sociability, and the relationship between parental and infant sociability could be mediated genetically rather than environmentally. That could not happen in adoptive families, because adoptive parents share family environment, but not heredity, with their children. The extent of genetic involvement in putative environmental relationships can be detected by comparing these relationships in adoptive families to those in non-adoptive families. Adoption studies are also useful in isolating genotype–environment interaction and correlation, as explained in the following section.

Other Behavioral–Genetic Analyses

The twin and adoption methodologies have been described with a focus on their usual use, untangling the threads of genetic and environmental influences on behavioral development. We maintain that this is a reasonable and important first step in understanding the etiology of individual differences in behavior. However, these behavioral-genetic methodologies can be extended in more sophisticated directions. We briefly discuss four of these: (1) genotype–environment interaction and correlation, (2) modeling, (3) multivariate extensions, and (4) developmental behavioral-genetic analyses.

Genotype–Environment Interaction and Correlation

Although little is yet known about the main effects of genetic and environmental influences, it is not too early to begin to think about more sophisticated interactional approaches. *Genotype–environment interaction* is one type of interaction that can be studied effectively using the adoption design. Genotype–environment interaction refers to the differential effectiveness of environmental factors for children of different genotypes: Different strokes for different folks. The typical environmental analysis, which we refer to as a "main-effects" analysis, determines whether an environmental influence has an average effect across all children. Such systematic influences are few and far between. It is more likely that environmental factors will be found that affect some children but not others. For example, explosive parental discipline may not be related importantly to children's emotionality on the average, but it might increase the emotionality of children who are predisposed to be emotional. Adoption studies can assess genetic and environmental main effects and their interaction by using measures on biological parents to estimate genetic propensities and by obtaining environmental measures in adoptive homes as described by Plomin, DeFries, and Loehlin (1977).

Genotype–environment correlation refers to the differential exposure of individuals to environments. For example, children with a genetic tendency toward sociability may receive feedback from their environment that fosters even greater social interaction. Thus, the term literally refers to the correlation between genetic propensities and environmental influences. Adoption studies also provide an opportunity to investigate the relationship between genetic estimates of behavioral traits in adoptees (based on measures obtained from their biological parents) and environmental influences measured in the adoptive homes. Genotype–environment correlation can be seen to be related to the issue of direction of effects in socialization (Bell, 1968) in that it estimates the extent to which environmental treatments reflect rather than affect behavior.

Three types of genotype–environment correlations have been proposed, and methods for assessing them have been discussed (Plomin, DeFries, & Loehlin, 1977). The passive type, which is most often considered in quantitative genetic analyses, emerges from the usual situation in which family members share both heredity and family environment. For example, sociable children are likely to have sociable parents and siblings who provide sociable environments for them. The other types of genotype–environment correlations, reactive and active, are likely to be even more important. The reactive type involves a differential response to children that is correlated with their genetic propensities. For example, school children might recognize emotional tendencies in one child and elicit such outbursts. The active type of genotype–environment correlation occurs when individuals actively seek out or create environments correlated with their genetic propensities. Active children, for example, are difficult to restrain because they can turn restrictive conditions, such as the back seat of a car, into highly active situations. Although we usually think of positive correlations between genetic predispositions and environmental factors, negative genotype–environment correlation is also possible; for example, teachers may attempt to dampen the bouncing of a highly active child. One general theory of development fashioned around these types of genotype–environment correlations posits a shift from the passive to the reactive and active varieties during childhood (Scarr & McCartney, 1983).

Structural Models

When we discussed family, twin, and adoption designs, we acknowledged that each method makes certain assumptions concerning assortative mating, additive and nonadditive genetic variance, the comparability of identical and fraternal twin environments, and selective placement. Rather than considering each experiment separately, behavioral geneticists have moved in the direction of analyzing the combined data from several experiments. Structural models (also called biometrical models, causal models, or path models) are superior to the piecemeal approach in several ways: They permit analysis of all data simultaneously, they make assumptions explicit, they permit tests of the relative fit of the model, and they allow tests of different models. Modeling basically involves fitting a series of overdetermined simultaneous equations in order to estimate genetic and environmental parameters that best fit observed familial correlations. Path analysis is typically used to derive the expectations for such equations.

In Chapter 6, a more sophisticiated model, one that closely follows the work of Sewall Wright (1931), who invented path analysis for the study of latent variables in intergenerational transmission, is applied to the CAP cognitive data. Longitudinal and multivariate extensions of structural modeling are also described at that time.

Although such analyses represent state-of-the-art techniques, the basic CAP results in the form of correlations are emphasized in this book because the CAP design is so powerful that these correlations often suggest interpretations without the need for more sophisticated analyses.

Multivariate Genetic–Environmental Analyses

As in most young fields, behavioral genetics has been univariate, analyzing the variance of characters considered one at a time. However, quantitative genetic methods can be readily extended to analyses of covariance among characters; the same principles apply, and the same quantitative genetic methodologies are applicable (e.g., DeFries, Kuse, & Vandenberg, 1979; Plomin & DeFries, 1979). It is extremely unlikely that completely different genes affect each character. Just as we study the factor structure of phenotypic variables, we can also study genetic and environmental factor structures that provide the foundation for the phenotypic factor structure.

A simple way of thinking about genetic analysis of covariance is that it can assess the extent to which the phenotypic or observed correlation between two traits is mediated genetically or environmentally. For example, is the correlation between shyness and fearfulness mediated genetically; that is, are the genes that affect shyness the same as those that affect fearfulness? Or is the covariance mediated by environmental factors that affect both traits?

The parent–offspring design of the CAP forces us to think about genetic covariance among different traits because we cannot assume that traits measured in the parents are the same as those measured in infants. Thus, as explained later, most of the parent–offspring analyses in this book are multivariate.

Developmental Behavioral Genetics

As mentioned earlier, genes are not running at full throttle at conception. The earliest twin studies by Galton and Thorndike at the turn of the century asked whether twin similarity changed with age. This developmental flavor was lost in the ensuing decades, but is seeing a resurgence (Plomin, 1983b). Using cross-sectional data, we can ask whether the relative mixture of genetic and environmental influences changes during development. For example, do twin studies find waning genetic influence on temperament as children experience more varied environments outside the home? Methods for answering such questions have been proposed (Ho, Foch, & Plomin, 1980).

Even more informative than cross-sectional analyses of change in the relative influence of genes and environment is the longitudinal analysis of genetic and environmental contributions to change and continuity in development. One approach has been used in the analysis of longitudinal data from the Louisville Twin Study (Wilson, 1983). Age-to-age changes (spurts and lags) have been analyzed using repeated-measures analysis of variance for identical and fraternal twins. Another approach to longitudinal analysis involves a simple extension of the multivariate genetic–environmental analysis discussed in the previous section: We merely need to consider measurements obtained at two different times rather than measurements of two different characters (Plomin & DeFries, 1981). Phenotypic stability can be mediated genetically or environmentally. An absence of stability indicates that the genetic and environmental factors that affect the character are not correlated across age. Genetic correlation provides a measure of the extent to which a character measured at two different ages is influenced by the same genes at both ages. Similarly, an environmental correlation denotes the extent to which environmental factors that affect a character at one age also affect the character at another age.

In addition to the basic analyses of genetic and environmental correlates of behavioral development, genotype–environment interaction and correlation, structural modeling, multivariate analyses, and developmental analyses have been applied to the CAP infancy data. In the next chapter, we describe the design of the CAP, its sample, and its measures. Then, in subsequent chapters, we turn to the results of our attempts to use this data set and these analyses to understand the origins of individual differences in infancy.

3

The Colorado Adoption Project: History and Design

Introduction

Skodak and Skeels' 1949 report of a longitudinal adoption study of IQ is one of the most frequently cited articles in developmental psychology. IQ scores of adopted children tested four times between early childhood and adolescence were compared to educational level and occupational status of their adoptive parents, to education and occupation of their birth parents, and to IQ scores of about two-thirds of the birth mothers. The results were impressive: The correlation between the IQ scores of birth mothers and IQ of their adopted-away children indicated increasing genetic influence during childhood and reached a correlation of .45 when the children were adolescents.

Despite the impact of Skodak and Skeels' study, over two decades elapsed before the adoption design was again employed to study psychological development. In the late 1970s, however, IQ data were reported for over 4000 pairings in studies that used the adoption design, although none of these studies considered infancy.

Table 3.1 lists 19 familial adoption studies of normal development. The table excludes reports of twins reared apart and studies of the extremes of behavioral variation such as psychopathology, criminality, and alcoholism. It also excludes all but two studies (Duyme, 1981; Hoopes, 1982) of the outcome of adoption (Bohman, 1970; Hoopes, Sherman, Lawder, Andrews, & Lower, 1970; Lawder, Lower, Andrews, Sherman, & Hill, 1969; McWhinnie, 1967; Seglow, Pringle, Kellmer, & Wedge, 1972; Witmer, Herzog, Weinstein, & Sullivan, 1963; Wittenborn, 1957). These adoption studies were not designed to evaluate genetic and environmental

TABLE 3.1

Summary of Previous Familial Adoption Studies of Normal Development

Reference	Full design?	Longitudinal?	Comparisons[a]	Sample size (pairs)	Age of children	Behavioral measures		Environmental measures[b]	Selective placement
						Parents	Children		
Theis, 1924	yes	no	AM/AF–AO BM/BF–AO	602 502	18–40 years	ratings of intelligence, income, education; "family background" for BM/BF sample	ratings of mental ability	none	no information reported
Freeman et al., 1928	no	no	AO–AO/CO AM–AO AF–AO AM–CO AF–CO	140 255 180 40 40	10–11 years (average) 2–22 years	IQ, interests, personality	IQ, school achievement interests	home index (includes education & occupation)	no direct information, but r = .34 between IQ of AO at time of placement & social status of AF
Burks, 1928	no	no	AM–AO AF–AO CM–CO CF–CO	204 178 105 100	5–14 years	IQ, interests	IQ, personality	home index, culture scale	r = .02 for occupations of AF and BF
Lawrence, 1931	no	no	BM–AO BF–AO	401 544	6–15 years	social class	IQ, performance tests for subsample	none	no information available

Study			Groups	N	Testing				Correlation
Leahy, 1935	no	no	AO–AO AM–AO AF–AO CM–CO CF–CO	35 186 178 191 175	5–14 years	IQ, vocabulary	IQ, personality, school progress	home, cultural, social status	$r = .09–.20$ for occupation & .20–.25 for education
Snygg, 1938	no	no	BM–AO	312	1–5+ years	IQ	IQ	none	no information available
Skodak & Skeels, 1949	yes	yes	AM–AO AF–AO BM–AO BF–AO	100 100 92 73	tested 4 times from 1–16 years	education, occupation; IQ for BM subsample	IQ	none	$r = .24–.27$ for education
Beckwith, 1971	yes	yes	AM–AO BM–AO	24 24	tested 2 times from 7–11 months	education, occupation	IQ, observational measures	self-report of childrearing, infants' social experiences, maternal observations	nonsignificant chi-square for occupation and education
Yarrow et al., 1973	no	yes	AM–AO	53	tested in infancy & at 10 years	occupation	IQ, observations, personality	observations, interviews	no information reported
Claeys, 1973	no	no	AM–AO AF–AO	84 84	4–8 years	social class	primary mental abilities	none	$r = .06–.66$
Munsinger, 1975	yes	no	AM–AO AF–AO BM–AO BF–AO	41 41 41 41	school-age	education, occupation	IQ	none	$r = -.22–-.07$
Casler, 1976	no	yes	BM–AO	151	tested 5 times from 2–27 months	IQ	IQ	none	no data, but "every attempt made to match"

(continued)

25

TABLE 3.1 (*Continued*)

Reference	Full design?	Longitudinal?	Comparisons[a]	Sample size (pairs)	Age of children	Behavioral measures		Environmental measures[b]	Selective placement
						Parents	Children		
Fisch et al., 1976	no	yes	AM–AO CM–CO	94 50	tested 2 times from 4–7 years	IQ	IQ, achievement, motor assessment	none	no information reported
Scarr & Weinberg, 1977	yes	no	AO–AO CO–CO AM–AO AF–AO AM–CO AF–CO BM–AO BF–AO	187 107 109 111 141 142 111 47	4–16+ years	IQ, personality; education only for BM–BF samples	IQ, personality, achievement	ratings of home & neighborhood	r = .22 for education
Scarr & Weinberg, 1978	yes	no	AO–AO CO–CO AM–AO AF–AO CM–CO CF–CO BM–AO	84 168 184 175 270 270 150	16–22 years	IQ subtests, specific cognitive abilities, personality, interests; education only for BM sample	IQ subtests, specific cognitive abilities, personality, interests	none	r = .24–.33 for education & .11 for occupation

Study			Comparison	N	Age				Results
Schiff et al., 1978	yes	no	AM–AO / AF–AO / CM–CO / BM–AO / BF–AO	32 / 32 / 20 / 28 / 28	2nd to 6th grade	occupation	IQ, school achievement	none	no information reported
Horn et al., 1979	yes	no	AO–AO/CO / CO–CO / AM–AO / AF–AO / AF–CO / AF–CO / BM–AO	330 / 46 / 459 / 462 / 162 / 163 / 345	3–26 years	IQ, personality	IQ, personality	none	r = .11–.25
Duyme, 1981	yes	no	AF–AO / BM–AO / BF–AO	87 / 74 / 54	14–15 years	occupation	school achievement & adjustment	none	r = .02–.08
Hoopes, 1982	no	yes	AF–AO / AM–AO	40–260 / 40–260	6 months, 2 & 5 years, 8–12 years	personality; self-concept for AM–AF	at 5 years: WISC vocabulary & block design; at 8–12 years: personality & self-concept	ratings from parental interviews	no information reported

[a] A = adoptive; B = biological; C = control; M = mother; F = father, O = offspring.
[b] Environmental measures other than education and occupation of the parents.

influences on development, but rather to compare mean outcomes of adoption. As a result, information usually was not obtained on the biological parents, and correlations between parental or environmental measures and measures on the adoptees were seldom reported.

Several conclusions emerge from the table:

1. Although 10 of the 19 studies include data from both biological and adoptive parents of adopted children (full adoption design), only 3 of these collected information other than education and occupation for biological parents.
2. None of the studies includes information other than education or occupation for biological fathers.
3. Only 6 of the studies followed adoptees longitudinally, and of these, there are only 3 long-term studies. The adoptees in the cross-sectional studies were generally distributed across a wide age range.
4. Only 1 large study considered infants.
5. Sample sizes were quite small in some studies.
6. IQ has clearly been the focus of previous studies.
7. Only 7 of the 19 studies obtained measures of the environment other than parental education or occupation.
8. Of the studies reporting information concerning selective placement, all but 3 showed some selective placement. With the exception of the Texas Adoption Project (Horn, Loehlin, & Willerman, 1979), selective placement estimates have been limited to measures of education and occupation.
9. Nearly all of the studies are retrospective.

In contrast to previous studies, the major features of the Colorado Adoption Project (CAP) may be summarized as follows:

1. The CAP uses a full adoption design. Moreover, the collection of data from parents and children in control (nonadoptive) families permits even more powerful tests of genetic and environmental influences.
2. Biological fathers are tested when possible.
3. The design is longitudinal, thus permitting analyses of the etiology of change and continuity in behavioral development.
4. Children are studied in their homes at 1, 2, 3, and 4 years of age, and it is our intent to conduct follow-up studies at 7, 11, and 16 years.
5. In terms of sample size, the present report includes 182 adoptive families and 165 nonadoptive families in which the children have been tested at both 12 and 24 months of age.
6. The CAP is multivariate. Behavioral assessments of the children at 12 and 24 months include standardized tests of mental and motor development, tester ratings, interview and questionnaire data provided by parents, and videotape recordings of mother–child interactions. Adoptive, biological, and control parents are administered a 3-hour battery of behavioral tests (specific cognitive abilities and personality), and questionnaire data pertaining to medical and social history, aptitudes, and interests are also obtained.

7. Observational, interview, and self-reported information concerning the home and family environment is collected.
8. Selective placement in the CAP is minimal, as indicated in later chapters.
9. The CAP is prospective.

Thus, the CAP differs from previous adoption studies in a number of respects, and it is these differences that make the CAP uniquely suitable for the study of the origins of individual differences in infancy.

History of the CAP

The design of the CAP was formulated by Plomin and DeFries in 1974. Because this took place over a decade ago, and because neither of us has an infallible memory, our recollections regarding the moment of conception of the study differ somewhat. Rather than write a composite history based upon a synthesis of our collective (but faulty) memories, we present our individual recollections and leave it to the reader to judge their plausibility.

The History according to Robert Plomin

When I came to the Institute for Behavioral Genetics in 1974 to interview for a position as assistant professor, I mentioned offhandedly during my colloquium that, although my research had previously employed the twin method, I was interested in conducting a longitudinal adoption study. I had not really given it much thought (if I had realized the time and effort involved in such a study, I never would have suggested it so breezily) and did not think about it again. However, shortly after arriving as a new faculty member fresh from graduate school, a full professor at the institute (John DeFries) asked how my research plans were coming along. Thinking that this was a thinly veiled inquiry into my plans for an adoption study, I choked a bit on my response and said something about laying the groundwork for the research. I felt even more pressured when John gave me a preprint of one of his papers that pointed out the importance and urgency of beginning a longitudinal adoption study. I slumped back to my office, pulling nervously on my beard, wondering how one begins an adoption study. Letting my fingers do the walking, I halfheartedly thumbed through a Denver telephone directory and, to my surprise, saw "Adoption Services." I sheepishly called the Colorado Department of Social Services, expecting them to think that I might be in need of services of an entirely different nature when asking how I could obtain information about pregnant unwed mothers. Instead, the first person with whom I talked suggested calling the director of adoption services of one of the largest adoption agencies in the Rocky Mountain area, Lutheran Social Services of Colorado. One more phone call, and a lunch meeting was arranged with Mr. John Califf, who was enthusiastic about participating in adoption research.

The timing was one of the charmed coincidences that seem to characterize the history of the CAP. Mr. Califf had been bemoaning the lack of good research on adoption, and, for him, the basic science questions that we were asking about nature and nurture were applied issues frequently asked by his adoptive parents. He was so excited about the proposed research that, back in his office after lunch, he called the director of the other major adoption agency in Denver, Catholic Community Services, in order to arrange their joint participation in the project. Together, the two agencies participated in the placement of over 100 "easily placed" infants (Caucasian infants with no known disabilities) each year. So, a few days following my fumbled fielding of John's question, I was able to report that progress on the adoption study looked promising.

The History according to J. C. DeFries

Early during the fall semester, 1974, a recently hired assistant professor (Robert Plomin) stopped by my office for a chat. Rather than engaging in small talk, I asked Robert about his research plans now that he had joined our faculty. Somewhat to my surprise, he responded by saying that he would like to conduct an adoption study. At that time, I was principal investigator of the Colorado Family Reading Study and a coprincipal investigator of the Hawaii Family Study of Cognition; it had been my intention to ask Robert to participate in one or both of these studies if he had no concrete plans for a research project of his own. Given his response, I decided to postpone that invitation. Instead, I gave him a copy of a preprint of a short note that I had recently written based upon a presentation at a workshop on developmental behavioral genetics sponsored by the National Institutes of Health, in April, 1974. At that meeting I had served as a discussant of a paper by Luigi Cavalli-Sforza in which he had mentioned the essential nature of adoption studies for disentangling genetic and environmental influences on complex behavioral characters. In order to elaborate on this point, I reviewed several recent examples of retrospective adoption studies and recommended that a prospective longitudinal adoption study be undertaken. I ended the commentary with a note of urgency because of the declining number of children available for adoption:

> The three studies reviewed above each provides convincing evidence for the presence of a heritable component in the characters under study. However, each of these studies has been *retrospective,* and thus suffers certain methodological inadequacies (incomplete information on biological and adoptive parents, etc.). In spite of these inadequacies, retrospective adoption studies have an important place in human behavioral genetics and clearly are worthy of continued support. Nevertheless, the time has come to also consider the merits of a *prospective* adoption study. In a prospective study, adoptive mothers, adoptive fathers, biological mothers, and even in some cases biological fathers could be administered a comprehensive battery of tests. Subsequently, data could be obtained from normal adoptees, as well as from those "at risk" for various characters of interest. Although longitudinal studies are rather unpopular with funding agencies, it seems to me that if a prospective adoption study is ever undertaken, it would be essential for at least some of the children to be tested at several different ages to assess for possible developmental differences.
>
> Data from a prospective adoption study could provide unambiguous evidence for the pres-

ence (or absence) of a heritable component in each of the behaviors under study. In addition, if comparable data were obtained on children reared by their biological parents, the relative roles of cultural versus biological inheritance could be assessed in the manner outlined by Professor Cavalli-Sforza. Such an undertaking would clearly represent a long-term commitment. Nevertheless, due to the potentially great value of such a study to the field of human behavioral genetics, it is at least worthy of consideration.

Immediate attention should be given to the merits of a prospective adoption study. Due to the increasingly widespread use of contraceptives among young people, as well as access to legalized abortion, we may be witnessing the last generation of adoptive placement of young illegitimate children in this country. Consider some data recently provided by the Colorado State Department of Social Services: During the past four years the Colorado County Departments of Social Services participated in the placement of the following numbers of children under one year of age: In 1970, 888 children were placed; in 1971, 581; in 1972, 406; and in 1973, 312. (These data were obtained from Program Evaluation Report, CS 73–1, and from A. Snook, personal communication.) According to the adoption consultant for this agency, this pattern is not unique to Colorado—it is being observed throughout the country. Thus, if a prospective adoption study is ever to be undertaken with a United States population, it may be necessary to do so within the relatively near future. (DeFries, 1975, pp. 147–148)

I had no intention of conducting such a study myself, but I believed that it could be a landmark study in human behavioral genetics. Therefore, I was pleased to recommend its general design to an eager young colleague.

Robert took the preprint to his office (next door to mine) and read it. Within five minutes he returned to my office and said, "Let's do it!" After suppressing a gulp, I said, "OK," or something to that effect, firmly believing it very unlikely that Robert would be able to convince adoption agency administrators to participate in such a project. Much to my astonishment, however, within only a few days he had met with administrators of two local adoption agencies and had obtained their full support, and we were on our way.

Initiation of the Project

We then began to plan the study in earnest and asked S. G. Vandenberg, who had founded the Louisville Twin Study in the late 1960s, to participate in the planning. Several months were required to work out the ethical complications of the project. The directors, who already knew the identity of the biological parents, agreed to provide us with code numbers for the biological parents so that we would have no identifying information. We developed a plan for the social workers at the agencies to explain the project to biological parents, who are typically counseled at the agency during the last trimester of pregnancy.

We agreed that we would not ask biological parents for blood samples to exclude paternity, because of legal implications as well as the negative effect such a request would have on participation rates. Thus, biological paternity is presumed on the basis of reports by the social worker, the birth mother, and the putative father himself. When a biological father verifies paternity, he is liable for support payments if the biological mother subsequently elects to retain the child; thus, affirmation of paternity is not taken lightly. Another fortuitous event facilitated the inclusion of at least some biological fathers in the CAP. In 1972, the Supreme Court (*Stanley v. Illinois*) ruled that biological fathers had the same rights as biological mothers concerning relinquishment and required that the biological father sign a release to facilitate the adoption of the child. When we began the CAP, this ruling had just begun to create changes in agency policies. However, after a couple of years, it became apparent that the decision was unworkable and unenforceable. Agencies began to slacken their efforts and simply published "John Doe" announcements as evidence of an attempt to locate the biological father. Nonetheless, we have tested approximately 25% of the biological fathers of adopted children in the CAP. Although this is a relatively small percentage, it represents the first attempt to obtain test data from biological fathers in an adoption study, data that are essential to determining birth parents' assortative mating—which affects genetic estimates and which cannot be presumed to be the same as for married couples.

Another ethical issue that had to be resolved was the possibility that asking adoptive parents to participate would make them feel compelled to do so for fear of jeopardizing the adoption process. We agreed to wait to contact the adoptive parents until after the court's final hearing concerning custody of the child, which usually occurs when the adopted infant is between 7 and 9 months of age. For this reason, we could not begin testing infants until they were 12 months old.

Many of our concerns were relieved when we conducted a study of likely participation rates. The project was explained to 23 biological mothers and 17 adoptive couples, who were then given an anonymous reply form asking if they would participate in the proposed study. They were asked to complete the form in private and mail it at their convenience in a stamped envelope addressed to the investigators. Of the 16 replies (70%) received from the biological mothers, all 16 indicated that they would participate and 8 indicated that the biological fathers would also participate. Of the 13 replies (77%) received from the adoptive couples, all 13 were positive and half included comments that emphasized their interest in the project.

We knew that it would be difficult to obtain a large research grant to fund the project because of its long-term nature; for example, over a year passes between the testing of a biological mother and the testing of her adopted-away infant. We also knew that we had to begin testing biological mothers soon because time was running out. As indicated in the above quotation, the availability of contraceptives, legalized abortions, and an increase in the number of unmarried mothers who keep their children had combined to lower drastically the number of infants available for adoption (Sklar & Berkoc, 1974). The decrease was most dramatic for Caucasian infants, for whom late placement and transracial adoption would not be likely to occur. Even though the Rocky Mountain area maintained a relatively high placement rate longer than other parts of this country because it has the largest ratio of easily placed infants to total adoptions (Hylton, 1965), we knew that the numbers showed a downward trend at our adoption agencies. The number of available adoptees has indeed steadily decreased since the CAP began, and it has been necessary to extend the number of years of the project in order to obtain the necessary sample size. This actually added another strength to the design, however, in that cohort effects can be analyzed to determine the generalizability of our results across a 7-year period.

The CAP began in 1976 with the aid of funds from the University of Colorado's Biomedical Research Support Grant and a small grant from the National Institute of Mental Health (MH-28076). The William T. Grant Foundation supported the project in 1977. On our third try, in 1977, the National Institute of Child Health and Human Development awarded a substantial 5-year grant (HD-10333) that launched the full-scale project and that has since been renewed. In 1978, the National Science Foundation provided funds to include videotape recordings of mother–infant interactions at 1, 2, and 3 years of age, a grant that also has been renewed (BNS-7826204 and BNS-8200310).

Design of the CAP

Overview

From the start, we viewed the CAP as a long-term commitment—fully intending to study this unique sample through adolescence to 16 years of age, when the children would be able to complete the same tests their parents had completed over a decade and a half earlier. This long-range goal led us to test the CAP children at 1, 2, 3, and 4 years of age, rather than testing more frequently, because the testing schedule had to balance frequency of testing and sample size. We had hoped to include 300 adopted probands and 300 matched nonadopted probands, which implied 2400 home visits if we tested once a year. This meant 10 tester-years and big budgets.

In retrospect, testing at 1 and 2 years has been especially valuable. Rapid development of symbolic and imitation capabilities occurs from 9 to 12 months, the age at which language, or at least symbolic communication of some kind, begins. The CAP 1-year-olds have thus passed that transitional period and are in the developmental plateau that continues until about 16 months of age, when another rapid period of change occurs as the infant begins the dramatic transition from infancy to childhood with its explosion of new abilities. This transitional turmoil has quieted down for most areas of psychological development by 24 months of age. Thus, our first two yearly tests permit assessment of individual differences in the periods of calm that follow two major transitional periods. In a study of individual differences in development, it is useful to avoid testing in the middle of a major transition because slight differences in timing of such transitions can create large differences among individuals tested at the same chronological age.

Adoption Design

The biological mothers of the CAP infants are tested on a 3-hour battery of psychological measures, as described later. Every attempt is made to test biological

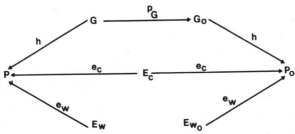

FIGURE 3.1   Path model illustrating parent–offspring resemblance in a nonadoptive family. (From Figure 1 in J. C. DeFries, R. Plomin, S. G. Vandenberg, & A. R. Kuse, "Parent-offspring resemblance for cognitive abilities in the Colorado Adoption Project: Biological, adoptive, and control parents and one-year-old children," *Intelligence*, 1981, 5, 245–277. Copyright 1981 by Ablex Publishing Corporation. Reprinted by permission.)

fathers as well. The adoptive parents of the infants are tested on the same 3-hour battery of tests. These tests fulfill two important conditions of the adoption design: Data are obtained on biological parents, who share heredity but not family environment with their adopted-away infants, as well as on adoptive parents, who share family environment but not heredity with their adopted infants. Another important feature of the CAP design is that nonadoptive families are matched to the adoptive families and studied in the same way. These families add an important control: parents who share both heredity and family environment with their infants. Adopted and nonadopted younger siblings of the probands are tested in the same manner as the probands and will provide developmental comparisons, although the sample size of younger siblings tested at both 1 and 2 years of age is not yet large enough for adequate analysis.

The CAP design can be visualized in terms of path diagrams that make the design and its assumptions more explicit. Figure 3.1 illustrates parent–offspring resemblance in a nonadoptive family: P represents a parent's observed phenotypic value, G is the additive genetic value (Falconer, 1981), E_c is common or shared family environmental influence that makes parents and offspring similar to one another, and E_w is within-family individual experience. The subscript o refers to corresponding values for a child. In nonadoptive families, parents and offspring share both genes and a common family environment. Thus, in path analytic terms, the expected parent–child correlation is

$$r_{PP_o} = h^2 p_G + e_c^2, \tag{3.1}$$

where h^2 is narrow-sense heritability, involving only additive genetic variance; p_G is a genetic path coefficient that equals .5 when mating is at random; e_c^2 is common family environmentality, the proportion of phenotypic variance due to environmental influences shared by parents and offspring; and e_w^2 is the rest of the environmental influence.

In contrast, as shown in Figure 3.2, adopted children share heredity with their biological parents and environmental influences with their adoptive parents. Thus, in

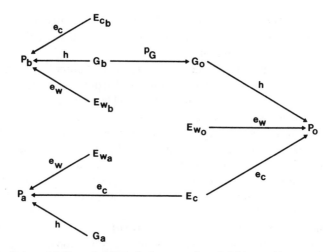

FIGURE 3.2   Path model illustrating biological parent–adopted child resemblance and adoptive parent–adopted child resemblance. (From Figure 2 in J. C. DeFries, R. Plomin, S. G. Vandenberg, & A. R.
Kuse, "Parent-offspring resemblance for cognitive abilities in the Colorado Adoption Project: Biological, adoptive, and control parents and one-year-old children," *Intelligence,* 1981, *5,* 245–277.
Copyright 1981 by Ablex Publishing Corporation. Reprinted by permission.)

the absence of selective placement, the expected correlation between adopted children and their biological parents is

$$r_{P_b P_o} = h^2 p_G, \qquad (3.2)$$

and the expected correlation between adoptive parents and their adopted children is

$$r_{P_a P_o} = e_c^2. \qquad (3.3)$$

Given these elementary models, the sum of the expected correlation for biological
parents and their adopted-away offspring and the expected correlation for adoptive
parents and their adopted offspring is equal to that for nonadoptive parents and their
children.

This model is affected by assortative mating because the phenotypes of mothers
and fathers are not independent if mating is not at random. This covariance inflates
correlations between each parent and the offspring (Plomin, DeFries, & Roberts,
1977). Thus, assortative mating inflates genetic estimates if biological parents mate
assortatively, and it also inflates estimates of common family environment if adoptive
parents mate assortatively (see DeFries, Plomin, Vandenberg, & Kuse, 1981). As
mentioned earlier, testing biological fathers is crucial in order to obtain estimates of
assortative mating for unwed parents, which cannot be presumed to be the same as for
wed couples.

The model is also affected by selective placement; that is, the matching of
biological and adoptive parents. If selective placement occurs, the phenotypes of
biological and adoptive parents are not independent, and covariance inflates both
biological parent–offspring correlations and adoptive parent–offspring correlations.

Thus, selective placement can inflate both genetic and environmental estimates in full adoption designs (see DeFries *et al.*, 1981). We present evidence that selective placement in the CAP is negligible.

It should be emphasized that the CAP design at this point is a parent–offspring design until the sample size of younger siblings of the probands increases. In terms of environmental analyses, this is a particularly useful feature. No one would doubt that the major systematic environmental force in the lives of infants is their parents. As just described, the adoption design facilitates estimates of common family environmental experiences that make parents and their children similar; socioeconomic status is often thought to be an influence of this type. In addition to this important component of variance, the parent–offspring adoption design is particularly useful for identifying specific environmental factors that affect development. Environmental assessments embedded in an adoption design of this type permit analyses of environmental influence free of genetic bias. Nearly all previous reports concerning the relationship between environment and children's development have been based upon studies of families in which both heredity and environment are shared by parents and their offspring. As long as heredity and environment are confounded, putative environmental relationships might well be mediated genetically. In addition to studying family environmental influences free of genetic confound, the CAP design permits estimation of the extent to which supposedly environmental influences are in fact genetically mediated by comparing such relationships in adoptive and nonadoptive families. This information is of considerable importance when it comes to thinking about intervention based on finding an environmental correlate of individual differences in development.

The parent–offspring design is not as powerful for detecting genetic influences in infancy, however. We cannot assume an isomorphism between the characters measured in parents and in their infants. It is more appropriate to consider the parental and

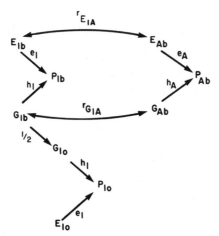

FIGURE 3.3   Path model illustrating correlations of biological parents as infants (P_{Ib}) and as adults (P_{Ab}) with their adopted-away offspring as infants (P_{Io}).

infant measures as representing different characters, although the logic of the adoption design remains the same. Figure 3.3 depicts a path model that emphasizes this point by adding a genetic correlation, $r_{G_{IA}}$, and an environmental correlation, $r_{E_{IA}}$, between infancy and adulthood. The e_A and e_I paths have been sufficiently described on page 34. Because genes can be expressed differentially during development, they contribute to differences from infancy to adulthood within an individual and thus between infant adoptees and their adult biological parents as well. In other words, significant resemblance between biological parents and their adopted-away infants requires that the genes that affect individual differences in infancy also affect individual differences in adulthood. Such resemblance implies genetic continuity between infancy and adulthoood within individuals. For example, if infant mental development scores for adoptees were correlated significantly with their biological mothers' IQ scores, we would predict a higher correlation between the infants' mental development scores and their own IQ scores as adults. This prediction follows from the fact that infants share only 50% of their genes with their biological mothers, whereas they share all of their genes with themselves as adults. In this way, the discovery of significant correlations between biological parents and their adopted-away infants suggests genetically mediated continuity between infancy and adulthood.

Instead of thinking about the adopted infant as an adult, which is implied by Equation 3.2, we should think about the adopted infant as an infant and add the genetic correlation $r_{G_{IA}}$, as depicted in Figure 3.3, in describing the correlation between the biological parent as an adult (P_{Ab}) and the adoptee as an infant (P_{Io}):

$$r_{P_{Ab}P_{Io}} = \tfrac{1}{2}h_A h_I r_{G_{IA}}. \tag{3.4}$$

In addition to the genetic correlation between infancy and adulthood, Figure 3.3 considers the likelihood that heritabilities differ in infancy and adulthood. Significant resemblance between biological parents and their adopted-away infants requires that the adult character and the infant character both be heritable. The three requirements for finding significant correlations between biological parents and their adopted-away offspring—heritability in infancy, heritability in adulthood, and a genetic correlation between infancy and adulthood—affect the power of the CAP design to detect significant genetic influence. Consider, for example, a character that shows 50% heritability in adulthood. We are unlikely to know the heritability of a character in infancy or its stability from infancy to adulthood. But suppose heritability in infancy is also 50% and that half of the genetic variance operates in common between infancy and adulthood (i.e., $r_{G_{IA}} = .50$). In this example, we would expect a correlation of .125 between parents and their infant offspring. Correlations of this magnitude would require a sample of over 500 biological mothers and their adopted-away infants to detect the correlation with 80% power given that $p < .05$ (Cohen, 1977). The CAP sample of biological mothers and their adopted-away infants provides 47% power to detect such correlations, meaning that half the time we will fail to detect significant genetic influence of this magnitude. However, the CAP design is a good deal more powerful than this would suggest because it includes nonadoptive parents and their children, a replication that adds considerable power when all the data are analyzed simultaneously using model-fitting approaches.

From the perspective of developmental behavioral genetics, the most interesting aspect of Figure 3.3 is the implication for estimating genetic continuity from infancy to adulthood when a significant correlation is found between biological parents and their offspring. By using published twin data to provide estimates of h_I and h_A, we can estimate the genetic correlation $r_{G_{IA}}$. At the extreme, if the parent–offspring correlation for biological parents and adopted infants equals $\frac{1}{2}h_I h_A$, the genetic correlation must equal 1.0, which means that the genes that affect individual differences in infancy are exactly the same as those that affect individual differences in adulthood. A more likely possibility involves the example mentioned earlier: If a correlation of .125 were observed between biological parents and their adopted-away infants and we knew that heritability in infancy and in adulthood was .50, we would estimate that the genetic correlation from infancy to adulthood is .50. At the other extreme, given the same constraints—heritability of .50 in infancy and in adulthood—a correlation of .00 between biological parents and their adopted-away infants suggests a genetic correlation of zero between infancy and adulthood. Although a fair amount is known about the adult heritabilities of the CAP measures, the fact that little is known about infant heritabilities limits our ability to explore these issues. Nonetheless, we do make some educated guesses along these lines for mental development and temperament and report some exciting results in subsequent chapters. Analyses of this type offer a promising approach for research in behavioral genetics.

The CAP Sample

The analyses summarized in this book are based on data from 182 adopted infants and 165 matched nonadopted (control) infants who have been tested at both 12 and 24 months of age, who had reasonably complete data, and for whom the testers indicated that the quality of testing was adequate. The sample also includes 179 biological mothers, 43 biological fathers, 177 adoptive mothers, and 174 adoptive fathers of the adopted infants, as well as 162 mothers and 162 fathers of the control infants. These 897 adults have participated in the 3-hour adult test session. Because nonadoptive families are matched to the adoptive families after the adoptive parents have been tested, the number of control families lags behind the number of adoptive families.

In this section the selection procedures are described, the sample's representativeness is discussed, and the selective placement issue is addressed.

Sample Selection

As mentioned earlier, biological parents are solicited through two Denver adoption agencies. Social workers encourage biological mothers to participate in the

CAP only if it is considered likely that they will relinquish their children for adoption. Of the biological mothers who have been tested, 74% decided to relinquish their children. We have found no important differences in either cognition or personality between those biological mothers who relinquish and those who do not, as described in Chapter 14. Biological parents are usually tested in small groups, ranging in size from 1 to 11, and they are paid for their participation. Seventy-one percent of the biological mothers are tested while pregnant; analyses indicate no significant differences in personality test scores between those tested while pregnant and those tested after delivery. Women tested after delivery are about half a standard deviation lower in their cognitive scores, however. Although it is not a testable hypothesis, we speculate that this difference can be attributed to a selection bias rather than to artifact in the testing procedure for three reasons. One might expect women in their last trimester of pregnancy to obtain lower scores because of the discomfort and stress of pending delivery and decisions about relinquishment; nonetheless, they scored higher than those women who were tested after delivery and after relinquishment had been settled. Motivational explanations of the difference between the two groups would predict differences on the personality questionnaires; however, no personality differences were detected. Therefore, it seems possible that women who were more difficult to schedule, missed testing appointments, and were thus tested after pregnancy may have been somewhat less intelligent on the average than those who participated punctually and eagerly.

For adoptive parents, the adoption process is lengthy; the average time from first contact with the agency to placement of an easily placed child is approximately 3 years. Although procedures for selecting adoptive parents have varied over the years, few potential adoptive parents (less than 10%) are denied a placement. General guidelines exist concerning age of the couple (combined age of adoptive parents less than 75 years); religion (one agency requires that both parents be Protestant and members of a church, whereas the other requires that at least one parent be a practicing Catholic); number of years that the couple has been married (more than 2); number of children already in home (not more than 1); and a medical reason making it undesirable or impossible for the couple to have a child. After waiting 2 to 3 years, a formal application is requested, and the home study, which includes an interview and home visit, begins. Criteria for placement include emotional stability, apparent stability of the marriage, and ability of the couple to meet their financial obligations. Income per se is not considered, and home ownership is not a criterion.

Adoptive parents are informed about the CAP during their orientation at the adoption agency, but they are not asked to participate until after the adoption of their child. At this time, adoptive parents are contacted by a social worker and are invited to visit the agency and be tested at their convenience. Of the adoptive parents who have been contacted, about 75% have agreed to participate. Adoptive couples are usually tested together in groups of 12 or less and are paid a small honorarium for their participation.

Immediately after release from the hospital ($\bar{X} = 4.2$ days; $SD = 3.5$ days; Range $= 1–33$ days), the adopted infants are taken to a foster home by a social worker.

Thus, the adopted infants in our sample are not taken home by their biological mothers. The infants remain in foster homes until the legal requirements concerning relinquishment are fulfilled ($\bar{X}$ = 24.1 days; SD = 20.7 days; Range = 0–156 days). The agencies used numerous foster homes for the children in our study; the average age of the foster parents is 45 and most foster parents have children of their own. Foster families never have more than one foster infant in their home at a time.

The children are placed in their adoptive homes at the average age of 29 days. The courts require three visits by a social worker after placement of the child in the adoptive home and before the court's final hearing concerning custody of the child. Terminations of placement are rare, and none occurred for infants in our study.

The nonadoptive (control) families are ascertained through local hospitals. Records of recently born children are surveyed by hospital staff to identify couples who have had a singleton birth and have no more than two other children in the home. These families receive a letter describing the project, a cover letter from the hospital, and a return postcard on which they may request that they be contacted to discuss the project in greater detail. Those parents who return the postcard are contacted by phone, and information is obtained in order to decide whether the family can be matched to an adoptive family based on the following criteria: sex of proband, number of children in family, age of father (± 5 years), National Opinion Research Center (NORC) rating of occupation status of the father (± 8 points), and total years of the father's education (± 2 years). This matching procedure ensures comparability between adoptive and nonadoptive families, but it is not used for the purpose of statistical analyses based upon paired observations. After a match between adoptive and control families is confirmed, the prospective control couple is contacted by phone and arrangements are made for testing in small groups (2–15 individuals) at the Institute for Behavioral Genetics. As is the case for other parents, nonadoptive couples are paid an honorarium for their participation.

Representativeness

Stereotypes abound in adoption. For example, adoptive parents are thought to be wealthy; biological parents are viewed as lower class. Educational and occupational status can be used to address the issue of representativeness of the CAP sample. We should first mention that the CAP families are not typical of all U.S. adoptions: Nearly 90% of the biological parents and over 95% of the nonadoptive parents report that they are Caucasian; the rest are primarily Hispanic and Oriental. The two adoption agencies participating in the CAP are Lutheran and Catholic, two religions that cut across a broad section of our society. As indicated in the description of the agencies' procedure for selecting adoptive parents, the agencies eliminate very few prospective parents and do not use wealth as a criterion. These considerations led us to expect CAP adoptive parents to be reasonably representative.

Education, occupation, and age of the biological, adoptive, and nonadoptive parents are described in Table 3.2. As a result of the matching procedures, adoptive and control fathers are similar with regard to education and occupational status, as

TABLE 3.2

Education, Occupation, and Age of CAP Parents

	Biological				Adoptive				Control			
	Mothers (N = 181)		Fathers (N = 44)		Mothers (N = 180)		Fathers (N = 177)		Mothers (N = 164)		Fathers (N = 164)	
	$\bar{X}$	SD	$\bar{X}$	SD	$\bar{X}$	SD	$\bar{X}$	SD	$\bar{X}$	SD	$\bar{X}$	SD
Education	12.0	1.9	12.4	1.9	14.8	2.1	15.7	2.5	15.1	2.0	15.7	2.2
Occupational NORC[a]	33.5	10.9	31.2	13.1	33.2	13.4	52.5	13.2	36.5	15.1	51.2	12.1
Age	19.4	3.0	21.1	4.8	32.5	3.5	34.1	4.1	29.6	6.5	31.8	4.3

[a]"Revised NORC" (Hauser & Featherman, 1977) based on occupational titles from the 1970 census.

TABLE 3.3

Education and Occupation of CAP "Grandfathers"

| | Biological | | | | Adoptive | | | | Control | | | |
| | Mothers' fathers (N = 167) | | Fathers' fathers (N = 39) | | Mothers' fathers (N = 176) | | Fathers' fathers (N = 163) | | Mothers' fathers (N = 155) | | Fathers' fathers (N = 152) | |
	$\bar{X}$	SD	$\bar{X}$	SD	$\bar{X}$	SD	$\bar{X}$	SD	$\bar{X}$	SD	$\bar{X}$	SD
Education	13.5	3.0	14.0	3.6	12.3	3.6	11.4	3.7	13.8	3.8	12.8	3.3
Occupational NORC[a]	47.9	14.7	50.3	14.4	48.2	13.0	45.2	12.4	49.8	13.0	48.3	13.5

[a] "Revised NORC" (Hauser & Featherman, 1977) based on occupational titles from the 1970 census.

TABLE 3.4

Occupational NORC Ratings of Males in the CAP
and in a Stratified Random Sample from Colorado[a]

	$\overline{X}$	SD
Biological fathers	60.9	8.8
Adoptive fathers	75.1	9.0
Control fathers	73.9	8.3
Biological fathers' fathers	72.7	8.8
Biological mothers' fathers	71.4	10.5
Adoptive fathers' fathers	69.0	9.8
Adoptive mothers' fathers	71.0	8.9
Control fathers' fathers	71.8	10.0
Control mothers' fathers	72.9	9.2
Denver random sample[b]	71.3	7.8

[a]"NORC" based on occupational titles from the 1950 census.
[b]From Crumpacker et al. (1979); $N = 162$.

are adoptive and control mothers. However, adoptive parents are slightly older than control parents and considerably older than biological parents. Because biological parents are often teenagers, their years of education and occupational status are lower than educational and occupational status of the adoptive and control parents. However, the data for the grandparents—that is, the parents of the CAP adults— indicate that the average years of education and occupational status of the biological grandparents are comparable to those measures for the control and the adoptive grandparents (see Table 3.3). These results lend no support to the stereotype of biological parents as lower class.

Because the biological, adoptive, and nonadoptive parents are similar in means and variances for these demographic measures (and for test scores, as we see in later chapters), the internal coherence of the CAP design is preserved. However, the issue of representativeness extends beyond such internal comparability. The CAP adult occupations would seem to span a broad section of society, ranging from occupations such as floor layer, farm worker, and miner to engineer, bank president, and surgeon. However, comparisons with other data sets are needed to evaluate CAP's representativeness.

Occupational ratings based on the NORC survey of occupational ratings of prestige that used the 1950 census classification of occupations (Reiss, 1961) were employed in an epidemiological study of smoking conducted in the Denver metropolitan area (Crumpacker et al., 1979). This study provides an important comparison group for the CAP sample because it was "selected by a stratified random sampling procedure in suburban Jefferson County, Colorado, using 1970 census data and a 1975 city directory, which referenced households geographically" (p. 183). Table 3.4 compares "NORC" occupational status of the CAP males, and of the fathers of the CAP males and females, to the occupational status of the stratified

TABLE 3.5

National Socioeconomic Comparisons to the CAP Males[a]

	NORC		SEI	
	$\overline{X}$	SD	$\overline{X}$	SD
Biological fathers	31.2	13.1	31.7	22.4
Adoptive fathers	52.5	13.2	63.4	20.5
Control fathers	51.2	12.1	61.9	18.2
Biological fathers' fathers	50.3	14.4	57.8	21.8
Biological mothers' fathers	47.9	14.7	54.7	24.0
Adoptive fathers' fathers	45.2	12.4	49.0	22.0
Adoptive mothers' fathers	48.2	13.0	54.6	22.2
Control fathers' fathers	48.3	13.5	54.7	23.1
Control mothers' fathers	49.8	13.0	56.7	21.9
1970 census white labor force	41.7	13.9	41.6	14.6

[a]"Revised NORC" and "revised SEI" from Hauser and Featherman (1977).

random sample of suburban Denver males in the Crumpacker *et al.* study. The average NORC rating for the adoptive and control fathers is about 75; their fathers' average rating is about 70. Because the biological fathers are only 21 years old on the average, a lower NORC is expected. However, the average NORC rating of their fathers and of the biological mothers' fathers is about 72, which is similar to the ratings of the fathers of the adoptive and control fathers. Most important, these mean occupational status ratings are quite similar to that of the stratified random sample of Denver males.

For the adoption design, variance is more critical than means. In every case, the standard deviations shown in Table 3.4 for the CAP sample are larger than that of the stratified random Denver sample. Thus, the parents in the CAP represent a broad cross section of the Caucasian population in the Denver metropolitan area.

This does not mean that the CAP sample is representative of the entire U.S. population, however, There are no nationwide comparisons for the NORC, so we converted the CAP adult occupations to other major indices of socioeconomic status (SES; see Table 3.5). For example, the NORC prestige rankings have been revised on the basis of the 1970 census occupational classification (Hauser & Featherman, 1977). For the U.S. white labor force, which includes rural as well as urban individuals, the mean "revised NORC" rating is 41.7 (*SD* = 13.9). For the CAP sample, the means are about 50 with standard deviations of about 13, suggesting that, although the CAP sample is somewhat above the national average in occupational status, it is nearly representative in terms of variance.

Other socioeconomic indices lead to a similar conclusion. The Socioeconomic Index (SEI), widely used in behavioral-genetic research, was initially developed by Duncan (in Reiss, 1961) using ratings of the 1950 census classification of occupations based on prestige, income, and education. Although national comparison samples are not available for the "SEI," it is noteworthy that Horn *et al.* (1979) reported a mean SEI of 65.0 (*SD* = 20.7) for adoptive fathers in the Texas Adoption

Project. CAP adoptive fathers have a mean SEI of 62.8 (*SD* = 22.0). The SEI was revised by Hauser and Featherman (1977) using the 1970 census classification of occupations. As indicated in Table 3.5, the 1970 white labor force yielded a mean of 41.6 (*SD* = 14.6) for this "revised SEI." The CAP adoptive and nonadoptive fathers yield a mean of approximately 62 on this index and a standard deviation of approximately 19. The mean revised SEI rating for the biological, adoptive, and control grandfathers is 54.6 (*SD* = 22.5). Thus, although the CAP means are above the national mean, the CAP variances are also larger than the national variance.

Another socioeconomic index that provides some comparison data is the revised Hollingshead four-factor index (Hollingshead, 1975) based on occupation, education, sex, and marital status. Gottfried (1984) reports a mean of 45.6 (*SD* = 11.7) for a sample of middle-class nonadoptive families from the Los Angeles metropolitan area. The CAP control fathers have a mean of 43.6 and a standard deviation of 13.4, indicating that the CAP sample is comparable to other samples of metropolitan families.

In summary, although the CAP families have a higher SES than the working U.S. population, the CAP variances tend to be similar to the U.S. population variance. We refer to the CAP sample as middle class, a group that is understudied, especially in terms of the development of individual differences, even though the middle class represents the majority of the population. Far more common are studies of lower-class samples and comparisons of averages for lower-class and middle-class samples. Although such studies are important, we cannot generalize from such average differences between groups to individual differences within groups, as discussed in Chapter 1. Historically, middle-class parents were viewed as providing home environments that maximally facilitate development (Metzl, 1980), but developmentalists have become aware of the obvious range of individual differences within middle-class populations, both in terms of infant development and home environments (Gottfried & Gottfried, 1984).

As an aside, we should mention that our analyses of five of the major measures of SES—the SEI and the revised SEI, the NORC and the revised NORC, and the revised Hollingshead four-factor index—reveal high intercorrelations, ranging from .85 to .98, with the exception of the revised Hollingshead, which yields correlations of .73 to .76 with the other measures. The reason for the lower correlations with the Hollingshead is that it is based directly on number of years of education and a 7-point classification of occupations, in contrast to the other measures, which include education only indirectly and provide much finer gradations of occupational status: For the SEI and the revised SEI, the occupational ratings range from 5 to 96 and 2 to 96, respectively; for the NORC and the revised NORC, the ratings range from 15 to 93 and from 9 to 82, respectively. The advantage of using the revised versions of the SEI and the NORC is that they include occupational titles based on the 1970 census (such as computer programmer) that were not included in the 1950 census classification of occupations. A 1981 review of SES measures argued that developmental psychologists should discontinue the use of older measures of SES, especially the old Hollingshead two-factor index, and recommend the revised SEI and revised NORC (Mueller & Parcell, 1981). However, Gottfried

(1984) suggests that the revised Hollingshead four-factor index is particularly useful because it is the only measure suitable for estimating the SES of unmarried individuals, female heads of households, and families in which both spouses are employed. Nonetheless, given the high intercorrelations among the various measures of SES, the particular measure one uses does not seem to be of critical importance.

Selective Placement

Another issue in adoption studies is selective placement—the matching of adoptive and biological parents. Positive selective placement will inflate estimates of both genetic and common family environmental influences. One of the reasons we were particularly excited about the two Denver adoption agencies participating in the CAP is that they, like other progressive agencies, do not attempt to match adoptees to adoptive parents, because they feel that this sets up false expectations in the adoptive parents that the baby will grow up to be just like them. Instead, the agency personnel believe that their resources are better spent counseling adoptive parents about the differences to be expected. Moreover, the pool of approved adoptive parents is kept small (10 couples or less), so that, when a child becomes available for placement, there are few parents from which to choose selectively even if the social workers might wish to do so. The only exceptions concern geographical area and height. Infants are not placed in the geographical area in which their biological parents reside. To the extent that this practice exists, it should result in some negative selective placement for traits associated with residence locale. Also, social workers intentionally avoid large mismatches in height. On the other hand, no conscious selective placement occurs with regard to mental ability, although some consideration is given to placing an infant in the best family for that particular child. Clearly, socioeconomic level is part of this consideration. Nevertheless, given the number of factors considered and the small number of adoptive couples among whom any selection can be practiced, it seems likely a priori that selective placement in the CAP for mental ability—and certainly for other characteristics such as personality—is minimal.

In subsequent chapters, we examine selective placement correlations for behavioral characteristics. Because social workers do not have access to behavioral test data, any selective placement they make would have to be based on demographic characteristics such as SES and education. Selective placement correlations for these variables are presented in Table 3.6. We report data for the revised SEI (Hauser & Featherman, 1977), the Hollingshead four-factor index (Hollingshead, 1975), and years of education; other socioeconomic indicators yielded similar results. Biological fathers' data are not reported because of the relatively small sample size.

The correlations between the biological mothers and adoptive parents are low and nonsignificant for education. Although selective placement for biological mothers' occupation is modest, it is significant. However, as mentioned earlier, biological

TABLE 3.6

Selective Placement Correlations for SES and Education in the CAP[a]

	Occupational indices		
	SEI	Hollingshead	Education
Biological mother vs. adoptive mother	.10	.21*	−.13
Biological mother vs. adoptive father	.17*	.21*	.08
Biological mothers' father vs. adoptive father	.02	.00	.08
Biological mothers' father vs. adoptive mothers' father	−.17*	−.14*	.02
Biological mothers' father vs. adoptive fathers' father	.01	.01	.12

[a] $N = 94-172$.
*$p < .05$.

mothers are young and their occupations might not adequately describe their social status. For these reasons, the most informative selective placement information may be obtained by comparing the biological mothers' fathers with the adoptive fathers and the fathers of the adoptive mothers and fathers. For both education and SES, these selective placement correlations are also low; the two that are significant are negative. Overall, the median selective placement correlation based on the data presented in Table 3.6 is .02. Thus, for those variables about which social workers have the best knowledge, selective placement in the CAP is negligible.

Summary

In this chapter we have presented an overview of the Colorado Adoption Project and a description of its sample and procedures. We began with a review of 19 previous adoption studies of normal behavioral variation that indicates the uniqueness of the CAP. We also have described the history and design of the project. Although design considerations can be complex, the major point of our description is that the CAP exemplifies a full adoption design that includes adoptive parents, who share only family environment with their adopted children; biological (birth) parents, who share only heredity with their adopted-away children; and control (nonadoptive) parents, who share both family environment and heredity with their children.

The sample selection procedures have been described, and data are presented indicating that, in terms of SES, the CAP sample is quite representative of metropolitan Caucasian families in the U.S., especially in terms of variance. Moreover, selective placement is negligible for SES and education, two variables most accessible to social workers. Other measures obtained in the CAP are described in detail in the following chapters.

4

The Colorado Adoption Project: Measures

Introduction

A broad array of data has been collected in the CAP for parents, infants, and their home environments. The breadth of the measures was our response to the challenge of creating a resource that could not be re-created: Given the drastic reductions in the availability of easily placed adoptees, we believed it highly unlikely that such a study could again be accomplished in the U.S. For this reason, we have attempted to collect as much valid and reliable data as possible during the relatively brief testing periods available to us. Our selection of measures was guided by an advisory committee including L. Heston, J. C. Loehlin, R. B. McCall, W. Meredith, and S. Scarr. We have also sought advice concerning our home visits from J. Block, W. Charlesworth, J. Kagan, and M. Weir.

This approach could be construed as a fishing expedition rather than a test of specific developmental theories. However, quantitative genetics provides a theory of unparalleled breadth for the study of individual differences in development in its approach to understanding genetic and environmental components of both variance and covariance and etiologies of change and continuity. The approach argues for including a broad, efficient battery of measures rather than attempting to test any one theory within one domain of development. Once the data are collected, it is possible to explore a variety of theoretical positions such as the ontogenetic hierarchical differentiation of abilities or the relationship between language and cognition, adding to these old issues the new perspective of quantitative genetics.

A related possible criticism is that some aspects of the vast amounts of data that have been collected in the CAP may be of minor interest. For example, in a review of one of our research proposals, musical interests, handedness, food preferences, religiosity, and television viewing were singled out for this criticism. Our reply is that we evaluated measures on the basis of a cost–benefit ratio. The food preference and religiosity items in the adult battery take only a few seconds to complete. Moreover, it is quite debatable how important such items might prove to be. Strong dislikes in food may be an important source of parent–child conflict that should be explored. Similarly, many in our society would argue that religiosity is one of the most important aspects of family life. Few child psychologists would argue that measuring television viewing is not worth the effort.

With the advantage of hindsight on a longitudinal study launched nearly a decade ago, we probably would have excluded some measures and included others. Still, we would defend our general goal of sampling extensively and broadly rather than intensively and narrowly in the CAP. In this section, the various measures used in the CAP for infants, adults, and to assess the home environment are described. Some of these measures are published; however, those that are unavailable or modified are reproduced in Appendices A through C. These appendices provide a fuller picture of the CAP's data set than does the following summary of measures. For example, we describe about 70 summary measures of the infants from each year's testing. However, the CAP data bank includes over 700 pieces of information concerning the infants' development at each year's home visits. Similarly, about 60 summary measures for the parents are listed even though the CAP data bank includes over 600 pieces of information from each adult's test booklet.

One final general issue concerning the CAP measures involves the preparation of data for analysis. With the assistance of gifted and dedicated data managers, especially Allan Kuse and Robin Corley, we have devised programs that not only routinely update the sample, but also simultaneously conduct numerous checks on the accuracy of the data. A systems information retrieval program has also been developed to permit easy access to the vast CAP data set using standardized variable labels that avoid confusion in the interpretation of printouts. In terms of preliminary analysis, one point should be emphasized: In all analyses reported in this book, we have eliminated outliers by using three standard deviations above or below the mean as a criterion. This screening was conducted at the level at which most analyses were to be done. For example, the screening was not conducted at the item level for personality measures, but rather at the level of scales, which is the level of analysis used in parent–offspring and environment–offspring analyses related to personality. The justification for eliminating such outliers is to avoid results based on individuals who are more rare than one in a thousand—results unlikely to be replicated. We explored more sophisticated methods of achieving this goal such as screening for bivariate outliers that contribute disproportionately to correlations; however, we found that simple univariate screening for individuals three standard deviations above or below the mean accomplished much the same results as did more sophisticated approaches.

TABLE 4.1

Summary of CAP Measures for 1- and 2-Year-Old Infants

Measure and reference	Age when administered (yr)	Scores obtained
Cognitive measures		
Bayley Mental Scale (Bayley, 1969)	1, 2	Age-normed Mental Development Index (MDI) score
Scale scores for Bayley items (Lewis, 1983)	1, 2	At 12 months, Means-End, Imitation, and Verbal Skill scores; at 24 months, Lexical, Spatial, Verbal, and Imitation scores
Uzgiris–Hunt Ordinal Scales of Psychological Development (Uzgiris & Hunt, 1975)	1	Visual Pursuit and the Permanence of Objects; Means of Obtaining Desired Environmental Events; Vocal Imitation; Gestural Imitation; Total score for these four scales
Communication measures		
Bayley communication items	1, 2	At 12 months, sum of items 84, 85, 89, 101, 106, 113, 116, 117, 124, 126, 127, and 130; At 24 months, sum of items 124, 126, 127, 128, 130, 132, 136, 138, 139, 141, 145, 146, 148, 149, 150, 158, and 163
Videotaped observations of mothers and infants interacting (Hardy-Brown et al., 1981)	1	Total vocalizations; communicative gestures; use of request prosody; vocal imitation; physical imitation; use of phonetically consistent forms; syllable structure; vocal signals; true words; vocalization context: objects vs. persons; unrotated principal component: infant communicative competence
Maternal interview concerning use of true words	1, 1½	Production of true words
Items from Sequenced Inventory of Communication Development (Hedrick et al., 1975)	2	Expressive scale; receptive scale
Personality–temperament measures Bayley Infant Behavior Record (Bayley, 1969)	1, 2	Three factors based on the 25 items rated by the Bayley tester as described by Matheny (1980): Affect–Extraversion; Task Orientation; Activity
Colorado Childhood Temperament Inventory (Rowe & Plomin, 1977)	1, 2	Parental ratings on 30 items scored on six scales: Emotionality; Activity; Sociability–Shyness; Attention Span; Reaction to Foods; Soothability

TABLE 4.1. (*Continued*)

Measure and reference	Age when administered (yr)	Scores obtained
Videotaped observations of mothers and infants interacting	1, 2	For each of the three situations, nine ratings based on the Infant Behavior Record that yield three scales: Affect–Extraversion; Task Orientation; Activity; plus rating of general difficultness
Behavioral problems		
Parental ratings on 23 items about infant's reaction to daily events	1, 2	Sleeping problems; eating problems; diaper problems
Parental ratings on nine dimensions of temperament and a general difficult temperament item	1, 2	Difficult temperament
Motor development measures		
Bayley Motor Scale (Bayley, 1969)	1, 2	Age-normed Psychomotor Development Index (PDI) score
Videotaped observations of mothers and infants interacting	1, 2	Hand preference for "tool use": relative strength of hand preference; absolute strength of handedness
Health measures		
Parental interview	1, 2	Common illnesses; general health factor
Miscellaneous measures		
Perinatal information	—	Clinical gestational age; birth weight
Maternal interview concerning infant's interests	1, 2	Infant's liking of gross motoric objects, fine motoric objects, cuddly objects, books, musical objects, artistic objects
Physical anchor variables	1, 2	Height, weight

Measures of Infant Development

Infant developmental data are obtained primarily during $2\frac{1}{2}$-hour visits to the adoptive and control homes by a full-time home tester. For the first visit, the average age of testing is 12.7 months, with a standard deviation of .68 months; at the time of the second visit, the average age is 24.6 months ($SD = .52$). An overview of the CAP infant measures is presented in Table 4.1.

The following protocol for the first-year home visit is followed in a flexible manner sensitive to the needs of infants and mothers: a health interview (10–15 min), the Bayley Scales of Infant Development (45 min), the Caldwell Home Observation for the Measurement of the Environment (45 min), interviews concerning the child's production of true words and the availability of and the infant's interest in different types of objects (10–15 min), four of the seven Uzgiris–Hunt

Ordinal Scales of Psychological Development (10 min), and three, 5-min mother–infant videotape sessions used to obtain information concerning language, personality, and mother–infant interactions. The home tester also collects parental rating forms, including the Colorado Childhood Temperament Inventory, the New York Longitudinal Study temperament ratings, and the Family Environment Scales, which were mailed 1 to 2 weeks prior to the home visit. The tester leaves with the parent an honorarium and a form concerning medical problems to be completed by the infant's pediatrician. Immediately after the home visit, the tester makes several ratings of the child (including the Bayley Infant Behavior Record) and of the home environment. Although this protocol taxes the limits of the infants' energy (not to mention its demands on the home testers), we have been able to collect nearly complete information for 99% of the first-year home visits. Incomplete information has been obtained for some measures, particularly the videotape measures, because of a lack of cooperativeness on the part of equipment, not the infants. Perinatal information, including gestational age and birth weight, is collected from adoption agency files for the biological mothers, and similar information is obtained from nonadoptive mothers.

The protocol for the second-year home visit is similar except that the Expressive and Receptive scales of the Sequenced Inventory of Communication Development are administered after the Bayley scales; the Uzgiris–Hunt Ordinal Scales Of Psychological Development are omitted because they are not appropriate for 2-year-olds. Nearly complete information has been collected for 94% of the second-year home visits.

Videotaped observations of mothers and their infants interacting in three situations during a 15-min period are used to obtain measures of several variables, such as language and communication, temperament, and handedness. The videotapes provide a permanent record of the children that has been rich in information and, unlike our other sources of data, permit us the luxury of going back to look at the tapes repeatedly to explore different behaviors and new ways of analyzing mother–child interactions. In order to maximize the utility of the videotapes, three situations that differ in structure and in behavioral content were chosen for videotaping at each age. For the 1-year-olds, we use *free play* as an unstructured setting in which the mother picks a play activity that the child typically enjoys. A *feeding* situation in which the infant is restrained in a high chair while the mother provides lunch or a snack for the child is used as a semistructured setting. *Teaching* is observed in a structured setting in which mothers are asked to teach their children a fine motor task—the "yellow pegboard" from the Bayley scales, a task that exceeds the ability of most 1-year-olds.

For the 2-year-olds, we chose three situations analogous to those for the 1-year-olds: free play, semistructured play (replacing the feeding situation), and teaching. During semistructured play, the mother is asked to engage the child in manipulative, symbolic play using a dollhouse. The teaching situation is similar to that for the first year, but the mother uses a xylophone (to teach sequences), an interactive book, and a fine motor toy (a wooden train that is to be assembled).

Despite their brevity, the videotaped situations have proven to be behaviorally intense. For example, language assessments during the 15 min average about 45 vocalizations per infant at 12 months and about 225 vocalizations for their mothers. We had questions concerning videotaped ratings: Would the presence of videotape equipment in the home inhibit the responding of the infant or mother? How much reliable information can be extracted from time-sampled videotapes? Nearly 1000 videotapes later, we are comfortable with the answers to these questions. Concerning the possible intrusiveness of videotape equipment, we found that the portable equipment was unobtrusive if the situations were engrossing for the mother and infant. The Sony videotape camera we used is not much bigger than a home movie camera, and we were able to obtain high quality sound and video recording without setting up a tripod or separate microphones. The field of vision of the camera is quite wide, so that the home tester is able to remain over 10 feet away and simply hand-hold the camera. When we question mothers who have participated in these videotaping sessions, they report that the videotaping had little effect on either their infant's behavior or their own. Part of the reason for this comfortable atmosphere is that we get to know the parents quite well; on the day of testing, the tester spends at least an hour and a half in the home before the videotaping begins.

In our initial work with the videotapes, we collected omnibus ratings that resulted from asking what we could assess from the tapes. Such analyses were useful in demonstrating that the videotapes can be a source of diverse, reliable information about the children and their mothers. However, such diverse ratings are difficult to combine into meaningful composite measures and are also difficult to use to address specific research questions. For these reasons, we began to direct our efforts toward specific variables such as infant and maternal communication, temperament, and handedness.

Details concerning the infant measures follow. Because test–retest reliability is generally not known for these measures, we obtained 2-week, test–retest reliability correlations for the first-year measures on 26 infants and their families.

Mental Development

There is general agreement that the 1969 revision and standardization of the Bayley Scales of Infant Development (Bayley, 1969) provides the best available measures of infant mental and motor development. The three Bayley measures are the Mental Development Index (MDI), the Psychomotor Development Index (PDI), and the Infant Behavior Record of personality ratings. The MDI at 12 months of age yields a split-half reliability coefficient of .82 (Bayley, 1969). We are aware of no reports of test–retest reliability; the CAP test–retest reliability for the MDI is .80.

As described in Chapter 7, we used factor analyses presented by Lewis (1983) to create three scales of Bayley items at 12 months and four scales at 24 months in order to measure some differentiated infant abilities. The CAP test–retest reliabilities for the three 12-month scales listed in Table 4.1 are .61, .75, and -.04, respectively. We have no explanation for the lack of significant reliability for the third scale, Verbal Skill; this result suggests caution in interpreting its results.

The Ordinal Scales of Psychological Development were developed by Uzgiris and Hunt (1975) from a Piagetian perspective. Competence in seven areas is assessed with ordinal scales for which the infant's score is the highest step achieved. We administer four scales deemed most appropriate for 1-year-olds. Few psychometric data have been reported for this measure. Although Uzgiris and Hunt do not advocate combining the scales, the intercorrelations of the scales are positive, and we present data for a total score based on the four scales as well as for the separate scales. The CAP test–retest reliability for the four scales listed in Table 4.1 are .44, .73, .38, and .16, respectively; for the total score, test–retest reliability is .52.

Communication

The Bayley scales include a number of communication-related items that we have pooled to create communication scores for infants at 12 and at 24 months of age. However, the videotapes provide a much richer source of information. Because the videotaped communication measures listed in Table 4.1 require transcripts and approximately 12 hours of coding per home visit, these measures have been analyzed for only 50 adopted and 50 nonadopted infants at 12 months of age (Hardy-Brown, 1982; Hardy-Brown et al., 1981). Similar work on the videotapes from the second-year visits is in progress. We also interview the mother concerning the child's production of true words during the first-year home visit, as well as during a telephone interview with the mother when the infant is 18 months old. At the second-year home visit, the Expressive and Receptive scales of the Sequenced Inventory of Communication Development (Hedrick, Prather, & Tobin, 1975) are administered in order to provide standardized measures of language production and comprehension.

Personality–Temperament

Temperament has become a focus of research on individual differences in personality development since 1970 (Plomin, 1983b). As explained in Chapter 9, the CAP measures were planned with the goal of permitting aggregation of ratings across items, across situations, and across sources of information (Rushton, Brainerd, & Pressley, 1983). We obtain information about temperament from three sources: testers, parents, and videotaped observations. Testers use the 30 items of the Infant Behavior Record (IBR; Bayley, 1969) to rate the children's behavior during the administration of the Bayley tests. The IBR is a promising measure of infant temperament because children are rated on the basis of their reaction to a standard, somewhat stressful situation. The Bayley manual indicates that "these scales focus on many areas of behavior, including the child's interpersonal and affective domains (Social Orientation, General Emotional Tone, Fearfulness), motivational variables (Goal Directedness, Attention Span, Endurance), and the child's interest in specific modes of sensory experience'' (Bayley, 1969, p. 99). A factor analysis of the 25 IBR items that are 5- or 9-point rating scales has been reported by Matheny (1980). The CAP data replicate Matheny's major factors of Affect–Extraversion, Activity, and Task Orientation, as described in Chapter 9. In the CAP, test–retest reliabilities for these scales are .76, .06, and .60, respectively.

The Colorado Childhood Temperament Inventory (CCTI; Rowe & Plomin, 1977) is a parental rating instrument. The CCTI is an amalgamation of the EASI Temperament Survey dimensions described by Buss and Plomin (1975) and the nine dimensions of temperament postulated by the New York Longitudinal Study (NYLS) researchers (Thomas & Chess, 1977). The median alpha reliability of the six scales is .80, and the median 1-week, test–retest reliability for children 2–6 years of age is .73. In the CAP sample, the median 2-week, test–retest reliability for 1-year-olds is .66.

A third source of information about infant temperament is our videotaped observations. We are using a rating scale modified from the work of Matheny and Wilson (1981), who developed an analog of the IBR that could be used for videotape ratings. Our "videotape-IBR" measure involves nine ratings that yield three scales plus a rating of the infant's general difficultness.

Behavioral Problems

Parents are asked to rate their children on 10 scales representing the nine NYLS dimensions of temperament as well as a general item of how difficult they perceive their infant to be. A first principal component of these items yields a dimension of difficult temperament similar to other measures of this construct (Daniels, Plomin, & Greenhalgh, 1984). In addition, mothers and fathers rate the infants' reactions to daily events such as sleeping, eating, and diapering, using items related to specific behavioral reactions similar to those used in questionnaires measuring the NYLS dimensions. A factor analysis of these items yielded three factors involving contextual behavioral problems described in Chapter 11. Unfortunately, these questionnaires were not included as part of the CAP test–retest reliability assessment.

Motor Development

The Bayley Motor Scale provides an easily obtained measure of motor development at 1 and 2 years. An interest in the development of handedness led to the use of the videotapes to record instances in which one hand is preferentially used in reaching for and playing with objects.

Health

A 10-min interview with the parent and a form for the infant's pediatrician cover major health-related aspects of development in infancy.

Miscellaneous

Perinatal information on the adoptees has been obtained from the adoption agency files and includes gestational age and birth weight. Similar information is obtained from the nonadoptive mothers. In addition, the child's interests in various objects and toys (see Table 4.1) are assessed during the interview with the mother. Finally, height and weight are measured for use as anchor variables.

Environmental Measures

As we have mentioned several times, the CAP design is as important for studying environmental influences as it is for understanding the role of heredity. In addition to isolating components of environmental variance, the inclusion of measures of specific environmental factors within the longitudinal adoption design provides several novel approaches to the analysis of environmental influences. For example, identifying environmental relationships in adoptive families, in which parents and their children share family environment but not heredity, eliminates the possibility that heredity underlies such relationships, a possibility that has begun to concern environmentalists (e.g., Gottfried & Gottfried, 1984). The design also permits assessment of the hereditary contribution to such environmental relationships by comparing the results in adoptive families to those in nonadoptive, control families. Other novel analyses, such as the analysis of genotype–environment interaction and correlation, are also possible.

The usefulness of these analyses depends directly upon the adequacy of the environmental assessments. In 1975 when the CAP began, we were fortunate that two measures, the Home Observation for Measurement of the Environment (HOME) and the Family Environment Scale (FES), had been developed to assess physical, social, and emotional–attitudinal aspects of the home environment that had been suggested as possible correlates of infant development. Our environmental data come from interviews and observations in the home, from parental questionnaires, and from analyses of videotaped interactions between mothers and their children. An overview of the environmental measures is presented in Table 4.2.

Home Observation for Measurement of the
Environment (HOME)

The core environmental measure is an observation–interview instrument known as the HOME (Caldwell & Bradley, 1978). The HOME is a semistructured interview consisting of 45 items, two-thirds of which are based on observations in the home and the remainder on parental reports. The measure was developed primarily to provide a more sensitive predictor of cognitive development than that provided by socioeconomic status. Despite its widespread use, there is some concern that the

TABLE 4.2

Summary of CAP Environmental Measures

Measure and reference	Age when administered (yr)	Scores obtained
Home Observation for Measurement of the Environment (Caldwell & Bradley, 1978)	1, 2	Traditional HOME scales: Emotional and Verbal Responsivity of the Mother; Avoidance of Restriction and Punishment; Organization of the Physical and Temporal Environment; Provision of Appropriate Play Materials; Maternal Involvement with Child; Opportunities for Variety in Daily Stimulation; Total HOME score Factors based on quantitative scoring system: HOME General Factor (unrotated first principal component); Toys; Maternal Involvement; Encouraging Developmental Advance; Restriction–Punishment
Family Environment Scales (Moos, 1974)	1	Relationship dimension: Cohesion; Expressiveness; Conflict Personal growth dimension: Independence; Achievement Orientation; Intellectual–Cultural Orientation; Active–Recreational Orientation; Moral–Religious Emphasis System maintenance dimension: Organization; Control Second-order factors: Personal Growth; Traditional Organization
Videotaped observations of mother and infant interacting (Hardy-Brown et al., 1981)	1	Counts of mothers': total vocalizations; sentence types; vocal imitation of infant; communicative gestures; tuitional modeling of language; contingent vocal responding to infant vocalization; mean length of utterance; self-repetition
Interview concerning availability of various objects	1, 2	Gross motoric objects; fine motoric objects; cuddly objects; books; musical objects; artistic objects
Gottfried and Gottfried's (1984) conceptualization of physical, social, and emotional–attitudinal environmental factors	1, 2	Variety of Experience; Provision for Exploration; Physical Home Setting

HOME "may be too gross and insensitive to reveal individual differences among middle-class homes and mothers" (Stevenson & Lamb, 1979, p. 347). In order to increase its sensitivity in middle-class homes, we use a quantitative scoring system in addition to the usual dichotomous scoring. That is, we can score the HOME items—such as "Mother spontaneously vocalizes to child at least twice during visit"—as *yes* or *no* as the HOME is usually scored. However, because such scoring of items yields little variability in middle-class homes, we also obtain quantitative scores for each item when possible. For the first HOME item (shown above) and the second HOME item, "Mother responds to child's vocalization with a vocal or verbal response," we use our videotapes of mother–infant interaction to provide an accurate count. The other HOME items have been modified in a similar manner to include quantitative information, although all of the items except the first two can be scored by the interviewer during the home visit.

The HOME has traditionally been scored for the six scales indicated in Table 4.2. Kuder–Richardson internal consistencies for the scales range from .44 to .89, with a median of .71; internal consistency for the total HOME score is .89. CAP 2-week, test–retest reliability at 12 months is .94 for the total HOME score, although the reliabilities of the individual scales are not as impressive: .65, .63, .89, .29, .69, and .57, respectively. The HOME is also quite stable: From 12 to 24 months in the CAP, the median stability correlation for the six scales is .56, and the correlation for the HOME total score is .89.

As discussed in the next chapter, we have conducted psychometric analyses of the HOME and have found the quantitative scoring system to be superior to the usual dichotomous scoring, at least for the range of families represented in the CAP. The factor structure of the HOME does not correspond closely to the six traditional scales. The dimensions that we have derived through factor analyses are shown in Table 4.2, and we discuss these analyses in the next chapter.

Family Environment Scale (FES)

This self-report questionnaire "focuses on the measurement and description of the interpersonal relationships among family members, on the directions of personal growth which are emphasized in the family, and on the basic organizational structure of the family" (Moos, 1974, p. 3). Form R consists of 90 true-false items, which are distributed on 10 scales (see Table 4.2). Factor analyses of the 90 items largely confirm the structure of these scales (Garfinkle-Claussner, 1979). The median Kuder–Richardson internal consistency for the 10 scales is .75, and the median 8-week, test–retest reliability has been reported to be .77 (Garfinkle-Claussner, 1979). The median CAP 2-week, test–retest reliability is .89 for the 10 scales.

We altered the FES from a true-false format to a 5-point rating scale (*strongly disagree* to *strongly agree*) because pilot work indicated that parents disliked answering *true* or *false* to such complex questions as "family members really help and support one another." An average rating for the two parents is obtained for each of the 10 FES scales and for two factors derived from a second-order factor analysis of the CAP data: Personal Growth and Traditional Organization, which are described in the next chapter. The two factors accounted for 45% of the rotated variance. The intercorrelations among the 10 FES scales are similar to those reported by Moos (1974) for 814 individuals in 285 families. This is noteworthy because the two matrices of intercorrelations differed in two important respects: Moos' correlations were based on individuals' scores and true-false items, whereas our correlations are based on midparent scores and 5-point rating scales. The similarity of results suggests that the correlational structure of the FES is quite robust.

Communication Environment

The videotapes of mother–infant interaction, discussed in the previous section on infant measures, have been useful for assessment of the language-learning environment. The time involved in obtaining transcripts and coding the videotapes has limited us to analyzing only a subsample of the CAP children's communication environment (Hardy-Brown, 1982; Hardy-Brown et al., 1981). As can be seen in Table 4.2, most of the commonly used measures of the language-learning environment have been included. Factor analyses of the various measures of communication environment did not yield readily interpretable factors; thus, the separate measures are used in analyses of the linguistic input available to the child as assessed during the videotaped interactions.

The videotapes will be valuable for analyzing other aspects of the maternal side of the mother–infant interaction. We have worked with a modification of the Hess and Shipman (1965) approach to assessing maternal teaching styles, obtaining measures of the mother's control system and techniques of influence; however, these measures did not offer sufficient reliability to continue their use. We have begun to collaborate with Judy Dunn of the University of Cambridge, who has published extensively on mother–infant interactions (e.g., Dunn & Kendrick, 1982), in order to use her methods for the analysis of our videotapes.

Gottfried and Gottfried (1984) Categories

In addition to these standard measures of environmental influence, we have collected information relevant to many other aspects of the environment that have been studied in relationship to infant development (e.g., Wachs & Gruen, 1982). For example, we conduct a lengthy interview with the mothers concerning the availability of various categories of toys and objects. We also obtain data on such ecological factors as noise levels, lighting, and neighborhood ratings. Rather than analyzing these various environmental measures independently, we have organized them according to a conceptualization suggested by Gottfried and Gottfried (1984), who conducted a systematic exploration of the HOME, the FES, and the Purdue Home Stimulation Inventory (PHSI; Wachs, 1979). The PHSI focuses on physical aspects of the infant's environment. The Gottfrieds' conceptualization attempts to merge these physical (PHSI), social (HOME), and emotional–attitudinal (FES) aspects of the environment that appear to be related to infant mental development. Although we were not able to include the PHSI in the CAP, we have collected information relevant to the measurement of similar aspects of the physical environment. Thus, we organized the CAP environmental measures into the Gottfrieds' conceptualization. We supplemented these measures with CAP analogs of additional environmental measures that Wachs and Gruen (1982) conclude to be "validated environmental components related to the development of general psychometric intelligence" (p. 214) at 12 to 24 months of age. Details concerning the measures and analyses, including factor analyses, of the various environmental measures are presented in the next chapter.

Adult Measures

The CAP parents—biological, adoptive, and control (nonadoptive)—complete the same 3-hour test battery, with tape-recorded instructions to standardize the administration of tests across test sessions and to set precise time limits. The various tests and questionnaires are reproduced on colored paper to facilitate the monitoring of time limits and performance on practice items and are bound into a test booklet. An overview of the adult measures is presented in Table 4.3.

Copies of the unpublished CAP measures are included in Appendix C for archival purposes and to provide a fuller description of the measures. For example, in Table 4.3 we mention the summary variable, "frequency of headaches"; however, the CAP booklet includes 12 questions about headaches of the subject as well as 12 questions about the subject's mother's and father's headaches.

Cognition

The CAP cognitive battery is largely based on the tests used in the Hawaii Family Study of Cognition (HFSC) that yielded a stable factor structure across ethnic groups (DeFries, *et al.,* 1974), sex, and age from adolescence to middle age (Wilson, *et al.,* 1975). Approximately 65% of the variance was accounted for by four factors: Spatial Visualization, Verbal, Perceptual Speed, and Visual Memory.

We attempted to improve upon the HFSC battery by dropping four tests and adding four new ones. We eliminated the Whiteman Test of Social Perception because of its low reliability, and Elithorn Mazes, Mental Rotations, and Number Comparisons were deleted because they correlated highly with other tests. We added the Colorado Perceptual Speed Test and the Educational Testing Service (ETS) Identical Pictures Test in order to broaden the Perceptual Speed factor to include tests with letters and geometrical designs. The Visual Memory factor in the HFSC was based upon an immediate and delayed version of a single test; thus, we

TABLE 4.3

Summary of CAP Adult Measures

Measure and reference	Scores obtained
Cognitive measures[a]	
PMA Vocabulary (50 multiple-choice items)—3 min	
ETS Vocabulary Test V-4 (abbreviated; 25 multiple-choice items)—4 min	Vocabulary (sum of PMA and ETS)
HFSC Picture Memory, Immediate and Delayed Recognition (40 illustrations; immediate recognition, 20 targets and 20 distractors; delayed recognition after 20 min, the remaining 20 targets and 20 new distractors)—45-sec exposure, 1-min recognition	Picture Memory (sum of immediate and delayed)
ETS Things Categories Test, revised by HFSC staff, "things round" and "things metal"—2 parts, 3 min	Things Verbal Fluency (sum of 2 parts)
ETS Card Rotations—2 parts, 3 min each	Card Rotations (sum of 2 parts)
ETS Subtraction and Multiplication—2 parts, 2 min each	Subtraction and Multiplication (sum of 2 parts)
ETS Word Beginnings and Endings—2 parts, 3 min each	Word Beginnings–Endings (sum of 2 parts)
PMA Pedigrees—2 parts, 2 min each	Pedigrees (sum of 2 parts)
ETS Hidden Patterns Test—2 parts, 2 min each	Hidden Patterns (sum of 2 parts)
Minnesota Paper Form Board Test, revised by HFSC staff—3 min	Paper Form Board
Raven's Progressive Matrices, shortened by HFSC staff—20 min	Progressive Matrices
Names and Faces, Immediate and Delayed Recall—1-min exposure to names and faces, 1-min recall name to face	Names and Faces (sum of immediate and delayed)
ETS Identical Pictures Test—2 parts, 90 sec each	Identical Pictures (sum of 2 parts)
Colorado Perceptual Speed Test—2 parts, 1 min each	Colorado Perceptual Speed (sum of 2 parts)
General cognitive ability	Unrotated first principal component
Specific cognitive abilities	Rotated factors: Verbal Reasoning; Spatial Visualization; Perceptual Speed; Memory
Personality measures	
Cattell's 16 Personality Factor Test (Cattell et al., 1970)	16 primary factors: A, Outgoing; B, Bright; C, Emotionally Stable; E, Assertive; F, Happy-Go-Lucky; G, Conscientious; H, Venturesome; I, Tender-Minded; L, Suspicious; M, Imaginative; N, Astute; O, Apprehensive;

(*continued*)

TABLE 4.3 (*Continued*)

Measure and reference	Scores obtained
	Q_1, Experimenting; Q_2, Self-Sufficient; Q_3, Controlled; Q_4, Tense
	Second-order factors: Q_I, Extraversion; Q_{II}, Neuroticism; Q_{IV}, Independence
EASI self-report and rating of other parent (Buss & Plomin, 1975)	Emotionality–Fear; Emotionality–Anger; Activity; Sociability; Impulsivity
Interests and talents	Interest and talent scales based on factor analyses: Artistic; Group Sports; Individual Sports; Mechanical; Domestic
Common behavioral problems	Frequency of headaches; speech problems (presence–absence); motion sickness (first principal component); sleep problems (time to get to sleep, how well sleeps); phobias (presence–absence); compulsions (presence–absence); depression (frequency); sociopathy; hysteria; menstrual problems
Commonly used drugs	Number of alcoholic drinks per month; nicotine (ex- or non-smoker vs. smoker); caffeine (cups of coffee per day)
Demographic information	Birth date; size of community in childhood; ethnicity; occupation and education of respondent and respondent's father
Miscellaneous	Relative and absolute strength of hand preference; food preferences (number of dislikes); hours of sleep; frequency of colds; tape-recorded oral reading score; height; weight

[a]Additional details concerning these measures and their sources are given in DeFries *et al.* (1981).

constructed the Names and Faces Test (immediate and delayed) in order to broaden this factor. Finally, because a ceiling effect was found for the Primary Mental Abilities (PMA) Vocabulary test used in the HFSC battery, a more difficult test (ETS's advanced vocabulary test) was added.

The 16 tests are listed in Table 4.3. Multiple-choice test scores (S) are adjusted for guessing by using the formula $S = R - W/(N-1)$, where R is the number of correct items, W is the number wrong, and N is the number of responses possible for an item. Details concerning the tests and their scoring are included in DeFries *et al.* (1981). Detailed instructions and examples were provided for each test. Appendix C contains reproductions of parts of each test. These 16 tests are used to obtain 13 scores. Scores on the immediate and delayed parts of the Picture Memory Test are summed to yield one score for Picture Memory; scores on the immediate and delayed versions of Names and Faces are combined to yield a single measure of recall; and PMA and ETS vocabulary test scores are combined.

Reliabilities, sex and age adjustment, and the factor structure of the CAP cognitive measures are discussed in Chapter 6. Although we describe results for the 13 individual test scores, most analyses are based on the unrotated first principal component as a measure of general cognitive ability, or IQ, and the specific cognitive abilities indexed by four rotated components: Verbal Reasoning, Spatial Visualization, Perceptual Speed, and Memory.

Personality

Self-report personality measures are also included in the test booklets. We used Form A of Cattell's 16 Personality Factor Questionnaire (16 PF; Cattell, Eber, & Tatsuoka, 1970), which contains 187 items that measure 16 primary personality factors and 4 second-order factors. The median 1-month, test–retest reliability for the 16 primary factors is .78. We score the 16 PF scales in accordance with the test manual (Cattell *et al.*, 1970). A second-order factor analysis of the 16 scales revealed three factors that are nearly identical to three of Cattell's "second stratum" factors—namely, Q_I (Invia–Exvia), Q_{II} (Adjustment–Anxiety), and Q_{IV} (Subduedness–Independence). The highest loading 16 PF scales on each of the CAP second-order factors correspond to those listed by Cattell *et al.* (1970, p. 116), and the congruence (Kaiser, Hunka, & Bianchini, 1971) between our loadings and the average of the male and female loadings presented by Cattell *et al.* (p. 121) is greater than .98 for the three second-order factors. We refer to the three second-order factors as Extraversion, Neuroticism, and Independence.

An adaptation of the EASI Temperament Survey developed by Buss and Plomin (1975) is also used to obtain self-report and "mate ratings" of personality. The CAP version of the EASI questionnaire consists of two, 25-item forms, one for parents to rate themselves and the other for them to rate the other parent for the same items. Factor analyses yielded a structure similar to the structure reported by Buss and Plomin (1975). Scale scores with unit weights were constructed for the five scales listed in Table 4.3.

Interests and Talents

The test booklet includes 40 items concerning interests and abilities in the domains of art, physical activities, and domestic and mechanical arts. Factor analyses of the items suggested several independent interest and ability scores. Other interest scores obtained include the amount of television viewing, reading, and religiosity.

Common Behavioral Problems

In order to conduct "at risk" studies with the large CAP sample, frequently occurring behavioral problems are assessed for the CAP parents. Detailed family histories are obtained for headaches and for speech problems (the latter in collaboration with Dr. Kenneth Kidd of Yale University). We also ask about depression, hysteria, sociopathy, phobias, sleep problems, compulsive behavior, motion sickness, and menstrual problems.

Commonly Used Drugs

Detailed questions concerning the parents' smoking history are included in the test booklet, and questions are also asked about alcohol consumption and coffee drinking.

Demographic Information

Background information such as education, occupation, and ethnicity is collected in order to characterize the CAP sample.

Miscellaneous Measures

The test booklet contains an 11-item questionnaire on handedness, questions about family history of handedness, and a 21-item questionnaire concerning food preferences. Parents are also asked to read aloud a section of the Gray Oral Reading Test that is tape-recorded to obtain a voice recording and for possible use as a screening tool for major reading problems.

Not all of these adult measures are related to infant measures in this book. Some parental measures, such as drug use and the tape-recorded reading sample, are not as relevant to infant behavior as they will be to later behavior of the CAP children. Moreover, this rich data set permits the exploration of many interesting possibilities such as possible relationships between parental interests and talents and the cognitive development of children; however, limitations of time and resources make it necessary for us to focus primarily on relatively straightforward comparisons between parents and their infants.

Summary

In this chapter the CAP measures have been described briefly. Copies of the unpublished measures are included in Appendices A–C. For the 12- and 24-month-old adopted and control (nonadopted) infants, the information obtained during a $2\frac{1}{2}$-hour home visit includes measures of mental development, communication, personality–temperament, behavioral problems, motor development, health, and miscellaneous measures such as the child's interest in various objects. These data are collected via standardized tests, tester ratings, parental ratings, interviews, and videotaped observations of mother–infant interaction. The infant's environment is assessed via observation, interview, parental report, and analyses of videotaped interactions. A 3-hour battery of tests and questionnaires administered to biological, adoptive, and control parents yields extensive information concerning cognitive abilities, personality, interests, talents, handedness, behavioral problems, and drug use.

The remainder of this book presents the results of analyses based on the measures described in this chapter. The following chapters describe intellectual development, communicative development, personality–temperament, behavioral problems, and motor development and their genetic and environmental etiologies in infancy. Change as well as continuity from 12 to 24 months are considered. Many of our analyses focus on relationships at the interface of nature and nurture and, for this reason, the next chapter continues our discussion of environmental measures.

5

Environment

Introduction

In his 1961 book *Intelligence and Experience,* Hunt reviewed previous research on early experience, related this research to the theories of Hebb and Piaget, and opened the floodgates for over a thousand studies of early experience (Hunt, 1979). This burst of interest in early experience was foreshadowed by a lengthy history, going back through Bloom (1964), Bowlby (1951), Freud (1949), and Watson (1928) to James Mill, John Locke, and Plato.

Although the popularity of the view of the primacy of early experience testifies to its reasonableness, doubts began to emerge in the 1970s and culminated in the book *Early Experience: Myth and Evidence,* edited by Clarke and Clarke (1976). The opening passage of the book states their position:

> During the last twenty-five years the impact of new biological and social knowledge has caused revision or reformulation of many theories about the development of behavioural processes. In particular the complexity of the interactions and transactions between nature and nurture are now more fully appreciated. There remains, however, one theory which is peculiarly resistant to change: that the environment in the early years exerts a disproportionate and irreversible effect on a rapidly developing organism, compared with the potential for later environmental influences. (p. ix)

They do not deny that early experience is important, only that its long-term role is limited.

In the wake of this dramatic reorientation, environmentalists have attempted to stop the pendulum from swinging all the way back to a position that ignores early environmental influence. In their book *Early Experience and Human Development,*

Wachs and Gruen (1982) summarize an impressive amount of research relating early experiences to cognitive and social development in infancy and early childhood. In addition to building an empirical case for the importance of early environment, they also argue for its importance on theoretical grounds such as the Hebbian notion of greater susceptibility of the central nervous system during its formative years in infancy and early childhood as well as the likelihood that early experiences will be maintained. Like other developmentalists, Wachs and Gruen (1982) note the need for studies at the interface of environment and heredity: "We accept the relevance of hereditary factors to development and the transaction of heredity with environment and will attempt to present data, whenever relevant, on the interaction of these two factors. Unfortunately, the available data is extremely limited" (p. 11).

Our goal for the CAP was to bridge this gap in our knowledge by studying the early environment and its developmental interactions. In the mid-1970s when the CAP began, we were surprised to find that, despite decades of research, there were few instruments available to assess the proximal environment of infants. It was as if the potency of the environment was assumed rather than assessed. Most of the evidence supporting the hypothesis of early environmental influence on infant development involved gross manipulations such as institutionalization rather than measured environmental variations. Other studies measured distal factors such as socioeconomic status (SES), although these showed few relationships with intellectual development until after the first 18 months of life (Golden & Birns, 1975). Such factors are important only if they impinge on the proximal environment of the infant (Wachs & Gruen, 1982).

In 1975, when we were searching for measures of the proximal environment of the infant, we noted that decades earlier there had been a few attempts to interview mothers to assess the home environment (Van Alstyne, 1929; Skodak, 1939), but that no measures had been developed in the ensuing years. However, just about that time, two measures of the home environment appeared that have since received wide acceptance: the Home Observation for Measurement of the Environment (HOME; Caldwell & Bradley, 1978), and the Family Environment Scale (FES; Moos, 1974). These measures were briefly described in the previous chapter. As we see in subsequent chapters, both measures yield some relationships with infant development. The purpose of this chapter is to discuss the CAP environmental assessments in greater detail before describing our application of these measures to the study of individual differences in infancy.

Family Environment Scale (FES)

The FES assesses the quality of social relationships among family members. As described in the previous chapter, we revised the FES from its true–false format to a 5-point rating scale that the CAP parents found more acceptable. Means and standard deviations for the 10 FES scales are listed in Table 5.1 for adoptive and control families, with ratings averaged for the mother and father in each family. Adoptive

TABLE 5.1

FES Means and Standard Deviations for Adoptive and Control Families

FES scale	Adoptive families (N = 167)		Control families (N = 160)	
	$\bar{X}$	SD	$\bar{X}$	SD
Cohesion	37.7	3.8	37.5	4.1
Expressiveness	32.0	3.8	32.3	4.3
Conflict	18.9	4.2	19.5	4.8
Independence	32.8	3.1	32.9	3.5
Achievement Orientation	29.8	3.8	29.6	3.8
Intellectual–Cultural Orientation	29.8	5.1	31.7	5.2
Active–Recreational Orientation	30.6	4.8	30.6	5.4
Moral–Religious Emphasis	34.4	5.7	29.7	8.0
Organization	33.3	4.3	31.0	5.1
Control	27.0	3.8	25.1	4.5

families are significantly higher and less variable on the Moral–Religious scale, which is not surprising given the religious affiliations of the two adoption agencies. Even so, the difference is only about two-thirds of a standard deviation. Other mean differences are smaller: Adoptive families are lower on the Intellectual–Cultural scale (one-third of a standard deviation) and higher on the Organization and Control scales (each about half a standard deviation). No mean or variance differences were observed for gender; that is, parents of boys responded similarly to parents of girls.

Intercorrelations among the 10 scales are presented in Table 5.2 for adoptive and control families combined because no correlational differences emerged for the two types of families. The intercorrelation matrix for the CAP families is similar to the

TABLE 5.2

Interrelations among the 10 FES Scales for Adoptive and Control Families Combined[a]

FES scale	FES scale									
	Coh	Exp	Con	Ind	Ach	Int	Act	Mor	Org	Ctl
Cohesion (Coh)		.60	−.37	.31	.10	.39	.36	.18	.39	−.14
Expressiveness (Exp)			−.11	.39	.04	.29	.33	−.03	.18	−.32
Conflict (Con)				−.14	.01	.00	−.02	−.21	−.29	.25
Independence (Ind)					.20	.17	.22	−.19	.13	−.38
Achievement (Ach)						−.06	.18	.01	.27	.18
Intellectual–Cultural (Int)							.38	.00	.06	−.11
Active–Recreational (Act)								.10	.16	−.06
Moral–Religious (Mor)									.35	.42
Organization (Org)										.28
Control (Ctl)										

[a] N = 323.

TABLE 5.3

Rotated Factor Loadings for the 10 FES Scales[a]

	Factor loading	
FES scale	Personal Growth	Traditional Organization
Relationship dimensions		
Cohesion	.80	.31
Expressiveness	.71	−.03
Conflict	−.31	−.14
Personal growth		
Independence	.53	−.16
Achievement Orientation	.11	.22
Intellectual–Cultural Orientation	.41	.03
Active–Recreational Orientation	.44	.03
Moral–Religious Emphasis	−.02	.61
System maintenance		
Organization	.29	.61
Control	−.46	.68

[a]$N = 323$ families (adoptive and control combined; ratings for mothers and fathers in each family have been combined in order to increase their reliability).

matrix reported in the FES manual (Moos & Moos, 1981), although the Cohesion and Expressiveness scales are not as highly correlated in the standardization sample ($r = .40$) as they are in the CAP sample ($r = .60$). Still, the correspondence between the two correlation matrices is remarkable, especially considering the fact that the CAP correlations are based on data averaged for mothers and fathers and using a 5-point rating scale rather than the FES true-false format.

However, the factor analysis of the 10 scales, summarized in Table 5.3, does not correspond closely to the major dimensions identified in the FES manual. The two factors described in Table 5.3 account for 45% of the rotated variance; factor scores were derived for these two dimensions and are used throughout this book for the purpose of data reduction. Loadings above .40 on the first factor were found for six FES scales: Cohesion, Expressiveness, Independence, Intellectual–Cultural Orientation, Active–Recreational Orientation, and Control (loading negatively). Although FES scales for each of the three dimensions identified in the FES manual are included in this factor, we chose to label the factor ''Personal Growth''; high scores indicate that parents are intellectual, active, permissive, and expressive. The other second-order scale was labeled ''Traditional Organization'' because the following scales loaded above .40: Moral–Religious Emphasis, Organization, and Control. These two FES factors are reminiscent of the two major dimensions of childrearing that typically emerge from the literature: love and control. Two-week, test–retest reliabilities of factor scores were .89 and .97, respectively, for Personal Growth and Traditional Organization.

Home Observation for Measurement of the
Environment (HOME)

The HOME is an observation–interview instrument constructed for the purpose of providing a more sensitive predictor of intellectual development than that provided by SES. The HOME was developed primarily for use in lower-class families; for example, the HOME manual reports psychometric characteristics of the HOME for 174 Arkansas families in which 66% were black, 34% on welfare, and 29% with no father present. The sensitivity of the HOME as a measure of environmental variation in middle-class families has been questioned (DeFries *et al.*, 1981).

Table 5.4 presents the HOME means and standard deviations at 12 and 24 months from the HOME manual and from the CAP data on adoptive and control homes; data from a study by Gottfried and Gottfried (1984) at 15 months are also included. The CAP means are higher and the standard deviations are lower than those reported in the HOME manual. Nonetheless, the CAP means and variances are quite similar to those of other middle-class samples, such as those of Gottfried and Gottfried, as well as for other samples (e.g., Hollenbeck, 1978; Ramey, Mills, Campbell, & O'Brien, 1975).

The table illustrates the limitations of the HOME for middle-class samples: A clear ceiling effect emerges with a consequent reduction of variance. For four of the HOME scales, the CAP mean is within one point of the highest possible score. For the other two scales, the CAP mean is within two points of the highest possible score.

At the item level, the problem of variability becomes even more apparent. For the four groups of adopted and control infants at 12 and 24 months, at least 8 of the 45 items have less than 1% variability and at least 30 items have less than 10% variability. As indicated in Chapter 3, the CAP sample is reasonably representative of metropolitan families; thus, these data suggest that the HOME is problematic from a psychometric point of view when used with middle-class families

Quantitative Scoring

In an attempt to analyze environmental variation in middle-class homes, we modified the HOME so that counts and ratings could be used rather than dichotomous scoring. The revised items are listed in Appendix B. For example, item 1 of the HOME, "Mother spontaneously vocalizes to child at least twice during visit (excluding scolding)," is scored as *yes* or *no*. We modified the item as follows: "Mother spontaneously vocalizes to child during visit (excluding scolding)." Then we count the number of such vocalizations from our videotapes. The traditional dichotomous scoring yields no variability for this item because all of the CAP mothers spontaneously vocalized to the child at least twice. However, this item was useful when scored quantitatively.

As indicated in Appendix B, some HOME items were changed to ratings. For

TABLE 5.4

Comparisons of Means and Standard Deviations for Traditional HOME Dichotomous Scores

HOME scale	Highest possible score	Colorado Adoption Project 12 Months Adoptive (N = 109–177) $\bar{X}$	SD	12 Months Control (N = 109–158) $\bar{X}$	SD	24 Months Adoptive (N = 113–176) $\bar{X}$	SD	24 Months Control (N = 107–158) $\bar{X}$	SD	Gottfried & Gottfried (1984) 15 Months (N = 129) $\bar{X}$	SD	HOME manual 12 Months (N = 50) $\bar{X}$	SD	HOME manual 24 Months (N = 50) $\bar{X}$	SD
Responsivity of Mother	11	9.1	1.3	9.2	1.2	9.5	1.2	9.4	1.1	8.7	1.5	8.0	2.2	8.6	2.0
Avoidance of Restriction and Punishment	8	6.8	1.0	6.9	1.0	6.5	1.0	6.8	0.9	6.4	1.1	5.3	1.6	5.2	1.6
Organization of the Environment	6	5.3	0.8	5.4	0.7	5.5	0.7	5.5	0.7	5.2	0.9	4.9	1.2	4.9	1.2
Appropriate Play Materials	9	8.6	0.6	8.7	0.6	8.7	0.5	8.7	0.5	8.6	0.7	6.4	2.4	6.4	2.0
Maternal Involvement	6	5.2	0.9	5.4	0.8	5.2	0.9	5.2	0.9	4.0	1.2	3.3	1.6	3.5	1.8
Variety in Daily Stimulation	5	4.0	0.9	4.0	1.0	4.6	0.6	4.6	0.6	3.4	1.1	3.0	1.1	3.0	1.5
HOME Total	45	39.1	2.8	39.6	2.8	39.9	2.4	40.0	2.4	36.4	3.7	30.6	7.6	31.7	7.5

example, HOME item 7, "Mother permits child occasionally to engage in 'messy' types of play" (scored as *yes* or *no*), was changed to "Mother permits child to engage in 'messy' types of play," and was rated on a 5-point scale in which a rating of 2 was defined as *occasionally*. A score of 0 was defined as *rarely* or *never*, and a rating of 4 indicated *very often*. We converted items 5, 7, 9, 11, 29, 35, 36, 37, 38, 39, 41, and 42 to 5-point ratings. The other HOME items were changed to permit counts, except items 4, 6, 21, 24, and 25, which were left unchanged because they could not be reasonably changed to a quantitative system. For example, item 4—"Mother's speech is distinct, clear and audible to interviewer"—was found in pilot work to be too difficult to rate on a continuous scale and was thus left as a dichotomous, yes-no item. However, all of these dichotomous items, except item 21, had to be deleted from analysis because of poor variability: *no* responses were recorded for only 1.2% for item 4, 0.3% for item 6, 5.2% for item 24, and 2.9% for item 25. In addition, three of the punishment items continued to show no variability even after conversion to a quantitative rating scale: item 12 (96.2% rated as *none),* item 13 (97.4%), and item 14 (96.0%). Item 45 was linearly dependent on item 34 and thus was deleted in subsequent analyses.

The remainder of the items (37 of 45) yielded reasonable variability with the quantitative scoring scheme. However, most of the quantitative item distributions were positively skewed and thus were transformed. Moderately skewed items (10, 22, 23, 30, 31, 32, 33, and 34) were transformed by square root, whereas log transformations were used for items skewed to a greater extent (3, 8, 15, 16, 17, 18, 20, 26, 27, 40, and 44).

Factor Analyses

Although the HOME manual indicates that factor analyses have been performed on the HOME items, the results have not been reported in detail. The internal consistencies of the six scales are moderately high, from .44 to .89, and the item–scale correlations are also moderately high. Both of these findings suggest a reasonable factor structure for the HOME. However, the scales are substantially intercorrelated—the median intercorrelation among the six scales at 12 months as reported in the HOME manual is .48; at 24 months, the median correlation is .44.

Because we found no published report of the HOME's factor structure, we considered conducting factor analyses of the dichotomous HOME items. However, the traditional dichotomous scoring leaves so few items with reasonable distributional properties that a factor analysis would be rendered nearly meaningless. Therefore, we performed factor analyses on the 37 quantitatively scored items with reasonable distributional properties. We began with a principal-component analysis to furnish an unrotated principal component at 12 and 24 months that could serve as a HOME general factor. The loadings on the unrotated first principal component are listed in Table 5.5. The highest loading items indicate that the factor is indeed general: item 5 (Mother initiates verbal interchanges with observer), item 11 (Moth-

TABLE 5.5

Loadings of HOME Items on Unrotated Principal Component for Quantitatively Scored HOME Items[a]

HOME item	12 Months	24 Months
1. Spontaneously vocalizes	.29	.17
2. Responds to child's vocalizations	.12	.19
3. Tells child names of objects	.37	.50
5. Initiates verbal interchanges with observer	.45	.60
7. Permits child to engage in "messy" play	.23	.03
8. Spontaneously praises child's qualities	.35	.51
9. Voice conveys positive feeling	.16	.48
10. Caresses or kisses child	.29	.41
11. Shows positive emotional responses	.41	.50
15. Physical punishment occurred	−.08	−.15
16. Scolds child	.10	.20
17. Interferes with child's actions	.01	−.02
18. Books present and visible	.36	.24
19. Family has pets	.00	−.05
20. Substitute care	.06	.13
21. Goes to grocery store	−.12	−.15
22. Gets out of house	.37	.10
23. Taken to doctor's office	.08	.20
26. Muscle activity toys	.43	.28
27. Push–pull toys	.34	.12
28. Strollers, scooter, etc.	.52	.31
29. Provides toys during interview	.37	.43
30. Learning equipment: mobile, etc.	.24	.42
31. Learning equipment: cuddly, etc.	.44	.33
32. Eye–hand coordination toys	.65	.45
33. Combinatorial toys	.47	.29
34. Toys for literature and music	.57	.48
35. Keeps child within visual range	.23	.21
36. Talks to child	.39	.49
37. Encourages developmental advance	.51	.52
38. Invests "maturing" toys with value	.54	.53
39. Structures child's play	.36	.32
40. Provides toys that challenge child	.51	.21
41. Caregiving by father	.29	.29
42. Mother reads books	.35	.47
43. Meals with mother and father	.16	.17
44. Visits by relatives or friends	.19	.20

[a]$N = 342$.

er shows positive emotional responses), item 32 (Eye–hand coordination toys), item 34 (Toys for literature and music), item 36 (Talks to child), item 37 (Encourages developmental advance), and item 38 (Invests "maturing" toys with value). Of the 37 items, 20 load above .30 at 12 months and 17 load above .30 at 24 months. The 12- and 24-month components are generally similar; however, at each age, the unrotated first principal component accounts for only 12% of the total variance.

We also undertook various types of rotations of the HOME dimensions in order to obtain more specific factors. The results of a Varimax rotated factor analysis are presented in Table 5.6 for adopted and control families combined. Among the items with the highest loadings on the first factor are items 33 (Combinatorial toys), 34 (Provides toys for literature and music), and 40 (Mother provides toys that challenge child). Although most of the items that load on this factor are included in the HOME scale Appropriate Play Materials, we refer to this factor with the more operational label, "Toys." The second factor includes high loadings at both ages for items 5 (Mother initiates verbal interchanges with observer), 8 (Mother spontaneously praises child's qualities), 9 (When speaking of or to child, mother's voice conveys positive feeling), and 11 (Mother shows positive emotional response to praise of child offered by visitor). Although the items that load on this factor are primarily included in the HOME Responsivity of Mother scale, the gist of the second factor appears to be more a matter of maternal involvement than responsivity per se. The highest loading items on the third factor at both 12 and 24 months were items 3 (Mother tells child the names of objects during visit), 36 (Mother "talks" to child while doing her work), 37 (Mother consciously encourages developmental advance), 38 (Mother invests "maturing" toys with value), and 42 (Times per week mother spends time with child with books). Although these items are part of the HOME Maternal Involvement scale, they and others loading on the third factor suggest maternal encouragement of developmental advance rather than general maternal involvement.

Other factor analyses, conducted separately for adoptive and control homes and using other rotational procedures, led us to create scales by summing the following items after transforming each to a z score in order to weight them equally: Toys (items 26, 27, 28, 31, 32, 33, 34, and 40), Maternal Involvement (items 1, 2, 8, 9, 10, and 11), and Encouraging Developmental Advance (items 3, 5, 29, 36, 37, 38, 39, and 42). Because the factor analyses yielded roughly similar factors at 12 and 24 months, the same items were used to construct the scales at both ages. In addition, because several factor analyses suggested the possibility of a Restriction–Punishment factor, we tentatively included such a scale based on items 15, 16, and 17.

Means and Variances

Table 5.7 presents means and standard deviations for the quantitatively scored HOME scales and the HOME General Factor at 12 and 24 months. No mean or variance differences emerged for families of boys as compared to families of girls or for adoptive versus control families.

Stability

One test of the utility of the quantitative scoring system is the stability of the HOME from 12 to 24 months. Table 5.8 lists stability correlations from the HOME

TABLE 5.6

Varimax Rotated Factors for Quantitatively Scored HOME Items for Adopted and Control Families[a]

HOME item number	12 Months			24 Months		
	Factor 1	Factor 2	Factor 3	Factor 1	Factor 2	Factor 3
1	—	—	.42	—	—	—
2	—	—	—	—	—	—
3	—	—	.53	—	—	.42
5	—	.52	—	—	.50	.33
7	—	—	—	—	—	—
8	—	.43	—	—	.59	—
9	—	.51	—	—	.79	—
10	—	—	—	—	—	—
11	—	.59	—	—	.54	—
15	—	—	—	—	—	—
17	—	—	—	—	—	—
18	.33	—	—	—	—	—
19	—	—	—	—	—	—
20	—	—	—	—	—	—
21	—	—	—	—	—	—
22	—	—	—	—	—	—
23	—	—	—	—	—	—
26	.51	—	—	.48	—	—
27	.55	—	—	.45	—	—
28	.57	—	—	.48	—	—
29	—	—	—	—	—	.38
30	—	.31	—	—	.31	.36
31	—	.41	—	—	.51	—
32	—	.66	—	—	.59	—
33	.49	—	—	.49	—	—
34	.55	—	—	.59	—	—
35	—	.46	—	—	—	—
36	—	.32	.41	—	.31	.39
37	—	.39	.35	—	—	.53
38	—	.39	.34	—	—	.62
39	—	—	—	—	—	.44
40	.66	—	—	.41	—	—
41	—	—	—	—	—	—
42	—	—	.55	—	—	.36
43	—	—	—	—	—	—
44	—	—	—	—	—	—

[a]N = 342. Only loadings of .30 or more are listed. HOME items with negligible variance were not included in the analysis.

manual and for the CAP sample using the traditional dichotomous scoring and the quantitative scoring. Except for the Avoidance of Restriction and Punishment scale, the HOME manual reports relatively high stability from 12 to 24 months. In contrast, probably because of the reduced variance in the middle-class homes of the CAP, stability of the traditional dichotomous scales for CAP families is consider-

TABLE 5.7

Means and Standard Deviations for Quantitatively Scored HOME Scales for Adoptive and Control Families

| HOME Scale | 12 Months | | | | 24 Months | | | |
| | Adoptive (N = 179–180) | | Control (N = 159–164) | | Adoptive (N = 177–181) | | Control (N = 161–164) | |
	$\bar{X}$	SD	$\bar{X}$	SD	$\bar{X}$	SD	$\bar{X}$	SD
General Factor	-.07	1.0	.06	0.9	.07	1.0	-.08	0.9
Toys	-.06	4.6	.05	4.3	-.23	4.6	.31	4.4
Maternal Involvement	.20	3.0	-.33	3.3	.48	3.5	-.31	3.0
Encouraging Developmental Advance	-.15	4.2	.27	4.6	.44	4.6	-.31	4.6
Restriction–Punishment	.04	1.7	-.38	1.5	.19	2.0	-.49	1.7

TABLE 5.8

Stability of the HOME from 12 to 24 Months for Traditional Dichotomous Scales and Factorially Valid Quantitative Scales

	HOME manual	CAP adoptive	CAP control
Traditional dichotomous scales			
Total score	.77	.49	.47
Responsivity of Mother	.55	.36	.22
Avoidance of Restriction and Punishment	.30	.36	.43
Organization of the Environment	.56	.43	.20
Appropriate Play Materials	.70	.21	.05
Maternal Involvement	.51	.12	.34
Variety in Daily Stimulation	.77	.23	.33
Factorially valid quantitative scales			
General Factor	—	.61	.55
Toys	—	.65	.61
Maternal Involvement	—	.45	.34
Encouraging Developmental Advance	—	.53	.56
Restriction–Punishment	—	.18	.36

ably lower. However, quantitative scoring yields better results. For the traditional HOME total score, the stabilities for the CAP adoptive and control homes are .49 and .47, respectively. However, for the unrotated principal-component score based on the quantitatively scored version of the HOME, the correlations are .61 and .55, respectively. For the traditionally scored scales, the median stability in the CAP is .29; for the quantitatively scored scales, the median stability is .48.

Conclusions

Thus, in terms of means, variances, factor structure, and stability, the quantitative scoring system appears to have advantages over the traditional method for scoring the HOME for middle-class families. We advocate the use of the quantitative scoring procedure because, in addition to these advantages, it permits scoring the HOME in the usual dichotomous manner. Thus, no information is lost. However, the quantitative system can be employed only if the HOME is modified to collect quantitative data. As indicated earlier, we obtained quantitative information concerning HOME items 1 and 2 from 15 min of videotaped interactions between the mother and infant. Researchers who do not plan to use videotapes could count the mother's spontaneous vocalizations and contingent vocalizations to the child during a 15-min observation period. Alternatively, these aspects of mother–infant interaction could be assessed during brief, time-sampled observations in between other measures obtained in the home. Tape recordings provide an inexpensive means of safeguarding the collection of these data in case on-the-spot counts prove to be too difficult to collect in a particular situation.

The Gottfried Categories of Environmental Influence

In addition to the HOME and FES measures, numerous environmental items—particularly items concerning the physical environment—were included in the CAP interviews and observations in order to assess a wide range of specific environmental influences that might be relevant to infant development. We adapted items from diverse sources such as research by Yarrow, Rubenstein, and Pedersen (1975) and White and Watts (1973). The danger in including such diverse items lies in the difficulty of distilling the items into composite scales; our factor analyses of the items exploit only a small portion of the variance of these heterogeneous measures.

Fortunately, as we were conducting these analyses, Allen and Adele Gottfried sent us drafts of chapters they had written for a book, *Home Environment and Early Cognitive Development: Longitudinal Research* (Gottfried, 1984). Their joint chapter summarizing the results of their study of home environment and mental development for 130 middle-class infants provided an approach to categorizing our diverse environmental measures. In their study, they included not only the HOME and the FES, but also the physical environment sections of the Purdue Home Stimulation Inventory (PHSI; Wachs, 1979) and they note: "The home stimulus variables that were positively related to cognitive development may be conceptualized into the following categories: variety of experience, stimulation of educational abilities, enhancement of skills, maternal involvement, provision for exploration and physical home setting" (Gottfried & Gottfried, 1984, p. 104). The Gottfrieds listed the PHSI and HOME variables that are related to infant mental development in terms of these six categories. The inclusion of several physical aspects of the infant home environment might prove to be an important addition. Although psychological studies of infant development tend to emphasize the social environment rather than the physical environment, a review of the environmental correlates of infant mental development by Wachs and Gruen (1982) revealed that mental development was related more consistently to the physical environment than to the social environment.

We constructed analogs of three of the Gottfried categories: variety of experiences, provision for exploration, and physical home setting. We were not able to construct scales for stimulation of educational abilities or enhancement of skills, because these categories rely primarily on the Gottfrieds' 39-month assessment items, which are not appropriate for infants. The maternal involvement category was not included because it merely sums two HOME scales and thus would create redundancy with our analyses of the HOME. Although the variety of experience category includes a HOME scale, it was used in our analyses because it also includes several other items. The other two categories, provision for exploration and physical home setting, also incorporate some HOME items; however, they generally represent dimensions untapped by the HOME and FES, and they include several CAP items involving the physical setting of the home.

Table 5.9 lists the items in the Gottfried categories of environmental influence

TABLE 5.9

Gottfried Categories of Environmental Influence and CAP Analogs

Gottfried categories and items	CAP items
Variety of experience	
HOME (15 & 39 month) opportunities for variety	HOME (12 or 24 month) opportunities for variety (quantitative scoring)
VEC[a] diversity of experiences outside the home	HOME items 20 (number of regular babysitters), 21 (number of trips to grocery store), 22 (times out of house), 23 (times to doctor)
PHSI visits neighbors	At 12 months only: FES items 4, 7, 8, 16, 27, 36, 37, 57, 66, 67, 77, which assess family activities[b]
PHSI taken out of neighborhood	At 24 months only: number of neighborhood children with whom infant played, total number of children with whom infant played, number of babysitters ever used, and times per month babysitter is used
Provision for exploration	
PHSI floor freedom	Percentage of rooms to which infant has access; Fine motor toys (sum of HOME items 32 and 33); Gross motor toys (sum of HOME items 26, 27, and 28); Number of windows
PHSI access to manipulable items	
PHSI view not restricted to interior	
Physical home setting	
PHSI rooms/people	Rooms/people
HOME (39-month environment clean, safe, conducive to development)	HOME item 25 (safe play environment)
PHSI number of noise sources (reversed)	External and internal noise
PHSI noise level (reversed)	Acoustical quality
PHSI number of children's books	Number of own books
PHSI access to newspapers, magazines, adult books	HOME item 18 (number of books present and visible)

[a]The VEC is the Variety of Experiences Checklist developed by the Gottfrieds to assess the total number of different experiences of the infant.

[b]FES items 4, 7, 16, 27, 36, and 57 were reversed in scoring so that the sum of the FES items indicates families with many activities.

and the CAP analogs. When HOME items were used, we employed the quantitatively scored versions. Separate scales were constructed at 12 and 24 months—the items were the same with the exception of the variety of experiences category. Several FES items were included in that category at 12 months, whereas four other items were used at 24 months as described in Table 5.9.

We explored the factor structure of the CAP items in order to assess the extent to which the items are related to each other in the manner proposed by the Gottfrieds. Factor loadings on the unrotated first principal component and on three rotated factors at 12 and 24 months are presented in Table 5.10. The unrotated first principal components at 12 and 24 months include loadings from most of the items, suggesting that a general factor exists among these items. However, the first principal components account for only 13% and 12% of the variance at 12 and 24 months, respectively. In general, the rotated factors do not correspond to their

TABLE 5.10 Factor Loadings of CAP Items for the Gottfried Categories of Environmental Influence[a]

Gottfried category	CAP item	Unrotated first principal component		Varimax rotated factors					
				Factor 1		Factor 2		Factor 3[b]	
		12 mo	24 mo	12 mo	24 mo	12 mo	24 mo	12 mo	24 mo
Variety of experience	HOME opportunities for experience	.56	.37	.49	.33	—	—	—	—
	Amount of public contact	-.58	—	—	—	.82	.83	—	—
	HOME item 20 (babysitters)	.33	.56	—	—	—	—	—	.60
	HOME item 21 (trips to store)	—	.30	—	—	—	—	—	—
	HOME item 22 (out of house)	.45	—	.35	—	—	—	—	—
	HOME item 23 (doctor's office)	—	—	—	—	—	—	—	—
	12 months only: FES items[c]	.42	—	—	—	—	—	—	—
	24 months only:								
	neighborhood children	—	.45	—	.35	—	—	—	—
	number of children	—	.55	—	.38	—	—	—	—
	number of babysitters ever	—	.59	—	—	—	—	—	.81
	times/month babysitter	—	.40	—	—	—	—	—	.51
Provision for exploration	Access to rooms	.30	—	—	—	—	—	.42	—
	Number of windows	.38	.50	.41	—	—	—	—	—
	Fine motor toys[d]	—	—	—	.49	—	—	—	—
	Gross motor toys[e]	.46	.62	.49	.68	—	—	—	—
Physical home setting	Rooms/people	—	-.35	—	—	—	—	.95	—
	HOME item 25 (safe play)	-.43	—	—	—	—	—	—	—
	External noise	—	—	—	—	.74	.72	—	—
	Internal noise	—	—	—	—	.32	—	—	—
	Acoustical quality	—	—	—	—	—	—	—	—
	Number of child's books	.56	.43	.64	.53	—	—	—	—
	Books visible	.34	.32	.37	—	—	—	—	—

[a] All CAP families when the proband was 12 months ($N = 250$) and 24 months ($N = 252$). Only loadings of .30 or more are listed.
[b] Factor 3 is different at 12 and 24 months.
[c] Sum of FES items 4, 7, 8, 16, 27, 36, 37, 57, 66, 67, 77.
[d] Sum of HOME items 32 and 33 (eye–hand, stacking, blocks toys).
[e] Sum of HOME items 26, 27, and 28 (muscle, push–pull, walker–scooter toys).

TABLE 5.11

Intercorrelations Among the Three Gottfried Categories for Adoptive and Control
Families Combined[a]

Gottfried category	12 Months			24 Months		
	VE	PE	PHS	VE	PE	PHS
Variety of experience (VE)	—	−.05	.13*	—	.24*	.19*
Provision for exploration (PE)	—	—	.17*	—	—	.13*
Physical home setting (PHS)	—	—	—	—	—	—

[a]$N = 256$.
*$p < .05$.

placement on the Gottfried categories. For example, the first factor at 12 months has two items loading above .30 from each of the three categories. The second factor at both 12 and 24 months basically involves two items—amount of public contact and external noise—that load negatively on the unrotated first principal component. The third factor differs at 12 and 24 months: At 12 months, it involves two items concerning room, whereas it involves babysitter items at 24 months.

We interpret these results to indicate that basically a single factor emerges from the items we used for the Gottfried categories. Nonetheless, we decided to use the three categories because their intercorrelations are low (see Table 5.11), and we can suggest no better way to organize these diverse data. Test–retest reliabilities for our three scales are reasonable—.82, .74, and .76, respectively—and comparable to those for the HOME and FES. However, the stability correlations from 12 to 24 months—.39, .42, and .18, respectively—are lower than for the HOME scales. The combination of high test–retest reliability and moderate stability suggests that the Gottfried categories may be more sensitive to environmental change than are the other measures. Means and standard deviations for the three Gottfried categories are listed in Table 5.12. Neither means nor variances differ significantly between adoptive and control families.

TABLE 5.12

Means and Standard Deviations for the Gottfried Categories of Environmental Influence for Adoptive
and Control Homes

Gottfried category	12 Months				24 Months			
	Adoptive (N = 146–155)		Control (N = 138–159)		Adoptive (N = 139–173)		Control (N = 131–157)	
	$\overline{X}$	SD	$\overline{X}$	SD	$\overline{X}$	SD	$\overline{X}$	SD
Variety of experience	.07	2.6	−.06	3.0	−.05	3.8	−.20	4.2
Provision for exploration	−.07	2.0	.00	2.2	−.11	2.1	.02	2.1
Physical home setting	.30	2.6	−.07	2.6	−.02	2.3	−.05	2.5

TABLE 5.13

Intercorrelations among Environmental Measures[a]

Environmental measure	HOME					FES		Gottfried		
	GF	T	MI	DA	R–P	PG	TO	VE	PE	PHS
12 months										
HOME General Factor (GF)	—	.66*	.44*	.75*	−.04	.12	.09	.39*	.41*	.23
HOME Toys (T)	.81*	—	−.07	.16	−.21	.00	.05	.11	.68*	.17
HOME Maternal Involvement (MI)	.59*	.28*	—	.37	.07	.14	.10	.29*	−.11	.12
HOME Encouraging Developmental Advance (DA)	.75*	.33*	.42*	—	.02	.10	.06	.24*	.09	.12
HOME Restriction–Punishment (R–P)	−.02	−.04	−.01	−.05	—	−.06	.11	.04	−.13	.07
FES Personal Growth (PG)	.18	.11	.01	.21	−.11	—	—	.30*	−.05	−.03
FES Traditional Organization (TO)	.06	−.01	.14	.04	.13	.34*	—	.16	.03	.00
Gottfried Variety of Experience (VE)	.37*	.16	.23	.31	−.08	.09	.05	—	−.02	.06
Gottfried Provision for Exploration (PE)	.58*	.73*	.24*	.24*	−.07	.01	.08	−.09	—	.23
Gottfried Physical Home Setting (PHS)	.25*	.22	.04	.15	.12	.01	.01	.23	.11	—
24 months										
HOME General Factor (GF)	—	.47*	.67*	.84*	−.08	—	—	.25*	.32*	.14
HOME Toys (T)	.55*	—	.09	.10	−.18	—	—	.37*	.61*	.15
HOME Maternal Involvement (MI)	.69*	.21	—	.48*	−.11	—	—	.14	.07	.11
HOME Encouraging Developmental Advance (DA)	.83*	.21	.41*	—	.05	—	—	.02	.11	−.01
HOME Restriction–Punishment (R–P)	−.02	−.04	−.07	.02	—	—	—	−.11	−.12	−.07
Gottfried Variety of Experience (VE)	.27*	.35*	.08	.13	.06	—	—	—	.22	.16
Gottfried Provision for Exploration (PE)	.41*	.77*	.11	.18	.00	—	—	.27*	—	.14
Gottfried Physical Home Setting (PHS)	.34*	.26*	.17	.23	.00	—	—	.23	.12	—

[a]Control families above diagonal; adoptive families below diagonal.

*p < .05.

TABLE 5.14

Correlations of Environmental Measures with Socioeconomic Status and Education[a]

Environmental measure[b]	Fathers' "revised NORC"		Grandfathers' "revised NORC"		Fathers' education		Grandfathers' education	
	A	C	A	C	A	C	A	C
HOME General Factor	-.02	.19*	.03	.04	.23*	.13	.13	-.03
HOME Toys	.06	.17*	-.05	-.04	.21*	.20*	.13	.04
HOME Maternal Involvement	-.07	.10	.04	.01	.04	-.07	.11	-.15*
HOME Encouraging Developmental Advance	-.06	.14*	.09	.10	.17*	.04	.04	.00
HOME Restriction–Punishment	-.11	-.15*	-.11	-.12	-.06	-.15*	-.09	-.14*
FES Personal Growth	.21*	.03	-.12	.15*	.35*	.19*	.01	.10
FES Traditional Organization	-.16*	.04	.08	-.01	-.11	-.03	-.01	-.10
Gottfried Variety of Experience	.19*	.09	.06	-.03	.31*	.18*	.13	.00
Gottfried Provision for Exploration	.04	.19*	.01	.02	.16*	.07	.03	-.04
Gottfried Physical Home Setting	.01	.17*	.15	-.04	.13	-.05	.03	-.12

[a] A = Adopted, C = Control.

[b] Environmental measures are from the 12-month home visit; the 24-month data yield similar results as do data for the mothers' education and her fathers' education and socioeconomic status.

*p < .05.

83

Intercorrelations among Environmental Measures

Our three environmental measures—the HOME, the FES, and the Gottfried scales—are not independent. Intercorrelations among the measures are listed in Table 5.13. Correlations for adoptive and control families are presented separately; however, they are sufficiently similar that we discuss them together. At 12 months of age, the correlations between the HOME General Factor and the two FES second-order factors are low, as were the correlations found by Gottfried and Gottfried (1984). The correlations between four specific HOME scales and the three Gottfried scales are only slightly higher. However, the correlations of the Gottfried scales with the HOME General Factor are substantial, and the correlations between the HOME Toys factor and the Gottfried Provision for Exploration scale exceed .60, due to the inclusion of several HOME Toys items in the Gottfried scale. Correlations between the two FES scales and the Gottfried scales are of low magnitude with the exception of a correlation of .34 between FES Personal Growth and Gottfried Variety of Experience. In general, the three types of measures are sufficiently independent to offer assessments of different facets of the environment.

The CAP environmental measures are also reasonably independent of paternal SES; however, correlations with education tend to be somewhat higher (see Table 5.14). The correlations with the HOME are lower than those reported in studies of disadvantaged homes (Elardo & Bradley, 1981). Although the correlations tend to be low, in the next chapter we discuss the relationship between measures of home environment and infant mental development independent of SES and parental education.

Perinatal Environment

Another type of environmental influence involves perinatal factors such as birth weight and gestational age. Birth history information was collected for adopted infants from hospital records kept on file at the adoption agencies. Control mothers were asked for the information directly. The average birth weight of the adoptees is 3221 g (range: 1724–4218 g); for the controls, the average birth weight is 3311 g (range: 1996–4354 g). Birth weight below 2500 g, thought to occur for about 7% of live births, is considered to be a risk factor. Five percent of the adopted infants and 3% of the control infants had birth weights below 2500 g.

Clinical estimates of gestational age were similarly representative. The average gestational age of the adoptees was 39.6 ($SD = 1.7$) with a range from 33 to 44 weeks. For the controls, the average was 39.7 ($SD = 1.5$) with a range from 34 to 43 weeks. Epidemiological data suggest that about 80% of all singletons are born at 40 or more weeks gestational age; in the CAP, this is true for 70% of the adoptees and 63% of the controls. A gestational age less than 36 weeks is often considered as a risk factor and occurs for about 3% of singleton births; in the CAP, 3.0% of the

TABLE 5.15

Correlations of Birth Weight and Gestational Age with Measures of the Home Environment

Environmental measure	Adoptees		Controls	
	Birth weight (N = 130–170)	Gestational age (N = 129–167)	Birth weight (N = 105–130)	Gestational age (N = 91–112)
12 months				
HOME General Factor	.00	.02	.06	.07
HOME Toys	.07	.06	.10	.02
HOME Maternal Involvement	−.12	−.03	−.02	.10
HOME Encouraging Developmental Advance	−.01	.00	.03	.06
HOME Restriction–Punishment	.03	.03	.01	−.03
FES Personal Growth	.13	.01	.03	−.07
FES Traditional Organization	−.05	.04	.04	.02
Gottfried Variety of Experience	.01	.07	−.08	.02
Gottfried Provision for Exploration	.06	.13	.19*	.11
Gottfried Physical Home Setting	.02	.05	.00	.01
24 months				
HOME General Factor	.00	.06	−.13	−.04
HOME Toys	.02	−.01	.01	.07
HOME Maternal Involvement	−.04	.07	−.05	.09
HOME Encouraging Developmental Advance	.01	.09	−.16*	−.11
HOME Restriction–Punishment	−.01	−.03	.01	.13
Gottfried Variety of Experience	−.01	−.06	.03	−.02
Gottfried Provision for Exploration	.05	.02	−.09	−.04
Gottfried Physical Home Setting	−.05	−.06	−.20*	−.16*

*$p < .05$.

adoptees and 2.7% of the controls had gestational ages less than 36 weeks. Thus, for both birth weight and gestational age, the CAP sample appears to be quite normal.

In order to explore the possibility that parents treat children differently on the basis of their perinatal status, we computed correlations of birth weight and gestational age with the other home environment measures (see Table 5.15). Only 4 of the 72 correlations are statistically significant, which is about the number of significant correlations that would be expected by chance. The one possibly systematic pattern of correlations is for the Gottfried Physical Home Setting scale at 24 months; infants with lower birth weights and gestational ages tend to have slightly better home settings in the sense of safer play environments and lower noise levels. However, parental measures such as Maternal Involvement and Encouraging Developmental Advance do not appear to be related to perinatal status.

Stability of the Environment and Interaction

Environmental measures used in the CAP are reasonably stable from 12 to 24 months. In the next chapter, we examine the extent to which environment at 12 months has an effect on infant mental development at 24 months.

Another issue related to the stability of the environment is the possibility that parental characteristics interact with stability. For example, Moss and Jones (1977) suggest that maternal education affects stability: More highly educated mothers are more stable in their parenting. In the analyses reported in this book, we employed hierarchical multiple regression to assess such interactions. Hierarchical multiple regression (HMR; Cohen & Cohen, 1975) permits evaluation of the significance of main effects and of their interaction by assessing the added predictiveness of the joint product of the main effects. Because this procedure is referred to frequently in this book, we describe it briefly at this time.

Hierarchical Multiple Regression for the Analysis of Interaction

By interaction, we mean conditional relationships: The relationship between X and Y depends upon Z. This is the usual meaning of *interaction* as the term is used in analysis of variance: "The phenomenon is well named. Interaction variations are those attributable not to either of two influences acting alone but to joint effects of the two acting together" (Guilford & Fruchter, 1973, p. 249). HMR provides linear regression results equivalent to those obtained by analysis of variance. A major advantage of HMR is that it permits the analysis of continuous variation. Dichotomizing continuous distributions by dividing the sample at the mean is a weak analytical procedure. Thus, although HMR can accommodate two-by-two dichotomous analyses, one of its virtues is its ability to analyze interactions involving continuous variation. Other advantages include its indication of the amount of variance explained by main effects and interactions and its exact tests of significance even with unequal subclass numbers.

The simplest HMR model of interaction predicts a dependent variable from two independent variables and their product:

$$\underbrace{\hat{Y} = b_1 X_1 + b_2 X_2}_{\text{Step One}} + \underbrace{b_3 X_1 X_2}_{\text{Step Two}} + \text{C}. \qquad (5.1)$$

Using the example at hand, we can predict later parental behavior (when the infant is 24 months old) from earlier parental behavior (when the infant is 12 months old); from parental characteristics such as education, SES, or IQ; and from the interaction between earlier parental behavior and other parental characteristics. More specifically, we can predict later parental behavior ($\hat{Y}$) from earlier parental behavior (X_1), parental IQ (X_2), and their interaction ($X_1 X_2$). C is the regression constant.

X_1 and X_2 are analogous to main effects in an analysis of variance. The two-way interaction (X_1X_2) is represented by the product of main effects (i.e., X_1 scores multiplied by X_2 scores) from which the main effects have been linearly partialed, as in the analysis of variance procedure for estimating interactions; b_1 is the partial regression of later parental behavior on earlier parental behavior, a measure of the main effect of stability of parental behavior; b_2 is the partial regression of later parental behavior on parental IQ, which indicates the main effect of IQ; and b_3 provides a measure of the conditional relationship between the main effects and $\hat{Y}$, that is, their interaction.

As indicated in the model, the significance of the main effects and the two-way interaction is tested sequentially, which is the reason why the analysis is referred to as *hierarchical* multiple regression. The b_1 and b_2 values are estimated from $\hat{Y}$, X_1, and X_2 during the first step. The product, X_1X_2, is added to the equation during the second step. The change in the multiple R^2 due to the product entered during this second step is attributed to the interaction between X_1 and X_2 and can be tested for statistical significance. A significant b_3 indicates that the relationship between earlier and later parental behavior changes as a function of parental IQ. In other words, a significant b_3 suggests that the stability of parental behavior depends upon parental IQ, which is precisely the question raised by Moss and Jones (1977).

The Interaction between Environmental Stability and Parental Characteristics

We conducted HMR analysis of the HOME and Gottfried-scale stabilities, looking for interactions with parental education, SES, and IQ. Combining adoptive and control data yielded a reasonably large sample size of nearly 350, which provides 80% power (with $p < .05$) to detect interactions that account for less than 2% of the variance of parental behavior—given a multiple R^2 greater than .30, which is quite reasonable for these variables. Nonetheless, when we conducted a total of 21 HMR analyses based upon pairings of our four quantitative HOME scales and three Gottfried scales with parental IQ, education, and SES, we found only one significant interaction, which is to be expected by chance ($p < .05$). Thus, our HMR approach does not confirm the hypothesis that environmental stability is moderated by parental characteristics such as IQ, education, and SES.

Genetic Mediation of Environmental Influences

Stepping back from these specific issues concerning the CAP environmental measures—descriptive statistics, intercorrelations, and stability—we can introduce the important role these measures play in the rest of this book. Correlations between these measures and infant development in adoptive homes assess environmental influence unbiased by hereditary similarity between parents and their children. Moreover, they permit exploration of possible genetic correlates of the environment. We can compare environmental relationships in control families to those in adoptive families to test the possibility of genetic influence in ostensibly environmental relationships with infant development. If heredity affects the relationship between an environmental measure and infant development, the relationship will be greater in control families than in adoptive families.

It is reasonable to consider this possibility. Certainly, environmental measures are not necessarily environmental because we name them as such. They usually involve parental behavior, and behavioral-genetic research has shown that genetic influences are ubiquitous for diverse domains of adult behavior. Suggestions of genetic influence on environmental measures can be found in the literature. David Rowe (1981, 1983) has sytematically explored the possibility of genetic influence on adolescents' perceptions of their parents' treatment, and, in two twin studies, he found that genetic factors affect children's perceptions of their parents' warmth and affection toward them. Even though an environmental measure is shown to be affected by heredity, this does not necessarily imply that the relationship between the environmental measure and infant development is mediated genetically, although it does add to the plausibility of the hypothesis. More to the point are two older studies of adoptive and control families that included environmental assessments (Burks, 1928; Leahy, 1935). Both studies found higher correlations between environmental indices and children's IQ in control families than in adoptive families. For example, Burks' study of 200 adoptive and 100 nonadoptive families included the Whittier Scale for Home Grading. The correlation between the Whittier Index and children's IQ in the adoptive homes was .21; the correlation was significantly higher, .42, in the control homes. Similarly, in the study by Leahy, a cultural index of the home correlated .21 with children's IQ in 194 adoptive homes and .51 in 194 control homes.

These results are not so surprising, because the measures of the home environment used in these studies are imbued with IQ-relevant factors such as parental education and economic status of the parents (see Chapter 6). Thus, the genetic influence suggested by the higher correlations in the control families than in the adoptive families may be mediated by parental IQ. Nonetheless, these studies attest to the reasonableness of considering possible genetic mediation of environmental influences.

Approaching the study of the environment from the novel perspective of genetics leads to interpretations, concepts, and methods not previously considered in environmental research. The approach is important as well because it makes a difference for intervention or application of environmental research if a supposedly environmental effect is in fact mediated genetically. In subsequent chapters, we develop a model of genetic mediation of environmental influences. It is our hope that this model will lead to a rapprochement between behavioral-genetic and environmental research. Ted Wachs, a well-known environmentalist who has written an important resource book on early environmental influence in psychological development (Wachs & Gruen, 1982), is encouraged about the prospects for such a rapprochement:

One major factor blocking this sorely needed integration of disciplines is a continued reliance on outmoded conceptions about the nature of each discipline. Thus, most environmentalists are more or less ignorant of current theories, concepts, and results in the area of behavior genetics. As a consequence, environmentalists all too often ignore the possibility of genetic influences in their research (Plomin *et al.*, 1980). Thus, correlations between parental behaviors and child development are commonly viewed as due solely to the contributions of the environment; rarely do we find consideration of the possibility that these correlations may reflect the contribution of shared genes that influence both the parents' behavior and the child's development. . . . In contrast, in behavioral genetic studies the environment is either estimated but not measured or is only measured indirectly. . . . Eventually, an understanding of the nature of human development will require the joint input of environmentalists and behavior geneticists. (Wachs, 1983, pp. 396–397)

Summary

Although it might seem odd to begin the substantive chapters of our behavioral-genetics book with a chapter on the environment, we believe that a major contribution of this book is its influence on the way we think about environmental effects on individual differences in infancy. We began the chapter with a brief review of changing conceptualizations of early environmental influences and then presented descriptive data concerning the second-order FES scales and a quantitative scoring scheme for the HOME. We have organized various measures of the physical environment using categories suggested by the Gottfrieds.

Although these environmental measures are somewhat interrelated, they add enough independent but reliable variance to justify inclusion in subsequent CAP analyses reported in this book. The environmental measures are also stable, with a median correlation from 12 to 24 months of about .50. We have explored the possibility that environmental stability interacts with parental characteristics such as social class, education, and IQ. Although we find no evidence to support this hypothesis, we have taken the opportunity to describe hierarchical multiple regression, a procedure for analyzing interactions that is referred to throughout the book.

In the final section of the chapter, we have discussed the possibility of genetic involvement in relationships between environmental measures and infant development. Possible genetic mediation of these relationships is explored by means of comparisons of environment–infant correlations in control families with those in adoptive families in the following chapters.

6

Development of General Cognitive Ability

Introduction

No issue in the behavioral sciences has received as much continuous attention as the nature and nurture of general mental ability. The first twin study and the first adoption study, both reported in 1924, focused on this trait, and data on about 50,000 individuals have subsequently been collected in dozens of family, twin, and adoption studies of IQ. Doubts raised about some of the older data (e.g., Kamin, 1974) led to the collection of data on larger samples during the 1970s than in the previous fifty years combined. Although the newer data suggest somewhat less genetic influence on IQ than did the older data, all the data converge on the conclusion of significant and substantial genetic influence (Plomin & DeFries, 1980).

The conclusion that heritable differences account for a significant portion of IQ variance is now generally accepted, at least in textbooks if not in the popular press (Herrnstein, 1982). However, this is not the end of the story; it is just the beginning, resulting in many more questions than answers. For example, what are the origins of specific mental abilities? For both general and specific mental abilities, what happens at the interface of heredity and environment? In other words, how do nature and nurture transact to affect the development of mental abilities? As we learn more about developmental behavioral genetics, the list of such questions grows longer. What is the developmental course of the relative influence of nature and nurture on individual differences in mental development; that is, does heritability change during development? Do genes mediate change as well as continuity; what are the longitudinal genetic correlations for mental development? Does heredity contribute to the developmental differentiation of mental abilities? As emphasized in Chapter 3, the study of genetic effects also leads to novel questions about environmental influence, questions that go well beyond the traditional question of the amount of variance that can be attributed to environment. What are the specific sources of environmental variance? Does heredity mediate some ostensibly environmental contributions to development? Are environmental influences experienced in common by children in the same family? Can specific genotype–environment interactions be isolated?

The purpose of this chapter is to present the results of the Colorado Adoption Project for general mental ability; the following two chapters consider specific cognitive abilities. For parents, general cognitive ability, or IQ, is indexed by scores on the first principal component (unrotated). For infants, general mental ability is assessed by standardized infant tests—most notably, the Bayley Mental Scale. The measures have been described in Chapter 4.

Continuity–Discontinuity

The zeitgeist in developmental psychology is such that one might ask who cares about individual differences in infant mental development, because infant test scores do not predict later IQ. Even if it were true that infant tests do not predict later IQ, we would nonetheless maintain that a developmental behavioral-genetic analysis of infant mental development might provide a basis for understanding the etiologies of developmental change. However, developmentalists may have permitted the pendulum to swing too far from an exaggeration of continuity to an exaggeration of discontinuity in mental development.

Infant tests are reliable. For example, Werner and Bayley (1966) reported that various infant tests of mental development had internal consistencies greater than .80 on the average during the first year of life. Test–retest reliability, although seldom reported, is usually greater than .75 (Thorndike, 1940). The disenchantment with infant tests came when longitudinal studies showed low predictive validity (Brooks & Weintraub, 1976). The expectation had been for constancy of IQ; instead, predictive correlations were too low for practical utility in predicting school-age IQ from infancy, one of the main goals of early infant test development. However, an important finding that went unnoticed was that certain items that correlated little with overall scores concurrently tended to be quite predictive of later IQ. For example, correlations of awareness items on the Gesell Developmental Schedule at 6 months (such as "regards pellet" and "splashes in tub") with the 6-month Gesell total score are much lower than are those for other items, but they predict 24-month Merrill–Palmer Scale scores and 36-month Stanford–Binet scores better than do any other items at 6 months (Nelson & Richards, 1939). These results were forerunners of the interest in preference for novelty as an early infancy predictor of school-age IQ (Fagan & Singer, 1983), discussed in the next chapter.

In fact, infant mental tests do predict later IQ, although not nearly as well as the early test constructors had hoped. For example, for 365 infants in the Louisville Twin Study (LTS), Wilson (1983) reported a correlation of .48 from 12 to 24 months. Also, 12-month Bayley scores significantly predicted school-age IQ—for example, a correlation of .33 with IQ at 9 years of age. Correlations of Bayley scores at 24 months with IQ at 36 months and at 9 years were .74 and .56, respectively. Stability was found to increase from infancy throughout childhood. In the first year, 3-month stability was about .50; 6-month stability was about .60 in the second year; 1-year stability was about .70 in early childhood and about .80 in middle childhood.

These LTS correlations are generally higher than those reported for other studies such as the Berkeley Growth Study (Bayley, 1949), the Berkeley Guidance Study (Honzik, Macfarlane, & Allen, 1948), and the Stockholm longitudinal study (Klackenberg-Larsson & Stensson, 1968). Although Bayley (1949) initially reported that the correlation between test scores at 1 year and 18 years is zero, a correlation of .25 was subsequently reported (Bayley, 1955). Furthermore, a review by McCall (1979) yielded a median correlation of .32 for three studies comparing infant test scores (13- to 18-month-old infants) to IQ scores at 8 and 18 years of age. Longitudinal correlations with IQ at maturity clearly increase after the first year of life. Bayley (1955) reported a correlation of .55 between mental scores at 2 years and 18-year-old IQ.

In summary, at least some continuity for infant mental development exists in the midst of considerable change. Both change and continuity are appropriate areas for developmental behavioral-genetic analyses.

Genetics of Infant Mental Development

Little is known about the etiology of individual differences in infant mental development. The famous Skodak and Skeels (1949) study did not begin until after infancy; the average age of the children at the first test was 27 months, and the ages varied from 6 months to 6 years. The biological mothers' IQ correlated .00 with the adoptees' scores on the Kuhlman Revision of the Binet test for 63 pairs. From the raw data provided by Skodak and Skeels, we computed the mother–child correlation for infants tested between 12 and 24 months of age. For 39 pairs, the correlation is −.01.

A cross-sectional study of the relationship between biological mothers' IQ and infant test scores for 227 infants from 1 to 2 years was reported by Snygg (1938). The Kuhlman test was used for the infants and the Stanford–Binet for the biological mothers. Unfortunately, there is no doubt that the biological mothers were a biased sample because "girls who had passed high school entrance examinations were seldom asked to take psychological tests" (Snygg, 1938, p. 403); their average IQ was only 78.3, and the range was probably restricted although no information concerning variance was provided in the brief report. The correlation for infants between 12 and 24 months and their biological mothers was .08. In order to learn more about this study, we corresponded with James J. Parry, assistant to the president, State University of New York at Oswego. We were informed that Professor Snygg died in 1967 (his wife died in the following year) and that the university's files contain no information concerning the 1938 study or any subsequent studies by him.

A third relevant study that obtained data on biological parents and infant adoptees was reported by Casler (1976). The infants, adopted at about 2 months of age, were tested on the Gesell; biological mothers were given the Stanford–Binet. The mean parent–offspring correlations for tests administered at 15 and 21 months for 150 pairs are .07 for the motor subtest, .13 for the language subtest, −.02 for the adaptive subtest, and .16 for the personal–social subtest. The mean of these correlations is .09. One problem with this study is that selective placement for IQ was intentionally practiced.

Thus, the three previous studies reporting IQ correlations for biological mothers and their adopted-away infants yielded correlations of −.01, .08, and .09. With regard to the environmental complement of the full adoption design (that is, comparisons between adoptive parents and their adopted infants), not a single study has been reported. More surprisingly, there appears to be only one small IQ study of control parents and their infant offspring (Eichorn, 1969). Gottfried and Gottfried (1984) reported a significant correlation ($r = .18$) between control mothers' scores on the Weschler Adult Intelligence Scale (WAIS) Vocabulary test and Bayley scores of their infants at 24 months of age ($N = 121$). However, the correlation with 12-month Bayley scores was −.01 ($N = 130$). WAIS Block Design yielded correlations of −.03 and .03 with the Bayley Mental Development Index (MDI) at 12 and 24 months, respectively.

There has been only one major longitudinal behavioral-genetic study that has involved infants, the Louisville Twin Study (LTS). Using the classical twin design, which compares similarity of identical twins and fraternal twins, this 20-year study has charted the developmental behavioral genetics of IQ as summarized in Figure 6.1. Correlations for both identical and fraternal twins are approximately .65 at 1 year of age, a pattern of correlations that suggests little genetic influence and very substantial shared family environmental influence. Another large-scale study, the Collaborative Perinatal Project (CPP), reported 8-month Bayley MDI correlations for 122 pairs of identical twins and 227 pairs of fraternal twins that confirmed the LTS results (Nichols & Broman, 1974). Although the twin correlations were .84 and .55, respectively, for the two types of twins, removal of severely retarded infants left the twin correlations much like those of the LTS.

After the first year, genetic influence can be detected in the LTS. Heritability continues at modest levels until 5 years of age, when the pattern of twin correlations for IQ begins to resemble that typically seen for adolescent and adult twins. In addition to documenting genetic influence on Bayley MDI scores in infancy, the LTS has demonstrated that genes are a source of change in infant mental development. Longitudinal profiles have been analyzed using a repeated-measures, analy-

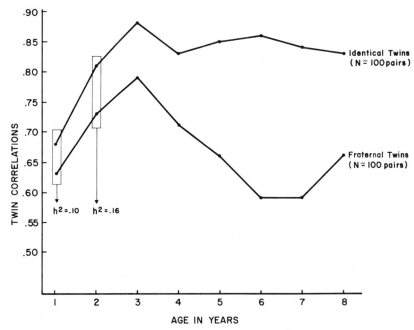

FIGURE 6.1   Summary of twin correlations from the longitudinal Louisville Twin Study. The symbol h^2 refers to heritability, the proportion of phenotypic variance that can be accounted for by genetic variance. (Data from Wilson, 1983, Table 2.)

sis-of-variance procedure that indicates greater profile similarity for identical twins than for fraternal twins (Wilson, 1983). The longitudinal profiles for MDI scores at 3, 6, 9, and 12 months yield twin correlations of .69 and .63 for identical and fraternal twins, respectively. The fact that the twin correlations do not differ significantly suggests that heritable differences are not an important source of variation in change during the first year of life; however, the twin correlations are interesting because they imply that environmental factors shared by twins living in the same family are closely related to differences in these longitudinal changes. Across the second and third years (at 12, 18, 24, and 36 months), the identical twin correlation (.80) for longitudinal profiles is significantly greater than the fraternal twin correlation (.72), suggesting that, in addition to substantial shared family environmental influences, genetic factors affect developmental profiles. Genetic regulation of the profiles increases throughout childhood. Although this analysis cannot be simply related to genetic and environmental longitudinal correlations, which are discussed in Chapter 3, the results indicate that by the second year of life genes are to some extent involved in developmental change.

In contrast to the parent–offspring design of the CAP, the twin design provides the important advantage of comparing individuals of the same age. However, twin correlations are suspiciously high in infancy—substantially higher than the 3-month stability for individuals. Moreover, twin correlations in infancy are almost twice as large as correlations for nontwin siblings. The LTS found twin correlations of about .65 in infancy, but nontwin sibling correlations of only .30 to .40. For over 3000 pairs of nontwin siblings in the CPP, the correlation at 8 months was only .22 compared to the CPP fraternal twin correlation of .55. Similarly, McCall (1972) reported a correlation of .24 for 142 pairs of nontwin siblings in the first year of life. Clearly, twins are special. The special environment of twins quite probably includes shared perinatal factors, such as prematurity, that are more common in twins (Wilson, 1977a). Identical twins actually experience greater differences prenatally than do fraternal twins—as indicated, for example, by the observation that birth weight and length differences are greater for identical than for fraternal twins (Wilson, 1976). Both physically and psychologically, identical twins become more similar throughout development and fraternal twins become less similar.

These factors that affect the results of twin studies, especially in infancy, make it particularly important to obtain comparison data using the adoption design.

CAP Infant Mental Development

In the CAP, the two measures of general mental development in infancy are the Bayley Mental Development Index (MDI; Bayley, 1969) and the Ordinal Scales of Psychological Development (OSPD; Uzgiris & Hunt, 1975), which are described in Chapter 4. Table 6.1 lists means and standard deviations for these two measures for adopted and control infants. A multivariate analysis of variance at each age indicated no significant effects due to gender, adoptive status, or their interaction. Also, variances for the groups were not significantly heterogeneous. Girls scored significantly higher than boys on the OSPD; however, the difference was less than half a standard deviation.

TABLE 6.1

Means and Standard Deviations for Bayley Mental Development Index (MDI) and Ordinal Scales of Psychological Development (OSPD)

	N	$\overline{X}$	SD
Bayley MDI			
12-month-olds			
Adopted	182	107.3	12.2
Control	165	109.1	12.7
24-month-olds			
Adopted	182	107.9	14.8
Control	163	109.5	15.7
OSPD Total for 4 Scales			
12-month-olds			
Adopted	148	27.8	2.6
Control	129	28.4	2.1

The Bayley (1969) manual reports a mean MDI of 101.1 for a stratified standardization sample that was representative of the 1960 U.S. census in terms of sex, color, urban–rural residence, and educational attainment of the head of the household. The mean MDI in the CAP is 108, about half a standard deviation above the mean of the standardization sample. However, at 12 months of age, the standardization sample consisted of only 94 children, 16% of whom lived in rural residences and 13% of whom were nonwhite; for 24% of the infants, the head of the household had an eighth-grade education or less. With these differences in mind, it again appears that the CAP sample is reasonably representative of the Caucasian, urban–suburban, middle-class population. In terms of variances, the standard deviation of the CAP sample at 12 months is about 12, only a quarter of a standard deviation less than the 16.0 standard deviation of the standardization sample. Moreover, at 24 months, the CAP variance is quite similar to that of the standardization sample.

Test–retest reliability information has not been reported previously for the MDI and OSPD measures. In the CAP, the 2-week, test–retest correlation for 12-month-olds is .80 for the MDI and .52 for the OSPD. The correlation between the MDI and OSPD is .38 for the entire sample at 12 months, and it remains the same when sex and adoptive status are partialed out ($N = 277$). These data support the hypothesis that Piagetian measures of cognitive development such as the OSPD are correlated at or near their reliability with psychometrically derived measures such as the Bayley scales (Gottfried & Brody, 1975). The longitudinal correlation for the MDI from 12 to 24 months, with linear effects of adoptive status and sex partialed out, is .40 ($N = 345$).

The factor structure of the Bayley Mental Scale has seldom been considered. For this reason, we explored the possibility of using the unrotated first principal component as a better measure of infant mental development than the Bayley MDI. Factor analytic work on the Bayley items is complicated by the fact that several items are interdependent. For example, at 12 months, items 90, 100, and 114 involve putting 1, 3 or more, or 9 cubes in a cup. An infant who puts 9 cubes in a cup obviously receives credit for the other two items. We sidestepped this problem by sorting such interdependent items into scales. In addition to the Cubes in Cup scale involving items 90, 100, and 114, the following 12 scales were created: Pegboard (items 87, 108, 118, 123, 134, and 156); Scribbles (95, 98, 112, 125, 135, and 147); Blueboard (110, 121, 129, 142, 155, 159, and 160); Tower of Cubes (111, 119, 143, and 161); Pinkboard (120, 137, and 151); Names Objects (124, 138, and 146); Names Pictures (130, 141, and 149); Points to Pictures (132, 139, and 148); Mends Doll (133, 140, and 153); Discriminates Cup, Plate, and Box (144 and 152); Names Watch (145 and 150); and Prepositions (158 and 163). If the infant does not pass any item on a scale, a score of zero is given, which is the same score given when an item is failed on the Bayley. If the lowest item is passed but the second item is failed, a score of 1 is given, the same score given for passing an item. A score of 1 is added for each additional item within a scale that is passed by an infant. Items and scales were deleted from factor analysis if they showed less than 10% variability. For 12-month-olds, this procedure resulted in the selection of 16 items and 6 scales; for 24-month-olds, 4 items and 12 scales were selected.

TABLE 6.2

Unrotated First Principal-Component Loadings for Items
and Scales of the Bayley Mental Scale

Item–scale	Loading
12 months	
94. Inhibits on command	.27
96. Unwraps cube	.13
97. Repeats performance laughed at	.30
99. Pushes car along	.26
101. Jabbers expressively	.18
102. Uncovers blue box	.34
104. Pats whistle doll in imitation	.22
105. Dangles ring by string	.05
106. Imitates words	.43
107. Puts beads in box (6 of 8)	.55
109. Removes pellet from bottle	.36
113. Says two words	.39
115. Closes round box	.38
116. Uses gestures to make wants known	.37
117. Shows shoes or other clothing	.34
122. Attains toy with stick	.38
Scale 1. Pegboard	.60
Scale 2. Cubes in Cup	.55
Scale 3. Scribbles	.53
Scale 4. Blueboard	.53
Scale 5. Tower of Cubes	.34
Scale 6. Pinkboard	.43
24 months	
131. Finds two objects	.12
136. Sentence of two words	.44
154. Train of cubes	.24
157. Folds paper	.15
Scale 1. Pegboard	.17
Scale 3. Scribbles	.28
Scale 4. Blueboard	.34
Scale 5. Tower of Cubes	.19
Scale 6. Pinkboard	.28
Scale 7. Names Objects	.75
Scale 8. Names Pictures	.86
Scale 9. Points to Pictures	.71
Scale 10. Mends Doll	.19
Scale 11. Discriminates Three	.48
Scale 12. Names Watch	.56
Scale 13. Prepositions	.41

Table 6.2 lists the loadings of all items and scales on the first unrotated principal component at 12 and at 24 months. Rotated factors are described in the next chapter. At 12 months, the general factor accounts for 18% of the variance. All but 6 of the items load above .30; the scale scores for Pegboard, Cubes in Cup, Scribbles, and Blueboard load most highly. At 24 months, the principal component

accounts for 23% of the variance. Again, the highest-loading items involve scales rather than individual items, especially language-oriented scales such as Names Pictures, Names Objects, and Points to Pictures.

These results, which suggest a change in infant general mental development, g, from 12 to 24 months, are similar to the results of analyses of Gesell items from the Fels study for 148 one-year-olds and 144 two-year-olds (McCall, Hogarty, & Hurlburt, 1972) and to the results of analyses of the Bayley precursor, the California First Year Test, for 70 infants in the Berkeley Growth Study (McCall, Eichorn, & Hogarty, 1977). In both studies, the principal component at 12 months largely involved fine motor and gross motor skills. At 24 months, the general factor was almost entirely verbal in nature.

Factor analytic scores were calculated for the first principal components at 12 and 24 months, and correlations with Bayley MDI scores were computed. The correlations exceed .90 at both 12 and 24 months for the adopted and control infants; thus, we utilize Bayley MDI scores as an index of infant general cognitive ability for all subsequent analyses.

CAP Adult General Cognitive Ability

The 16 CAP cognitive tests and the 13 scores they yield are described in Chapter 4. Although the means and variances of these scores are described in the next chapter when we focus on specific cognitive abilities, it should be noted here that the adoptive, biological, and control parents do not differ in variance for the 13 cognitive scores. Age is significantly related to cognitive scores, however, and is confounded with parental type because the biological parents are about 10 years younger than the other parents. For this reason, the 13 scores were adjusted for age, age squared, and sex separately for each group of parents. The resulting standard scores thus do not differ in terms of means or variances for the three types of parents.

Table 6.3 lists the loadings of the individual tests on the unrotated first principal component for the entire sample. The first principal component accounts for 36% of the variance and has high loadings for all tests with the exception of the memory tests (Picture Memory, and Names and Faces). When principal-component analyses were conducted separately for the adoptive, biological, and control parents, the loadings were virtually identical, yielding factor similarity indices exceeding .90 for the three types of parents, as well as for males and females, according to the maximum congruence factor structure comparison method of Kaiser, Hunka, and Bianchini (1971).

A first principal component based on similar cognitive measures was found to be correlated .73 with WAIS full-scale IQ, a correlation that is comparable to correlations reported between WAIS IQ and other standard tests of intelligence (Kuse, 1977). Thus, we consider the first principal component score to be a measure of general cognitive ability or IQ.

TABLE 6.3

Unrotated First Principal-Component Loadings
for Adult Cognitive Tests[a]

Test	Factor loading
Things Categories	.45
Card Rotations	.53
Subtraction and Multiplication	.59
Word Beginnings and Endings	.63
Picture Memory	.30
Pedigrees	.77
Hidden Patterns	.67
Paper Form Board	.61
Progressive Matrices	.68
Vocabulary	.65
Identical Pictures	.64
Colorado Perceptual Speed	.71
Names and Faces	.41

[a]$N = 910$.

As discussed in Chapter 3, assortative mating and selective placement can affect estimates of quantitative genetic parameters from adoption studies. Age-adjusted assortative mating correlations for IQ are .27, .24, and .17, respectively, for the adoptive, biological, and control parents. The correlations do not differ significantly among the three types of parents. Although the effects of selective placement can be incorporated into model-fitting approaches to the analysis of adoption data, the clean separation of genetic and environmental influences is attenuated when adoptive parents resemble biological parents. Fortunately, selective placement is negligible in the CAP: Biological mothers' IQ correlates .02 with the adoptive mothers' IQ and −.01 with the adoptive fathers' IQ. The biological fathers' IQ correlates −.09 and −.05 with the adoptive mothers' and fathers' IQ, respectively.

Parent–Offspring Correlations for IQ

The parent–offspring design of the CAP is described in Chapter 3. The essence of the design lies in comparisons of correlations for three types of parents and their offspring: controls, who share both heredity and family environment; adoptive parent–adoptee pairs, who share only family environment; and biological parent–adopted-away offspring, who share only heredity. The limitations of this design for studying infancy were discussed earlier: Genetically, the design is limited to genetic variance shared by infants and adults; environmentally, the design is limited to parental behavior that is related to mental development of their infants. However, these limitations add to the excitement of finding either genetic or environmental influences using this design because genetic findings imply some genetically mediated continuity between infancy and adulthood. Environmental findings imply that parents do something that affects infant mental development independent of heredity; moreover, the adoption design provides an opportunity to isolate specific environmental factors (regardless of their relationship to parental behavior) devoid of genetic bias.

As mentioned earlier, few behavioral-genetic studies have involved infants; thus, it is difficult to predict what may be found in the CAP. If we believed that infant scores are not related to later IQ, we would predict no significant genetic influence as estimated from the correlation between biological parents and their adopted-away infants. However, we have seen that greater continuity exists than one would gather from a cursory review of contemporary developmental writing. We cannot rely much on the three previous adoption studies correlations for IQ measures between biological mothers and their adopted-away infants (Casler, 1976; Skodak & Skeels, 1949; Snygg, 1938), because tests other than the Bayley were used. Nonetheless, the median correlation between biological mothers and their adopted-away infants was .08. Data from the LTS (Wilson, 1983), reviewed earlier, suggest an average heritability of .13 in infants between 12 and 24 months old. Assuming genetic continuity between infancy and adulthood, these twin data suggest that the correlation between biological parents and their adopted-away offspring should be approximately .07, very close to the median correlation of .08 found in previous adoption studies in infancy. It should be noted that a sample size in excess of 600 pairs is needed to detect a correlation of this magnitude with 80% power ($p < .05$, one-tailed; Cohen, 1977).

It is not possible to predict parent–offspring correlations for adoptive or control relationships. There are no previous studies comparing infant adoptees to their adoptive parents. Moreover, the one small IQ study of control parents and their infant offspring yielded mixed results (Eichorn, 1969). The twin data do not help to predict parent–offspring correlations for adoptive and control families, because twins share at least twice as much family environmental variance as do nontwin siblings; in addition, siblings have more of these influences in common than do parents and their offspring (Plomin et al., 1980). Nonetheless, studies of preadolescent adoptees yield a median IQ correlation between adoptive parents and adopted children of about .15, although we might expect the correlation to be somewhat lower for infants.

If the upper-limit estimate of the biological parent–adopted-away offspring correlation is about .10 and if that for the adoptive parent–adopted infant correlation is .10, the correlation between control parents and their infants should be no greater than .20.

Table 6.4 lists the CAP parent–offspring correlations for the MDI at 12 and 24 months and for the OSPD at 12 months. At 24 months, the results are suggestive of both genetic and environmental influences. The ''heredity'' correlation (weighted biological parent–adoptees correlation) is about .10; the ''environmental'' correlation (adoptive parents–adoptees) is about .10; and the ''heredity plus environment'' correlation (control parents–control infants) is about .20. At 12 months, however,

TABLE 6.4

Parent–Offspring Correlations for Parents' IQ and Infants' Bayley MDI and Uzgiris–Hunt OSPD

	Biological		Adoptive		Control	
	Mother	Father	Mother	Father	Mother	Father
Bayley MDI						
12-month-old	.12	.29*	.12	.00	.04	.09
24-month-old	.06	.38*	.10	.08	.22*	.21*
Uzgiris–Hunt OSPD						
12-month-old	.16*	.23	−.04	.01	.00	.09
N for MDI =	176	41	177	169	157	157
N for OSPD =	144	36	143	138	122	123

$^*p < .05$.

the results are less straightforward. The weighted biological parent–adoptee correlation is .17, suggesting genetic influence; the adoptive parent–adoptee average correlation is .06, suggesting slight family environmental influences; but, the average control parent–offspring correlation is only .07. Nonetheless, the hypothesis of genetic influence at 12 months is supported by maximum-likelihood, model-fitting analyses described later, which have considerably more power to detect relationships as weak as these. At 24 months, the pattern of correlations clearly is consistent with the hypothesis of some hereditary influence and some effect of family environment on infant mental development. Taken at face value, these results suggest that about 20% of the variance of MDI scores in infancy is due to genetic variance (about 15% after adjusting for assortative mating), and that about 10% is due to familial environmental factors shared by parents and their infant offspring. The majority of the variance is unexplained.

We have indicated in Chapter 3 that the CAP parent–offspring design is best viewed in terms of a genetic correlation between infancy and adulthood for two different characters. We showed how significant correlations between biological parents and their adopted-away offspring can be used to estimate the genetic correlation between infancy and adulthood if heritabilities in infancy and in adulthood are known. In the case of mental development, we can assume a heritability of about .15 for Bayley MDI scores and a heritability of .50 for adult IQ scores. Given a correlation of .10 between biological parents and their adopted-away offspring, the genetic correlation between infant Bayley MDI scores and adult IQ scores is about .75. This means that the genes that affect Bayley MDI scores in infancy, although weak in their overall effect in infancy, continue to affect IQ scores in adulthood.

g Clusters of Bayley Items

As mentioned earlier, the total MDI score might not maximally predict *g*; certain Bayley items might predict later IQ or parental IQ better than the MDI. Although no one has reported items that best predict parental IQ, several attempts have been made to isolate infant mental test items that are better predictors of later IQ than is the MDI total score (Anderson, 1939; Cameron, Livson, & Bayley, 1967; Fillmore, 1936; Moore, 1967; Nelson & Richards, 1939; Siegel, 1979; Wilson, 1977a).

In an analysis of the Fels data, Nelson and Richards (1939) selected Gesell items for 80 one-year-olds that best predicted 36-month Stanford–Binet scores. The three items that were the best predictors involved communication: says three words (r = .42), scribbles imitation (r = .37), and says "bye-bye" or "hello" (r = .32). Together, these three items yielded a multiple correlation of .48 with 36-month IQ; in contrast, the total Gesell at 12 months correlated only .33 with IQ at 36 months. Nelson and Richards also make the important point that, at several ages in infancy, the items most predictive of later IQ are not the items that correlate most highly with total scores on the infant mental tests. For example, the three 12-month items listed above ranked 14, 11, and 16 out of 29 items ordered in terms of their correlation with total 12-month Gesell scores. These results suggest that 12-month items that correlate best with 12-month total scores are not the most effective for predicting later IQ.

For 91 children tested from infancy to 5 years of age, Anderson (1939) selected children one standard deviation or more above or below the mean for 5-year-old IQ and selected items from the 12- and 24-month infant tests that showed the greatest difference in percentage passing between the low and high IQ groups. Only 5 out of 97 items from various tests were selected for 12-month-olds; 46 out of 183 items were selected for 24-month-olds. For the 12-month-olds, the selected items were: imitates sounds, reacts to question "where is mother," places cubes into cup, uses spoon, and asks for things by pointing. For 24-month-olds, language items were also predominant among the 46 selected items, although motoric items and form-board items also were selected. Anderson (1939) concludes that "the most signifi-cant early indicator of future intelligence appears to be the acquisition of language habits, both in terms of use and understanding language symbols" (p. 207).

Wilson (1977a) used a similar technique. He established the upper and lower quartiles on the 3-year Stanford–Binet as a criterion to select Bayley items. Of 38 items administered, none was found to discriminate the two groups at 12 months. At 24 months, Wilson found that nearly all items differentiated the two groups.

However, a longitudinal analysis by Bayley (1949, 1955) that employed an approach similar to that of Anderson and Wilson led to inconclusive results. Items on the Bayley test were selected that had been passed earlier by the six Berkeley Growth Study subjects who, at 14 to 16 years of age, had the highest and lowest IQs at 14 to 16 years. The 31 test items thus selected were heterogeneous in content and yielded no obvious interpretation (Bayley, 1949); furthermore, when the items were combined into a single scale, the scale was no more predictive of later IQ than were the other items (Bayley, 1955).

Siegel (1979) concluded that by 12 months of age language items become predic-tive of 36-month IQ. In a study of 148 infants, Siegel used the Kohen-Raz (1967) scoring of the Bayley items to predict later IQ. The Kohen-Raz system classifies items into five subscales: eye–hand coordination, manipulation, conceptual relations, imitation–comprehension, and vocalization–social. At 12 months, all five scales predicted 36-month IQ ($r = .22–.45$); at 24 months, the imitation–comprehension and vocalization–social scales predicted 36-month IQ better than did the other three scales ($r = .63$ and $.55$). However, these analyses involve a priori scales of items rather than true item analyses as in the other studies of this genre.

Other studies also support the hypothesis that infant verbal behavior might be predictive of later IQ. Moore (1967) reported a correlation of .50 between a speech scale at 18 months and IQ at 8 years for girls, although the correlation was only .20 for boys. Cameron, Livson, and Bayley (1967), in an analysis of data from the Berkeley Growth Study, found that age of passing items during the first 12 months yielded a vocalization cluster (e.g., vocalizes eagerness, displeasure, interjections; says "da-da," two words) that correlated from .40 to .60 with adult IQ for girls, but the correlations for boys were nonsignificant. The small sample size (about 20 boys and 20 girls) and the absence of significant relationships for boys suggests caution in the interpretation of these results.

Thus, item analyses and other research converge on the conclusion that the best predictor of later IQ after the first year of life might be measures of language–communication. We continue to obtain cognitive ability data on the CAP children at 3 and 4 years of age and thus will be able to perform similar analyses of Bayley items as they predict later cognitive ability for a large and representative sample. However, a conceptually similar analysis, and one that potentially yields even more intriguing information, involves the selection of infant items that best predict parental IQ within the adoption design.

CAP Genetic Clusters of Bayley Items

Parent–offspring analyses of the total MDI score indicate some genetic continuity for IQ from infancy to adulthood. Using the CAP design, we can ask whether some Bayley items are better than the MDI total for predicting parental IQ. For control families, both genetic and environmental influences are shared by parents and infants; the CAP design permits separation of these genetic and environmental influences by means of comparisons between biological parents and their adopted-away offspring and between adoptive parents and their adopted offspring.

Selection of items in such an analysis is not an easy choice. Simply selecting items that correlate most highly with IQ as in the study by Nelson and Richards (1939) presents two problems: It capitalizes on chance, and correlations greater than .50 are not expected on genetic grounds. Discriminating extremes of the IQ distribution as in the studies by Anderson and by Wilson does not avoid these problems and adds the problem that only a small amount of the information available in the continuous distribution of IQ is used.

We used a modification of Nelson and Richards' procedure, adding replication to minimize the problem of capitalizing on chance. Bayley items that showed the

TABLE 6.5

Correlations between Adoptees' Bayley Items and Biological Mothers' IQ[a]

	Biological mother (N = 174)	Control parents		
Bayley item or scale		Midparent (N = 155)	Mother (N = 155)	Father (N = 156)
12 months				
Tower of Cubes scale	.10*	.21**	.17**	.16**
Pinkboard scale	.11*	.18**	.10	.17**
Closes round box (item 115)	.13**	.16**	.11*	.14**
24 months				
Blueboard scale	.15**	.21**	.22**	.12*
Pinkboard scale	.15**	.21**	.22**	.08
Prepositions scale	.12*	.18**	.19**	.12*
Tower of Cubes scale	−.03	.20**	.17**	.14**
Names Objects scale	−.05	.15**	.08	.15**
Names Pictures scale	−.10	.21**	.14**	.18**
Points to Pictures scale	−.02	.18**	.19**	.12*
Folds paper (item 157)	.07	.14**	.21**	.01*

[a]Biological mother–infant correlations for Bayley items–scales that yield significant correlations between control midparent IQ and control infants.

*$p < .10$; **$p < .05$.

highest correlations with control parents' average IQ score were selected, and then replication was sought for biological parents and for adoptive parents. We have 80% power to detect control parent–offspring correlations of .20 or greater (Cohen, 1977); correlations of .10 can be detected with 33% power. In control families, parent–offspring correlations are functions of both genetic and family environmental sources of similarity. If the control parent–offspring correlations are due to genetic resemblance, they should replicate for biological parents; if family environment underlies the resemblance in control families, the correlations should be replicated for adoptive parents.

Because of the dependencies among the items of the Bayley as discussed earlier, our analyses were conducted on the 16 items and 6 scales at 12 months and the 4 items and 12 scales at 24 months that avoid item interdependencies. Table 6.5 lists the Bayley items and scales at 12 and 24 months that correlate significantly with control midparent IQ scores. The correlations shown in the table for biological mothers for the same items enable us to determine whether replication of the control correlations suggests genetic continuity from infancy to adulthood.

Only one significant correlation was expected by chance at either age, yet three significant correlations with control midparent IQ scores emerged at 12 months and eight at 24 months. All three of the significant correlations at 12 months in the control families were replicated in analyses of the biological mothers and their adopted-away infants ($p < .10$), suggesting genetic mediation between these Bayley scores and adult IQ. The three Bayley scores are the Tower of Cubes scale; the Pinkboard scale; and item 115, which involves closing the lid on a round container.

At 24 months, three of the eight significant correlations in the control families were replicated in comparisons between biological mothers and their adopted-away infants: the Blueboard scale, the Pinkboard scale, and the Prepositions scale.

These results suggest that insofar as infant items predict adult IQ, the prediction involves genetic influence. Substantively, the genetically influenced precursors of adult IQ appear to involve spatial processes, such as those measured by the Bayley formboard items, rather than other processes such as language.

CAP Environmental Clusters of Bayley Items

A formally similar analysis can be conducted for adoptive families to identify environmental clusters of Bayley items; that is, to determine the extent to which control parent–offspring resemblance is mediated by family environmental influences. However, because adoptive and control parents contribute to the immediate environment of their infants, items so selected would not necessarily represent environmental continuity of g in the same way that correlations between biological parents' IQ and adopted-away infants' Bayley scores denote genetic continuity. The analysis in adoptive families isolates Bayley items that are maximally sensitive to environmental influences or, alternatively, suggests environmental influences that are maximally expressed by Bayley items.

The same procedure was followed: Bayley items and scales that correlated significantly with control midparent IQ were submitted for replication in the adoptive families. Table 6.6 lists the Bayley items and scales again, but this time, it includes

TABLE 6.6

Correlations between Adoptees' Bayley Items and Adoptive Parents' IQ[a]

Bayley item or scale	Adoptive mother (N = 177)	Adoptive father (N = 177)
12 months		
Tower of Cubes scale	.08	−.19**
Pinkboard scale	−.01	−.05
Closes round box (item 115)	−.05	.05
24 months		
Blueboard scale	.01	.08
Pinkboard scale	.04	.08
Prepositions scale	.16**	.05
Tower of Cubes scale	−.12*	−.08
Names Objects scale	.05	.00
Names Pictures scale	.11*	.03
Points to Pictures scale	.16**	−.08
Folds paper (item 157)	−.05	−.03

[a]Adoptive parent–infant correlations for Bayley items–scales that yield significant correlations between control midparent IQ and control infants.
*$p < .10$; **$p < .05$.

the parent–offspring correlations for adoptive relationships rather than biological relationships. The fact that the only significant adoptive parent–adoptee correlation at 12 months is negative suggests that family environment does not mediate the three significant parent–offspring correlations found in control families. However, at 24 months, three language-related Bayley scores yield significant adoptive parent–adopted child correlations (Prepositions scale, Names Pictures scale, and Points to Pictures scale), suggesting the importance of shared family environmental influences for these lexical measures.

Specific Environmental Correlates of Infant Mental Development

Literature Review

The CAP design is particularly useful for identifying specific environmental factors unconfounded by hereditary influences that may affect the results of studies of nonadoptive families. This search is not limited to the 10% of the MDI variance identified from the adoptive parent–adopted infant correlations as being due to common family environment. That component of variance refers to environmental influences shared by parents and offspring that make them similar in IQ; it is the portion of the control parent–control infant IQ correlation that is mediated environmentally. Environmental influences relevant to mental development are likely to include many factors that do not lead to phenotypic resemblance between parents and their offspring. In other words, environmental factors uncorrelated with parental IQ may well affect infant mental development.

As discussed in the preceding chapter, a major shift has occurred in thinking about the importance of early environment. Based primarily on results of deprivation studies, both psychoanalytic and learning theories emphasized the importance of early experience, even though the empirical foundations for this assumption were weak. In the 1960s and 1970s, the foundation began to show cracks that finally led to a denial of any special role for early environment (Clarke & Clarke, 1976). That challenge spurred environmentalists to begin a more systematic study of early environmental influences in the normal range of variation (Wachs & Gruen, 1982). This research has found environmental factors that account for significant amounts of variance in infant mental development, although the strength of these relationships has not as yet been given much attention.

Wachs and Gruen (1982) present a list of "validated environmental components related to the development of general psychometric intelligence" (p. 214) at 12 and 24 months of age (see Table 6.7). The list includes physical as well as social aspects of the infants' environment and emphasizes proximal factors that can be observed. It can be seen that this list agrees with common sense, although one might wonder about the direction of effects in such relationships, To what extent does the social environment reflect rather than effect differences among infants? Also, to what

TABLE 6.7

List of "Validated Environmental Components
Related to the Development of General
Psychometric Intelligence"[a]

Social environment
   Quantity of primary caretaker–infant interaction
   Responsivity to infant's social signals
   Verbal stimulation
   Encouragement of exploration
   Promotion of specific skills
   Avoidance of restriction–coercion
Physical environment
   Variety of objects
   Variety of activities
   Responsiveness of objects
   Floor freedom
   Lack of crowding
   Temporal–spatial regularity
   Avoidance of noise–confusion

---

[a]At 12 to 24 months of age. From Wachs and
Gruen (1982).

extent are such apparently environmental relationships mediated genetically? For example, measures of the infants' physical environment might be related to parental characteristics such as IQ that are linked genetically to the infants' mental development. The CAP, which includes measures similar to those listed in Table 6.7, is ideally suited for answering such questions.

The most widely used measure of family environmental factors is the HOME, which is described in Chapter 5. Elardo and Bradley (1981a) have reviewed 32 studies relating HOME scores and mental development (see also Elardo & Bradley, 1981b; Zimmerman, 1981a, 1981b). Gottfried (1984) summarized data from five studies in which the HOME was administered at 1 year of age and the Bayley test at 1 year and from four studies in which the Bayley test also was given at 2 years of age. Table 6.8 lists Gottfried's mean correlations across the studies and the correlations for the Gottfried and Gottfried (1984) study in which the middle-class sample is similar to the CAP sample. At 1 year, the HOME is not related to MDI scores; however, the 1-year HOME significantly predicts 2-year MDI. At both 1 and 2 years, the middle-class sample of Gottfried and Gottfried yields lower correlations than other studies that involve lower-class samples. Other measures of the environment do not do much better than the HOME in predicting MDI scores. For example, Gottfried and Gottfried found that scores on the Purdue Home Stimulation Inventory, which focuses on physical rather than social aspects of the environment, correlates .05 with the MDI at 12 months and .18 at 24 months. Gottfried and Gottfried also report correlations between the MDI and Moos' FES, which is described in Chapter 5. The correlations are nonsignificant at 12 months, although 3 of the 10 scales reach significance at 24 months.

TABLE 6.8

Correlations between 1-Year HOME Scores and Bayley MDI Scores at 1 and 2 Years
in Control Families

	1-year Bayley MDI scores		2-year Bayley MDI scores	
HOME measure	Gottfried review of five studies ($N = 626$)	Gottfried & Gottfried (1984) ($N = 129$)	Gottfried review of four studies ($N = 455$)	Gottfried & Gottfried (1984) ($N = 128$)
Maternal Responsivity	.12	−.04	.17	.09
Restriction–Punishment	.02	−.06	.16	.08
Organization	.10	−.07	.17	.00
Play Materials	.18	−.13	.23	.02
Maternal Involvement	.14	−.05	.25	.10
Variety	.10	.12	.24	.31
HOME Total	.17	−.07	.32	.20

These environmental correlates of infant mental development are modest; more-over, the results are based on studies of families in which both heredity and environ-ment are shared by parents and their offspring. As long as heredity and environment are confounded, putative environmental relationships might well be mediated genet-ically. In two earlier adoption studies (Burks, 1928; Leahy, 1935), measures of the home environment correlated substantially higher with children's IQ scores in con-trol families than in adoptive families, suggesting that some of the relationship between home environment and children's IQ is mediated genetically. Two other studies of environmental influences in adoptive families did not include control families and obtained conflicting results. Beckwith (1971), in a study of 24 adopted infants, found few significant environmental correlates of infant mental develop-ment. In contrast, Yarrow's (1963) study of 40 adopted 6-month-olds found strik-ingly high correlations between various maternal measures, such as those shown in Table 6.7, and infant Cattell IQ scores. The median correlation between maternal care variables and infant test scores was .55; a correlation of .72 was reported between "achievement stimulation" and test scores of the infants. These correla-tions are considerably higher than those reported in numerous studies conducted subsequently (Wachs & Gruen, 1982). Unfortunately, the procedure was not re-ported in detail by Yarrow (1963) nor in a 10-year follow-up report (Yarrow et al., 1973). For example, no indication is given as to whether the environmental ratings were based on interviews or observations; if they were based on observations, the amount of time and type of situations in which the observations were made are not specified.

CAP Results

The CAP is the first investigation of environmental correlates of infant mental development for adoptive and matched control families using standardized mea-

TABLE 6.9

CAP Environmental Correlations with Bayley MDI Scores[a]

	12-month MDI		24-month MDI	
Environmental measure	Adopted infants	Control infants	Adopted infants	Control infants
HOME				
General factor	.11	.09	.29*	.44*
Toys	.12*	.19*	.22*	.16*
Maternal Involvement	.11	.01	.23*	.25*
Developmental Advance	.09	−.01	.22*	.44*
Restriction–Punishment	−.06	−.09	−.01	.02
FES second-order factors[b]				
Personal Growth	.12	−.12	—	—
Traditional Organization	−.16*	−.09	—	—
Gottfried scales				
Variety of Experience	.04	−.11	.05	.08
Provision for Exploration	.12	.15*	.17*	.12
Physical Home Setting	.01	.07	.10	.11

[a]N = 139–180 for adoptive families; 130–163 for control families.

[b]The FES was administered only when the infants were 12 months of age.

*$p < .05$.

sures of the home environment. The need for information concerning possible genetic confounding of relationships between environmental measures and infant mental development led us to focus on environmental assessments in the CAP. The three types of CAP environmental measures have been described in Chapter 5: Caldwell and Bradley's (1978) Home Observation for Measurement of the Environment (HOME), a 45-item observation–interview measure for which we also developed a quantitatively scored version with scales based on the results of factor analysis; the Family Environment Scale (FES; Moos, 1974), a 90-item measure of family relationships and attitudes, for which we created two second-order factors; and scales based on three categories of physical and social environmental influences suggested by Gottfried and Gottfried (1984).

The correlations between these environmental measures and Bayley MDI scores of adopted and control infants at 12 and 24 months are presented in Table 6.9. Beginning with the most widely used measure, the HOME, Table 6.9 indicates that few significant correlations emerge at 12 months of age, a result similar to those of other studies. The only significant correlations occurred for the first rotated factor that we call, Toys.

At 24 months, the HOME becomes more predictive of the MDI. All correlations are significant except for the Restriction–Punishment factor. Most noteworthy are the significant correlations for the adopted children that allow us to conclude for the first time that the widely reported relationship between the HOME and infant mental development is indeed environmental in origin to some extent. However, heredity is also important. For 2-year-olds, the correlation for the HOME General Factor is significantly greater for control infants than for adopted infants. This suggests that the relationship between HOME and MDI scores for 2-year-olds is partially mediated by hereditary factors. However, the fact that the correlation is significant for the adopted infants suggests that some of the relationship between the HOME and the MDI is mediated via family environment as well as by heredity. A similar pattern of results, significantly higher correlation for the controls as compared to the adoptees, occurred for the Developmental Advance factor.

Correlations with the MDI are mostly nonsignificant for the FES and Gottfried measures. The Gottfried categories, which include physical as well as social aspects of the home environment, yield significant correlations only for the Provision for Exploration scale, which is highly correlated with the HOME Toy factor.

In summary, the CAP results lead to three conclusions: (1) Environmental relationships for the HOME are stronger at 24 months than at 12 months; (2) Environmental influences can be found that are related to infant mental development independent of heredity, as shown by the correlations in adoptive families; and (3) Genetic factors are involved in correlations between the HOME and infant mental development.

Multiple regression analyses provide support for these conclusions. Although none of the various environmental measures explains much variance in infant mental development, a reasonable question to be asked is the extent to which the environmental measures taken together can predict infant development. We regressed Bayley MDI scores on the HOME General Factor, on FES Personal Growth and Traditional Organization, and on the three Gottfried scales in the adoptive and control homes. At 12 months, the multiple correlation in the adoptive families was .27, the adjusted R^2 was .00, and the regression was nonsignificant. In the control families, the multiple correlation was statistically significant ($R = .36$), and the adjusted R^2 was .06. At 24 months, the multiple correlations were substantially greater in both the adoptive homes ($R = .39$) and control homes ($R = .65$). Both of these multiple correlations are statistically significant, and the adjusted R^2 values are .16 and .25, respectively.

We now discuss several subsidiary analyses of environmental influence. The first explores whether parental IQ might mediate the relationship between the HOME and infant mental development.

Parental IQ as a Mediating Factor

In control families, the hereditary underpinnings of relationships between environmental measures and children's mental development might involve parental IQ, as suggested by Longstreth *et al.* (1981). As indicated in Table 6.10, the HOME is not highly correlated with parental IQ in the CAP. It is interesting that in both the adoptive and control homes, the HOME General Factor and the Gottfried Variety of Experience scale tend to be positively correlated with parental IQ, whereas the HOME Restriction–Punishment factor and the FES Traditional Organi-

TABLE 6.10

Correlations between Environmental Measures and Parental IQ

	Parental IQ			
	Adoptive		Control	
Environmental measure from 12-month home visit	Mother ($N = 142–175$)	Father ($N = 140–167$)	Mother ($N = 131–156$)	Father ($N = 132–157$)
HOME				
General Factor	.08	.19*	.14*	.09
Toys	.23*	.14*	.12	.04
Maternal Involvement	−.07	.07	−.04	.08
Developmental Advance	.04	.18*	.05	.05
Restriction–Punishment	−.23*	.05	−.10	−.18*
FES second-order factors				
Personal Growth	.12	.14*	.13	.16*
Traditional Organization	−.26*	−.11	−.09	−.18
Gottfried scales				
Variety of Experience	.14*	.24*	.23*	−.01
Provision for Exploration	.09	.08	.13	.11
Physical Home Setting	−.07	.01	−.03	.01

*$p < .05$.

zation factor tend to correlate negatively. However, when parental IQ was partialed out of the relationship between the HOME and MDI scores, the correlations reported in Table 6.9 changed very little, less than .05, for both the adoptive and control families. Thus, contrary to the results for older children of varied ages as reported by Longstreth *et al.*, we do not find that the relationship between the HOME and MDI scores is mediated importantly by parental IQ. This interpretation is buttressed by our model-fitting path analyses, which are discussed later, as well as by results reported by Gottfried and Gottfried (1984).

The results described in the previous section indicate that genetic influence is in part responsible for the relationship between environmental measures and infant mental development. The results in this section suggest that parental IQ is not the factor that mediates this genetic relationship. Thus, one question for future research is: What are the processes by which heredity comes to influence the relationship between home environment and infant mental development? This issue is discussed in more detail in Chapter 15.

Curvilinear Relationships between Home Environment and Infant Mental Development

Wachs, Uzgiris, and Hunt (1971), following Hunt's (1961) concept of the importance of the match between environments and infants' abilities, suggested that the relationship between environmental measures and cognitive development might be curvilinear rather than linear. For example, what might be important beyond the linear relationship between HOME and infant Bayley MDI scores is the match between HOME stimulation and infants' inherent abilities—bright children might profit disproportionately from substantial stimulation; less bright children might be affected adversely by such stimulation.

We examined this hypothesis using HMR procedures (Cohen & Cohen, 1975), described in the previous chapter, in which the linear relationship between an environmental measure and Bayley scores is removed in the first step. In the second step, the environmental measure squared is tested for significance as an index of a quadratic relationship. We conducted these analyses, separately for adoptive and control families, at 12 and 24 months for the HOME General Factor and four rotated factors and for the three Gottfried scales; the second-order FES factors were examined at 12 months only. Of these 36 HMRs, only two significant curvilinear relationships emerged; on average, the curvilinear terms yielded an R^2 change of only .007. Thus, we conclude that the relationships between environmental measures and infant mental development are almost wholly linear in nature.

Family Environment beyond SES and Parental Education

Construction of measures of environmental influence relevant to mental development has been guided by two goals: (1) to develop a measure that predicts infant mental development better than does socioeconomic status (SES), and (2) to understand the mechanisms underlying the correlation between SES and mental development in families. The first issue is important from a practical viewpoint: If hour-long visits to the home do not yield information more predictive of mental development than does a 30-sec phone call asking about occupation and education, there would be little justification for the new wave of home environment measures. The second goal, however, would still be important.

The HOME manual (Caldwell & Bradley, 1978) states:

> The HOME Inventory was generally a better predictor of mental test performance than a combination of socioeconomic status variables (maternal education, paternal education, occupation of head of household, and amount of crowding). (p. 50)

> The multiple correlation between HOME subscale scores and IQ was generally as high as the multiple correlation between HOME plus SES variables and IQ. However, there was usually a loss in predictive power when the combination of SES variables was used apart from the HOME. (p. 56)

In a review of six studies, Gottfried (1984) concludes:

> The results invariably showed that home environmental variables related to mental development independent of SES. While reductions in the frequency of significant correlations were found when SES was partialed out . . . . the large majority of the correlations remained significant. (p. 8)

Gottfried also notes that SES measures are correlated with mental development after the effects of home environmental measures are removed.

TABLE 6.11

Stepwise Multiple Regressions of Infant Mental Development on SES, Parental Education, and HOME General Factor

	Adoptive homes		Control homes	
	R	adj. R^2	R	adj. R^2
Predicting 12-month MDI				
SES and parental education (step one)	.19	—	.22	—
HOME General Factor (step two)	.22	.02	.24	.02
Predicting 24-month MDI				
SES and parental education	.16	—	.28*	—
HOME General Factor	.35*	.09	.49*	.21

*Significance ($p < .05$) of term added to the multiple regression.

A report from the LTS (Wilson & Matheny, 1983b) generally confirms this conclusion and begins to pinpoint the relative additional variance explained by the HOME over SES and parental education. The HOME was administered to over 200 families with children of various ages who had participated in the longitudinal twin study. The HOME total score correlated .39 with Bayley scores at 24 months of age; fathers' education, mothers' education, and SES correlated .40, .36, and .42, respectively, with the 24-month Bayley scores. Although multiple regression analyses testing the increment in predictive power of the HOME over SES and education were not reported, the authors indicate that 20% of the variance of 24-month Bayley scores is accounted for by parental education and SES; the variance accounted for by these measures plus the HOME scales is 30%. Thus, the HOME scales increase the predictive power by about half.

The CAP data are unique in that they permit exploration of the etiology of these relationships. Regressions in adoptive families indicate environmental relationships unbiased by heredity, and comparisons of regressions in adoptive and control families suggest the extent of hereditary involvement in these relationships. We conducted stepwise multiple regressions for Bayley MDI scores at 12 and 24 months, removing SES and parental education in the first step and then testing the significance of the relationship between the HOME General Factor and the MDI independent of SES and parental education. The results of these analyses are summarized in Table 6.11.

At 24 months in the control families, the CAP results replicate those of the LTS. SES and parental education and the HOME General Factor each make a significant contribution to the prediction of infant mental development. Together, they account for 21% of the variance. However, as in Table 6.9, these data suggest genetic mediation of the environmental relationships because SES, parental education, and the HOME account for only 9% of the variance in adoptive homes. At 12 months, none of the environmental measures accounts for a significant amount of variance.

TABLE 6.12

Correlations between Perinatal Factors and Infant Mental Development

	Adopted infants		Control infants	
	r	N	r	N
12-month Bayley MDI correlated with:				
Birth weight	.10	172	.13	131
Gestational age	.03	166	.32*	129
24-month Bayley MDI correlated with:				
Birth weight	.05	172	.04	129
Gestational age	.08	166	.05	111

*$p < .05$.

Birth Weight and Gestational Age

A different set of environmental influences involves perinatal factors such as birth weight and gestational age. These factors are different from others in our analyses in that they do not permit differentiation of genetic and environmental influences upon infant development. Correlations between perinatal measures and Bayley MDI scores are listed in Table 6.12. In general, the correlations tend to be low and nonsignificant, although the correlation between gestational age and 12-month Bayley MDI for control infants is .32.

Longitudinal Analyses of Specific Environmental Factors

The environmental analyses described previously in this chapter were cross-sectional. The longitudinal nature of the CAP permits us to explore the effect of early environmental influences in adoptive homes on later behavioral outcomes without the usual genetic confounds that occur when parents and their children share heredity as well as family environment. By comparing these data from adoptive families to data from control families, we can also identify any genetic involvement in such longitudinal environmental relationships.

In Table 6.9, we presented contemporaneous correlations between specific environmental measures and infant mental development. Table 6.13 extends these analyses longitudinally. Although the 12-month environmental measures are generally unrelated to 12-month MDI scores, they predict 24-month MDI scores almost as well as do the 24-month environmental measures. This is especially noteworthy given the moderate stability of the environmental measures from 12 to 24 months, which is also indicated in Table 6.13. The significant longitudinal correlations in the adoptive homes suggest that the ability of early environmental measures to predict later MDI scores is mediated environmentally. The fact that the correlations in the control homes are of a similar magnitude suggests that heredity is not involved in these longitudinal relationships, even though the contemporaneous correlations show genetic influence. As observed at 24 months, the HOME Develop-

TABLE 6.13

CAP Longitudinal Correlations for Environmental Measures and between Environmental Measures and Infant Bayley MDI Scores

| | | Correlation between environmental measure at 12 months and MDI at 24 months | |
| | Correlation from 12 to 24 months | Adoptive families | Control families |
Environmental measure	($N = 224–342$)	($N = 139–180$)	($N = 130–163$)
HOME			
General Factor	.58	.25*	.25*
Toys	.63	.18*	.10
Maternal Involvement	.40	.24*	.01
Developmental Advance	.55	.19*	.30*
Restriction–Punishment	.28	−.02	.02
FES second-order factors[a]			
Personal Growth	—	.21*	.08
Traditional Organization	—	.03	−.15*
Gottfried scales			
Variety of Experience	.38	.09	.09
Provision for Exploration	.42	.22*	.13
Physical Home Setting	.18	−.01	.03

[a]The FES was administered only when the infants were 12 months of age.

mental Advance factor correlated more highly with MDI scores in the control homes than in the adoptive homes; however, the difference in these longitudinal correlations (.19 vs. .30) is not significant.

Early Environment

Another issue concerning the longitudinal relationship between home environment and infant mental development is the extent to which early environment per se is important as compared to the possibility that the effect of early environment is mediated by stability of the environment. In his review of the literature, Gottfried (1984) concludes, "Most of the findings support the view that early home environment is related to later intellectual development because of the stability of home environment" (p. 11). Although we could address this and other longitudinal questions using longitudinal path models, the issue of the independent effect of early environment can be studied in a simpler manner through the use of partial correlations. For example, to what extent is the relationship between 12-month HOME scores and 24-month Bayley MDI (Table 6.13) due to the relationship between 12-month and 24-month HOME scores? The answer may be found by partialing out the 24-month HOME scores from the zero-order correlation of .25 between 12-month HOME and 24-month Bayley MDI. This zero-order correlation will be reduced if the relationship between the 12-month HOME scores and 24-month MDI is mediated by the 24-month HOME scores. In the adoptive families, the correlation between the 12-month HOME General Factor and 24-month Bayley MDI scores drops from .25 to .10 when the effect of 24-month HOME General Factor is removed; in the control families, the correlation changes from .25 to .01. Thus, our analyses offer support for Gottfried's hypothesis that the relationship between early environmental measures and later infant mental development is mediated by contemporaneous environmental influences.

Predicting Changes in Infant Mental Development

The literature contains examples of attempts to predict increasing and decreasing patterns of mental development. For example, McCall, Appelbaum, and Hogarty (1973) concluded that measures of the home environment can predict change in mental development. Similarly, Caldwell and Bradley (1978) divided their sample of infants and toddlers into those who, from 6 to 36 months, increased 20 IQ points or more, those who decreased 20 IQ points or more, and those who changed by less than 20 IQ points. They concluded on the basis of discriminant analyses that "the HOME appears to provide a rather sensitive index of change in relative mental test performance from the first year of life to age three" (p. 47). However, the results of such analyses of change scores are dubious because change scores can be highly correlated with IQ scores at either age, and we already know that the HOME is correlated with 36-month IQ. The issue is whether the HOME is related to IQ changes independently of its simple relationship to IQ.

A more appropriate analysis rephrases the question in interaction terms and uses HMR, asking whether the relationship between 12-month and 24-month Bayley MDI scores differs as a function of the HOME scores. The main effects of 12-month MDI scores and the HOME as they predict 24-month MDI scores are removed in the first step. The interaction between 12-month MDI and the HOME is tested in the second step. A significant interaction indicates a conditional relationship between 12- and 24-month MDI scores that would be expected if environmental measures show their greatest impact on children who were brightest at 12 months of age. Such an interaction would also be predicted from the conclusion reached by McCall et al. (1973) and by Caldwell and Bradley(1978): The relationship between 12- and 24-month MDI scores (i.e., increases or decreases) depends to some extent on the home environment. However, our HMR analysis using the HOME General Factor found no significant interaction: The interaction term yielded an R^2 change of only .003 for adoptees and .001 for controls.

Genotype–Environment Interaction

Interaction is similar to the weather in Samuel Clemens' remark that everyone talks about it but no one does anything about it. Behavioral-genetic analyses offer one clear and novel approach to studying genotype–environment interaction, which refers to the possibility that individuals of different genotypes respond differently to environmental factors. We utilize the adoption method proposed by Plomin, De-Fries, and Loehlin (1977) to isolate environmental influences that differentially affect individuals who differ genetically. Our approach uses HMR to remove main effects of genotype and environment and then to assess their interaction, the joint influence of genotype and environment, in predicting infant mental development.

We conducted 15 analyses of genotype–environment interaction using biological mothers' IQ as an estimate of genotype and several indices of environmental influence in the adoptive homes: adoptive mothers' and fathers' IQ, HOME General Factor, FES Personal Growth, and FES Traditional Organization. The dependent measures were 12-month MDI, 24-month MDI, and the average of 12- and 24-month MDI scores. None of the interactions was significant. Thus, systematic, nonlinear effects of various combinations of genetic and environmental influences on infant mental development are not apparent in the CAP. Although it is certainly possible that other measures might reveal significant genotype–environment interactions, it is noteworthy that this first attempt to assess the effects of genotype–environment interaction on infant mental development found no significant interaction.

Direction of Effects

Causality cannot be assumed on the basis of correlations between environmental measures and infant mental development even when we show in adoptive families that the relationship is not mediated genetically. It is possible that variations in the environmental measures reflect rather than effect differences in the infants' mental development, an issue that has been referred to as the *direction of effects* (Bell, 1968). For example, it is quite plausible to suppose that the relationship between the HOME Maternal Responsivity factor and infant MDI scores is due to greater responsivity of adults to brighter infants.

Developmentalists have attempted to use longitudinal data to resolve the direction-of-effects issue. For example, cross-lagged panel analysis (Kenny, 1979) has been used to evaluate the causal direction underlying longitudinal relationships between HOME scores and Bayley MDI scores in infancy (Bradley, Caldwell, & Elardo, 1979). In general, results have been inconclusive in that the two cross-correlations in each analysis were similar; for example, the correlation between 12-month HOME Maternal Responsivity and 24-month Bayley MDI scores was .21, and the correlation between 12-month Bayley MDI and 24-month HOME Maternal Responsivity was .31. Moreover, cross-lagged panel analysis has been subjected to severe criticism because of the assumptions it requires (Rogosa, 1980).

Behavioral genetics offers the concept of genotype–environment correlation as one clear type of "child effect" in the direction-of-effects issue. As described in Chapter 3, genotype–environment correlation includes the reaction of environmental agents to genetic predispositions, thus creating a correlation between environmental measures and genotype. For example, using the example above, HOME

Maternal Responsivity scores might be correlated with infants' inherent brightness because parents are more responsive to brighter infants. How can we measure infants' genetic predispositions or inherent brightness? A method has been proposed to assess such reactive genotype–environment correlations simply by studying the correlation between any measurable aspect of the environment of adoptees and some measure on their biological parents (Plomin, DeFries, & Loehlin, 1977). For example, if HOME scores for adoptive families reflect genetic differences relevant to MDI scores of adopted infants, HOME scores should be correlated with IQ of the biological parents (which is a genotypic estimate of the adoptees' IQ). In the absence of selective placement, this test will detect genotype–environment correlation only when there is a heritable relationship between the phenotypes of the biological parent and the adopted child and when there is a relationship between the environmental measure and the adopted infant's phenotype. Although these appear to be quite restrictive limitations, they really define genotype–environment correlation: Genetic differences among children are correlated with differences among their environments.

We used the three CAP environmental measures (HOME, FES, and the Gottfried scales) to explore genotype–environment correlations relevant to infant mental development. For example, we examined the relationship between HOME scores in the adoptive families and IQ of the biological mothers. Although MDI scores of the infants are related to biological mothers' IQ (suggesting genetic influence) and also to HOME scores in the adoptive homes (suggesting family environmental influence), no evidence for significant genotype–environment correlation emerged. That is, correlations between IQ scores of the biological mothers and the HOME scores were not significant, as shown in Table 6.14. The only significant correlation involves FES Personal Growth. Although it is tempting to interpret this relationship in terms of adoptive parents' response to genetic predispositions of their adopted infants, it is more prudent to ascribe the result to chance because only 1 of 18 correlations was significant and because FES Personal Growth is not significantly related to infants' Bayley MDI scores (see Table 6.9).

Path Models and Maximum-Likelihood Estimates of Genetic and Environmental Parameters

The adoption design leads to straightforward interpretations of correlational data because control relationships include both heredity and family environment, adoptive relationships include family environment alone, and biological relationships include heredity alone. However, a more powerful estimation procedure utilizes path models and the simultaneous analysis of data on the adoptive, biological, and control parents and their children, as well as measures of specific environmental factors. Model-fitting approaches are particularly useful because, in addition to analyzing all of the data simultaneously, they make assumptions explicit and permit tests of the relative fit of different models. With the help of David W. Fulker,

TABLE 6.14

Genotype–Environment Correlation: Correlation between Biological
Mothers' IQ Scores and Environmental Measures in Adoptive Homes

	Genotype–environment correlation	
Environmental measure	12 Months $(N = 141-174)$	24 Months $(N = 135-175)$
HOME		
General Factor	−.06	−.02
Toys	−.02	.05
Maternal Involvement	−.04	.03
Developmental Advance	−.06	−.08
Restriction–Punishment	.06	−.09
FES second-order factors[a]		
Personal Growth	.13*	—
Traditional Organization	.05	—
Gottfried scales		
Variety of Experience	.11	−.01
Provision for Exploration	−.10	.03
Physical Home Setting	.05	.07

[a]The FES was administered only when the infants were 12 months of age.
*$p < .05$.

formerly of the Institute of Psychiatry, University of London, and now at the
Institute for Behavioral Genetics, we have developed path models and have applied
maximum-likelihood estimation procedures to the CAP data.

Path models were first applied to the analysis of adoption data by Sewall Wright
(1931). Barbara Burks (1928) had conducted a primitive path analysis using only
manifest variables such as parental IQ, a measure of home environment, and children's IQ in her classic adoption study. Wright reanalyzed Burks' data, introducing
latent genetic and environmental variables useful for analysis of quantitative genetic
parameters. Subsequent applications of models that incorporate assortative mating
and selective placement parameters and employ procedures that explicitly evaluate
the fit between the model and the observed data have been described by Jencks
(1972); Rao, Morton, and Yee (1974); Eaves, Last, Young, and Martin (1978);
Cloninger, Rice, and Reich (1979); and Loehlin (1979).

The basic path model for analysis of the CAP data is described by Fulker and
DeFries (1983). In addition to providing tests of hereditary and environmental
influences, the model includes parameters for passive genotype–environment correlation, direct effects of parental phenotype on the child's environment, assortative
mating, and selective placement. The path model for control families is illustrated
in Figure 6.2. The model includes only two latent variables, additive genetic value
G and environmental deviation E, and these totally determine the phenotype P with
paths h and e, respectively. Although the model appears complex, the basic idea
retains the simple point that control parents contribute both heredity and environ-

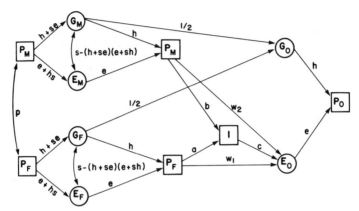

FIGURE 6.2   Path model including an environmental index (I) in control families. (From Figure 3 in D. W. Fulker & J. C. DeFries, "Genetic and environmental transmission in the Colorado Adoption Project: Path analysis," *British Journal of Mathematical and Statistical Psychology*, 1983, *36*, 175–188. Copyright 1983 by The British Psychological Society. Reprinted by permission.)

ment to their children. The novel features of the model are primarily on the environmental side, allowing parental phenotypes to have a direct effect w on children's environment as well as an effect a or b mediated by an environmental index I such as the HOME. The complexities on the left side of the path model arise from consideration of assortative mating and genotype–environment correlation, presenting these complex issues in the simplest possible terms using *reverse path analysis* (see Fulker & DeFries, 1983, for details). This presentation facilitates the derivation of the six expected correlations among the four manifest variables (P_M, P_F, I, and P_O) following the rules of path analysis (Li, 1975).

Figure 6.3 illustrates the path model for adoptees. The basic idea is that adoptees have one set of parents P_{BM} and P_{BF} who contribute genes and another set P_{AF} and P_{AM} who contribute environmental influences. Because assortative mating may differ in wed and unwed couples, different assortative mating parameters p and q are included in the model. The extent of selective placement x is also determined. The six manifest variables in Figure 6.3 potentially yield 15 correlations for which expectations may be derived. The expectations for both the control and adoptive correlations are presented in the article by Fulker and DeFries (1983).

Parameters are estimated by equating expectations for control and adoptive relationships to observed covariances employing a maximum-likelihood estimation procedure similar to that discussed by Jöreskog and Sörbom (1976) for the analysis of structural equation models. An additional feature of the maximum-likelihood analysis employed is that it permits the simultaneous analysis of covariance matrices of different size that occur when data are missing. For example, in the case of adoptive families, a full 6×6 matrix requires data from biological mothers and fathers, adoptive mothers and fathers, an environmental index, and adoptees' mental development scores; many more families provide data for a 5×5 matrix, missing only data for biological fathers.

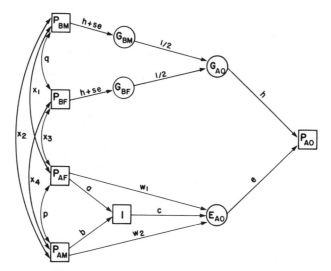

FIGURE 6.3   Path model including an environmental index (I) in adoptive families. (From Figure 4 in D. W. Fulker & J. C. DeFries, "Genetic and environmental transmission in the Colorado Adoption Project: Path analysis," *British Journal of Mathematical and Statistical Psychology*, 1983, *36*, 175–188. Copyright 1983 by The British Psychological Society. Reprinted by permission.)

Fulker and DeFries applied this model and procedure to CAP data for parental IQ, the Maternal Responsivity scale of the HOME as an environmental index, and MDI scores of the CAP children at 12 and 24 months for a slightly smaller data set than the present one. Estimates of the parameters of the model and their standard errors are presented in Table 6.15. The χ^2 values indicate an adequate fit of the model at both 12 and 24 months. The most prominent results are the highly significant genetic effect h and environmental effect c of HOME Maternal Responsivity. Assortative mating p and q is modest, and selective placement x is negligible, as is passive genotype–environment correlation s.

In brief, the model-fitting approach confirms the conclusions reached earlier: At 12 and 24 months, genetic and environmental influences are both significant. In fact, the confirmation extends even to the rough estimates of genetic and environmental components of variance discussed earlier. The maximum-likelihood estimate of genetic influence h^2 on children's MDI is approximately .15 at both 12 and 24 months; family environmental variance $w_1^2 + w_2^2 + c^2$ accounts for approximately 5% of children's MDI variance at 12 months and 8% at 24 months, with nearly all of the environmental variance mediated through the environmental index I.

An example of a longitudinal model-fitting approach to the analysis of the CAP data in 12- and 24-month-olds has been presented by Baker, DeFries, and Fulker (1983). A model similar to but simpler than the one depicted in Figures 6.2 and 6.3 was developed that does not include latent variables, but rather considers both the 12- and 24-month MDI scores simultaneously and leads to expectations for phenotypic correlations among the three types of mothers and fathers and their children.

TABLE 6.15

Maximum Likelihood Parameter Estimates ± SE from CAP Cognitive Data on Biological, Adoptive, and Control Parents and Their Children[a]

	12-month-olds	24-month-olds
h	0.38 ± 0.14	0.41 ± 0.13
s	0.03 ± 0.02	0.04 ± 0.03
w_1	-0.02	0.05
w_2	0.10 ± 0.07	0.03 ± 0.08
p	0.22 ± 0.06	0.21 ± 0.06
q	0.22 ± 0.29	0.24 ± 0.17
x_1	0.02 ± 0.08	0.01 ± 0.09
x_2	0.09 ± 0.09	0.09 ± 0.09
x_3	-0.09 ± 0.18	-0.14 ± 0.15
x_4	0.17 ± 0.20	0.54 ± 0.15
a	0.13 ± 0.06	0.25 ± 0.06
b	-0.02 ± 0.07	-0.04 ± 0.06
c	0.20 ± 0.07	0.28 ± 0.08
χ^2	$49.97, p > .40$	$55.75, p > .20$
df	50	50

[a]Adapted from Table 5 in D. W. Fulker & J. C. DeFries, "Genetic and environmental transmission in the Colorado Adoption Project: Path analysis," *British Journal of Mathematical and Statistical Psychology,* 1983, *36,* 175–188. Copyright 1983 by The British Psychological Society. Reprinted by permission.

The analysis using this model generally yielded results similar to those presented above; additionally, it indicated that stability between 12 and 24 months is largely independent of both genetic and environmental influences shared between parents and their infant offspring, an issue to which we return later.

Models of Developmental Behavioral Genetics

As discussed in Chapter 2, genes can be a source of change as well as continuity in development. Beginning with Francis Galton's twin study in 1875, the earliest human behavioral-genetic studies focused on developmental change, although this developmental flavor was lost in ensuing decades (Plomin, 1983a). One developmental question concerns cross-sectional changes in the relative mixture of genetic and environmental influences (Ho *et al.,* 1980); however, longitudinal analyses of genetic and environmental contributions to change and continuity in development are more informative (Plomin & DeFries, 1981). In this section we consider the implications of the CAP data for understanding continuity from 12 to 24 months and from infancy to adulthood.

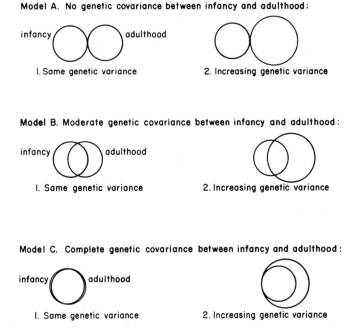

FIGURE 6.4   Models of developmental behavioral genetics. See text for explanation.

Genetic Continuity from Infancy to Adulthood

Figure 6.4 describes a few of the possible models relating genetic variance in infancy and adulthood to genetic covariance from infancy to adulthood. Because the CAP is a parent–offspring design, we chose to focus on the longitudinal relationship between infancy and adulthood, although it is interesting to consider these issues for all the intervening ages as well. Figure 6.4 considers two dimensions of the issue: genetic variance in infancy and in adulthood (same or increasing), and genetic covariance (zero, moderate, or complete). For example, Model A posits no age-to-age genetic covariance, so that genetic variance in infancy is unrelated to the genes that affect IQ in adulthood. In contrast, Model C assumes complete age-to-age genetic covariance; that is, once any genes come to affect mental development in infancy, they continue to affect IQ in adulthood.

We believe that Model C.2 best explains the behavioral-genetic data on infant mental development. First, it seems clear from both the CAP results reviewed in this chapter and from the results of the LTS (Wilson, 1983) that genetic influence, although significant, is slight in infancy, at least as compared to later in life. Thus, we conclude that heritability increases from infancy to adulthood. Second, the fact that both studies suggest only slight heritability in infancy leads to an interesting hypothesis: Even though genetic variance is relatively less important for infant mental development than it is for later IQ, the little genetic variance that does exist in infancy is largely related to the genetic variance that affects IQ later in life. The reasoning behind this radical conclusion is that the CAP parent–offspring correlations suggest the existence of genetic continuity from infancy to adulthood; the amount of genetic variance shared by adult parents and their infant offspring is nearly the same as the amount of genetic variance in infancy found in the LTS. The CAP maximum-likelihood, model-fitting results reviewed earlier suggest that genetic variance accounts for about 15% of the variance of Bayley scores at 12 and 24 months. The LTS results (see Figure 6.1) suggest that genetic variance accounts for about 10% of the variance of Bayley scores at 12 months and about 16% of the variance at 24 months.

This evidence favors Model C.2 in that any genetic variance that affects infant mental development continues to affect adult IQ. It suggests an amplification model of genetic variance in which genes relevant to IQ during infancy and childhood exert even greater effects during adulthood.

Additional support for this hypothesis comes from the Berkeley and Fels two-generational longitudinal studies. Parents of the infants had been tested since infancy. Although these parent–offspring correlations involve control families and are thus functions of both genetic and family environmental influences, the results are consistent with our hypothesis. If genetic variance affecting Bayley scores were specific to infancy (i.e., if the genetic correlation between infancy and adulthood was negligible), parent–offspring correlations should be greater when parents' scores as infants are used rather than the parents' adult scores. Instead, Eichorn (reported in McCall, 1979) found no difference in parent–offspring correlations in the Berkeley study when parents' infant scores or adult scores were used. In the Fels study, McCall et al. (1973) found an effect in the opposite direction: Parents' adult scores yielded greater parent–offspring correlations than did parents' scores as infants.

Because this finding is counterintuitive, at least from the perspective of current developmental theory, additional discussion might not be overly redundant. What we are saying is that the set of genes that creates differences among infants in their scores on the Bayley test also affects scores on adult IQ tests. We cannot say that this same set of genes continues to affect scores on IQ tests throughout childhood and adolescence, although it would seem reasonable to make this prediction given that the genes affect scores both in infancy and adulthood. However, we need to keep in mind that infant scores are measures of developmental rate, not final level; all human beings are eventually able to stick the yellow pegs in the pegboard of the Bayley test. It is possible that differences in developmental rates on the Bayley test at certain points in development provide a window through which we can view individual differences that are indicative of differences in adult IQ. The window provided by other ages might not present a similar view.

It is not quite correct to say that precisely the same genes that affect mental ability are expressed during both infancy and adulthood. It may be that the relevant genes have an irreversible effect in infancy that simply continues to affect test scores throughout life. For example, the genes might affect the way in which dendritic spines on neurons develop and such structural changes could continue to affect test scores throughout life. However, it is also possible that genes are actively involved in both infancy and adulthood. Perhaps a set of genes that affects uptake of a particular neurotransmitter in infancy continues to have the same effect in adulthood. The point is that, although we conclude that the genes that affect infant scores on the Bayley test are correlated with the genes that affect adult IQ scores, the mechanisms by which this occurs are unknown.

To a limited extent, we can examine the question of psychological mechanisms: Do the genes expressed during both infancy and adulthood have an effect upon the same psychological mechanism, such as memory or some other cognitive ability, or are different psychological mechanisms involved in the genetic correlation between infant Bayley scores and adult IQ scores. For example, the genes expressed during infancy might affect rate of acquisition of language, whereas those expressed during adulthood might affect symbolic reasoning, yet the two sets of genes are highly correlated; that is, positive deviations on the Bayley test created by genetic variance in infancy correlate highly with positive deviations on adult IQ tests. We examine this important issue in the next chapter.

Genetic Continuity from 12 to 24 Months

If Bayley MDI scores at 12 months and at 24 months are both genetically related to adult IQ, it would seem reasonable to expect that genetic variance affecting 12-month MDI scores is substantially correlated with the genetic variance that affects 24-month MDI scores. However, this does not necessarily have to be the case. Thinking about the component processes tapped by infant mental tests at 12 and 24 months makes it more plausible to think that the genes that affect both 12-month MDI scores and adult IQ are not highly related to the set of genes that affects 24-month MDI scores and adult IQ. At 12 months, the Bayley Mental Scale includes numerous sensorimotor items such as putting beads in a box, imitating scribbles, and some rudimentary expressive communication; all of these items probably involve a large motivational, social, and personality component that could be the basis for the relationship between 12-month MDI scores and adult IQ. At 24 months, the Bayley test includes much more symbolic activities—such as naming objects, understanding prepositions, and using two-word sentences—that might be the basis for a different relationship between 24-month MDI scores and adult IQ.

If MDI scores at 12 and 24 months are related to different components of genetic variance, we would predict that the sum of 12- and 24-month MDI scores would yield a higher parent–offspring correlation than the separate parent–offspring correlations for 12-month MDI and 24-month MDI. However, the average of the 12-month and 24-month MDI shows no greater parent–offspring correlation than we would expect on the basis of its increased reliability. Thus, we can conclude that the small but important components of genetic variance for 12-month and 24-month Bayley MDI scores are correlated with one another.

In an earlier paper (Plomin & DeFries, 1983), we addressed this question in a different way. We reasoned that if the genetic variance shared by infant offspring and their adult parents is also shared at 12 and 24 months, we would expect the longitudinal correlation for adopted infants between 12 and 24 months to be reduced when the biological mothers' IQ—an estimate of adult genotype—is removed from the longitudinal correlation. Height shows such an effect: The zero-order correlation for height from 12 to 24 months is .44 for the adopted probands; partialing out biological mothers' height reduced the longitudinal correlation to .36. This suggests that genetic variance that affects height both in infancy and in adulthood also mediates genetic continuity from 12 to 24 months to some extent. Removal of the effects of maternal height produced a similar reduction in the longitudinal correlation for height in the control families, which would be expected if genetic factors are involved in the stability of height from 12 to 24 months. Not surprisingly, partialing out adoptive parents' height had no effect on the adoptees' longitudinal correlation for height.

For the Bayley MDI, the longitudinal correlation between 12 and 24 months is .47 for adopted probands. When we partialed out the biological mothers' IQ from the longitudinal correlation, no effect was observed (the partial correlation was .46), and we concluded that the set of genes that affects both 12-month MDI scores and adult IQ are largely independent of the set of genes that affect both 24-month MDI scores and adult IQ. However, we now realize that this approach is too weak to be useful when heritability is low and when stability from infancy to adulthood also is low. For height, the heritability at 24 months is about .70, the heritability of adult height is about .90, and the correlation between height at 24 months and adult height is about .80 (Plomin & DeFries, 1981). The CAP height correlation between biological mothers and their adopted-away 2-year-old infants is .33. Despite these conditions, the longitudinal correlation for height from 12 to 24 months was reduced only from .44 to .36 when the effect of biological mothers' height was removed. Given a heritability of about .15 for infant mental development, a heritability of about .50 for adult IQ, and stability of not more than .30 from infancy to adulthood, the expected effect of partialing out biological mothers' IQ from the longitudinal 12- to 24-month Bayley MDI correlation is negligible.

Environmental Continuity from Infancy to Adulthood

Environmental continuities and discontinuities can be viewed in terms of similar models. However, we have no empirical basis upon which to hypothesize a development model for environmental influence from infancy to adulthood. Adoptive parent–adoptee correlations do not provide environmental information comparable to the genetic information obtained from biological parents and their adopted-away infants, because adoptive parents supply the immediate environment of their adopted children. However, as explained by Plomin and DeFries (1981), phenotypic stability is composed of genetically mediated continuity and environmentally mediated continuity. To the extent that we know the phenotypic stability and the genetic contribution to the stability, we can estimate environmentally mediated continuity. The highest phenotypic correlations for mental ability between infancy and adulthood that have been reported were mentioned earlier: .25 from the first year to adulthood and .55 from the second year to adulthood (Bayley, 1955). A review by McCall (1979) yielded a median correlation of .32 for three studies comparing test scores of 13- to 18-month-old infants to their IQ scores at 8 to 18 years of age.

If we use .30 as the upper-limit estimate of phenotypic stability from infancy to adulthood, there is substantial room for some environmental mediation of the stability. As explained by Plomin and DeFries (1981), genetic mediation of phenotypic stability is a multiplicative function of the square root of the heritability at the first age, the square root of the heritability at the second age, and the genetic correlation between the ages. We have said that heritability in infancy is low (about .15), heritability in adulthood is moderate (about .50), and the genetic correlation between infancy and adulthood is substantial. Earlier, we estimated that the genetic correlation between infancy and adulthood is about .75. Thus, the genetic contribution to phenotypic stability from infancy to adulthood is about .20, that is, $\sqrt{.15} \times \sqrt{.50} \times .75$. This means that about one-third of the phenotypic stability could be attributed to environmental factors. This environmental contribution to phenotypic stability can also be partitioned to estimate the environmental correlation between infancy and adulthood: $\sqrt{1 - .15} \times \sqrt{1 - .50} \times r_E = .10$. Solution of this equation suggests that the environmental correlation is relatively low, that is, about .15.

The Amplification Model of Developmental Genetics and Canalization

The developmental genetic model that we have proposed to account for CAP results is an amplification model in which genes relevant to mental development during infancy and childhood exert even greater effects during adulthood. Thus, although genetic variance is less in infancy than in adulthood, genetic factors in infancy covary highly with those in adulthood. This model is profoundly different from the evolutionary model of canalization that suggests that infant intellectual development is so tightly programmed that variability, both genetic and environmental, is curtailed (Scarr, 1975). This view implies that variability among infants is relatively unimportant:

> The evidence suggests to me that there is less genetic variability in infant than in later intelligence, that much of the genetic variability that exists is hidden in a well-buffered, epigenetic system, and that many environments are indeed functionally equivalent for the development of sensorimotor skills. (pp. 185–186)

> Differences in rates of sensorimotor development are not yet assignable to genetic or environmental causes, but they are relatively unimportant variations on a strong primate theme. (p. 194)

In contrast, the amplification model suggests that the origins of genetic variance lie in infancy, and like streams tumbling and diverging down the mountainside from their glacial source, these primordial genetic differences among children continue to diverge during development. Until these early genetic differences are amplified during development, they are small and thus difficult to detect. However, the amplification model suggests that genetic differences that are manifested during infancy, far from being unimportant, covary closely with genetic differences later in life.

This conclusion depends on data that were obtained using the Bayley Mental Scale. Other measures of infant mental development might yield different results. This possibility is the topic of the following two chapters. We also suggest that the amplification model we posit for infant mental development need not be a general model; it is possible that other domains of development, such as temperament, will be better explained by other developmental genetic models.

7

Development of Specific Cognitive Abilities

Introduction

In the preceding chapter on general cognitive ability *(g)*, we concluded that genetic variance accounts for a small but significant proportion of individual differences among infants on the Bayley MDI. Moreover, the results suggest the intriguing hypothesis that this genetic variance in infancy continues to affect individual differences in IQ from infancy to adulthood.

Behavioral-genetic studies of cognition in older children and adults have shifted from a preoccupation with *g* to the study of specific cognitive abilities (DeFries, Vandenberg, & McClearn, 1976). This transition in research attention is so clear that it would presage a similar change in the study of infant mental development were it not for the difficulty of measuring specific cognitive abilities in infancy, the general disenchantment with tests of infant mental development, and the belief that specific cognitive abilities are not differentiated developmentally until after infancy.

For adult cognitive tests, a lively controversy pitting *g* against specific cognitive abilities existed for several decades. Spearman (1904, 1927), who first developed factor analysis, emphasized the low but consistent correlation among all cognitive tests and extracted a factor that typically accounts for 30% of the shared variance of cognitive tests. Spearman's two-factor theory identified this first factor as general intelligence—that part of a test common to other cognitive tests. The second factor is unique to each test. In contrast, Thurstone (1938) emphasized the correlations among tests that clustered into seven or eight groups such as verbal, spatial, and memory factors. The debate continues today, although the possibility that both sides are partially correct is generally accepted. A rapprochement was suggested as early as 1949 by Burt, who argued for a hierarchical model in which individual tests can be viewed as clustering into group factors, group factors cluster into higher-order factors such as verbal and performance, and these group factors in turn are components of g. Although testers continue to employ IQ tests that provide a measure of g—or, at most, verbal and nonverbal IQ—researchers who study adult mental ability have generally come to focus on group factors interpreted as specific cognitive abilities.

Developers of infant tests, limited by the amount of time one can test infants, have emphasized g, although factor analytic work has rarely been conducted. Nevertheless, infancy researchers disagree about the importance of g in infancy. Some researchers have argued that there is no such thing as g in infancy (McCall et al., 1977; McCall et al., 1972) because the composition of a general factor changes from age to age. Others argue that extant infant tests do not adequately assess basic processes involved in g (Fagan, 1984). Lack of satisfactory alternatives for testing specific cognitive abilities of infants leads most researchers to continue to focus on g. Although there may well be developmental changes in the composition of g as McCall et al. suggest, it is safe to predict that some sort of hierarchical model that recognizes both g and specific abilities will eventually emerge from research on this topic.

In this chapter, we explore specific cognitive abilities, both in parents and in infants, in a more fine-grained approach to the study of infant mental development. We begin with the application of the CAP design to specific cognitive abilities of parents as they relate to infant Bayley MDI scores in order to investigate the nature of the relationship between adult IQ and infant MDI scores described in Chapter 6. Then we consider clusters of Bayley items and other analyses of these items as they relate to specific cognitive abilities of parents as well as to measures of the home environment. CAP cognitive measures other than the Bayley test, namely, measures of language–communication and attention to novel stimuli, are discussed in Chapter 8.

CAP Specific Cognitive Abilities for Adults

Many of the analyses in this chapter make use of factor scores based on the 13 cognitive test scores described in Chapter 4 (see also DeFries et al., 1981). The unadjusted means, variances, and reliabilities of the 13 scores are listed in Table 7.1 for biological, adoptive, and control mothers and fathers. As indicated previously, age is significantly related to cognitive scores, although age is confounded with parental type because the biological parents are about 10 years younger than the other parents. For this reason, the 13 scores were adjusted for age, age squared, and sex separately for each group of parents. The resulting standard scores thus do not differ in terms of means or variances for the three types of parents. Even without standardization, the groups of parents do not differ significantly in terms of the

TABLE 7.1

Means, Standard Deviations, and Reliabilities for 13 CAP Cognitive Test Scores for Parents

| | Biological | | | | Adoptive | | | | Control | | | | Internal reliability[a] | Test–retest reliability[a] |
| | Mother (N = 178–181) | | Father (N = 42–44) | | Mother (N = 180–181) | | Father (N = 173–178) | | Mother (N = 162–164) | | Father (N = 161–164) | | | |
Test	$\overline{X}$	SD	$\overline{X}$	SD	$\overline{X}$	SD	$\overline{X}$	SD	$\overline{X}$	SD	$\overline{X}$	SD		
Paper Form Board	10.4	(3.4)	11.0	(3.1)	10.8	(3.8)	12.5	(4.0)	11.6	(3.9)	12.9	(4.1)	.86	.76
Card Rotations	93.5	(35.3)	109.9	(27.6)	90.7	(31.8)	111.9	(30.8)	92.2	(30.8)	112.3	(29.8)	.88	.81
Hidden Patterns	65.6	(21.5)	72.3	(20.0)	76.0	(18.8)	83.5	(19.6)	80.8	(19.0)	83.9	(21.0)	.94	.84
Identical Pictures	80.9	(11.0)	82.3	(9.7)	81.3	(11.7)	81.3	(11.4)	83.7	(10.0)	83.5	(10.7)	.86	.72
Progressive Matrices	20.1	(3.8)	21.4	(3.5)	20.9	(3.6)	21.6	(4.4)	21.2	(3.6)	22.2	(4.0)	.84	.71
Things	27.2	(8.3)	27.4	(9.0)	32.6	(10.0)	34.7	(10.0)	35.0	(9.6)	36.4	(9.9)	.72	.76
Vocabulary	33.2	(14.0)	32.1	(15.4)	49.0	(12.6)	46.9	(13.8)	51.6	(12.0)	51.6	(13.2)	.88	.88
Word Beginnings and Endings	17.2	(5.9)	16.4	(5.4)	19.5	(7.0)	18.4	(7.5)	20.8	(7.0)	19.9	(7.0)	.76	.81
Subtraction and Multiplication	47.1	(17.4)	49.5	(20.8)	62.7	(20.4)	65.0	(21.6)	63.3	(19.7)	62.5	(19.6)	.96	.91
Colorado Perceptual Speed	37.1	(6.6)	33.9	(7.2)	39.7	(6.5)	36.4	(7.7)	41.2	(6.5)	37.7	(7.2)	.86	.81
Pedigrees	28.7	(6.9)	24.7	(7.6)	29.1	(7.3)	26.6	(7.6)	32.2	(5.9)	30.2	(6.8)	.85	.76
Picture Memory	25.7	(5.7)	25.8	(5.8)	26.5	(5.7)	24.5	(5.2)	26.9	(4.7)	25.4	(5.7)	.65	.63
Names and Faces	13.2	(5.8)	12.0	(5.5)	15.5	(6.0)	12.4	(6.1)	15.2	(5.4)	12.5	(5.9)	.93	.80

[a]From DeFries et al., 1981.

TABLE 7.2

Loadings on Varimax Rotated Factors[a]

	Factor loading			
Factor/test	Spatial	Verbal	Perceptual Speed	Memory
Spatial				
Paper Form Board	.76	—	—	—
Card Rotations	.73	—	—	—
Hidden Patterns	.71	—	—	—
Identical Pictures	.66	—	—	—
Progressive Matrices	.43	.34	.32	—
Verbal				
Things	—	.78	—	—
Vocabulary	—	.65	.48	—
Word Beginnings and Endings	—	.63	.40	—
Perceptual Speed				
Subtraction and Multiplication	—	—	.80	—
Colorado Perceptual Speed	—	—	.80	—
Pedigrees	.39	.41	.47	—
Memory				
Picture Memory	—	—	—	.85
Names and Faces	—	—	—	.68

[a] $N > 900$. Only loadings of .30 or more are listed.

variances of their test scores. The internal and test–retest reliabilities are high enough to make the individual test scores, as well as the factor scores, useful for analysis.

The CAP test battery was developed primarily from the Hawaii Family Study of Cognition (HFSC) conducted in the 1970s (DeFries, Ashton *et al.*, 1976) to measure four specific cognitive abilities: Verbal, Spatial, Visual Memory, and Perceptual Speed. The factor structure is robust, surviving several changes made for the CAP battery as discussed in Chapter 4. Table 7.2 lists the loadings for the four components following a principal component analysis with Varimax rotation. The items were z scored within groups of biological, adoptive, and control parents and corrected for sex and age as explained elsewhere (DeFries *et al.*, 1981). Also, as in all CAP analyses, individual scores three standard deviations or more above or below the mean were eliminated from analyses to ensure that the results would not be affected by rare outliers. Four factors, accounting for 61% of the total variance, were rotated and can be interpreted as Spatial, Verbal, Perceptual Speed, and Memory. The Spatial factor has its highest loadings on Paper Form Board, Card Rotations, and Hidden Patterns. Identical Pictures, which has been assumed to be primarily a test of perceptual speed, also correlates highly with the Spatial dimension; however, in retrospect, the loading is not so surprising, because the test consists of geometric designs, often differing in orientation, which are to be matched. The Verbal factor is defined largely by Things, Vocabulary, and Word Beginnings and Endings. Two tests, Subtraction and Multiplication and Colorado Perceptual Speed, primarily account for the Perceptual Speed factor. The Memory factor is defined almost completely by Picture Memory and Names and Faces. Pedigrees and Progressive Matrices have moderate loadings on the Spatial, Verbal, and Perceptual Speed dimensions, a finding similar to the HFSC results (DeFries *et al.*, 1974). The factor structures for the three types of parents, as well as for males and females, were nearly identical (DeFries *et al.*, 1981). The rotated principal-component scores for these four dimensions are used throughout this chapter as measures of specific cognitive abilities.

Selective placement and assortative mating correlations for the four specific cognitive abilities and 13 test scores are presented in Tables 7.3 and 7.4, respectively. The results are quite similar to those previously reported for IQ: Of the 68 selective placement correlations, 10 are significant; however, half of the significant correlations are negative in sign. Assortative mating for perceptual speed and verbal abilities appears to be similar to assortative mating for IQ. The correlations for vocabulary are .32, .36, and .44, respectively, for the biological, adoptive, and control couples.

TABLE 7.3

Selective Placement Correlations for Cognitive Measures

Measure	Biological mother vs. adoptive mother ($N = 178$)	Biological mother vs. adoptive father ($N = 173$)	Biological father vs. adoptive mother ($N = 42$)	Biological father vs. adoptive father ($N = 41$)
Factors				
Spatial	.14*	−.03	.20	−.04
Verbal	−.01	.07	−.03	.28*
Perceptual Speed	−.08	.02	.05	−.20
Memory	−.11	.00	.18	−.11
Tests				
Paper Form Board	.18*	−.03	.00	.03
Card Rotations	.15*	−.04	.20	−.34*
Hidden Patterns	.00	−.08	.05	.02
Identical Pictures	−.02	.00	−.26*	−.26
Progressive Matrices	.15*	.08	.09	−.08
Things	.00	.10	−.02	.23
Vocabulary	−.05	.07	−.12	−.20
Word Beginnings and Endings	−.01	.00	.01	.22
Subtraction and Multiplication	−.02	.00	.23	−.09
Colorado Perceptual Speed	−.17*	−.01	−.11	−.01
Pedigrees	.09	.01	−.01	−.27*
Picture Memory	−.04	.04	.25	−.34*
Names and Faces	−.11	.00	−.25	.09

*$p < .05$.

TABLE 7.4

Assortative Mating Correlations for Biological, Adoptive, and Control Parents
for Cognitive Measures

Measure	Biological couples	Adoptive couples	Control couples
Factors			
Spatial	−.12	.04	.05
Verbal	−.02	.34*	.23*
Perceptual Speed	.14	.14*	.23*
Memory	.06	.08	.22*
Tests			
Paper Form Board	−.11	.14*	.00
Card Rotations	−.12	.08	.01
Hidden Patterns	.10	.06	−.03
Identical Pictures	.19	.27*	.25*
Progressive Matrices	.40*	.18*	.06
Things	.02	.28*	.25*
Vocabulary	.32*	.36*	.44*
Word Beginnings and Endings	.27*	.19*	.21*
Subtraction and Multiplication	.03	.07	.15*
Colorado Perceptual Speed	.07	.19*	.27*
Pedigrees	.43*	.16*	.11
Picture Memory	.13	.08	.08
Names and Faces	.21	.08	.14*

*$p < .05$.

For some analyses, we present results for the 13 test scores as well as for the four factor scores. Although group factor scores provide useful summaries of the data on specific cognitive abilities, a substantial amount of variance is unique to each test. As indicated in Table 7.1, the tests themselves are sufficiently reliable to permit parent–offspring analyses for the individual tests. One rationale for considering this level of detail comes from the finding of the HFSC (DeFries, Johnson *et al.*, 1979) that the Spatial factor, which showed moderately high parent–offspring resemblance on the whole, contained one test with high parent–offspring resemblance (a midchild–midparent regression of .61) and another test with low parent–offspring resemblance (regression of .27).

Parent–Offspring Correlations for the Bayley MDI

Although construction of the infant tests was primarily guided by a notion of g, it is nonetheless possible that the Bayley MDI is more closely related to some specific cognitive abilities of parents than it is to parental IQ. If this were true, it would shed some light on the nature of infant mental development as measured by the Bayley test, as well as suggest a psychological process mediating the genetic relationship between infant MDI scores and adult IQ.

TABLE 7.5

Parent–Offspring Correlations for Cognitive Measures

	12-month Bayley MDI						24-month Bayley MDI					
	Biological		Adoptive		Control		Biological		Adoptive		Control	
Parent measure	Mother (N = 175)	Father (N = 40)	Mother (N = 176)	Father (N = 171)	Mother (N = 157)	Father (N = 154)	Mother (N = 175)	Father (N = 40)	Mother (N = 176)	Father (N = 171)	Mother (N = 156)	Father (N = 154)
Factors												
Spatial	.06	.19	.02	.08	.11	.05	.02	.28*	.03	.12	.22*	.06
Verbal	.00	−.05	.00	.06	.05	−.03	.07	.45*	.02	.08	.10	.09
Perceptual Speed	.07	.16	.15*	.00	−.09	.06	.05	−.08	.13*	.03	.05	.19*
Memory	.09	.42*	.06	−.09	−.02	.14*	.09	.15	.03	.01	−.05	.09
Tests												
Paper Form Board	.09	.21	−.03	−.02	.07	.02	.05	.20	.06	.05	.10	.09
Card Rotations	.04	.21	.04	.06	.00	−.02	.04	.31*	.08	.10	.12	.06
Hidden Patterns	.07	.03	.11	.11	.05	.13	.06	.29*	.06	.15*	.28*	.11
Identical Pictures	.00	.18	.06	.04	.04	.00	−.07	.06	.07	.01	.11	.02
Progressive Matrices	.06	.35*	−.03	.03	.08	.05	.02	.24	−.05	.04	.24*	.11
Things	.02	.03	.05	.14*	.03	−.04	.02	.33*	.03	.12	.11	.03
Vocabulary	.10	−.05	.09	.01	−.04	.04	.18*	.37*	.04	.03	.09	.14*
Word Beginnings and Endings	.04	.06	.03	.02	.01	.03	.09	.33*	.04	−.02	.07	.13
Subtraction and Multiplication	.15*	.18	.16*	.01	−.11	.01	.00	−.10	.06	.04	.06	.07
Colorado Perceptual Speed	.04	.35*	.14*	.01	−.08	.10	.07	.09	.09	.08	.07	.22*
Pedigrees	.06	.36*	.21*	.04	.13*	−.05	.02	.37*	.15*	.13*	.30*	.13*
Picture Memory	.12	.40*	.08	−.10	.00	.10	.12	.11	.01	.00	.06	.04
Names and Faces	.07	.34*	.05	−.03	−.05	.05	.03	.21	.05	.04	−.14*	.12

*p < .05.

Parent–offspring correlations between the Bayley MDI scores and parents' cognitive measures are listed in Table 7.5 for the three types of CAP relationships. The pattern of results at 12 months differs from those for IQ. Of the 34 control parent–offspring correlations, only 2 are statistically significant. Although some significant relationships are observed for biological parents or for adoptive parents, these relationships generally are not replicated in the control families. The only exceptions at 12 months are the Pedigrees test and the Memory factor. At 24 months, 9 of the 34 control parent–offspring correlations are statistically significant in a positive direction. The highest correlations emerged for the Pedigrees test, which, interestingly, is the highest-loading test on the unrotated principal-component measure of g (Table 6.3). Other measures yielding significant correlations in the control families and in the biological or adoptive parent–offspring relationships include the Spatial and Perceptual Speed factors and the Hidden Patterns and Vocabulary tests. The Memory factor and the individual memory tests, which load lowest on g, show the least parent–offspring resemblance.

These results imply that the nature of infant intelligence involves g. The finding that infant intelligence as measured by the Bayley MDI is correlated with IQ of the biological parents suggests that there is genetic covariance between infant and adult intelligence. The finding that Bayley MDI scores are not correlated systematically with parents' specific cognitive abilities, especially at 12 months, suggests that genetic covariance between infant and adult intelligence involves general cognitive ability rather than differentiated abilities. This hypothesis is supported by the fact that the least parent–offspring resemblance is found for memory tests, which show the lowest g loadings, and that the greatest parent–offspring resemblance occurs for Pedigrees, which has the highest g loading.

Factor Analyses of Bayley Mental Scale Items

Perhaps because of the emphasis on g, few factor analyses of the Bayley Mental Scale items have been reported. The best-known report is that of Stott and Ball (1965), who obtained test protocols on 1926 infants and young children for an early version of the Bayley test (the California First-Year Test) as well as other tests— including the Cattell Infant Scale, the Gesell Developmental Schedules, the Merrill–Palmer Scale, and the Stanford–Binet. Their general conclusions include the following: (1) The nature of the item groupings suggests that the infant tests involve intellectual, "thinking process," tasks; (2) factor content differs by age and for particular tests; and (3) some tests include highly correlated items that yield large general factors. However, "these general factors do not necessarily test 'g' or general intelligence content, but, rather, are merely so narrow in their coverage of abilities, that there is little variation in their meaning" (Stott & Ball, 1965, p. 137).

The forerunner of the Bayley Mental Scale fared moderately well in factor analyses of the items for 12-month-olds ($N = 137$), offering "a rich variation in test meaning" (p. 90). However, of the 31 items appropriate for 12-month-olds, all but

TABLE 7.6

Stott and Ball's (1965) Varimax Factor Loadings of 11 Bayley Items for 12-Month-Olds[a]

Suggested factor name	Item	Factor loading
Deduction, Concepts of Relationships	88. Picks up cup, secures cube	.89
	82. Attempts to secure three blocks	.78
	96. Unwraps cube	.76
	90. Puts cube in cup on command	.58
	98. Holds crayon adaptively	.53
	106. Imitates words	.50
	92. Stirs with spoon in imitation	.43
Language, Communication	113. Says two words	.81
	101. Uses expressive jargon	.72
	106. Imitates words	.53
Inhibits on Command, Goal Directed Behavior	94. Inhibits on command	.66
	98. Holds crayon adaptively	.64
	101. Uses expressive jargon	.72
Imitation, Immediate Memory	105. Dangles ring by the string	.66
	92. Stirs with spoon in imitation	.52
	90. Puts cube in cup on command	.45

[a]The listed item numbers are from the Bayley (1969) test. Only 11 items loading on the four factors are listed.

13 were eliminated because of experimental deficiencies. As discussed in Chapter 6, several items, such as putting 1, 3 or more, or 9 cubes in a cup, are interdependent—an infant who puts 9 cubes in a cup of course gets credit for the other items as well. Table 7.6 lists the 11 Bayley items (with their 1969 item numbers) that yielded Varimax factor loadings greater than .40 in the factor analyses performed by Stott and Ball.

Four factors emerged. Naming factors is always a risky business, but especially so when the items are infant mental test items. As Stott and Ball (1965) point out concerning the first factor, "While one might be tempted to call this 'cube behavior,' more careful scrutiny gives insight into the possible processes involved. The scoring of the items is not based upon the degree of skill shown, but upon whether the baby can do the task because he *understands* what to do" (pp. 93–94). The second factor clearly involves language or, more generally, communication. The third factor "seems to involve an adaptive response to the directions of the examiner" (p. 95). The fourth factor is similar to the third, although its items also involve imitative responses.

Some other infant tests yield more factors. However, most do not separate motor items from mental items as the Bayley does. For example, items of the Gesell Developmental Schedules were grouped into four subtests: motor items, including posture and locomotion; adaptive items, among which Gesell (1954) included "alertness, intelligence, and various forms of constructive exploration" (p. 338); language items, which include facial expressions as well as gestures and vocalizations; and personal–social items that include play, feeding, and dressing. However, Stott and Ball (1965) suggest that Gesell's item groupings bear little relationship to the factor structure of the items: "Observational guessing about related item meanings is shown to have little validity in grouping together items in terms of the fundamental item relations, as shown by the factor analyses. For example, the Gesell items are quite differently classified by factor selectivity than they are by the labels in the Developmental Schedules" (p. 137). Moreover, the Gesell Developmental Schedules were considered to be less standardized and more subjective than the other infant tests (Anastasi, 1961). A more rigorous version of the Gesell test, the Cattell Infant Scale, was developed by P. Cattell (1960) and became one of the most widely used infant tests. However, the Cattell test has been shown to measure "a particularly narrow range of ability . . . the interitem correlations were all very high" (Stott & Ball, 1965, p. 85), although it should be pointed out that Stott and Ball included only the 3-month and 6-month items in their analyses.

Other approaches to grouping Bayley items into clusters have been suggested (e.g., Bayley, 1970; Kohen-Raz, 1967; Yarrow & Pedersen, 1975), but none has gained general acceptance.

CAP Factor Analyses

We attempted to develop psychometrically valid factors from the Bayley items at 12 and 24 months using the items and scales of interdependent items discussed in Chapter 6. Although our analyses did not yield evidence for a clear factor structure, we present the results of these analyses because published factor analyses of the Bayley items are rare. We present the factor analytic results for sexes combined and for adopted and control infants combined because preliminary analyses indicated no systematic correlational differences among the groups. As described in Chapter 6, 16 independent items and 6 scales were analyzed for 12-month-olds and 4 items and 12 scales were used for 24-month-old analyses, after items and scales showing less than 10% variability were eliminated.

At 12 months, seven principal components were found with eigenvalues greater than 1.0; however, a three-factor solution appeared to be more interpretable. Table 7.7 lists the Varimax factor loadings for a principal factoring solution involving 32% of the total variance. Three factors based on 290 CAP probands at 12 months of age were rotated. The first factor correlates most highly with the Pinkboard, Blueboard, and Pegboard scales; the second involves imitation somewhat more in that it includes high loadings for Cubes in Cup and Puts beads in box, measures that involve modeling; and the third is a lexical factor involving two items, Imitates words and Says two words. In the seven-factor solution, similar factors emerged, and subsequent factors were primarily test specific.

The factor analytic results for the 24-month-olds are not much more satisfactory (see Table 7.8). Six components had eigenvalues greater than 1.0; however, the most interpretable solution occurred when four factors involving 41% of the total

TABLE 7.7

CAP Varimax Loadings for 12-Month Bayley Items–Scales[a]

	Factor loading		
Item–scale	Factor 1	Factor 2	Factor 3
94. Inhibits on command	—	.45	—
96. Unwraps cube	—	—	—
97. Repeats performance laughed at	—	.32	—
99. Pushes car along	—	.31	—
101. Jabbers expressively	—	—	—
102. Uncovers blue box	.33	—	—
104. Pats whistle doll in imitation	—	—	—
105. Dangles ring by string	—	—	—
106. Imitates words	—	—	.84
107. Puts beads in box (6 of 8)	.30	.49	—
109. Removes pellet from bottle	.40	—	—
113. Says two words	—	—	.63
115. Closes round box	.40	—	—
116. Uses gestures to make wants known	—	—	—
117. Shows shoes or other clothing	—	—	—
122. Attains toy with stick	.41	—	—
Scale 1. Pegboard	.48	.38	—
Scale 2. Cubes in Cup	—	.56	—
Scale 3. Scribbles	.36	.38	—
Scale 4. Blueboard	.55	—	—
Scale 5. Tower of Cubes	—	—	—
Scale 6. Pinkboard	.69	—	—

[a]$N = 290$. Only loadings of .30 or more are listed.

variance were rotated. The first factor, with highest loadings for Sentence of two words, Names Objects, Names Pictures, and Names Watch, is clearly lexical. The second factor is more symbolic in nature, with high loadings for Discriminates Three and Points to Pictures. The third factor, similar to the first factor at 12 months, has high loadings for the Pinkboard and Blueboard scales, which may require spatial ability. Also similar to a 12-month factor is the fourth factor, which involves Tower of Cubes, Folds paper, and Scribbles—all measures that involve imitation.

We tried alternative approaches such as using tetrachoric correlations for the dichotomous items, as well as different methods of factor extraction and rotation. None of these procedures improved the solution.

Lewis–Enright Factors

Although our solution was far from simple structure, confidence in our results was buoyed when we learned that Michael Lewis had conducted similar research. He kindly sent us a draft of a paper with Mary Enright that was based on a

TABLE 7.8

CAP Varimax Loadings for 24-Month Bayley Items–Scales[a]

	Factor loading			
Item–scale	Factor 1	Factor 2	Factor 3	Factor 4
131. Finds two objects	—	—	—	—
136. Sentence of two words	.50	—	—	—
154. Train of cubes	—	—	—	—
157. Folds paper	—	—	—	.34
Scale 1. Pegboard	—	—	—	—
Scale 3. Scribbles	—	—	—	.32
Scale 4. Blueboard	—	—	.60	—
Scale 5. Tower of Cubes	—	—	—	.44
Scale 6. Pinkboard	—	—	.62	—
Scale 7. Names Objects	.81	—	—	—
Scale 8. Names Pictures	.87	—	—	—
Scale 9. Points to Pictures	.43	.62	—	—
Scale 10. Mends Doll	—	—	—	—
Scale 11. Discriminates Three	—	.74	—	—
Scale 12. Names Watch	.58	—	—	—
Scale 13. Prepositions	—	.34	.30	—

[a]$N = 328$. Only loadings of .30 or more are listed.

TABLE 7.9

Lewis and Enright's (1983) Hierarchical, Oblique Rotated Factor Loadings
for 12-Month Bayley Items

Suggested factor name	Item	Factor loading
Means-End	114. Puts nine cubes in cup	.75
	115. Closes round box	.64
	100. Puts three or more cubes in cup	.63
	107. Puts beads in box (6 of 8)	.58
Imitation	108. Places one peg repeatedly	.60
	120. Pinkboard: Places round block	.52
	125. Imitates crayon stroke	.50
	118. Pegs placed in 70 sec	.44
	112. Spontaneous scribble	.39
	105. Dangles ring by string	.38
	111. Builds tower of two cubes	.36
	109. Removes pellet from bottle	.33
	122. Attains toy with stick	.31
Verbal Skill	106. Imitates words	.58
	113. Says two words	.55
	117. Shows shoes or other clothing or own toy	.51
	101. Jabbers expressively	.32

TABLE 7.10

Lewis and Enright's (1983) Hierarchical, Oblique Rotated Factor Loadings
for 24-Month Bayley Items

Suggested factor name	Item	Factor loading
Lexical	132. Points to three pictures	.82
	139. Points to five pictures	.80
	141. Names three pictures	.78
	149. Names five pictures	.68
	148. Points to seven pictures	.62
	130. Names one picture	.60
	138. Names two objects	.43
	146. Names three objects	.40
	145. Names watch, fourth picture	.38
	143. Builds tower of six cubes	.34
	150. Names watch, second picture	.33
	154. Train of cubes	.32
Spatial	155. Blueboard: completes in 150 sec	.65
	159. Blueboard: completes in 90 sec	.61
	160. Blueboard: completes in 60 sec	.58
	142. Blueboard: places six blocks	.55
	151. Pinkboard: reversed	.41
	129. Blueboard: places two round and two square	.39
	126. Follows directions, doll	$-.38$
	124. Names one object	$-.35$
	128. Points to parts of doll	$-.31$
Verbal (symbolic)	144. Discriminates two: cup, plate, box	.59
	136. Sentence of two words	.55
	127. Uses words to make wants known	.53
	146. Names three objects	.49
	156. Pegs placed in 22 sec	.46
	134. Pegs placed in 30 sec	.45
	124. Names one object	.42
	152. Discriminates three: cup, plate, box	.41
	128. Points to parts of doll	.38
	126. Follows directions, doll	.32
Imitation	147. Imitates strokes: vertical and horizontal	.68
	135. Differentiates scribble from stroke	.63
	156. Pegs placed in 22 sec	.58
	125. Imitates crayon stroke	.57
	161. Builds tower of eight cubes	.42
	162. Concept of one	.35

presentation by Kreitzberg (1978). A new factor analytic procedure, *resistance fitting,* developed by A. Yates (1977), was used "in order to control for specific interitem variance resulting from natural item dependencies from entering into the common factor solution" (p. 3), and a hierarchical analysis with oblique rotation was employed. This procedure resulted in a reasonable factor structure in an analysis of data from 166 one-year-olds and 139 two-year-olds (see Lewis, 1983).

The Lewis–Enright factors for 12- and 24-month Bayley items are listed in Tables 7.9 and 7.10, respectively. Three factors were identified at 12 months: Means-End, Imitation, and Verbal Skill. Except for the Verbal Skill factor, there is little correspondence with the CAP factors at 12 months. However, it should be noted that Lewis and Enright used items 100 through 125, which correspond to age placements of 11.3 to 17.8 months, indicating that their sample was above average in performance (no means were reported). Although we might quibble with some factor names—for example, the second factor seems to be more cognitive than the name "imitation" suggests—the factor structure in general is quite reasonable.

For 24-month Bayley items (Table 7.10) the factor structure is more differentiated, involves more items, and is more similar to the CAP results. The first factor, called "Lexical," involves verbal production. The second factor, "Spatial," is somewhat dubious because its highest-loading items involve dependencies created by the Blueboard task. Moreover, the items other than the Blueboard load negatively on the factor, something never seen in other analyses of mental items. The third factor, "Verbal (symbolic)," appears to involve verbal comprehension items; and the fourth factor, "Imitation," again seems to be more general and cognitive than the name would imply.

As reported by Lewis and Enright, intercorrelations among these oblique factors within each age are low. Nevertheless, at 12 months, two of the three correlations are significant: .31 between Means-End and Imitation and −.16 between Means-End and Verbal Skill. At 24 months, only one of the six intercorrelations is significant: .31 between Lexical and Verbal. Correlations between the 12-month factors and the 24-month factors are also low: The highest correlation is only .21, between the Imitation factors at 12 and 24 months. The only other significant correlations are

TABLE 7.11

Means and Standard Deviations of the CAP Lewis–Enright
Bayley Scale Scores

Lewis–Enright Bayley Scale	Adopted infants (N = 182)		Control infants (N = 165)	
	$\overline{X}$	SD	$\overline{X}$	SD
12 months				
Means-End	1.9	1.2	1.9	1.2
Imitation[a,b]	1.9	1.5	2.5	1.8
Verbal Skill	1.7	1.2	1.7	1.1
24 months				
Lexical	8.5	3.1	8.8	2.7
Spatial	0.9	2.0	1.0	2.0
Verbal (symbolic)[a]	8.1	1.6	8.1	1.6
Imitation	2.5	1.1	2.4	1.1

[a]Significant gender difference ($p < .05$).
[b]Significant difference between adopted and control infants ($p < .05$).

TABLE 7.12

Intercorrelations among Lewis–Enright Bayley Scale Scores and Total MDI Scores within and across 12 and 24 Months for CAP Infants[a]

Measure	12 Months				24 Months				
	MDI	Means-End	Imitation	Verbal	MDI	Lexical	Spatial	Verbal (symbolic)	Imitation
12 Months									
MDI total	—	.63	.69	.49	.39	.31	.23	.24	.21
Means-End		—	.42	.24	.21	.13	.20	.16	.10
Imitation			—	.23	.37	.27	.17	.19	.22
Verbal Skill				—	.30	.21	.22	.23	.12
24 Months									
MDI total					—	.72	.59	.68	.49
Lexical						—	.12	.62	.27
Spatial							—	.18	.19
Verbal (symbolic)								—	.24
Imitation									—

[a] N = 341–347.

between the 12-month Verbal Skill factor and the 24-month Lexical factor (.19) and Verbal factor (.17).

We constructed scales based on the Lewis–Enright factors, using unit weights and summing the items listed in Tables 7.9 and 7.10. Means and standard deviations for the CAP adopted and control infants are presented in Table 7.11. The 12-month Imitation scale and the 24-month Verbal scale showed a significant sex difference in that girls scored about one-quarter of a standard deviation higher than boys. One significant difference emerged between adopted and control infants: The control infants scored higher than the adopted infants on the Imitation scale at 12 months of age. However, the 24-month Imitation scale revealed no such difference. The same scales yielded significant heterogeneity of variance among the four groups of adopted and control boys and girls; however, a multivariate test of the homogeneity of the variance–covariance matrices was nonsignificant.

The intercorrelations among the scales (see Table 7.12) are generally higher than those mentioned earlier. This was to be expected because we used scale scores comprised of unit-weighted sums of the highest-loading items, whereas Lewis and Enright employed factor scores. The longitudinal correlations of Lewis–Enright scales from 12 to 24 months are similar to those reported by Lewis and Enright: The greatest longitudinal correlation, between 12-month Imitation and 24-month Lexical, is .27.

In the following section, we discuss the relationship of these Lewis–Enright Bayley scales to specific cognitive abilities of parents and to environmental measures.

Parent–Offspring Correlations for the Lewis–Enright Bayley Scales

The goal of our analyses was to determine whether the Lewis–Enright Bayley scales correlate differentially with parents' specific cognitive abilities. Earlier in this chapter, we saw that the total Bayley MDI score correlated with IQ of the parents, but not with the parents' specific cognitive abilities. Nonetheless, it is possible that specific clusters of the Bayley items (for example, the Verbal factor) might correlate more highly with one or more specific cognitive abilities of the parents (for example, verbal ability).

The parent–offspring correlations are presented in Table 7.13 for 12-month-olds and in Table 7.14 for 24-month-olds (reported previously by Thompson, Plomin, & DeFries, 1984). Parental IQ is included in addition to parental specific cognitive abilities in order to determine whether Bayley clusters correlate more highly with specific cognitive abilities of the parents than with parental IQ. At 12 months, there are few significant parent–offspring correlations. For control parents, only 3 of the 30 correlations are significant in a positive direction. These 3 significant correlations involve the Means-End scale as related to parental IQ and parental memory and are replicated for biological parents, suggesting possible genetic influences.

TABLE 7.13

CAP Parent–Offspring Correlations for Specific Cognitive Abilities: 12-Month-Old Infants[a]

Measure		Biological		Adoptive		Control	
Parent	Infant	Mother	Father	Mother	Father	Mother	Father
IQ	Means-End	.20*	.18	−.02	−.01	.05	.13*
	Imitation	.07	.03	−.01	−.09	.03	.06
	Verbal Skill	.17*	.31*	.02	.06	.01	.07
Verbal	Means-End	.17*	−.16	−.03	−.05	.00	.04
	Imitation	.11	.04	−.07	−.01	.03	.03
	Verbal Skill	.02	.09	−.04	.08	.10	−.01
Spatial	Means-End	.09	−.04	−.06	.10	.03	.03
	Imitation	−.05	−.13	.00	−.07	.06	.06
	Verbal Skill	.10	.26*	.04	.09	.11	.08
Perceptual	Means-End	.09	−.02	−.01	−.03	−.10	−.03
Speed	Imitation	.09	−.02	−.01	−.03	−.10	−.03
	Verbal Skill	.08	.05	.06	.01	−.16*	.05
Memory	Means-End	.16*	.31*	.06	.02	.17*	.18*
	Imitation	.03	.30*	.10	.00	.12	.08
	Verbal Skill	.10	.34*	−.03	.04	−.09	.01

[a]Lewis–Enright Bayley scales for 12-month-old adopted and control infants and CAP specific cognitive ability factors for biological, adoptive, and control parents.

*$p < .05$.

The correlation between parental memory and infant Means-End remains significant when parental IQ is partialed out, which suggests that this relationship may be specific to adult memory.

At 24 months, more significant parent–offspring correlations emerge in the control families; 13 of the 40 correlations are significant. However, little replication occurs for either the biological or the adoptive parents. One replicated relationship involves the Bayley Spatial scale and parental IQ for both control and biological relationships, suggesting genetic influence. The control infants' Spatial scores are significantly correlated with control mothers' Spatial score; however, when the control mothers' IQ is partialed out, the correlation is no longer significant, which suggests that the relationship is to some extent a reflection of IQ rather than specific to spatial ability.

In general, when the Bayley scales are related to parental cognitive abilities, they tend to be related to general cognitive ability (IQ) rather than to specific cognitive abilities of the parents. There are more relationships at 24 months than at 12 months. The 24-month Spatial scale appears to be related genetically to adult IQ. No systematic pattern of results is observed for the infant Verbal scales and adult verbal ability. These results agree with our emerging hypothesis that mental abilities during infancy that are predictive of adult intellectual functioning are precursors of g, rather than specific cognitive abilities.

TABLE 7.14

CAP Parent–Offspring Correlations for Specific Cognitive Abilities: 24-Month-Old Infants[a]

Measure		Biological		Adoptive		Control	
Parent	Infant	Mother	Father	Mother	Father	Mother	Father
IQ	Lexical	−.06	.15	.09	.02	.12	.17*
	Spatial	.18*	.37*	.02	.09	.23*	.14*
	Verbal (symbolic)	−.01	.12	.12	.08	.07	.11
	Imitation	−.04	.12	−.02	−.02	.21*	.03
Verbal	Lexical	−.02	.35*	.03	.07	.04	.10
	Spatial	.12	.20	−.02	.03	.14*	.00
	Verbal (symbolic)	.10	.28	.08	.05	.07	.02
	Imitation	−.04	.39*	−.02	.06	.05	−.05
Spatial	Lexical	−.05	.19	−.05	.10	.08	.01
	Spatial	.13*	.06	−.03	.04	.24*	.07
	Verbal (symbolic)	−.05	.00	.02	.16*	.08	.03
	Imitation	.01	.00	.08	−.03	.13*	−.09
Perceptual	Lexical	−.02	−.25	.17*	−.04	.14*	.24*
Speed	Spatial	.10	.34*	.10	.16*	.00	.15*
	Verbal (symbolic)	−.04	−.04	.06	−.03	.00	.18*
	Imitation	−.07	−.24	−.03	−.08	.15*	.12
Memory	Lexical	.07	.04	.06	−.08	−.13	−.08
	Spatial	.06	.08	.00	.06	−.03	.08
	Verbal (symbolic)	.02	−.03	.09	.02	−.04	−.06
	Imitation	.05	.16	−.08	−.07	.03	.14*

[a]Lewis–Enright Bayley scales for 24-month-old adopted and control infants and CAP specific cognitive ability factors for biological, adoptive, and control parents.

*$p < .05$.

Correlations between Environmental Measures and the Lewis–Enright Bayley Scales

Other than in the area of language development, few attempts to assess the relationship between environmental measures and infants' specific cognitive abilities have been reported. Bradley and Caldwell (1980) used two Bayley clusters of items at 12 months suggested by Yarrow *et al.* (1975): goal directedness and language use. For a lower-class sample of 72 infants, Bradley and Caldwell found that the HOME scales correlated more highly with the total MDI at 12 months (median correlation of .31) than with either the goal directedness cluster (median correlation of .12) or the language use cluster (median correlation of .22). Differential environmental influence on specific cognitive abilities is suggested by the higher correlations between HOME scales and language use than between HOME scales and goal directedness.

Correlations between the major CAP environmental measures and the 12-month Lewis–Enright Bayley scales are presented in Table 7.15; correlations for 24-

TABLE 7.15

Correlations between 12-Month Lewis–Enright Bayley Scales and Environmental Measures for Adoptive and Control Families

Measure		Correlation	
Environmental	Infant	Adoptive families ($N = 144–180$)	Control families ($N = 138–161$)
HOME General Factor	Means-End	−.01	.05
	Imitation	.07	.15*
	Verbal Skill	.14*	.03
HOME Toys	Means-End	.02	.10
	Imitation	.03	.17*
	Verbal Skill	.14*	−.06
HOME Maternal Involvement	Means-End	.01	.01
	Imitation	.10	.03
	Verbal Skill	.19*	.00
HOME Developmental Advance	Means-End	−.02	.02
	Imitation	.07	.07
	Verbal Skill	.13*	.15*
HOME Restriction–Punishment	Means-End	−.02	−.04
	Imitation	−.06	−.03
	Verbal Skill	.05	−.02
FES Personal Growth	Means-End	−.09	−.16*
	Imitation	.08	−.15*
	Verbal Skill	.15*	−.04
FES Traditional Organization	Means-End	−.01	−.15*
	Imitation	−.08	−.19*
	Verbal Skill	.06	.07
Gottfried Variety of Experience	Means-End	−.04	−.14*
	Imitation	.06	−.05
	Verbal Skill	−.10	−.02
Gottfried Provision for Explora-tion	Means-End	−.07	.15*
	Imitation	.05	.14*
	Verbal Skill	.22*	−.06
Gottfried Physical Home Setting	Means-End	.00	−.03
	Imitation	.11	.03
	Verbal Skill	.07	.03

*$p < .05$.

month-olds are listed in Table 7.16. The results are presented separately for adoptive and control families in order to explore genetic influence, which, as seen in Chapter 6, can play a major role in ostensibly environmental relationships.

At 12 months, significant relationships tend to occur primarily for the infants' Verbal Skill scale, especially in the adoptive families. However, although 10 of the 30 correlations are significant in the control families and 6 of the 30 correlations are significant in the adoptive families, only 1 of these is significant in both: The infant Verbal Skill scale correlates significantly with HOME Developmental Advance in

TABLE 7.16

Correlations between 24-Month Lewis–Enright Bayley Scales and Environmental Measures for Adoptive and Control Families

Measure		Correlation	
Environmental	Infant	Adoptive families ($N = 138–181$)	Control families ($N = 129–163$)
HOME General Factor	Lexical	.26*	.34*
	Spatial	.15*	.19*
	Verbal (symbolic)	.19*	.36*
	Imitation	.14*	.23*
HOME Toys	Lexical	.13*	.17*
	Spatial	.17*	.02
	Verbal (symbolic)	.06	.13*
	Imitation	.19*	.18*
HOME Maternal Involvement	Lexical	.23*	.16*
	Spatial	.14*	.06
	Verbal (symbolic)	.24*	.21*
	Imitation	.08	.16*
HOME Developmental Advance	Lexical	.23*	.36*
	Spatial	.08	.23*
	Verbal (symbolic)	.14*	.37*
	Imitation	.09	.14*
HOME Restriction–Punishment	Lexical	−.04	.09
	Spatial	−.14*	−.01
	Verbal (symbolic)	−.03	.14*
	Imitation	−.05	−.08
Gottfried Variety of Experience	Lexical	.17*	−.01
	Spatial	−.02	.09
	Verbal (symbolic)	−.07	.01
	Imitation	.08	.03
Gottfried Provision for Exploration	Lexical	.07	.15*
	Spatial	.18*	.04
	Verbal (symbolic)	.00	−.01
	Imitation	.18*	.17*
Gottfried Physical Home Setting	Lexical	.14*	.12*
	Spatial	.03	.03
	Verbal (symbolic)	.04	−.02
	Imitation	−.12*	.12*

*$p < .05$.

both adoptive and control families. There is some suggestion of genetic mediation of the relationships involving the two FES scales in that 4 of the 6 correlations are significant in control families and only 1 is significant in adoptive families. Similarly, 3 of the 9 correlations involving the Gottfried categories of environmental influence are significant in the control families, whereas only 1 is significant in the adoptive families.

TABLE 7.17

Correlations between Perinatal Factors and Bayley Scales

Lewis–Enright Bayley Scale	Birth weight				Gestational age			
	Adopted		Control		Adopted		Control	
	r	N	r	N	r	N	r	N
12 Months								
Means-End	.10	172	.09	131	.00	166	.16*	113
Imitation	−.06	170	.14	131	−.04	164	.27*	113
Verbal Skill	.15*	172	.00	131	.06	166	.00	113
24 Months								
Lexical	−.04	172	.08	127	−.03	166	.13	110
Spatial	.17*	172	.06	129	.19*	166	.03	111
Verbal (symbolic)	.04	171	.06	129	.06	165	.00	111
Imitation	.05	172	−.02	129	.07	166	−.13	111

*$p < .05$.

At 24 months, many more correlations are significant, and replications in adoptive and control families are common. Significant correlations occur with regard to each of the HOME scales, although fewer of the correlations are significant for Restriction–Punishment. For each HOME scale, correlations also occur with regard to more than one of the four Lewis–Enright Bayley scales, which suggests that environmental influence measured by the HOME is general rather than specifically tailored to one infant ability rather than another. However, the Lexical and Verbal scales yield higher correlations, especially with the HOME General Factor, Maternal Involvement, and Developmental Advance. Genetic influence is implied by the higher correlations in the control families as compared to the adoptive families, especially for the HOME General Factor and Developmental Advance. Fewer correlations are significant for the Gottfried scales, although, in both the adoptive and control families, the Provision for Exploration scale is related to Imitation and Physical Home Setting is related to the Lexical scale.

In summary, environmental relationships are considerably stronger and more frequent at 24 months as compared to 12 months. Most interestingly, the results—particularly for the HOME scales at 24 months—suggest that genetic factors in part mediate the relationship between environmental measures and infant mental abilities as assessed by the Lewis–Enright Bayley scales.

We have indicated in Chapter 6 that the correlations of birth weight and gestational age with Bayley MDI scores are generally low and nonsignificant. The results for the Lewis–Enright scales are much the same, as shown in Table 7.17. Although 5 of the 28 correlations are significant, the significant correlations are not replicated across adopted and control infants. Thus, it does not appear that perinatal factors differentially affect scores on the Lewis–Enright Bayley scales.

Path Analysis of Verbal and Nonverbal Bayley
Clusters

As another approach to the issue of infant specific cognitive abilities, we considered the possibility that the distinction between verbal and nonverbal Bayley items might be useful because, for adults, specific group factors cluster into distinct higher-order verbal and performance factors. Dissertation research by Baker (1983) utilized verbal and nonverbal clusters of Bayley items in a bivariate path analysis of the CAP data that compares infant verbal and nonverbal scores to parental verbal and nonverbal scores. Although multivariate models and analyses have previously been applied to family and twin data, no research of this type has been reported using the adoption design. Baker developed a model that estimates genetic and environmental variances as well as covariances between verbal and nonverbal scores of infants and their parents. The parent–offspring correlations and cross-correlations (verbal vs. nonverbal) are listed in Table 7.18. At both 12 and 24 months, the parent–offspring correlations for verbal and nonverbal scores suggest a pattern of results similar to those found for the Bayley MDI total score; that is, both genetic and shared family environmental influences appear to be influential. The fact that the cross-correlations (i.e., parental verbal vs. infant nonverbal; parental nonverbal vs. infant verbal) are about the same as the isomorphic correlations (parental verbal vs. infant verbal; parental nonverbal vs. infant nonverbal) for all three sets of parents suggests that verbal and nonverbal abilities are not differentiated genetically or environmentally.

Maximum-likelihood, model-fitting procedures indicated significant genetic influence on both verbal and nonverbal abilities. Most interestingly, the analyses suggested that the genetic correlation between verbal and nonverbal abilities in 12-month-olds is nearly unity, suggesting that the genetic factors that affect individual differences in verbal abilities overlap almost entirely with the genetic factors that affect nonverbal scores. A somewhat lower genetic correlation at 24 months leads to

TABLE 7.18

Parent–Offspring Correlations and Cross-Correlations for Verbal and Nonverbal Scores[a]

Measure		Biological		Adoptive		Control	
Parent	Infant	Mother	Father	Mother	Father	Mother	Father
Verbal	12-month verbal	.12	.10	.13	.10	.11	.04
	12-month nonverbal	.11	.24	.04	.01	.04	.01
	24-month verbal	.14	.08	.14	.07	.20	.22
	24-month nonverbal	.22	.41	.04	.13	.21	.07
Nonverbal	12-month nonverbal	.09	.18	.06	.00	.01	.11
	12-month verbal	.09	.34	.14	.08	−.08	.14
	24-month nonverbal	.22	.25	.01	.12	.20	.14
	24-month verbal	.07	.07	.16	.05	.12	.15

[a]Maximum-likelihood estimates of pooled correlation matrix from Baker, 1983.

the hypothesis that genetic differentiation of verbal and nonverbal abilities occurs during the second year of life.

Genetic and Environmental Clusters of Bayley Items

In previous analyses described in this chapter, Bayley items have been clustered on the basis of their conceptual and empirical intercorrelation—for example, by factor analysis. Another, potentially important, approach is to select Bayley items on the basis of their correlations with parental cognitive abilities. In Chapter 6, we reviewed studies that used infant test items to predict later IQ and presented parent–offspring data for selected Bayley items that predict adult IQ in the CAP. Bayley items that correlate with parental IQ in control families could do so for either genetic or environmental reasons. The adoptive relationship tests the origins of the control family results. Bayley items for adoptees that correlate with biological parents' IQ can be thought of as measuring genetically mediated precursors of adult IQ. Correlations between adoptees' Bayley items and adoptive parents' IQ suggest environmental mediation of the infant–adult cognitive relationship. The analyses reported in Chapter 6 revealed some genetically influenced precursors of adult IQ, and these precursors appear to involve spatial processes rather than other processes such as language. Results of these analyses also revealed correlations between lexical Bayley items and adoptive parents' IQ scores, which suggests that family environment mediates the relationship between infant lexical factors and adult IQ.

We now report on analyses in which Bayley items are selected on the basis of their correlation with specific cognitive abilities of parents. The items and scales, procedures, and analyses are the same as those described in Chapter 6, but the focus of the analyses is on specific cognitive abilities of parents rather than IQ.

Genetic Clusters of Bayley Items

As in the analyses of IQ, we begin with items that correlate significantly ($p < .05$) with control midparent specific cognitive abilities. We then look for replication in the correlations between biological mothers and their adopted-away infants as an index of genetic continuity from infancy to adulthood. These correlations for 24-month-old infants, based on previous analyses reported by Rice, Plomin, and DeFries (1984b), are presented in Table 7.19. The results are quite different from those of the analyses in which parental IQ was predicted from Bayley items. No 12-month-old Bayley items or scales are listed in Table 7.19 because there are fewer significant correlations between specific cognitive abilities of control parents and their infants' 12-month Bayley scores than expected by chance. At 24 months, there are fewer correlations between each of the specific cognitive abilities of the control parents and 24-month Bayley scores than were found for general cognitive ability. Only two control family correlations are replicated for

TABLE 7.19

Correlations between Bayley Items–Scales and Specific Cognitive Abilities of Biological Mothers and Control Parents[a]

Parent factor	Bayley item–scale	Biological mother ($N = 175$)	Control parents		
			Midparent ($N = 157$)	Mother ($N = 157$)	Father ($N = 157$)
Spatial	Mends Doll scale	.01	.19*	.16*	.11
	Pinkboard scale	.13*	.19*	.20*	.07
	Blueboard scale	.07	.16*	.21*	.01
	Prepositions scale	.08	.17*	.17*	.11
	Train of cubes (item 154)	−.04	.14*	.05	.17*
Verbal	Tower of Cubes	−.02	.19*	.14*	.13*
	Names Objects scale	−.04	.21*	.12*	.22*
	Names Pictures scale	−.04	.24*	.12*	.26*
	Points to Pictures scale	−.03	.21*	.12*	.21*
Perceptual	Names Objects scale	.06	.16*	.11*	.13*
Speed	Points to Pictures scale	−.12	.15*	.12*	.10
	Finds 2 objects (item 131)	−.10	.24*	.19*	.17*
Memory	Pinkboard scale	.17*	.19*	.12*	.15*

[a]Biological mother–infant correlations for Bayley items–scales that yield significant correlations between control midparent specific cognitive abilities and Bayley scores of control infants at 24 months. Only 24-month measures are presented because fewer significant parent–offspring correlations were found at 12 months than expected by chance. Data from Rice, Plomin, and DeFries, 1984b.
*$p < .05$.

biological mothers; both involve the Pinkboard scale, which, as indicated previously, is also significantly correlated with biological mothers' IQ and can thus be ascribed to g rather than to specific cognitive abilities.

Environmental Clusters of Bayley Items

The correlations for the adoptive parents' specific cognitive abilities presented in Table 7.20 permit us to determine the importance of family environment in mediating the control family relationships described in Table 7.19. As in the IQ analyses described in Chapter 6, these analyses in adoptive families select Bayley items that are maximally sensitive to environmental influence. For IQ, we found that three lexical Bayley measures yield significant parent–offspring correlations in adoptive families, suggesting the importance of shared family environmental influences. The results in Table 7.20 replicate this finding and extend it by suggesting that the environmental relationship primarily involves parental verbal ability: The Names Pictures and the Points to Pictures scales are significantly correlated with the adoptive mothers' Verbal factor, although these correlations are nonsignificant for adoptive fathers.

TABLE 7.20

Correlations between Bayley Items–Scales and Specific Cognitive Abilities of Adoptive Parents[a]

		Correlation	
		Adoptive mother (N = 177)	Adoptive father (N = 177)
Parent factor	Bayley item–scale		
Spatial	Mends Doll scale	.03	.06
	Pinkboard scale	.05	.10
	Blueboard scale	−.04	.06
	Prepositions scale	.13*	.06
	Train of cubes (item 154)	.07	.06
Verbal	Tower of Cubes	−.10	−.12
	Names Objects scale	.11	−.06
	Names Pictures scale	.16*	−.03
	Points to Pictures scale	.15*	−.03
Perceptual Speed	Names Objects scale	.03	.02
	Points to Pictures scale	.03	−.03
	Finds 2 objects (item 131)	−.01	−.02
Memory	Pinkboard	−.01	−.01

[a]Adoptive parent–infant correlations for Bayley items–scales that yield significant correlations between control midparent specific cognitive abilities and Bayley scores of control infants at 24 months. Only 24-month measures are presented because fewer significant parent–offspring correlations were found at 12 months than expected by chance. Data from Rice, Plomin, and DeFries, 1984b.

*$p < .05$.

Summary

Our goal has been to utilize items of the Bayley Mental Scale to explore specific cognitive abilities in infancy. The results generally indicate that g dominates infant mental development, especially that portion of variance that predicts later cognitive abilities. We have seen, for example, that the total Bayley MDI score correlates only with IQ of parents, not with parental specific cognitive abilities. For the biological parents and their adopted-away infants, this finding suggests genetic continuity between infancy and adulthood.

Factor analysis of items from the Bayley Mental Scale yields no strong general component, unlike cognitive measures for adults. The items of the Bayley test are factorially diverse; thus, we report parent–offspring results for scales based on the Bayley items. These results demonstrate that Bayley scales in infancy are more strongly related to parental IQ than to parental specific cognitive abilities, again supporting a view of infant mental development in terms of g. Although specific cognitive abilities exist in infancy, to the extent that they are correlated with adult cognitive ability they predict adult g rather than specific cognitive abilities. Our analyses of the items of the Bayley rather than scales derived from tbe Bayley items also support this view of infant mental development.

It is possible, of course, that the items on the Bayley test lack sufficient diversity to assess adequately the structure of specific cognitive abilities in infancy. In the next chapter, we explore this possibility by comparing the results using Bayley scales and items reported in this chapter to those obtained for subsamples of the CAP using intensive measures of two domains of infant mental development: language–communication and attention to novel stimuli.

8

Language–Communication and Attention to Novel Stimuli

Introduction

The CAP parent–offspring design facilitates an "instant" longitudinal study and thus permits a unique test of continuity from infancy to adulthood. Two domains included in the CAP data bank have been suggested as infant precursors of later cognitive ability, but warrant treatment in a separate chapter because they both go beyond the Bayley test, which has been the focus of the preceding two chapters, and they both involve intensive analyses limited to subsamples of the CAP. The first area encompasses language (verbal behavior, which includes linguistic as well as nonlinguistic vocalizations such as babbling) and, more broadly, all communicative behaviors—including nonverbal communicative gestures, such as pointing, as well as verbal behavior. Analyses of infant-to-adult longitudinal data obtained in the Berkeley Growth Study suggest that infant expressive vocalizations predict adult IQ, at least for females, better than any other measure in the study (Cameron *et al.*, 1967). The second area evolved from Fagan's (1984) research with the infant visual recognition memory paradigm, a task that uses novelty preference as a tool to assess infants' ability to discriminate, categorize, and retain information. Twelve studies using different procedures and samples yield a mean correlation of .44 in predicting IQ at 2 and 7 years of age from scores on the infant recognition memory task during the first few months of life. In this chapter, we focus on CAP data relevant to these two topics—language–communication and attention to novel stimuli.

Language–Communication

One of the most impressive normative changes in infancy is the development of language. Infants typically say "ma-ma" or "da-da" at 12 months, two words are usually said by 14 months, and two-word sentences begin to be used at 20 months. These beginnings of language balloon to about 100 to 200 words by 2 years, 1000 by 3 years, 8000 by 6 years, and 18,000 by 8 years. Given this imposing average increase with age, it is surprising that earlier infant tests did not fully exploit language development in the study of individual differences in mental development. Infant tests emphasize motoric and sensorimotoric items much more than language items, especially during the first 18 months of life. In 1954 in England, Griffiths criticized previous tests for their lack of language items and incorporated in her test twice as many language and communication items as other tests, including imitation, listening to sounds and conversation, repetition of single sounds, and babbling. However, Griffiths' Mental Development Scale has rarely been used in the United States because the test was sold only to those trained by Griffiths. The Bayley test includes some language and communication items: The number of such Bayley items with 10% to 90% pass rates is 12 at 12 months and 17 at 24 months.

The only previous adoption study relevant to language development reported correlations between the Gesell language scale for adoptees and their biological mothers' IQ for 151 mother–infant pairs (Casler, 1976). When the infants were 6 weeks of age, the Gesell scale correlated significantly with biological mothers' IQ; however, the correlation was not significant at 9 or 15 months. At 21 and 27 months of age, the correlations were significant for females but not for males.

Reprise of CAP Results for Bayley Items

The Bayley language–communication items yielded some interesting results in the CAP analyses reported in the previous chapter. In our factor analyses of the items, verbal factors emerged at 12 months and at 24 months. Analyses of results for the CAP Lewis–Enright Verbal Skill scale at 12 months and the Lexical and Verbal (symbolic) scales at 24 months revealed that they are not related genetically either to adult IQ or to adult verbal ability. That is, in no case are the correlations of 12- or 24-month Verbal or Lexical scale scores with parents' IQ or verbal ability significant for both the control parent–offspring and biological mother–offspring comparisons. For example, in the control families, scores on the 24-month Lexical scale are correlated .12 and .17 with mothers' and fathers' IQ, respectively; the biological mother–adopted-away infant correlation is −.06. The analogous correlations with parents' Verbal factor scores are .04 and .10 for control mothers and fathers and −.02 for biological mothers. The 24-month Verbal scale yielded similar results.

We also presented results based on Bayley items rather than factorially derived scales. Bayley items were identified for which control infants' scores are significantly correlated with their parents' cognitive abilities and then replication was sought for the adoptees and their biological mothers. Such items were found; however, language–communication items are not among them. Thus, it appears that individual differences in the Bayley language–communication items at 12 and 24 months are not genetic precursors of differences in adult IQ or adult verbal ability.

The only evidence from CAP Bayley data that appears to support a hypothesis of genetic influence for verbal development came from an analysis of 12- and 24-month scales based on all of the Bayley language–communication items (Baker, 1983). In this case, the results are similar to those reported in Chapter 6 for the Bayley MDI total score; both genetic and shared family environment are implicated in the relationship between infant language–communication and adult verbal IQ. At 12 and 24 months, the parent–offspring correlation for biological mothers and their adopted-away offspring is about .10, the correlation for adoptive parents and their adopted infants is about .10, and the correlation for control parents and their offspring is about .20, although the control family correlation is lower than expected at 12 months (see Table 7.18). However, a scale based on the nonverbal Bayley items yielded similar results in predicting parental nonverbal IQ; moreover, the cross-correlations between infant verbal scores and parental nonverbal IQ and between infant nonverbal scores and parental verbal IQ are also much the same. These results, as well as the results of maximum-likelihood, model-fitting analyses, indicate that the Bayley verbal and nonverbal items are not differentiated genetically or environmentally. In other words, the verbal and nonverbal items are isomorphic etiologically and yield patterns of results similar to results obtained using the total Bayley MDI. Thus, these analyses do not provide much support for genetic influence on infant language–communication per se.

The environmental analyses of the Bayley items produced an interesting twist. Although scores on the CAP Lewis–Enright verbal scales at 12 and 24 months are not significantly correlated with either IQ or verbal ability of the adoptive parents, analyses of the Bayley items at 24 months isolated two lexical scales that appear to be most susceptible to environmental influence. Scores on the Bayley measures that involve naming and pointing to pictures are significantly correlated with parental verbal ability for both the control parent–offspring and adoptive mother–adoptee relationships. Naming things might be hypothesized to be susceptible to parental influence in the direct form of coaching.

This hypothesis receives support from the analyses of the HOME environmental measure. At 12 months, the only relationship between Lewis–Enright Bayley scales and HOME factors that is replicated in adoptive and control homes is the relationship between the Verbal Skill scale and the HOME factor that assesses parental encouragement of developmental advance.

At 24 months, most of the Lewis–Enright scales are significantly correlated with most of the HOME factors. However, the correlations for the Verbal and Lexical scales are particularly interesting. Although significant correlations emerged in the adoptive families for the HOME General Factor and for the HOME factor of

Developmental Advance, the correlations are greater in the control families. In the adoptive homes, the HOME General Factor correlates .26 with the 24-month Lexical scale and .19 with the Verbal scale. However, the correlations in the control homes are .34 and .36, respectively. In the adoptive homes, the HOME Developmental Advance factor correlates .23 with the 24-month Lexical scale and .14 with the Verbal scale; the comparable correlations in the control families are .36 and .37. Thus, the environmental analyses suggest both influence of the family environment (indicated by significant correlations in the adoptive families) and genetic mediation of these environmental relationships (indicated by the higher correlations in the control families).

Sequenced Inventory of Communication Development

At the 24-month home visit, the CAP includes a measure of communication development that is similar to the Bayley language–communication items but contains many additional items. The measure is the Sequenced Inventory of Communication Development (SICD; Hedrick *et al.*, 1975), which includes Expressive and Receptive scales. As indicated in Chapter 4, the CAP uses 20 items from the Expressive scale (such as imitation of sounds and words) and 16 items from the Receptive scale, which primarily assesses comprehension of commands. Means and standard deviations for the Expressive and Receptive scales and a total communication development score for the SICD are listed in Table 8.1. These data suggest, as usual, that adopted and control infants are similar for means and variances. Girls score higher than boys, particularly on the Expressive scale. The correlations of gender (boys = 1, girls = 2) with the SICD total, Receptive, and Expressive scores are .23, .16, and .23, respectively ($N = 333$).

The intercorrelation between the Receptive and Expressive scales of the SICD is .45. The SICD scales also correlate substantially with the Lewis–Enright scales. With the effects of gender removed, the SICD total, Receptive, and Expressive scores correlate .60, .43, and .58, respectively, with the Lewis–Enright Lexical scale; the comparable SICD correlations with the Lewis–Enright Verbal scale are .57, .42, and .50. Importantly, the correlations of the SICD total, Receptive, and Expressive scores with the total Bayley MDI are even higher: .66, .56,

TABLE 8.1

Means and Standard Deviations of Scores on the SICD for Adopted and Control Infants at 24 Months

SICD measure	Adopted ($N = 175$)		Control ($N = 159$)	
	$\overline{X}$	SD	$\overline{X}$	SD
Receptive scale	14.6	3.6	15.1	4.0
Expressive scale	16.9	5.6	17.1	5.6
Total score	31.5	8.0	32.2	8.3

and .58. The fact that the SICD total score correlates .66 with the Bayley MDI affects our interpretation of the SICD results described in the following section.

Parent–Offspring Correlations

Correlations between infant SICD scores and cognitive abilities of parents are presented in Table 8.2. The results differ from those based on the Lewis–Enright Verbal and Lexical scales at 24 months. In the control families, the SICD measures are significantly correlated with parental IQ and, to a lesser extent, with parental spatial and verbal abilities. A similar pattern of results in adoptive families suggests a role for family environmental influences. The correlations between scores of adopted infants and their biological parents suggest the possibility of genetic involvement in the relationship of the SICD Receptive scale with adult IQ and verbal ability.

These results are reminiscent of results presented earlier for a verbal scale based on all of the Bayley language–communication items (Baker, 1983) that implicated both genetic and shared environment in the relationship between infant language–communication and adult verbal and nonverbal IQ. At 24 months, that analysis revealed a parent–offspring correlation for control parents and their offspring of about .20, a parent–offspring correlation for biological mothers and their adopted-away offspring of about .10, and a correlation between adoptive parents and their adopted infants of about .10. However, results of a bivariate path analysis of verbal and nonverbal Bayley scales led to the conclusion that these results are not specific to language acquisition.

We explored the extent to which the SICD contributes to parent–offspring correlations independently of the Bayley MDI by partialing out the 24-month Bayley MDI from the parent–offspring correlations reported in Table 8.2. In general, partialing out the Bayley MDI removes the significant and systematic results reported in the table. For example, the correlations between control mothers' IQ and the SICD total, Receptive, and Expressive scores are .24, .26, and .17, respectively. However, with 24-month Bayley MDI scores partialed out, the correlations are .12, .16, and .04. For the control fathers, the pattern of results is similar: The correlations of .20, .20, and .16 in Table 8.2 are reduced to .09, .10, and .04, respectively. This suggests that the SICD adds little beyond what is already measured by the Bayley MDI. Of course, this is a severe test of the SICD's predictive power because the Bayley MDI includes more than a dozen language-related items.

Correlations between Parental Speech Problems and Infant SICD Scores

We also examined the relationship between parents' speech problems and infants' SICD scores. As mentioned in Chapter 4 and described in Appendix C, the CAP includes 11 items concerning parental speech problems such as personal and family histories of stuttering. A scale of parental speech problems was created by summing the 11 speech problems. The means (and standard deviations) for biological mothers

TABLE 8.2

Parent–Offspring Correlations between Infant SICD Scores and Cognitive Abilities of Biological, Adoptive, and Control Parents

Infant SICD score	Parental measure	Biological		Adoptive		Control	
		Mother (N = 169–172)	Father (N = 40)	Mother (N = 169–171)	Father (N = 162–165)	Mother (N = 152–153)	Father (N = 152)
SICD total score	IQ	-.02	.36*	.20*	.11	.24*	.20*
	Spatial	-.01	.23	.02	.14	.18*	.00
	Verbal	.04	.14	.17*	.22*	.19*	.04
	Perceptual Speed	-.12	-.14	.13	.00	.03	.20*
	Memory	.12	.34*	.08	-.09	.02	.10
SICD Receptive scale	IQ	.10	.39*	.12	.12	.26*	.20*
	Spatial	.02	.16	.00	.20*	.18*	.08
	Verbal	.10	.33*	.08	.17*	.23*	-.02
	Perceptual Speed	.02	.04	.10	.01	.01	.19*
	Memory	.15*	.37*	.08	-.12	.08	.15*
SICD Expressive Scale	IQ	-.08	.24	.21*	.07	.17*	.16*
	Spatial	-.02	.22	.03	.08	.14*	-.06
	Verbal	.00	.36*	.19*	.20*	.12	.07
	Perceptual Speed	-.18*	-.23	.12	-.02	.04	.25*
	Memory	.07	.22	.07	-.04	-.02	.04

$^{*}p < .05.$

TABLE 8.3

Correlations between Infant SICD Scores and Speech Problems of Biological, Adoptive, and Control Parents

Infant measure	Biological		Adoptive		Control	
	Mother (N = 141)	Father (N = 37)	Mother (N = 163)	Father (N = 158)	Mother (N = 157)	Father (N = 147)
SICD total score	−.15*	−.26	−.07	−.15*	−.02	−.03
SICD Receptive scale	−.19*	−.26	−.03	−.09	−.06	.03
SICD Expressive scale	−.09	−.19	−.09	−.16*	.01	−.07

*$p < .05$.

and fathers are 1.2 (1.4) and 1.4 (1.8), respectively; for adoptive mothers and fathers, 1.0 (1.3) and 0.8 (1.2); and for control mothers and fathers, 1.0 (1.2) and 1.0 (1.4). These results indicate similar means and variances for the three types of parents, and also suggest the presence of some self-reported speech problems and variability in these problems among the parents.

Table 8.3 lists parent–offspring correlations between parental speech problems and infant SICD scores. The results are odd in that the biological parent correlations suggest genetic influence and the adoptive parent correlations suggest some influence of the family environment, but the correlations for the control parents hover around zero. Despite the lack of replication in the control families, these results merit further exploration because of the possibility that the SICD could yield early markers of adult speech problems.

Environment–Infant Correlations

The parent–offspring results for the SICD indicate significant family environmental influence. These results are consistent with those described earlier that showed that two Bayley measures—Naming, and Pointing to Pictures—are significantly correlated with parental verbal ability for both the control parent–offspring and adoptive mother–adoptee relationships. However, the SICD data suggest that the effect may not be specific to parental verbal ability, because the parent–offspring correlations are generally similar for parental IQ.

Our previous analyses of the relationship between the Lewis–Enright verbal scales and HOME measures of the environment yielded an intriguing pattern of results. At 24 months, the Lewis–Enright Verbal and Lexical scales are significantly correlated with most of the HOME factors. Signficant correlations emerged in both the adoptive homes and in the control homes for the HOME General Factor and for the HOME factor, Developmental Advance. However, the correlations in the control families are higher. Thus, the Lewis–Enright scale analyses suggest the influence of both family environment and heredity.

Correlations between the HOME factors and the SICD scales, listed in Table 8.4, yield similar and even more striking results. Many of the correlations between the

TABLE 8.4

Correlations between 24-Month SICD Scores and HOME Environmental Measures for Adoptive and Control Families

Measure		Correlation	
		Adoptive families	Control families
Environmental	Infant SICD	($N = 172–174$)	($N = 156–159$)
HOME General Factor	total	.32*	.50*
	Receptive	.24*	.42*
	Expressive	.29*	.44*
HOME Toys	total	.22*	.08
	Receptive	.07	.04
	Expressive	.26*	.09
HOME Maternal Involvement	total	.20*	.31*
	Receptive	.16*	.29*
	Expressive	.19*	.26*
HOME Developmental Advance	total	.27*	.50*
	Receptive	.25*	.44*
	Expressive	.22*	.43*
HOME Restriction–Punishment	total	−.12	−.01
	Receptive	−.14*	−.13*
	Expressive	−.08	.08

*$p < .05$.

HOME factors and the SICD scales are significant in adoptive families, suggesting family environmental influence. However, several of these correlations are significantly higher in the control families than in the adoptive families. For example, the HOME General Factor correlates .32 with the SICD total score in the adoptive homes; in the control homes, the correlation is .50. This suggests that to some significant extent heredity mediates the relationship between HOME scores and SICD scores in control families. This pattern of results does not apply to the HOME Toys or Restriction–Punishment factors.

Videotape Analyses

The Bayley and SICD items by no means provide an exhaustive assessment of the development of communicative behaviors, nor does the HOME provide specific measures of the infant's language-learning environment. For example, the Bayley items do not attempt to evaluate number of vocalizations, the use of request prosody, syllable structure, and communicative gestures. Although the HOME assesses the number of parental vocalizations, other measures of the language-learning environment that could be assessed are type of sentence structure, use of tuitional modeling, contingent vocal responding, and mean length of utterance.

Do these fine-grained measures of communication and language-learning environment yield results different from those described for the Bayley items and the SICD? The answer appears to be affirmative in research that began with a dissertation by Hardy-Brown (1981) involving analyses of videotapes of 50 one-year-old adoptees and their mothers. The CAP videotapes, described in Chapter 4, include 15 min of mother–infant interaction in unstructured, semistructured, and structured situations. At 12 months, the contexts relevant to language are free play, feeding, and mother teaching the infant how to use a pegboard, and these proved to be rich sources of information about individual differences in language development as well as the language-learning environment. For example, on the average, the CAP infants emit about 45 vocalizations, and their mothers vocalize over 200 times. Individual differences are striking: The standard deviation for infant vocalizations is about 25, and the standard deviation for maternal vocalizations is about 80.

Studies of language development have utilized a universals perspective even though individual differences in the development of language are so dramatic (Hardy-Brown, 1983; Nelson, 1981). One practical reason for reluctance to address individual differences is the time-consuming nature of the analyses. Complete analysis of the CAP videotape records for each mother–infant pair at each year requires 8 to 10 hours of transcribing, rating, and scoring for 15 min of videotape. Although 50 adoptive families and 50 control families represent less than a third of the current CAP sample, analyses of data on the 100 families makes this the largest study in the field. Some of the following results have been published previously by Hardy-Brown *et al.* (1981).

Table 8.5 lists the major infant measures and describes means and standard deviations for the adopted and control infants (as reported by Hardy-Brown, 1982). Although the control infants appear to be slightly slower than the adoptees in communicative development, with fewer vocalizations and fewer true words at 12 months, they score higher on a scale of communication items from the Bayley test (items 89, 101, 106, 113, 116, 117, 124, and 126).

Table 8.5 also lists factor loadings of these measures on an unrotated first principal component that accounts for 29% of the variance (Hardy-Brown, 1980). The highest-loading items are maternal reports of a word diary, vocal imitation, and the scale of Bayley items; these are followed by several videotape assessments such as the use of phonetically consistent forms, vocalization context, vocal signals, true words, use of request prosody, and syllable structure. The breadth of this component and the absence of reasonable rotated factors led us to use the unrotated first principal-component score as a measure of infant communicative behavior.

Parent–Offspring Correlations

Correlations between infant communicative behavior and parental cognitive abilities are reported in Table 8.6 (from Hardy-Brown, 1982). In contrast to the results described earlier in this chapter, infant communicative behavior is significantly correlated with parental IQ for the control parents and their infants and for biolog-

TABLE 8.5

Means and Standard Deviations of Measures of 12-Month-Old Communicative Performance
and Loadings on the Unrotated First Principal Component[a]

Measure	Adopted ($N = 50$)		Control ($N = 50$)		Loading on the unrotated first principal component
	$\overline{X}$	SD	$\overline{X}$	SD	
Videotape assessment					
Total vocalizations	50.0	26.7	39.2	23.1	.28
Communicative gestures	7.4	6.9	4.4	3.7	.09
Use of request prosody	yes = 42%		yes = 26%		.44
Vocal imitation	.92	1.6	.86	1.7	.64
Physical imitation	1.0	1.2	.66	1.0	.36
Use of phonetically consistent forms	yes = 42%		yes = 38%		.58
Syllable structure					.44
c, v, or shrieks	28.0	16.7	24.4	16.4	
cv, vc, cvc	15.4	11.3	9.2	7.4	
cvcv, vcvc	3.0	3.5	3.0	3.4	
compounds	3.5	3.1	1.6	3.0	
Vocal signals	17.4	12.8	17.3	11.6	.46
True words	3.0	3.8	.76	1.9	.46
Vocalization context					.52
"objects"	22.4	13.9	19.0	14.8	
"persons"	23.7	14.6	17.6	10.1	
Other CAP assessments					
Productive word diary	4.7	3.1	3.3	2.4	.74
Bayley scale of communication items	2.4	1.3	3.2	1.5	.59

[a]Data from Hardy-Brown, 1980, 1982; Hardy-Brown, Plomin, and DeFries, 1981.

TABLE 8.6

Parent–Offspring Correlations Between Infant Communicative Behavior At 12 Months and Cognitive
Abilities of Biological, Adoptive, and Control Parents[a]

Parental measure	Correlation				
	Biological mother ($N = 50$)	Adoptive		Control	
		Mother ($N = 50$)	Father ($N = 50$)	Mother ($N = 50$)	Father ($N = 50$)
IQ	.36*	−.15	.07	.31*	.29*
Spatial	.19	.01	.13	.24*	−.01
Verbal	−.08	−.01	.21	.20	.18
Perceptual Speed	.22	−.19	−.22	−.05	.32*
Memory	.29*	−.14	−.07	−.06	.18

[a]Data from Hardy-Brown, 1982.
*$p < .05$.

ical mothers and their adopted-away offspring. The infant measure does not predict specific cognitive abilities of the parents. Most notably, the correlation for control parents' verbal ability is nonsignificant, and for biological mothers the correlation is −.08. No significant correlations emerged in comparisons between the adopted infants' communicative behavior and their adoptive parents' cognitive abilities. For parental IQ, the midparent–offspring correlation for adoptive parents is −.06, which is significantly lower than the midparent–offspring correlation of .42 for control parents.

The genetic relationships reported in Table 8.6 are among the strongest observed in the CAP infancy data. In fact, the biological mother–adoptee correlation is too large to fit a reasonable developmental genetic model. Given that the heritability of parental IQ is about .50, both the genetic correlation and heritability of infant communicative behavior must be about 1.0 to produce a biological mother–adoptee correlation of .36. If, however, the heritabilities of adult IQ and infant communicative behavior are both about .50, the biological mother–adoptee correlation should not exceed .25, even if the genetic correlation between infant communicative behavior and adult IQ is almost 1.0.

Thus, the results of this intensive analysis of data on 50 adopted and 50 control 12-month-old infants suggest quite substantial genetic continuity between infant communicative performance and adult IQ. Why do these results differ from those described earlier for Bayley items and factors even though a scale consisting of the Bayley communication items loads highly on the principal component derived from the measures of infant communicative behavior? We suggest that the resolution to this seemingly paradoxical result lies in the possibility that the videotaped data and the Bayley items provide different information; the correlation of the Bayley communication scale with the communicative behavior factor (factor loading) is .59, which leaves substantial room for additional contributions by the videotaped data. The relevant Bayley items used in these analyses at 12 months are Responds to verbal request, Jabbers expressively, Imitates words, Says two words, Uses gestures to make wants known, Shows shoes or other clothing or own toy, Names one object (ball, watch, pencil, scissors, cup), and Follows directions with doll. These Bayley items do not assess other facets of the infant communicative behavior factor such as the use of phonetically consistent forms, vocalization context, vocal signals, use of request prosody, and syllable structure.

Earlier, we reported that a scale based on all of the 12-month Bayley verbal items yields evidence for genetic influence in its relationship with adult IQ, although we suggested that this result is not specific to the verbal items but rather reflects nonspecific results for the Bayley MDI as a whole. Similarly, the SICD does not predict parental cognitive abilities when the Bayley MDI is partialed out. Because the infant communicative behavior factor includes the Bayley verbal items, it is important to ask the extent to which scores on the communicative factor are correlated with adult IQ independently of the Bayley verbal items. We therefore computed the parent–offspring correlations between this infant measure and parental IQ when the effect of Bayley verbal items is partialed out. The parent–offspring correlations reported in Table 8.6 were lowered only slightly—from .36 to .28 for biological mothers and from .31 to .25 and .29 to .25 for control mothers and fathers, respectively. This supports the hypothesis that the videotape analyses assess genetic precursors of adult IQ at 12 months of age that are independent of the processes assessed by the Bayley items.

The Relationship between Language and Mental Development

These results have important implications for understanding the developmental relationship between individual differences in language and in cognition. Although the issue is usually considered at the level of universals for the human species (e.g., Harris, 1983), recasting the issue in terms of individual differences leads to an interesting question: To what extent are rates of language acquisition related to rates of mental development? If infants who develop more rapidly than others in terms of nonverbal mental functions are also more advanced linguistically, then one could argue that language development depends upon cognitive development or, more likely, that they both depend upon a third factor.

As we have seen, various measures of language acquisition in the CAP are substantially correlated with Bayley MDI scores. These data are not particularly useful, because the Bayley MDI involves language items. However, the Lewis–Enright Lexical and Verbal scales also correlate significantly with nonverbal scales based on Bayley items, although the magnitude of the correlations is low (about .20). The results reported by Baker (1983) that we discussed earlier suggest that Bayley verbal items overlap both phenotypically and genetically with nonverbal items. Taken together, these data imply that individual differences in rates of language acquisition and mental development are to some extent related. Of course, we cannot conclude that one causes the other, because "both domains may be influenced by some hitherto unexamined third variable, such as environmental stimulation; or, more likely, the two domains may share a common skill that is ignored by the hypothesis under scrutiny" (Harris, 1983, p. 763). CAP data suggest that unexamined third variables underlying the relationship between language ac-quisition and mental development are neither environmental stimulation nor com-mon skills. Both language acquisition and Bayley MDI scores in infancy are related to adult IQ. They are not related to parental specific cognitive abilities; most notably, they are not related to verbal ability. Furthermore, the significant correla-tions of biological parents' IQ with language and mental development of their adopted-away offspring indicate that the continuity between infancy and adulthood is mediated genetically. Thus, these data suggest that a common factor shared by language measures and Bayley MDI scores is a genetic *g* factor involving processes in infancy that are genetically related to adult IQ.

Environment–Infant Correlations

Language-learning environment—including total vocalizations, sentence types, vocal imitation of the infant, communicative gestures, tuitional modeling of lan-

TABLE 8.7

Videotape Assessments of Language-Learning Environment: Means, Standard Deviations, and Correlations with Infant Communicative Behavior

Maternal measure	Adoptive (N = 50)		Control (N = 50)		Correlation	
	$\overline{X}$	SD	$\overline{X}$	SD	Adoptive	Control
Vocalizations	220.5	75.2	227.7	83.1	−.09	.01
Sentence types						
Single word utterances	26.6	14.8	41.3	21.3	.06	.16
Imperatives	49.1	31.6	52.1	32.0	−.11	−.05
Declaratives	53.0	27.4	51.6	24.3	−.07	.11
Questions	44.9	24.7	38.7	24.5	.24*	−.22
Wh- questions	10.3	7.4	8.0	6.7	.22	.02
Yes-no questions	24.9	13.4	23.9	15.7	−.01	−.10
Imitation of infant vocalizations	2.5	3.0	2.0	2.9	.19	.29*
Contingent vocal responsivity (%)	25.0	14.0	21.5	14.7	−.11	.23*
Tuitional modeling of language	13.9	11.2	13.3	10.2	.10	.15
Mean length of utterance	3.5	0.5	3.7	0.7	−.04	−.19
Communicative gestures	16.3	10.1	12.4	8.7	−.12	−.10
Self-repetition (%)	26.2	8.3	25.9	7.8	.15	−.10

*$p < .05$.

guage, contingent vocal responding, mean length of utterance, types of questions, and type of self-repetition—was also assessed from the videotapes of mother–infant interaction (Hardy-Brown, 1981; Hardy-Brown et al., 1981). It is interesting that, unlike the various measures of infant communicative behavior, the linguistic environmental measures are not intercorrelated and yield no general principal component.

Table 8.7 lists the means and standard deviations of the environmental measures and their correlations with infant communicative behavior (from Hardy-Brown, 1982). In general, no significant and systematic relationships emerged. Only 3 of the 26 correlations are significant. However, maternal imitation of infant vocalizations is significant in control families and marginally significant in adoptive families. The other 2 significant correlations involve correlations of reversed signs in the adoptive and control families and are thus attributed to chance.

In addition to examining these measures of the language-learning environment derived from assessments of videotaped interactions, we analyzed the relationship between infant communicative behavior at 12 months and other environmental measures such as time reading books with the infant, presence of an older sibling in the family, and parental education and occupation. Here again, no significant and systematic pattern of results was observed in the adoptive and control families. However, one relationship is worth mentioning even though it involves nonsignificant correlations: Time spent reading books with the infant yields a correlation of .16 in the control homes and .18 in the adoptive homes.

Although other studies have reported relationships between measures of the language-learning environment and infants' verbal development, these studies frequently involve large correlation matrices and small samples. For example, five of the most frequently cited studies had samples of 3, 7, 15, 16, and 18 (Hardy-Brown, 1983). The CAP results based on a reasonably representative sample of 100 one-year-olds lead us to conclude that variability in language-learning environments is generally unrelated to individual differences in language acquisition at 12 months of age.

Attention to Novel Stimuli

One advance in identifying infant precursors of later cognitive ability has resulted from Fagan's research on novelty preference using a recognition memory paradigm (Fagan, 1982, 1984; Fagan & Singer, 1983):

> To predict later intelligence, the task is to tap processes during infancy which are similar in kind to processes known to be related to later intelligence. On later intelligence tests, children are asked, for example, to discriminate among stimuli, to retain new information, to identify similarities, and to categorize. Over the last decade, methodological advances and empirical studies in the field of infant visual perception and recognition memory have made it possible to ask an infant to exhibit discrimination, retention, identification, and categorization. (Fagan, 1982, p. 22)

The technique is based on the observation that infants tend to gaze longer at novel stimuli than at familiar ones. The key to the technique was Fantz's (1964) insight that infants must be able to perceive and remember a stimulus in order to treat it as familiar. The method used by Fagan involves a box in which stimuli are presented to the infant and a peephole in the box through which the tester views the corneal reflection of the infants' pupils to record how long an infant gazes at a target stimulus—for example, a photo of a face. The stimulus is displayed until the infant has looked at it for a specified time during the training period. Later in the session, the target stimulus is presented again, this time paired with another stimulus. The length of time that the infant looks at each of the two stimuli or at neither stimulus is recorded; differential looking time is used as the measure of novelty preference.

With increasing age, infants are able to distinguish between pairs of stimuli with fewer distinguishing features. In addition to displaying finer discriminations, older infants need relatively less time to study a target stimulus before being able to recognize it as familiar (Fagan, 1974). At 5 months, as little as 4 sec of prior study time are needed to differentiate a novel from a target stimulus when the stimuli vary widely. Furthermore, with increasing age, infants are able to retain visual information for longer periods of time and such retention is not easily disrupted. For example, Fagan (1973) found that infants 5 and 6 months of age recognized after 2 days which member of a pair of abstract stimuli they had originally studied even when the stimuli differed only in patterning. A second experiment reported by Fagan (1973) demonstrated delayed recognition of photos of faces by 5-month-old infants after a 2-week interval. Findings such as these have now been replicated by several other investigators (reviewed by Fagan, 1984).

The complex cognitive processes that can be assessed with this task led Fagan to consider its use as a probe for mental ability in infancy. Previous research showed strong relationships with age and discrimination between retarded and normal infants. Twelve follow-up studies yielded a mean correlation of .44 between recognition memory performance at 3 to 7 months and IQ scores at 2 to 7 years of age (Fagan, in press). Moreover, these correlations very likely underestimate the predictive value of infant recognition memory tests because of restriction of range and the low reliability of the tests due to the small number of stimuli upon which the infant memory scores were based.

Fagan (in press) suggests that:

> The discovery that intelligence is continuous from infancy also has implications for the questions of the contribution of genetic endowment and environmental circumstance to intellectual functioning. In general, tests of infant intelligence based on recognition memory should allow a more accurate determination of the relative influence of genetics and environment on intelligence from infancy to adulthood. Estimates of genetic and environmental influences on infant intelligence are currently based on tests of sensori-motor functioning, tests which are not predictive of later intelligence.

Some support for this hypothesis comes from a study of the offspring of highly intelligent parents who were compared with offspring of women of average intelligence (Fantz & Nevis, 1967). This longitudinal study suggested that a preference for novelty is exhibited earlier by the offspring of highly intelligent parents.

A collaborative project with Joseph Fagan began in 1981 with support from the Spencer Foundation to test the remaining infants in the CAP using newly developed stimuli for infant recognition memory at 5 and 7 months of age. Parent–offspring correlations between infant recognition memory scores (combined for 5- and 7-month testing in order to increase their reliability) and adult cognitive ability scores in control families are presented in Table 8.8 (previously reported by Thompson & Fagan, 1983). The results indicate positive correlations between the infant scores and parental IQ: The correlations for control mothers and fathers are .13 and .30,

TABLE 8.8

Parent–Offspring Correlations between Infant Novelty Preference Scores and Parental Cognitive Abilities in Control Families[a]

	Correlation		
Parental measure	Midparent ($N = 31$)	Mother ($N = 31$)	Father ($N = 31$)
IQ	.25	.13	.30[*]
Spatial	.29[*]	.21	.27
Verbal	−.03	.01	−.05
Perceptual Speed	.16	−.03	.29
Memory	−.03	−.01	−.03

[a]Infant scores combined for 5- and 7-month testing. Data from Thompson and Fagan, 1983.

[*]$p < .05$.

respectively, and the midparent correlation is .25. The infant recognition memory scores also are positively correlated with parental spatial ability; however, they are not systematically correlated with other parental specific cognitive abilities.

These preliminary CAP analyses of the relationship between attention to novel stimuli in infancy and adult cognitive abilities suggest that Fagan's measure may predict adult IQ and that the relationship between infant novelty preference and adult IQ involves a familial component. When a sufficient number of adoptive families have been tested, it will be possible to assess the extent to which genetic factors account for this familial component.

Summary

In this chapter, we have examined two areas of cognitive development for which measurement does not rely upon the Bayley test: language–communication measures and Fagan's measure of attention to novel stimuli. We began with a review of the CAP results involving the Bayley language items: analyses of the items themselves, analyses of scales derived from factor analyses of the Bayley items, and analyses of a verbal scale that includes all language–communication items on the Bayley test. Results of the first two analyses provide little evidence for genetic influence on language acquisition. However, the relationship between the HOME scales and the factorially derived verbal scales is mediated genetically as well as environmentally. The third type of analysis, involving a verbal scale consisting of all Bayley language–communication items, suggests genetic influence, although the effect appears to be general for cognitive development rather than specific to language acquisition.

CAP results for the Sequenced Inventory of Communication Development at 24 months of age yield results similar to those for the Bayley verbal scale. The SICD correlates with parental IQ and with parental spatial and verbal abilities; both heredity and shared family environment are implicated in the relationship. However, partialing out the Bayley MDI total score vitiates the relationships between the SICD and the parental cognitive abilities, thus suggesting that the SICD contributes little to parent–offspring correlations beyond that which is already attributable to the Bayley test.

In contrast, fine-grained analyses of language acquisition from videotaped mother–infant interactions for a sample of 50 adopted and 50 control 12-month-olds suggest substantial genetic influence. Infant communicative behavior is significantly related to parental IQ for biological parents and control parents, but not to parental verbal ability. Moreover, the parent–offspring correlations are not diminished when the Bayley MDI score is partialed out. These results suggest that infant communicative behavior is genetically related to adult IQ and imply that communicative and cognitive development are virtually isomorphic. Analyses of measures of the language-learning environment suggest that variability in these measures in middle-class homes is generally unrelated to individual differences in language acquisition at 12 months of age.

The second type of cognitive measure explored in this chapter is attention to novel stimuli. Fagan adapted an infant recognition memory task to assess individual differences in infants' ability to discriminate, categorize, and retain information as early as 3 months of age. Fagan's measure at 3 to 7 months of age correlates .44 with IQ from 2 to 7 years of age. Preliminary CAP results using this measure at 5 and 7 months of age for 31 control families yield a midparent–offspring correlation of .25 between infant novelty preference and parental IQ.

In the present and previous chapters, cognitive measures obtained in the CAP have been emphasized. Personality and temperament measures are discussed in the following two chapters.

9

Personality and Temperament: Background and Descriptive Data

Introduction

If you ask parents about the ways in which their children differ, their answers are not likely to refer to general mental development or specific cognitive abilities such as memory, spatial ability, or language (other than the age at which the first words were spoken). They will describe behavioral differences of another sort: Some children are remarkably easygoing, rarely becoming upset; others are so easily upset that any new situation invites distress; some are content to sit still; other dynamos electrify even the most tranquil situations, such as the back seat of an automobile; some play happily by themselves for hours on end; other socialites are happy only in the presence of others. These examples of emotionality, activity, and sociability are part of the enormous domain of behavior that includes all personality traits.

Personality

Although everyone knows what personality is, no adequate definition exists. Dictionary definitions refer to the sum total of the characteristics of an individual. In the East, the term is used in this global way (Mangan, 1982). In the West, however, personality refers to individual differences in characteristics other than traits such as mental, sensory, and motoric abilities. This leaves an incredible amount of behavior to study, and dozens of personality traits have been proposed—including such diverse dispositions as sensation-seeking, masculine–feminine, and the hard-driving "type A" personality that is said to be related to heart attacks. Each of the dozens of personality traits could turn out to be as complex as intelligence, and, in many ways, they are more difficult to study. For example, personality is more difficult to measure: Because intelligence involves reasoning and problem-solving skills, problems can be posed and solutions recorded; for personality, however, there are no right or wrong answers, nor is there a single class of stimuli (such as problems to be solved) that elicits behaviors that can be used to index personality. For intelligence, scholastic achievement has been used as a validation criterion; for personality, no validation criteria exist. Furthermore, tests of intelligence intercorrelate highly and thus permit comparisons among studies; with the possible exception of extraversion and neuroticism, two "super-factors" studied for 35 years by Eysenck (1947, 1967, 1983), the field of personality has no such general factor to draw researchers together. Extraversion (essentially sociability) and neuroticism (essentially emotionality) account for a substantial amount of the variance in responses to self-report personality questionnaires, are virtually identical to the first two second-order factors that emerge from the other major system of personality developed by Raymond Cattell (Cattell *et al.*, 1970; Royce, 1973), and appear to be the two most heritable facets of personality (Loehlin, 1982).

During the 1970s, a malaise settled over the field of personality, brought on to some extent by a chronic lack of progress in surmounting these difficulties. The acute cause of the malaise was a book by Walter Mischel (1968), *Personality and Assessment,* which attacked the concept of traits—the heart of personality research. Traits are collections of individual differences in responses that show consistency across time and across situations. Mischel argued that there is much less consistency across situations than trait theorists suppose. He rejected self-report questionnaire data—the mainstay of personality research—because he felt that such data represent mental constructions of traits rather than accurate reflections of behavior. For this reason, Mischel's argument rests on laboratory assessments of personality, which often show substantial situational specificity; for example, children who are honest in one situation are not especially likely to be honest in another. Furthermore, the correlation between self-report questionnaire scores and laboratory assessments is often in the vicinity of .30, a value that Mischel dubbed the "personality coefficient."

The issues raised by Mischel have dominated the field since 1970, resulting in hundreds of articles and several books (e.g., Magnusson & Endler, 1977). At first, the research showed the importance of context in laboratory settings; later, studies suggested that traits, situations, and trait-by-situation interactions can all be shown to account for significant variance in personality.

Most of this research was conducted in the laboratory, and no one seriously questioned Mischel's contention that questionnaire data are invalid. However, an important development in the past few years is the recognition that the reason for the low correlations between self-report and laboratory assessments is that laboratory assessments—not the self-report questionnaire data—are often invalid and unreliable. Laboratory situations often cut such a thin slice of behavior that there is no hope of obtaining measurements that will show consistency across time and situations. Laboratory measures are often analogous to one item on a questionnaire. Questionnaires, however, sample responses across time and across many situations and thus yield trait assessments that are often stable across time and situations. The major proponent of this view has been Seymour Epstein (1980, 1983), who has emphasized the need to aggregate laboratory assessments made at different times in a variety of situations. Epstein found that one-time laboratory measures are seldom reliable in the test–retest sense; however, aggregation of several laboratory assessments results in improved reliabilities and higher correlations with self-report measures (see also Rushton *et al.*, 1983).

Temperament

While the study of adult personality was suffering its decade of self-doubt, the study of personality in children enjoyed an exhilarating decade of escalating enthusiasm. Hiding behind an alias, temperament, the field managed to ignore the problems plaguing the study of adult personality. The excitement was enhanced by multidisciplinary contributions from pediatric, infancy, and personality researchers. Pediatric researchers were interested in behavioral problems in infancy and in the possibility of isolating predictors of later adjustment problems. Infancy researchers extended their laboratory studies beyond perception and cognition to include social–emotional development. Personality researchers thought that their research might yield more definitive results if they studied the unadorned foundations of personality in young children rather than studying personality in adults. For all three groups, two general developmental trends added to the interest in temperament: the tendency to view the child as an active participant with the environment, reinforcing environmental agents and modifying the impact of the environment; and a shift from exclusive reliance on environmental explanations of development to a more balanced perspective that recognizes the possibility of biological influences.

However, this multidisciplinary convergence of interest in personality development in young children has been offset by a divergence of perspectives, methodologies, and criteria. Because pediatric researchers are primarily interested in predicting adjustment problems, they tend to use interviews to assess temperament. Infancy researchers are interested in arousal phenomena, which they study in the laboratory. Personality researchers are primarily concerned with distinguishing temperament from the rest of personality and usually employ parental rating questionnaires in their research.

The best-known approach to temperament is the pediatric research of Thomas and Chess (1977), whose pioneering infancy-to-adulthood New York Longitudinal Study (NYLS) marks the beginning of the modern era of temperament research. The NYLS is known for its nine dimensions of temperament (activity, rhythmicity, approach, adaptability, intensity of reaction, threshold of responsiveness, quality of mood, distractibility, and attention span–persistence), for its emphasis on a global dimension of difficultness, and for the widely used parental rating questionnaires based on this approach that have been developed by Carey and his colleagues (Carey & McDevitt, 1978; Fullard, McDevitt, & Carey, 1978; Hegvik, McDevitt, and Carey, 1982).

In their early writing and in some later material, Thomas and Chess (1977) concur in the general opinion that the origins of temperament lie in constitutional factors: "Temperamental individuality is well established by the time the infant is two to three years old. The origins of temperament must therefore be sought in the factors reviewed in this chapter: genetic, prenatal, and early postnatal parental influences" (pp. 152–153). However, Thomas and Chess have generally down-played genetic or constitutional origins of temperament and have opted for an "interactionist" position that temperament is inextricably intertwined in interactions with the environment. Rather than emphasizing genetic origins as the hallmark of temperament, Thomas and Chess (1977) suggest that "temperament can be equated with the term *behavioral style*. Each refers to the *how* rather than the *what* (abilities and content) or the *why* (motivation) of behavior" (p. 9). However, many dimensions of personality (e.g., femininity) are stylistic but are not considered to be temperaments, and several of the nine NYLS temperaments (e.g., mood) involve content as well as style (Buss & Plomin, 1984).

Other theories have been developed by infancy and personality researchers. Several infancy researchers have proposed theories (Coll, Kagan, & Reznick, 1984; Goldsmith & Campos, 1982; Rothbart & Derryberry, 1981) that generally focus on infant arousal (Buss & Plomin, 1984). The only theory of temperament developed by personality researchers is that of Buss and Plomin (1975, 1984).

Aside from their united interest in early appearing personality traits, these theories of temperament have, on the surface at least, little in common. Although they tend to mention Allport's (1937) definition of temperament as personality traits that are hereditary in origin, most theorists shy away from explicit statements concerning the origins of temperament and prefer interactionist explanations. Nevertheless, at the 1980 Temperament Research Symposium in New Haven, a definition of temperament modeled after Allport's received considerable consensus: "Temperament involves those dimensions of personality that are largely genetic or constitutional in origin, exist in most ages and in most societies, show some consistency across situations, and are relatively stable, at least within major developmental eras" (Plomin, 1981, p. 269).

The temperament theory of Buss and Plomin (1984) defines temperament as genetically influenced, early appearing personality traits and suggests that three broad traits meet these criteria: emotionality, activity, and sociability (EAS). Sociability is the key component of extraversion in infancy when the impulsivity facet of adult extraversion is not important; similarly, emotionality is the stripped-down version of adult neuroticism with its anxiety component removed. Activity, although obviously important, is simply not measured in many personality questionnaires for adults, although it is nearly always included in ratings of children. In addition to being related to the adult superfactors of extraversion and neuroticism, the EAS traits also give some orderliness to the diverse approaches to temperament in infancy and early childhood. The infancy researchers' interest in arousal lies in the domain of emotionality. One approach (Coll *et al.*, 1984), for example, focuses on shyness, which involves emotionality in social settings. Similarly, factor analyses of items on NYLS questionnaires yield a major factor of shyness (Buss & Plomin, 1984). The difficultness construct of the NYLS primarily involves emotionality (Bates, 1980), although it also includes other behavioral problems as discussed in Chapter 11.

What do we know about temperament? In terms of measurement, mothers and fathers agree reasonably well (correlations of about .40 to .50) in their ratings of their children (Field & Greenberg, 1982) even when the opportunity for collusion between the parents is attenuated (Lyon & Plomin, 1981). Significant relationships also are found between parental ratings and teacher ratings of children's temperament (Field & Greenberg, 1982; Keogh, 1982). Although only modest relationships have been observed between parental ratings and laboratory observations (reviewed by Plomin, 1983a), few systematic attempts have as yet been made to aggregate responses across situations and time, a step that has proven to be necessary in personality research with adults as described earlier. Thus, there are enough data to conclude that temperament measures show significant concurrent validity—significant does not mean substantial, however. The modest relationships among various sources of information about temperament suggest that an eclectic, multimethod approach is needed (Plomin, 1983a).

Concerning the etiology of temperament, it appears that heredity influences the EAS traits, at least after infancy (Buss & Plomin, 1984). However, this conclusion is based exclusively on twin studies and largely on studies using parental ratings of children's temperament. Adoption studies or studies using laboratory and observational data might yield different results (Plomin, 1981, 1982). Two ongoing longitudinal twin studies of temperament are employing measures other than parental ratings (Goldsmith, 1983; Wilson & Matheny, 1983a).

Concerning the developmental course of temperament, it is clear that there is less stability than originally assumed. In the NYLS, for example, the median year-to-year correlation during infancy and early childhood is only .30; the median correlation from 12 to 24 months is .38. Activity and adaptibility, a dimension related to both sociability and emotionality, show greater stability than do the other NYLS dimensions (Thomas & Chess, 1977). One reason why temperament was expected to be stable is the common misconception that genetically influenced characters do not change. Although genes can contribute to change as well as continuity in development, it does appear that the EAS traits, which show the greatest genetic influence, also show the greatest stability, at least after infancy (Buss & Plomin, 1984). There is, however, a need for more longitudinal data, particularly for the EAS traits and particularly in infancy.

A related issue is the ability of infant temperament to predict later adjustment problems, a major impetus behind clinical interest in temperament. However, the premier study on this topic, the NYLS, has found no relationship between infant temperament and later adjustment, although temperament in childhood begins to become predictive of adjustment (Thomas & Chess, 1982; see also review by Plomin, 1983a).

Finally, little is known about the relationship between temperament and the environment. This is odd, given the frequency with which one reads that the developmental course of temperament is greatly influenced by transactions with the environment. A major new direction for temperament research is the study of the interface between temperament and environment in development. In a review of the effects of early experience on human development, Wachs and Gruen (1982) conclude that this is the highest priority for environmental research:

> Both from basic and applied data it has become increasingly clear that the relationship of early experience to development will be mediated by the nature of the organism on which the experience impinges. Unfortunately, virtually nothing is known about the specific organismic characteristics which mediate differential reactivity to the early environment. (p. 247)

Temperament is likely to be an important component of such organismic characteristics.

Although temperament researchers view the development of temperament in terms of its interaction with the environment, there have been remarkably few studies that measure both temperament and the environment (Buss & Plomin, 1984). If it is true that, despite two decades' intensive work to isolate environmental correlates of mental development, "the discipline is still very much in its infancy" (Wachs & Gruen, 1982, p. 250), then the study of environmental correlates of personality development is still in its neonatal period.

This brief review of personality and temperament research indicates some of the reasons why we made the domain a major focus of the CAP: The CAP's full adoption design provides a needed comparison to the twin studies of temperament; the CAP employs tester ratings and videotaped observations in addition to parental ratings; the CAP is a large, longitudinal study, with over 300 children tested at both 12 and 24 months; its emphasis on environmental assessment provides the unique ability to study relationships between temperament and environment in adoptive homes in which hereditary similarity cannot influence the results; and the inclusion of nonadoptive families facilitates assessment of the impact of heredity on temperament–environment relationships by comparing data on adoptive and nonadoptive families. Because the CAP data set on personality and temperament is so voluminous, we have divided the presentation of these data into two parts. In the remainder of this chapter, we present descriptive data—such as means, variances, and factor structures—for the infant and adult measures. The next chapter focuses on the causes and correlates of individual differences in infancy.

CAP Infant and Adult Measures

In overview, the personality and temperament measures for the infants (described in Chapter 4) include information from three sources. Parental ratings are obtained using the Colorado Childhood Temperament Inventory (CCTI), an amalgamation of the EASI and NYLS approaches to temperament (Rowe & Plomin, 1977). The second source of information is tester ratings of the infants on Bayley's Infant Behavior Record (IBR). The third source is videotaped observations of mother–infant interactions that are rated using a modification of the IBR. For the parents, the CAP data set includes scores on Cattell's 16 PF questionnaire and self-report and mate ratings on the EASI Temperament Survey of Buss and Plomin.

Infant Measures

Factor Structures

As mentioned in Chapter 4, factor analyses of the CAP data at 12 and 24 months largely supported published reports of the factor structures of the CCTI, of tester ratings on the IBR, and of videotape ratings using the modified IBR. The results of exploratory factor analyses for these three measures are described in this section. In general, we present results for the entire sample because few adopted–control or gender differences were observed for means, variances, or covariance structures; chapters 13 and 14 focus on such group differences.

Concerning the factor analysis of the CCTI (see Table 9.1), the results are similar to those reported by Rowe and Plomin (1977) for an older sample, and their published scoring scheme was used to create the six CCTI scales. The CCTI factor structure at 12 and 24 months shows only one item with a loading above .30 on any factor other than the intended one. As mentioned earlier, the CCTI was constructed as a factor analytic amalgamation of the EASI and the NYLS dimensions of temperament. The EASI scales emerged as independent factors; however, the NYLS items contributed only to two factors, Soothability and Reaction to Foods, which are discussed in Chapter 11.

Table 9.2 contains the loadings that resulted from a Varimax rotation of the 25 items of the IBR that are 5- and 9-point rating scales. At both 12 and 24 months, the CAP data replicate the three major factors reported by Matheny (1980): Affect–Extraversion, Activity, and Task Orientation. The Affect–Extraversion factor is somewhat unusual in that it conveys a dual nature. Half of its name refers to affect because high scores include ratings of *happy* on the emotional tone item. However, this aspect of the factor is better considered as indicative of low emotionality because it includes low fearfulness rated on an item from *no evidence of fear* to *strong indication of fear;* other items also convey a low emotionality component. The other half of the factor is clearly relevant to extraversion or sociability as expressed in a testing situation. We summed the highest-loading IBR items reported by Matheny to produce scale scores. At both 12 and 24 months, using twin data from the Louisville Twin Study, Matheny (1980) reported heritabilities greater than .50 for Affect–Extraversion and Task Orientation; although heritability was negligible for Activity at 12 months, it too was substantial at 24 months.

The videotapes of mother–infant interactions were rated for seven items using a

TABLE 9.1 Factor Loadings of the Colorado Childhood Temperament Inventory (CCTI) at 12 and 24 Months for the Combined Sample[a]

CCTI scale	Item number	Descriptor	12 Months						24 Months					
			Emo	Act	Soc	AtSp	Sooth	RF	Emo	Act	Soc	AtSp	Sooth	RF
Emotionality (Emo)	2.	Cries easily	.67						.73					
	15.	Often fusses	.66						.70					
	9.	Somewhat emotional	.64						.54					
	24.	Upset easily	.64											
	28.	Reacts intensely when upset	.57						.44					
Activity (Act)	3.	Always on the go		.73						.76				
	20.	Very energetic		.66						.79				
	10.	Moves slowly		-.60						-.61				
	27.	Prefers quiet, inactive games		-.55						-.54				
	14.	Off and running when wakes up		.52						.42				
Sociability (Soc)	30.	Very friendly with strangers			.89						.88			
	23.	Slow to warm up to strangers			-.80						-.88			
	19.	Very sociable			.78						.75			
	1.	Tends to be shy			-.76						-.81			
	11.	Makes friends easily			.71						.72			
Attention Span (AtSp)	5.	Gives up easily				.74						.79		
	4.	Persists at a task				-.73						-.77		
	17.	With a difficult toy, gives up				.64						.80		
	21.	Plays with a single toy for long												
	8.	Goes from toy to toy quickly												
Soothability (Sooth)	12.	Easily distracted when starts crying					.64						.75	
	16.	If talked to, stops crying					.61						.68	
	26.	Stopped fussing when picked up					.55						.60	
	7.	When upset, quickly calms down					.48						.47	
	22.	Tolerates frustration well	-.54						-.44			-.32		
Reactions to Foods (RF)	6.	Consistently dislikes many foods						.81						.84
	25.	Strong likes and dislikes in food						.74						.74
	18.	Rarely takes new food without fuss						.70						.72
	29.	Makes faces at new foods						.61						.66
	13.	Once dislikes, no getting to like it						.31						.50

[a] N = 325; midparent ratings. Only loadings of .30 or more are listed.

TABLE 9.2

Factor Loadings of the Infant Behavior Record at 12 and 24 Months for the Combined Sample[a]

Item placement (Matheny, 1980)	Item number	Descriptor	12 Months			24 Months		
			AfEx	Act	TO	AfEx	Act	TO
Affect–Extraver-	2.	Responsiveness to examiner	.77			.68		
sion (AfEx)	7.	General emotional tone	.65			.82		
	5.	Fearfulness	−.63			−.67		
	4.	Cooperativeness	.61			.82		
	13.	Endurance	.36			.63		
	6.	Tension		.46		−.57		
Activity (Act)	14.	Activity		.83			.82	
	21.	Body motion		.82			.81	
	25.	Level of energy		.65			.64	
	19.	Producing sounds—banging						
Task Orientation	8.	Responsiveness to objects			.78			.71
(TO)	12.	Attention span			.78			.76
	11.	Goal directedness			.65			.58
	15.	Reactivity						

[a]N = 335. Only loadings of .30 or more are listed.

modified version of an IBR-like instrument developed by Matheny and Wilson (1981). The average item intercorrelations among the four videotape situations at 12 months (free play, roughhouse, feeding, teaching) and the three situations at 24 months (free play, dollhouse play, teaching) are listed in Table 9.3. They indicate some consistency across situations for the seven rating items. At 12 months, the free play and teaching situations yield the highest average correlations for the seven items ($r = .37$); at 24 months, the highest correlation ($r = .39$) occurs between the teaching and dollhouse play situations. The positive manifold among the situations permitted aggregation across the situations; sums across the situations for each of

TABLE 9.3

Average Item Intercorrelations among Videotape Situations at 12 and 24 Months[a]

Item	12 Months	24 Months
Emotional tone	.29*	.40*
Attentiveness	.21*	.17*
Activity	.18*	.21*
Locomotion	.20*	.18*
Orientation to parent	.28*	.38*
Cooperativeness	.25*	.35*
Goal directedness	.23*	.37*

[a]N = 228–261.
*$p < .05$.

TABLE 9.4

Factor Loadings of Videotape Rating Items at 12 and at 24 Months[a]

	12 Months			24 Months		
Videotape scale–item	AfEx	Act	TO	AfEx	Act	TO
Affect–Extraversion						
Cooperativeness	.87	—	—	.64	−.44	—
Orientation to parent	.86	—	—	.82	−.41	—
Emotional Tone	.69	—	—	.54	—	—
Activity						
Locomotion	—	.67	—	—	.54	—
Task Orientation						
Goal directedness	—	—	.63	—	—	.74
Activity	—	—	.67	—	—	.68
Attentiveness	.53	−.35	.53	—	−.61	.40

[a]$N = 228-261$. Only loadings of .30 or more are listed.

the seven items were submitted to factor analysis. The unrotated first principal component accounted for 41% of the variance at 12 months and 45% of the variance at 24 months. This general factor replicates the unrotated principal component derived from videotape ratings in the work of Wilson and Matheny (1983a).

The rotated factor structures at 12 and at 24 months for the seven items are described in Table 9.4. The factors at 12 and 24 months are reasonably similar to the IBR factors, although the Activity factor consists solely of locomotion; an activity item involving self-initiated activity was expected to load on the Activity factor, but appeared instead as part of the Task Orientation factor. Videotape scales of Affect–Extraversion, Activity, and Task Orientation were constructed by summing scores on the items as indicated in Table 9.4.

Means and Standard Deviations

Considering adopted and control boys and girls at 12 and at 24 months, multivariate analysis-of-variance procedures revealed no significant mean differences for gender or adopted–control status. The few significant univariate mean differences are considered in Chapters 13 and 14. Cochran's C and Bartlett's Box F yielded no more than a chance number of significant departures from homogeneity of variance. A multivariate test for the homogeneity of dispersion matrices was nonsignificant, indicating that the variance–covariance structures for the adopted and control boys and girls are similar.

The means and standard deviations for the infant measures for the entire sample are presented in Table 9.5. Both mothers and fathers rate their children's temperament on the CCTI at 12 and 24 months; the median correlation between the spouses for the four CCTI scales is .42 at both 12 and 24 months. The parental agreement for Sociability is significantly higher than for other traits, .67 at 12 months and .59 at 24 months. In accord with our general principle of aggregating data whenever

TABLE 9.5

Means and Standard Deviations for Infant Temperament Measures

Measure	12 Months			24 Months		
	N	$\overline{X}$	SD	N	$\overline{X}$	SD
CCTI						
Emotionality	329	12.4	3.2	333	13.4	3.0
Activity	322	21.1	2.6	322	21.2	2.3
Sociability	323	19.5	3.7	333	19.6	3.5
Attention Span	317	17.3	2.2	318	17.7	2.6
IBR						
Affect–Extraversion	337	35.4	5.0	342	35.6	6.5
Activity	332	17.7	3.0	344	16.2	3.4
Task Orientation	335	21.9	3.3	341	23.6	3.1
Videotape						
Affect–Extraversion	251	18.0	1.9	267	18.2	1.8
Activity	251	3.5	1.0	267	3.4	0.8
Task Orientation	248	12.6	1.9	266	16.4	1.9

possible, midparent CCTI ratings are used in all analyses. The CCTI data in Table 9.5 are similar in all respects to those published by Rowe and Plomin (1977): Means are similar even though the CAP sample consists of infants rather than young children and singletons rather than twins; standard deviations are similar when one takes into account the reduced variance caused by use of midparent ratings rather than ratings by each parent; and no age effect can be detected.

No comparison data are available for the CAP means and standard deviations for the tester ratings on the IBR or for videotape ratings using the modified IBR. Again, with the exception of Task Orientation, differences between 12 and 24 months are negligible.

Intercorrelations

Table 9.6 lists intercorrelations among the infant temperament measures at 12 and at 24 months of age. These correlations are in fact second-order partial correlations with mean effects of gender and adopted–control status removed, but these correlations seldom differ by more than .01 from the zero-order correlations because gender and adopted–control differences are slight.

Correlations among the CCTI scales are similar to those reported by Rowe and Plomin (1977). For example, significant correlations at both ages are observed for Activity and Sociability.

Correlations among the three IBR factors have not been reported previously, and it is noteworthy that Affect–Extraversion and Task Orientation correlate .44 at 12 months and .36 at 24 months.

Although correlations between tester ratings on the IBR scales and midparent

TABLE 9.6

Intercorrelations among Infant Temperament Measures[a]

Measure	CCTI				IBR			Video		
	Emo	Act	Soc	AtSp	AfEx	Act	TO	AfEx	Act	TO
CCTI										
Emo	—	-.04	-.32*	-.18*	-.16*	.09	.03	-.02	-.02	-.09
Act	.07	—	.25*	.12*	-.05	.07	.05	-.11	.12*	.00
Soc	-.17*	.33*	—	.09	.24*	-.01	-.01	.05	-.01	.11
AtSp	-.17*	.01	.04	—	.11	-.07	.13*	.01	-.06	.05
IBR										
AfEx	-.06	.11	.31*	-.04	—	-.13*	.44*	.23*	-.13*	.19*
Act	.05	.08	.03	-.01	-.04	—	-.11	-.02	.16*	.09
TO	-.04	.03	.18*	.11	.36*	.04	—	.13*	-.05	.32*
Video										
AfEx	-.07	-.08	.17*	.02	.19*	-.05	.16*	—	-.21*	.40*
Act	-.04	.10	.01	.02	.06	.15*	-.01	-.26*	—	-.27*
TO	.03	-.15*	.07	.03	.06	-.08	.06	.57*	-.21*	—

[a] 12-month data above diagonal, 24-month data below diagonal. $N = 302-343$ (correlations involving videotape ratings are based on $N = 228-261$). Correlations are partial correlations with gender and adopted–control status removed.

*$p < .05$.

ratings on the CCTI are low, the differences in the context of the ratings are so great that any significant correlations are noteworthy. Testers complete the IBR ratings on the basis of an hour's observation of the infant in the test situation; in contrast, the CCTI asks parents to rate broad dimensions averaged across time and situations. Despite these differences, IBR Affect–Extraversion at 12 months is significantly correlated with CCTI Emotionality (negatively) and Sociability (positively); also, IBR Task Orientation correlates significantly with CCTI Attention Span. At 24 months, IBR Affect–Extraversion correlates .31 with CCTI Sociability.

The videotape ratings are even more limited than the IBR in that they are based on 15 min of observation; nevertheless, the observations include several situations that were designed to elicit rich samples of behavior. The videotape scales are significantly correlated with the appropriate IBR scales at 12 and 24 months, with the exception of Task Orientation scales at 24 months. As for the IBR, videotape Affect–Extraversion and Task Orientation are significantly correlated at both 12 and 24 months.

At 12 months, the only significant relationship between the videotape ratings and the CCTI scales is for Activity. At 24 months, similar to IBR Affect–Extraversion, videotape Affect–Extraversion is correlated with CCTI Sociability. Although these correlations for both IBR and videotape ratings would suggest Affect–Extraversion is more a matter of extraversion (sociability) than affect (emotionality), it should be noted that CCTI Sociability is in fact a measure of shyness, which includes high emotionality as well as low sociability (Buss & Plomin, 1984).

Aggregation

Wilson and Matheny (1983a) also found low correlations between laboratory-based ratings and parental ratings on the NYLS questionnaire at 12 months. However, aggregation had an important effect: A first principal-component score for the laboratory ratings correlated .52 with a first principal-component score for the parental ratings. In an attempt to aggregate personality measures across situations, we used standardized scores from the parental, tester, and videotape ratings to construct scales: Affect–Extraversion, Activity, and Task Orientation. Even though analogous measures from the parental, tester, and videotape ratings are not in all cases significantly correlated, they can be viewed as measures of a single construct assessed in quite different situations. Aggregating conceptually similar measures across these situations could thus increase the generality of the measure. Aggregate Affect–Extraversion, like shyness, involves low emotionality and high sociability and is the sum of standardized measures of IBR Affect–Extraversion, videotape Affect–Extraversion, and CCTI Emotionality (reversed) and Sociability. Aggregate Activity is the sum of the IBR, videotape, and CCTI Activity, and aggregate Task Orientation consists of CCTI Attention Span and the IBR and videotape Task Orientation scales. These aggregate scores are used in subsequent analyses of parent–infant and environment–infant relationships. Although we could have aggregated 12- and 24-month measures, our interest in developmental changes in relationships and etiologies led us to keep measures at the two ages separate.

Longitudinal Correlations from 12 to 24 Months

Table 9.7 lists correlations between 12 and 24 months for the infant measures and their aggregates. The CCTI midparent ratings show impressive stability, with correlations of .57, .52, and .57 for the major variables of Emotionality, Activity, and Sociability, respectively. These correlations contrast favorably with the median correlation of .38 from the first to the second year reported by Thomas and Chess (1977) for the NYLS interview measures of temperament and the median correlation of .38 reported for the revised Infant Temperament Questionnaire based on the NYLS dimensions (McDevitt & Carey, 1981). The higher CAP stability may be due to the use of broad questions that ask parents to aggregate across responses, situations, and time; it is not due to the aggregation involved in midparent ratings, because the longitudinal correlations for the single-parent ratings are nearly as high as the correlations for the midparent ratings seen in Table 9.7.

The issue of aggregation might also be relevant for the low stability correlations for the IBR and the videotape ratings. Although these factors represent aggregations of behaviors, they are limited in terms of situations. We had hoped that aggregating the CCTI, IBR, and videotape ratings would improve their stability. However, the correlations from 12 to 24 months for the aggregate measures are close to the average of their separate stabilities.

The low stabilities for the IBR and videotape ratings make us less optimistic about finding genetic influences using the CAP parent–offspring design. As discussed in

TABLE 9.7

Correlations for Infant Temperament Measures[a]

Measure	Correlation from 12 to 24 months
CCTI	
Emotionality	.57
Activity	.52
Sociability	.57
Attention Span	.39
IBR	
Affect–Extraversion	.14
Activity	.17
Task Orientation	.10
Videotape	
Affect–Extraversion	.20
Activity	.10
Task Orientation	.04
Aggregate	
Affect–Extraversion	.44
Activity	.27
Task Orientation	.29

[a]$N = 294–330$ (N for videotape ratings = 213–221 and N for aggregates = 179–192).

earlier chapters, it is possible that parental genotype as expressed in adulthood could be correlated with infant genotype at 24 months even in the absence of stability from 12 to 24 months. However, this possibility seems remote. Nonetheless, low stability does not weaken interest in relationships between these measures and the home environment that may have effects upon developmental changes.

Adult Measures

Two approaches have dominated personality research. One is Hans Eysenck's (1967, 1983) "top-down" approach that focuses on two major higher-order factors, extraversion and neuroticism, and also considers component dimensions—for example, extraversion includes sociability and several types of impulsivity (Eysenck, 1983). Raymond Cattell has promulgated the major "bottom-up" approach, beginning with ratings of traits identified by the major adjectives of the English language and using factor analysis to sift through the multitude of dimensions to suggest the 16 major factors that are measured by his 16 Personality Factor Questionnare (16 PF; Cattell *et al.*, 1970). Referring to these two approaches as top-down and bottom-up suggests their complementary nature: the first two second-order factors of the 16 PF are virtually identical to extraversion and neuroticism (Royce, 1973). Our analyses focus on these second-order factors, although we also report data for the primary scales of the 16 PF.

In addition, the CAP adult measures include a version of the EASI Temperament Survey (Buss & Plomin, 1975), which has the advantage of being the only personality questionnaire that has adult and infant versions with similar factor structures. Thus, it permits parent–offspring comparisons for scores that are at least similar in a factorial sense for parents and their infant offspring. Another attractive feature of the EASI is that it has a self-report and "rating-by-other" version with similar factor structures. Thus, in the CAP, we obtain self-report and mate ratings ("mate" rather than "spouse" because the biological parent couples are not spouses) for both mothers and fathers. This feature has two advantages: First, aggregation of "self" and "other" ratings may improve the reliability of the personality ratings. Second, it permits the analysis of a full sample of biological fathers by using the biological mothers' ratings of their mates.

Factor Structures

Exploratory factor analyses yielded structures similar to those published for the 16 PF and the EASI. We report results of second-order factor analyses of the 16 PF scales for males and females separately in Tables 9.8 and 9.9 because the 16 PF

TABLE 9.8

Second-Order Factor Analysis of the 16 PF Questionnaire for Males[a]

| 16 PF Scale[b] | 16 PF placement[c] | Factor loading | | | | |
		Extraversion	Neuroticism	Independence	?	?
A. Outgoing	E+	.58	—	—	—	—
B. Bright		—	—	—	—	—
C. Emotionally Stable	N−	—	−.74	—	—	—
E. Assertive	E+, I+	—	—	.73	—	—
F. Happy-Go-Lucky	E+	.58	—	.36	—	—
G. Conscientious		—	—	—	.74	—
H. Venturesome	E+, N−	.60	—	.48	—	—
I. Tender-Minded		.32	—	—	—	.33
L. Suspicious	N+, I+	—	.48	.33	—	—
M. Imaginative	I+	—	—	—	—	.52
N. Astute		—	—	−.43	—	—
O. Apprehensive	N+	—	.72	—	—	—
Q_1. Experimenting	I+	—	—	.45	—	—
Q_2. Self-Sufficient	E−, I+	−.56	—	—	—	—
Q_3. Controlled	N−	—	−.38	—	.51	—
Q_4. Tense	N+	—	.82	—	—	—

[a]$N = 274$–297. Only loadings of .30 or more are listed.

[b]Rather than using the technical psychological titles (such as sizothymia vs. affectothymia for Factor A), we list the popular translations.

[c]Second-order factors with significant loadings by primary scales (from Table 10.3 in the 16 PF handbook): E = Extraversion, N = Neuroticism, I = Independence. Positive and negative loadings are indicated by + and −.

TABLE 9.9

Second-Order Factor Analysis of the 16 PF Questionnaire for Females[a]

16 PF Scale[b]	16 PF placement[c]	Factor loading				
		Extraversion	Neuroticism	Independence	?	?
A. Outgoing	E+	.44	—	—	—	—
B. Bright		—	—	—	—	—
C. Emotionally Stable	N−	—	−.74	—	—	—
E. Assertive	E+, I+	.35	—	.71	—	—
F. Happy-Go-Lucky	E+	.62	—	—	—	—
G. Conscientious		—	—	—	.75	—
H. Venturesome	E+, N−	.68	—	.44	—	—
I. Tender-Minded		—	—	—	—	.58
L. Suspicious	N+, I+	—	.57	—	—	—
M. Imaginative	I+	—	—	.36	—	.33
N. Astute		—	—	−.36	—	—
O. Apprehensive	N+	—	.63	—	—	—
Q$_1$. Experimenting	I+	—	—	.33	—	—
Q$_2$. Self-Sufficient	E−, I+	−.61	—	—	—	—
Q$_3$. Controlled	N−	—	−.37	—	.54	—
Q$_4$. Tense	N+	—	.75	—	—	—

[a]N = 404–416. See footnotes for Table 9.8.

handbook describes the normative factor analytic results in this manner; however, it is clear that the factor structures for males and females are virtually identical. Following the 16 PF scale names in the tables are the 16 PF placements of the scales, and it can be seen that the CAP loadings correspond well to the 16 PF placements for Extraversion, Neuroticism, and Independence. The remaining two second-order factors with eigenvalues greater than 1.0 each includes only two items with loadings greater than .30; these represent the eighth (Superego Strength) and fifth (Prodigal Subjectivity) second-order factors of the 16 PF. We scored the Extraversion, Neuroticism, and Independence second-order factors as indicated in the administrator's manual for the 16 PF, which weights the primary scales separately for males and females.

Results of the EASI factor analyses are reported in Table 9.10 for self-ratings and Table 9.11 for mate ratings. EASI factors clearly emerge for both males and females and for both types of ratings. As suggested by the EASI theory of temperament, there are two emotionality factors: Emotionality–Fear and Emotionality–Anger, although one of these fear items (number 25) would be better scored as an anger item. The factor structure is not nearly as clear for Impulsivity as it is for the other EASI traits; this reason and the difficulty of conceptualizing impulsivity in infancy led Buss and Plomin (1984) to drop impulsivity from consideration as a temperament trait in a revision of their theory.

Because these factor analyses largely verified the conceptual groups of items from the EASI approach, EASI scales were created as suggested by Buss and

TABLE 9.10

Factor Analyses of the Adult EASI Temperament Survey: Self-Report Ratings[a]

EASI scale	Item number	Descriptor	Males (N = 368)					Females (N = 502)				
			EF	EA	Act	Soc	Imp	EF	EA	Act	Soc	Imp
Emotionality– Fear (EF)	4.	insecure	.38					.44				
	9.	feel like crying	.38	.31				.51				
	14.	easily frightened	.64					.65				
	20.	panic when scared	.43					.50				
Emotionality– Anger (EA)	25.	always calm (−)		−.47					−.42			
	6.	not often mad (−)		−.68					−.66			
	11.	quick-tempered		.64					.67			
	15.	many things annoy		.43				.39	.48			
	19.	let know displeased		.33					.42			
	22.	yell and scream		.52					.48			
Activity (Act)	2.	like to keep busy			.62					.48		
	8.	bursting with energy			.49					.61		
	13.	like exertion			.35					.37		
	18.	do things vigorously			.50					.59		
	21.	usually in a hurry			.49							
Sociability (Soc)	1.	make friends quickly				.73					.80	
	7.	do things alone (−)				−.68						
	12.	sociable				.75					.71	
	16.	have many friends				.67					.75	
	24.	tend to be loner (−)				−.70					−.51	
Impulsivity (Imp)	3.	plan things ahead (−)										
	5.	hard to control			.33		.47			.36		.63
	10.	see things through (−)										
	17.	try anything once										
	23.	impulsive					.54					.62

[a]Only loadings of .30 or more are listed.

188

TABLE 9.11

Factor Analysis of the Adult EASI Temperament Survey: Mate Ratings[a]

EASI scale	Item number	Descriptor	Males (rated by females) (N = 501)					Females (rated by males) (N = 370)				
			EF	EA	Act	Soc	Imp	EF	EA	Act	Soc	Imp
Emotionality—Fear (EF)	4.	insecure	.45					.45				
	9.	feel like crying	.52					.66				
	14.	easily frightened	.62					.57				
	20.	panic when scared	.58					.59				
Emotionality—Anger (EA)	25.	always calm (−)		−.59					−.57			
	6.	not often mad (−)		−.74					−.69			
	11.	quick-tempered		.80					.64			
	15.	many things annoy		.63					.53			
	19.	let know displeased		.55					.48			
	22.	yell and scream		.69					.54			
Activity (Act)	2.	like to keep busy			.61					.76		
	8.	bursting with energy			.73					.65		
	13.	like exertion			.64					.51		
	18.	do things vigorously			.60					.62		
	21.	usually in a hurry		.32	.39					.52		
Sociability (Soc)	1.	make friends quickly				.81					.81	
	7.	do things alone (−)				−.50					−.45	
	12.	sociable				.83					.72	
	16.	have many friends				.70					.70	
	24.	tend to be loner (−)				−.64					−.48	
Impulsivity (Imp)	3.	plan things ahead (−)					−.51					−.35
	5.	hard to control		.56			.43			.36		.50
	10.	see things through (−)					−.49					−.37
	17.	try anything once								.42		
	23.	impulsive		.53			.46					.58

[a]Only loadings of .30 or more are listed.

189

Plomin (1975) using unit weights and summing the scores for the items listed in Tables 9.10 and 9.11.

Means and Variances

Tables 9.12 and 9.13 present means and standard deviations for the 16 PF and EASI measures. Although no norms are available for the form of the EASI that is used in the CAP, 1967 norms are available for the 16 PF. The *Norms for the 16 PF, Forms A and B (1967–68 Edition)* includes norms separately by sex for high-school juniors and seniors (average age of 17) and for the general population (average age of 30). The former norms are the most appropriate comparison for the biological parents; the latter are used for the adoptive and control parents. For all groups, the CAP parents are quite representative of the 16 PF means. The CAP means differed from the norms by more than half a standard deviation for only 9 of 64 comparisons: In comparison with the normative data, biological mothers are less outgoing and more self-sufficient, biological fathers are more self-sufficient, and adoptive and control mothers are more intelligent. Four of the differences involve adoptive and control fathers who, compared to the general population, are less outgoing, more intelligent, more dominant, and more self-sufficient.

The CAP sample also appears to be representative in terms of variances on the 16 PF. Most of the standard deviations are within 10% of the appropriate 16 PF norm. For IQ scores, with a standard deviation of 16, this criterion would mean that the standard deviation would not be less than 14.4 or greater than 17.6. The exceptions for the 16 PF are as follows: Biological mothers are more variable in self-sufficiency; adoptive mothers show less variability on the Conscientious, Tender-Minded, and Experimenting scales; control mothers are less variable in imagination and control; adoptive fathers are less variable in conscientiousness and control and show more variability on the Venturesome scale; and control fathers are less variable in imagination and show more variability on the Venturesome scale. Although standard deviations for 6 of the 16 scales for the biological fathers are not within the ±10% range, 2 are higher and 4 are lower than the normative standard deviations. A ± 20% criterion yielded only one difference: Biological fathers are less variable on the Experimenting scale. The fact that only 12 of the 96 comparisons yield departures from the normative variances—and the fact that those deviations are unsystematic—speaks to the representativeness of the CAP sample with regard to personality.

We used both the 16 PF and EASI data to make comparisons among the three types of parents. For the six groups (mothers and fathers of each of the three types), homogeneity of variance could be rejected for only 6 of the 31 comparisons—1 of the self-report EASI scales, 3 of the EASI mate-rating scales and 2 of the 16 PF scales—which is noteworthy given the power of tests of homogeneity of variance. The heterogeneity of variance is due to the fact that the adoptive parents show less variability on the self-report EASI Sociability and 16 PF Conscientious scales; males are less variable than females on the 16 PF Tender-Minded scale and on the

TABLE 9.12

Means and Standard Deviations for the 16 PF Questionnaire for CAP Parents

	Biological				Adoptive				Control			
	Mother		Father		Mother		Father		Mother		Father	
Measure	$\bar{X}$	SD	$\bar{X}$	SD	$\bar{X}$	SD	$\bar{X}$	SD	$\bar{X}$	SD	$\bar{X}$	SD
Primary scales												
A. Outgoing[a]	9.6	(3.1)	7.6	(2.8)	10.3	(3.3)	7.8	(3.4)	9.4	(2.9)	7.8	(3.3)
B. Bright[b]	8.0	(2.0)	7.8	(2.4)	8.1	(1.9)	8.6	(1.9)	9.1	(1.9)	9.2	(1.8)
C. Emotionally Stable	16.0	(4.0)	15.5	(3.5)	16.5	(3.6)	17.1	(3.7)	15.9	(3.7)	16.7	(3.9)
E. Assertive[a,b]	11.1	(4.1)	14.3	(3.4)	11.3	(4.9)	14.1	(4.2)	12.3	(4.4)	15.8	(4.4)
F. Happy-Go-Lucky[b]	16.4	(4.3)	16.1	(3.6)	14.4	(3.8)	13.2	(4.0)	14.1	(4.1)	14.1	(4.5)
G. Conscientious[b]	11.8	(3.4)	11.6	(3.8)	14.0	(2.8)	14.0	(2.8)	13.0	(3.1)	13.6	(3.4)
H. Venturesome	12.7	(5.7)	13.8	(5.5)	14.6	(4.8)	14.1	(6.0)	13.5	(6.1)	14.6	(6.4)
I. Tender-Minded[a]	13.2	(2.7)	9.1	(3.3)	14.2	(2.8)	8.2	(3.4)	13.6	(3.2)	8.6	(3.8)
L. Suspicious[a,b]	8.0	(3.1)	10.0	(3.2)	6.6	(3.1)	7.6	(3.5)	6.9	(3.1)	7.6	(3.7)
M. Imaginative[b]	11.7	(3.5)	11.2	(4.0)	12.1	(3.7)	13.0	(3.3)	13.1	(3.4)	13.5	(2.7)
N. Astute[a]	9.5	(2.5)	8.8	(2.3)	9.2	(2.9)	8.3	(2.7)	9.1	(2.9)	8.1	(2.9)
O. Apprehensive[a,b]	12.1	(3.7)	10.6	(4.2)	10.4	(4.0)	8.1	(3.8)	10.7	(3.7)	8.6	(4.1)
Q₁. Experimenting[a,b]	8.3	(2.7)	10.5	(2.2)	6.3	(2.6)	8.8	(3.1)	7.7	(3.0)	9.6	(3.3)
Q₂. Self-Sufficient[a]	10.8	(3.8)	11.9	(3.0)	11.0	(3.7)	11.7	(3.3)	12.4	(3.6)	12.4	(3.6)
Q₃. Controlled[b]	11.7	(3.0)	11.7	(2.6)	13.5	(2.9)	14.0	(2.7)	12.9	(2.7)	12.8	(3.1)
Q₄. Tense[a,b]	14.2	(4.4)	13.7	(4.4)	13.2	(4.8)	11.4	(5.0)	14.8	(4.5)	12.2	(5.1)
Second-order factors												
Q₁. Extraversion	47.7	(17.5)	53.3	(13.2)	58.7	(17.7)	51.2	(17.4)	54.7	(19.4)	51.8	(17.1)
Q₁₁. Neuroticism	52.4	(18.1)	57.0	(14.1)	54.3	(18.2)	53.4	(16.3)	55.9	(16.3)	55.2	(16.5)
Q₁ᵥ. Independence[a,b]	53.8	(16.0)	57.0	(11.7)	52.8	(15.2)	59.6	(14.6)	59.2	(16.0)	63.2	(16.2)
N 16 PF Primary scales	162–164		37–38		134–136		134–153		139–140		131–132	
N 16 PF Second-order factors	152–154		36		126–128		129–130		116–118		131–135	

[a]Significant gender difference ($p < .01$).

[b]Significant difference among biological, adoptive, and control parents ($p < .01$).

TABLE 9.13

Means and Standard Deviations for the EASI Temperament Survey for CAP Parents

| | Biological | | | | Adoptive | | | | Control | | | |
| | Mother | | Father | | Mother | | Father | | Mother | | Father | |
Measure	$\bar{X}$	SD	$\bar{X}$	SD	$\bar{X}$	SD	$\bar{X}$	SD	$\bar{X}$	SD	$\bar{X}$	SD
EASI (self-rating)												
Emotionality–Fear[a,b]	13.8	(3.8)	11.7	(2.7)	12.5	(3.1)	10.4	(2.6)	13.1	(3.4)	10.2	(2.9)
Emotionality–Anger	12.1	(3.8)	13.0	(3.3)	11.6	(3.3)	11.4	(3.4)	11.8	(3.8)	11.7	(3.3)
Activity	15.9	(3.0)	17.6	(3.6)	16.9	(3.1)	17.2	(3.0)	16.3	(3.5)	17.9	(3.4)
Sociability[b]	17.9	(4.3)	16.4	(3.5)	18.6	(3.4)	16.3	(3.8)	17.6	(4.0)	16.2	(4.1)
Impulsivity[b]	13.2	(2.9)	14.0	(3.0)	11.6	(2.9)	11.7	(2.7)	12.4	(2.8)	12.5	(3.1)
EASI (mate-rating)												
Emotionality–Fear[a,b]	15.9	(3.4)	11.3	(3.2)	14.3	(3.3)	8.9	(2.8)	14.5	(3.7)	9.3	(3.1)
Emotionality–Anger[b]	14.2	(3.7)	15.3	(4.1)	13.1	(3.6)	10.9	(4.1)	12.9	(3.7)	12.0	(4.7)
Activity	15.9	(3.8)	16.2	(3.7)	16.5	(3.4)	16.6	(3.6)	16.1	(3.8)	16.8	(4.1)
Sociability[a]	18.2	(3.3)	17.7	(4.2)	18.9	(3.5)	17.8	(4.2)	18.6	(3.9)	17.6	(4.7)
Impulsivity[a,b]	13.8	(2.3)	16.6	(3.5)	12.2	(3.0)	12.9	(3.5)	13.0	(3.2)	13.5	(3.7)
N EASI self-ratings	170–173		40–42		172		170		157–161		157–161	
N EASI mate ratings	37–40		153–161		165–179		165–179		157–162		157–162	

[a]Significant gender difference ($p < .01$).
[b]Significant difference among biological, adoptive, and control parents ($p < .01$).

TABLE 9.14

Selective Placement Correlations for EASI and 16 PF

Measure	Biological mother–adoptive mother	Biological mother–adoptive father	Biological father–adoptive mother	Biological father–adoptive father
EASI Emotionality–Fear	.07	.01	.03	.28*
Emotionality–Anger	−.09	.03	.01	−.05
Activity	.11	−.10	−.22	.07
Sociability	.02	.11	−.22	−.22
Impulsivity	−.08	−.01	.05	−.17
16 PF Extraversion	−.21*	.03	.03	−.24
Neuroticism	.02	.19*	.15	−.05
Independence	−.06	.07	.11	.15
N for EASI	158–163	159–164	38–42	37–40
N for 16 PF	103–106	109–114	29	25–27

*$p < .05$.

mate-rating EASI Sociability scale; and males are more variable on the mate-rating EASI scales of Impulsivity and Emotionality–Anger.

Numerous significant mean differences for gender and for parental type emerged, although it should be remembered that samples of this size have considerable power to detect mean differences that account for only a small amount of variance. The largest mean difference in Tables 9.12 and 9.13—the greater EASI Emotionality–Fear of females—is less than one standard deviation for the self-report measure and about one and a half standard deviations for the mate-rating measure. Most of the other significant group differences, such as the greater EASI sociability of females, represent less than half a standard deviation mean difference. In addition to these two EASI gender differences, which are similar to those reported by Buss and Plomin (1984), the 16 PF yielded significant gender effects suggesting that females are more outgoing, tender-minded, apprehensive, and tense than males and that they are less dominant, suspicious, astute, and experimenting. These gender differences are similar both in direction and magnitude to those reported in the *Norms for the 16 PF, Forms A and B (1967–68 Edition)*. For the second-order 16 PF factors, no significant gender differences emerged for Extraversion or Neuroticism, although females are less independent than males.

Selective Placement and Assortative Mating

As indicated in previous chapters, selective placement—correlations between biological and adoptive parents—can inflate both genetic and family environmental estimates in the CAP design. For cognitive abilities, selective placement is negligible, and Table 9.14 suggests a similar result for personality. For the 20 EASI selective placement correlations, only 1 is significant, as would be expected by chance. The median correlation is .01. Although 2 of the 16 PF selective placement

TABLE 9.15

Assortative Mating Correlations for EASI and 16 PF

Measure	Biological parents	Adoptive parents	Control parents
EASI			
Emotionality–Fear	.11	−.12	−.07
Emotionality–Anger	−.13	−.06	−.09
Activity	−.01	.01	.03
Sociability	−.11	.07	.23*
Impulsivity	−.31*	.08	.10
16 PF			
Extraversion	.05	.21*	.09
Neuroticism	.25	.16	−.06
Independence	.13	.23*	.24*
N for EASI	34–41	162–165	153–156
N for 16 PF	31	94–101	98–111

*$p < .05$.

correlations are statistically significant, 1 is negative; moreover, the median correlation is only .02.

Assortative mating also affects parent–offspring resemblance. Correlations for the three types of parents are listed in Table 9.15. As in other studies, little assortative mating is found for personality. The median correlations for the biological, adoptive, and control parents are .02, .08, and .06, respectively. The significant negative correlation between biological parents for the EASI Impulsivity appears to be a fluke. Negative assortative mating is rarely found; the adage that opposites attract is weak compared to the maxim that birds of a feather flock together. Moreover, impulsivity-related scales of the 16 PF do not replicate this EASI result: Assortative mating correlations for 16 PF Happy-Go-Lucky and Controlled scales are −.04 and .03, respectively, for the biological parents.

Although assortative mating for personality is generally low, the data hold open the possibility of greater assortative mating for some traits than for others. For example, as shown in Table 9.15, 16 PF Independence yields correlations of .13, .23, and .24 for the three types of parents. The 16 PF primary scales also vary in amount of assortative mating. Not surprisingly, 16 PF Scale B, which is a measure of general intelligence, shows an average assortative mating correlation of .24. Although the Happy-Go-Lucky scale correlates −.04 for the biological parents, the correlations are .32 and .29 for the adoptive and control couples. Another 16 PF scale that yields somewhat higher than average assortative mating correlations is the Experimenting scale (.13, .20, and .30).

Summary

This chapter provides background material concerning individual differences in personality and temperament. The modern history of research in the areas of adult personality and infant temperament is briefly described. The rationale for emphasizing temperament in the CAP lies in the fact that so little is known about either environmental or hereditary influences on temperament in infancy.

The chapter also describes the CAP measures for infants and adults. The measures were selected to converge on four traits—emotionality, activity, sociability, and impulsivity (EASI)—that were suggested by a theory of temperament proposed by Buss and Plomin (1975). Three sources of information are used in the assessment of these traits for infants: parental reports, tester observations, and videotaped observations. Aggregated scores across these sources of information are used in order to test the hypothesis that multiple methods will produce more orderly results.

In general, factor structures, means, and variances indicate that the CAP sample is reasonably representative of other samples. Assortative mating and selective placement are negligible.

The following chapter considers the causes and correlates of individual differences in infant temperament.

10

Personality and Temperament: Etiology

Introduction

We have presented an overview of research in personality and temperament and described the CAP measures in the preceding chapter. We now turn to the focal issue of this book: the etiology of individual differences in infancy. Parent–offspring relationships in the adoptive and control families are considered first and then specific environmental influences are addressed.

Twin studies using parental ratings of temperament typically support the hypothesis that emotionality, activity, and sociability (EAS) are heritable, although fraternal twin correlations are too low—typically near zero—to fit the twin model unless some contrast effect is taken into account (Buss & Plomin, 1984). Twin studies using Infant Behavior Record (IBR) ratings also suggest significant genetic influence in infancy. The Louisville Twin Study yielded the following median identical and fraternal twin correlations, respectively, for the three IBR factor scores at 6, 12, 18, and 24 months of age: .52 and .20 for Task Orientation, .46 and .18 for Affect–Extraversion, and .32 and .18 for Activity (Matheny, 1980). Activity showed a consistent pattern of increasing heritability during infancy. Twin studies using observational measures other than the global IBR ratings have found no genetic influence on social responding by infants to their mothers (Lytton, Martin, & Eaves, 1977; Plomin & Rowe, 1979), although the latter study also considered social responding to strangers (i.e., shyness) and found evidence for heritability. Two other longitudinal observational twin studies of emotionality are in progress (Goldsmith, 1983; Wilson & Matheny, 1983a).

As in most areas of personality research, considerably more data have been collected for twins than for other family relationships. Two small studies found significant and substantial parent–offspring resemblance for activity in infants and children (Caldwell & Herscher, 1964; Willerman, 1973). Only one study has reported parent–offspring correlations for the EAS traits using mothers' and fathers' ratings of infants and young children (mean age of 54 months) in 137 families (Plomin, 1974). The parent–offspring correlations were low, .10 to .20 on the average, and maternal effects were suggested by consistently higher correlations for mothers than for fathers. Similar results were obtained when different procedures were used: individual parents' self-reports, one spouse's rating of the other spouse, midparent ratings of the children, and "cross ratings" (for example, mothers' self-report with fathers' ratings of the children). The study also yielded some relevant methodological information: Parental self-reports correlated .54 on the average with their spouses' ratings of them. Correlating parents' self-report with the parents' ratings of the spouse revealed no tendency for parents to project their personality into their ratings of the spouse. Similar analyses yielded no evidence that parents project their own personality into ratings of their children (Lyon & Plomin, 1981).

Parent–offspring data have also been collected in studies of older children, adolescents, and adults, including two adoption studies. On average, parent–child correlations in control families for self-report personality questionnaires are .14 (Loehlin, Horn, & Willerman, 1981). Two adoption studies of adolescents and young adults using self-report questionnaires obtained control parent–offspring correlations of a similar magnitude for extraversion and neuroticism. Scarr, Webber, Weinberg, and Wittig (1981) reported a parent–offspring correlation of .13 for extraversion and .18 for neuroticism in 120 control families; for 115 adoptive families, the correlations were .01 and .02, respectively. Similarly, Loehlin *et al.* (1981; see also, Loehlin *et al.,* 1982) found control parent–offspring correlations of .12 for extraversion and .08 for neuroticism; for adoptive parent–offspring comparisons, the correlations were .06 and .04, respectively. In the study by Loehlin *et al.,* the adult extraversion and neuroticism scores were based on the Cattell 16 PF scales that loaded on second-order factors and the children's scores were based on a general rating on each of the 16 PF scales, thus raising the possibility that the adult and child scores are not comparable. However, for a "well-measured" subsample in which children exhibited consistent scores on two measures, parent–offspring correlations were substantial: for extraversion, .40 in the control families and .06 in the adoptive families; for neuroticism, .22 and .15, respectively. In a follow-up study of the sample using the California Psychological Inventory and the Thurstone Temperament Schedule, similar results were found, with control parent–offspring correlations of about .15 and adoptive parent–offspring correlations of about .05. In contrast to Plomin's (1974) findings, these studies do not provide evidence for maternal effects; however, the study by Plomin involved infants and young children for whom a maternal effect might be more evident than for adolescents and young adults.

Although these parent–offspring results suggest less heritability than do the twin data, studies involving separated identical twins suggest genetic influence of about the same magnitude as in studies of twins reared together. In two older studies, identical twins reared apart are as similar as identical twins reared together for extraversion and neuroticism (Newman, Freeman, & Holzinger, 1937; Shields, 1962). In the Minnesota study of separated identical twins, the median correlation for 30 pairs of twins reared apart was .49 for Tellegen's Differential Personality Questionnaire as compared to a correlation of .51 for identical twins reared together (Bouchard, 1983). Similar results appear to be emerging from ongoing studies of separated twins in Sweden (Pedersen, Friberg, Floderus-Myrhed, McClearn, & Plomin, 1983) and Finland (Langinvainio, Kaprio, Koskenvuo, & Lonnqvist, 1983).

Thus, there appears to be reason to expect genetic influence on personality traits in adolescence and adulthood. The previous adoption data would suggest a correlation of about .15 in control families and about .05 in adoptive families when self-report questionnaires are used. However, we would not be surprised to see different parent–offspring correlations for the CAP families and their adopted and non-adopted infants. Parental personality may have a greater effect in infancy than later in life, as children begin to experience social influences outside the home; this could lead to higher parent–offspring correlations in the control and adoptive relationships in infancy than later in development. The genetic estimates from the biological parents (and included in the control relationships) might well be lower if the genes that influence infant traits are not highly correlated with those that influence adult traits. Affecting both environmental and genetic estimates in unknown ways is the fact that self-report questionnaires cannot be administered to infants. The use of parental ratings, tester ratings, and videotaped observations to assess temperament in infancy would, most likely, lead to lower parent–offspring correlations to the extent that these measures differ from self-report measures.

The CAP data provide the first opportunity to apply the adoption design to the study of infant temperament. As discussed in previous chapters, the parent–offspring design of the CAP makes three demands before significant biological parent–offspring resemblance will be found: The trait must be heritable both in infancy and adulthood, and a substantial genetic correlation must exist between the infant and adult measures. In other words, genes that affect the trait in infancy must be correlated with the genes that affect the trait in adulthood. For mental development, we were forced to the surprising conclusion that genetic factors that influence infant mental test scores also influence adult IQ scores; that is, the genetic correlation between infancy and adulthood is nearly 1.0, which implies that genes contribute more to continuity than to change.

For mental development, there is a striking increase in heritability after infancy. For temperament, no clear developmental trend in heritability can be seen, and we would not be surprised to find the opposite tendency, that is, greater heritability in infancy than later in life, for some temperaments. In order to estimate a reasonable range of biological parent–adoptee correlations, we need to consider heritability in infancy and in adulthood, and the genetic correlation between infant and adult measures. If temperament were similar to mental development, we would suggest a heritability in infancy of about .15, an adult heritability of about .50, and a genetic correlation of 1.0, which would lead to an estimate of about .14 for the biological parent–adoptee correlation. The same estimate would be made if the heritability of infant temperament were .50 and the adult heritability were .15. If the genetic correlation was 1.0, but the heritabilities in infancy and adulthood were both .50, the expected correlation for biological parents and their adopted-away offspring would be .25. The present size of the CAP sample has 80% power to detect correlations of .20 or greater and about 35% power to detect correlations of .10 or greater. If the genetic correlation between infancy and adulthood is less than 1.0, the expected parent–offspring correlation is lower; in the above two examples, the parent–offspring correlations would be halved (.07 and .13, respectively) if the infancy–adulthood genetic correlation were .50 rather than 1.0.

The point of this extended discussion is that the CAP design will not detect genetic effects unless these three conditions are met; however, when significant genetic influence is detected in the CAP, the results are of key interest because they suggest genetically induced continuity from infancy to adulthood.

In this section, the CAP parent–offspring correlations in infancy are presented separately according to the three major sources of temperament data in infancy: parental ratings, tester observations, and videotaped observations. We also attempt to aggregate assessments across these three methods.

Parent–Offspring Correlations

Parental Ratings

Because the temperament theory of Buss and Plomin (1984) focuses on EAS as likely dimensions of temperament, our discussion of parent–offspring correlations will be organized around these three traits. We begin with parental measures as they relate to corresponding ratings of their children and then we consider parental 16 PF measures.

EASI

Buss and Plomin's theory (1975, 1984) suggests only that EAS show evidence of hereditary influences after infancy because so few data are available to evaluate their heritability in infants. Impulsivity was provisionally considered as a temperament in their 1975 book, but was dropped in their 1984 book because the intervening years had not clarified the conceptual nature of impulsivity or its etiology. A modification of the EASI Temperament Survey (Buss & Plomin, 1975) is used in the CAP to obtain self-report and mate ratings for the parents, and the corresponding parental ratings of infants on the CCTI are included in order to investigate the etiology of these traits.

The fact that all parents rated themselves and their mates, and the adoptive and control parents also rated their children, creates several possibilities for analyses of parent–offspring similarlity. We can compare parents' self-ratings to their ratings of their children: These comparisons could be inflated because the same individual provides ratings of the parent and the child. We can also compare cross ratings of several types in which the parent and child are rated by different individuals; for example, the father rates himself and the mother rates the child. We can also aggregate ratings in an attempt to improve their validity by using midparent ratings of the infants' temperament and combining parents' self-report ratings with the mate ratings. In fact, all of these analyses are presented for the EASI traits. In order to simplify this complex presentation, we focus first on parent–offspring correlations in the control families. EASI traits that show no familiality for the controls are dropped before we consider the data on adoptive families. We have the greatest power to detect parent–offspring correlations in control families because control parents and their offspring share both heredity and environment and are expected to yield higher parent–offspring correlations than those for biological or adoptive relationships. With data for 150 control families, as mentioned previously, we have 80% power to detect correlations of .20 or greater but only 35% power to detect correlations of .10. If we cannot detect parent–offspring correlations in control families, it is unlikely that we can reliably detect parent–offspring correlations between adoptees and their biological or adoptive parents. Moreover, looking for either genetic or family environmental influences in control families and then attempting to find genetic influence in the biological parent–adoptee relationship and family environmental influences in the adoptive parent–adoptee relationship permits replication of the results and increased confidence in the findings.

Table 10.1 lists correlations between parental EASI and infant CCTI in control families. In addition to the usual ''same-rater'' data (for example, a mother rates herself and her child), cross ratings are included in the table. Although it would be reasonable to expect that the same-rater data would yield higher correlations than the cross ratings, the values are similar for the two types of data. Generally, the correlations are low—.08 on the average. The correlations are similar for mothers and fathers and at 12 and 24 months. The one obvious exception to this general pattern of very low parent–offspring correlations is Sociability, especially at 24 months. The same-rater data for Emotionality suggest some familiality; however, the cross-rating data do not agree. The data for Activity are also interesting in that they suggest father–offspring resemblance (regardless of whether the father rates himself or is rated by his spouse), but not mother–offspring resemblance: The mean activity correlation for fathers is .11 at both 12 and 24 months; for mothers, the mean correlations are .01 and −.05. Correlations for Impulsivity are the lowest and least systematic.

Table 10.2 begins to aggregate ratings by combining mothers' and fathers' ratings of their infants' temperaments into a midparent rating. Nonetheless, the results are similar although somewhat more systematic: The average correlation is .10; mothers' and fathers' correlations are similar; correlations at 12 and 24 months are similar; Sociability yields the highest correlations, although in this case they appear

TABLE 10.1

Parent–Offspring Correlations in Control Families: Correlations between Parents' EASI Ratings and Infants' CCTI Ratings[a]

Parent EASI	Infant CCTI	"same-raters"			"cross-ratings"		
		M → M / M → I	F → F / F → I	F → M / M → I	M → F / F → I	M → M / F → I	F → F / M → I
12 Months							
Emotionality–Fear	Emotionality	.03	.18*	.16*	.01	−.06	.08
Emotionality–Anger	Emotionality	.16*	.11	−.01	−.02	.03	.11
Activity	Activity	−.07	.22*	−.01	.19*	.10	.13
Sociability	Sociability	.20*	.09	.06	.03	.24*	.05
Impulsivity	Attention Span	.12	.04	.14*	.15*	.01	−.03
24 Months							
Emotionality–Fear	Emotionality	.10	.19*	.04	.05	−.09	.15*
Emotionality–Anger	Emotionality	.16*	.04	.07	.00	.00	.14*
Activity	Activity	−.11	.12	−.13	.04	.08	.17*
Sociability	Sociability	.15*	.14*	.16*	.15*	.26*	.14*
Impulsivity	Attention Span	.00	−.05	.04	.02	.07	−.03

[a]$N = 145$–156. M = Mother, F = Father, and I = Infant; arrow indicates direction of rating. Thus, "same-raters" involves, for example, mothers rating themselves and their infants; "cross-ratings" occur when, for example, fathers rate the mothers and mothers rate their infants.

* $p < .05$.

TABLE 10.2

Parent–Offspring Correlations in Control Families: Correlations between Parents' EASI Ratings and Infants' CCTI Midparent Ratings[a]

Parent EASI	Infant CCTI	M → F	F → F	F → M	M → F
12 Months					
Emotionality–Fear	Emotionality	−.02	.17*	.07	.06
Emotionality–Anger	Emotionality	.08	.12	.10	.06
Activity	Activity	.02	.21*	.08	.22*
Sociability	Sociability	.23*	.09	.24*	.09
Impulsivity	Attention Span	.08	.00	.07	.10
24 Months					
Emotionality–Fear	Emotionality	.01	.21*	.08	.02
Emotionality–Anger	Emotionality	.11	.11	.14*	.10
Activity	Activity	−.03	.19*	−.08	.14*
Sociability	Sociability	.22*	.13	.22*	.15*
Impulsivity	Attention Span	.06	−.06	.06	.00

[a]$N = 141–157$. M = Mother, F = Father; arrow indicates direction of rating.
*$p < .05$.

higher for mothers than for fathers; Activity shows significant correlations for fathers but not mothers; and Impulsivity shows the least familiality. Emotionality–Anger shows some evidence of familiality. Finally, the self-report and mate ratings also yield similar results.

The next step in aggregation is to combine parents' self-report and mate ratings as indicated in Table 10.3. Again, the average correlation is slightly higher, .12; the other results remain the same.

TABLE 10.3

Parent–Offspring Correlations in Control Families: Correlations between Average of Parents' EASI Self-Report and Mate Ratings and Infants' CCTI Midparent Ratings[a]

Parent EASI	Infant CCTI	Control mothers	Control fathers
12 Months			
Emotionality–Fear	Emotionality	.05	.15*
Emotionality–Anger	Emotionality	.11	.09
Activity	Activity	.05	.23*
Sociability	Sociability	.24*	.09
Impulsivity	Attention Span	.07	.08
24 Months			
Emotionality–Fear	Emotionality	.09	.14*
Emotionality–Anger	Emotionality	.16*	.12
Activity	Activity	−.05	.18*
Sociability	Sociability	.24*	.15*
Impulsivity	Attention Span	.07	−.04

[a]$N = 139–152$.
*$p < .05$.

We can safely drop Impulsivity from further analysis because it yields correlations of less than .10 at both 12 and 24 months. Activity is retained even though it does not conform to a genetic hypothesis because the father–offspring correlation suggests environmental influence that ought to be replicated in the adoptive families.

Table 10.4 presents parent–offspring correlations for biological and adoptive parents using midparent ratings of the adopted infants as in Table 10.2. Because the sample size of biological fathers is small, we cannot combine biological parents' self-report and mate ratings as we did in Table 10.3. It should also be noted that, unlike the control and adoptive relationships, the parent–offspring correlations for biological parents in Table 10.4 are actually cross-correlations because the self-reports of the biological parents are related to the adoptive midparent rating of the adoptee. In Table 10.2, the average parent–offspring correlation for control mothers and their infants for the EAS traits (excluding Impulsivity from the EASI) was .08 at both 12 and 24 months. The average biological mother–adoptee correlation in Table 10.4 is .02 at 12 months and .08 at 24 months. The results for biological mothers at 24 months thus suggest at most a trace of genetic influence. The only statistically significant correlation is for Sociability, which also showed the greatest familiality in the control families. This significant correlation is particularly noteworthy because it is based on self-report ratings of biological mothers and adoptive midparent ratings of the adopted-away infant over 2 years later. The small sample of biological fathers yields no systematic pattern of results, nor do the biological mothers' ratings of the biological fathers.

Several parent–offspring correlations for the adoptive relationships are significant. In fact, the adoptive correlations are larger (but not significantly) than those in control families. Although we assume this is due to chance, it could, at least in theory, be caused by negative genotype–environment correlation. For Emotionality–Fear, all of the adoptive mother–infant correlations are significant at 12 and 24 months. The average adoptive parent–adoptee correlation is .12 for Emotionality–Fear and .14 for Emotionality–Anger. No family environmental influence is suggested for Activity: The correlations for adoptive fathers did not confirm the suggestion from the control parent data of paternal environmental influences relevant to infant activity level. All but one of the correlations for Sociability are significant, which replicates the results for control families.

In summary, these EASI analyses suggest some environmental influence of parental temperament on infant Emotionality and Sociability. The only hint of genetic influence is for Sociability at 24 months.

Multiple Regressions

Although the evidence for an influence of parental personality on infant temperament is weak, we conducted multiple regression analyses of infant temperament on several parental traits to explore their combined ability to predict infant temperament. Rather than blindly including the hundreds of possible combinations of parental personality measures, we chose combinations that make conceptual sense—such as using parental sociability and emotionality to predict infant sociability. Infant

TABLE 10.4

Parent–Offspring Correlations for Biological and Adoptive Relationships: Correlations between Parents' EASI Ratings and Infants' CCTI Midparent Ratings

		Biological relationships				Adoptive relationships			
		"same-raters"		"cross-ratings"		"same-raters"		"cross-ratings"	
Parent EASI	Infant CCTI	M → M	F → F	F → M	M → F	M → M	F → F	F → M	M → F
12 Months									
Emotionality–Fear	Emotionality	.00	.08	−.13	−.02	.16*	.14*	.23*	.05
Emotionality–Anger	Emotionality	.01	.15	−.22	.02	.17*	.19*	.12	.06
Activity	Activity	.06	−.09	−.09	.00	−.10	.01	−.03	−.03
Sociability	Sociability	.02	−.18	.06	−.09	.19*	.15*	.21*	.11
	N =	151–168	39–42	36–42	142–153	152–168	154–166	156–166	159–173
24 Months									
Emotionality–Fear	Emotionality	.04	−.20	.06	.10	.15*	.00	.14*	.06
Emotionality–Anger	Emotionality	.06	.02	−.07	.08	.12	.15*	.10	.09
Activity	Activity	.05	.09	.07	−.02	.02	.01	−.05	.05
Sociability	Sociability	.15*	−.06	−.14	−.05	.24*	.25*	.18*	.17*
	N =	151–168	39–42	36–42	142–153	152–168	154–166	156–166	159–173

*$p < .05$.

TABLE 10.5

Multiple Regressions of Infant CCTI Sociability (Shyness) on Parental EASI Sociability and Emotionality–Fear

	Biological mothers		Adoptive mothers		Control mothers	
Regression	R	adj. R^2	R	adj. R^2	R	adj. R^2
12 Months						
CCTI midparent Sociability on:						
EASI Sociability	.02		.20*		.23*	
EASI Emotionality–Fear	.08	.00	.20	.03	.24	.04
24 Months						
CCTI midparent Sociability on:						
EASI Sociability	.16*		.25*		.20*	
EASI Emotionality–Fear	.16	.01	.25	.05	.27*	.06

*Significance ($p < .05$) of term added to multiple regression.

CCTI Sociability is a measure of shyness rather than gregariousness; shyness has been conceptualized as a combination of emotionality–fearfulness and low sociability (Buss & Plomin, 1984). In Table 10.5 we present the results of using both maternal Sociability and Emotionality–Fear to predict midparent ratings of shyness (CCTI Sociability). The control mothers' Sociability and Emotionality–Fear both add significantly to the prediction of midparent ratings of infant shyness at 24 months; together these two parental personality traits account for 6% of the variance in infant shyness. Both genetic and family environmental influences are suggested by the regressions for the biological mothers and adoptive mothers, although EASI Emotionality–Fear does not add significantly to EASI Sociability in predicting infant shyness at either 12 or 24 months.

In general, other attempts to find combinations of parental personality traits that yield more powerful predictions of infant temperament were unsuccessful.

16 PF

Rather than listing all possible intercorrelations between parental scores on the scales of the 16 PF and the infants' CCTI, we focus on the second-order 16 PF factors of Extraversion and Neuroticism. The other 16 PF second-order factor, Independence, consists of the Assertive, Suspicious, Imaginative, Experimenting, and Self-Sufficient primary scales of the 16 PF, which have no analogs in infancy. As indicated earlier, sociability can be viewed as an infant version of extraversion, and emotionality may be an infant analog of neuroticism. Table 10.6 contains correlations for 16 PF Extraversion and Neuroticism for the three types of parents and the midparent ratings of infants' Sociability and Emotionality.

The 16 PF Extraversion and Neuroticism results are somewhat different from those previously described for the EASI. The control mother correlations are signif-

TABLE 10.6

Parent–Offspring Correlations between Parents' 16 PF Second-Order Factor Scores and Infants' CCTI Midparent Ratings

Parent 16 PF	Infant CCTI	Biological		Adoptive		Control	
		Mother (N = 135–151)	Father (N = 35–36)	Mother (N = 119–122)	Father (N = 121–130)	Mother (N = 121–133)	Father (N = 107–123)
12 Months							
Extraversion	Sociability	−.03	−.07	.02	.07	.24*	.05
Neuroticism	Emotionality	.07	−.11	.16*	.09	.25*	.07
24 Months							
Extraversion	Sociability	.02	.05	−.08	.14	.22*	.17*
Neuroticism	Emotionality	.20*	−.11	.07	.03	.10	.14

*p < .05.

icant for both Extraversion and Neuroticism at 12 months and for Extraversion at 24 months; control fathers' correlations suggest familiality at 24 months. This suggestion of familial influence implies that these results should be replicated in the biological or adoptive relationships. However, few systematic replications were observed for biological parents or adoptive parents. In terms of genetic influence, biological mothers' Neuroticism correlated significantly with infant Emotionality at 24 months; however, the EASI suggestion of genetic influence for Sociability is not replicated for Extraversion. In terms of family environmental influence, the only replication of the control parent correlations is a significant correlation for adoptive mothers' Neuroticism with 12-month infant Emotionality; this replicates the EASI Emotionality results, although the finding is not replicated at 24 months, nor is the influence of family environment on EASI Sociability replicated for Extraversion.

In summary, the EASI results suggest some family environmental influence on infant emotionality and sociability at both 12 and 24 months, and the possibility of genetic influence on infant sociability at 24 months. The 16 PF results suggest links between parental extraversion and infant sociability and between parental neuroticism and infant emotionality in the control families. Although these relationships in control families point to the influence of either heredity or family environment, the biological parents' and adoptive parents' 16 PF data provide little insight into the etiology of these familial influences. The only significant correlations suggest the influence of family environment on neuroticism–emotionality at 12 months and genetic influence on neuroticism–emotionality at 24 months.

What may we conclude concerning the etiology of temperament in infancy? It should be emphasized that these analyses only bear on infant temperament as it relates to adult temperament. We can safely assert that no strong relationships of this type can be found using parental ratings of infant temperament and self-report ratings of parents' personality. However, it should also be stressed that biological parent–adoptee correlations reflect only half of the additive genetic variance. Given the exciting possibilities of isolating infant-to-adult relationships, whether they are mediated genetically or environmentally, the hints of genetic influence on sociability and neuroticism–emotionality at 24 months and the family environmental influences on emotionality and sociability at 12 and 24 months merit attention in future research.

Tester Observations

The Infant Behavior Record (IBR) of Bayley's Scales of Infant Development (Bayley, 1969) is becoming more widely used as a measure of temperament that differs importantly from parental ratings. The IBR involves ratings of the infants' reactions to a specific and somewhat stressful situation, the hour-long administration of the Bayley Mental and Motor Scales. In contrast, parental ratings involve broad dimensions averaged across time and situations. Matheny (1980) reported heritabilities greater than .50 for three factors derived from the IBR: Affect–Extra-

TABLE 10.7

Parent–Offspring Correlations between Parents' EASI and 16 PF Measures and Infants' IBR Scores

Parent measure	Infant IBR measure	Biological Mother (N = 149–171)	Biological Father (N = 36–42)	Adoptive Mother (N = 122–170)	Adoptive Father (N = 127–171)	Control Mother (N = 128–158)	Control Father (N = 112–155)
12 Months							
EASI Emotionality–Fear	Affect–Extraversion	.01	-.02	-.05	-.01	.06	.15*
EASI Sociability	Affect–Extraversion	.05	.24	.06	.03	.05	.12
16 PF Neuroticism	Affect–Extraversion	.12	.06	.09	.03	-.07	.05
16 PF Extraversion	Affect–Extraversion	.01	.11	-.03	-.09	.12	.04
EASI Activity	Activity	.05	.01	-.05	.11	-.07	.10
EASI Impulsivity	Task Orientation	.05	.03	-.10	.06	.02	.08
24 Months							
EASI Emotionality–Fear	Affect–Extraversion	-.09	.18	-.03	.02	.06	-.03
EASI Sociability	Affect–Extraversion	.02	.06	-.01	.02	.14*	-.09
16 PF Neuroticism	Affect–Extraversion	.03	.07	-.04	.06	-.04	-.03
16 PF Extraversion	Affect–Extraversion	-.08	.12	-.02	.06	.13	.00
EASI Activity	Activity	-.10	-.21	.04	.14*	-.03	.08
EASI Impulsivity	Task Orientation	.00	.07	.06	-.12	-.07	-.13*

*$p < .05$.

version and Task Orientation at both 12 and 24 months, and Activity at 24 months but not 12 months. We used the scoring of these three IBR factors suggested by Matheny (1980) and related the IBR Affect–Extraversion factor to parental EASI Emotionality–Fear and Sociability as well as to 16 PF Neuroticism; IBR Task Orientation to parental EASI Impulsivity; and IBR Activity to parental EASI Activity.

Parent–offspring correlations are listed in Table 10.7. In the control families, 3 of the 24 correlations are significant. However, these correlations are not replicated for the biological mothers (for whom none of the 12 correlations is significant) or for the adoptive parents (for whom only 1 of 24 correlations is significant). Thus, infants' temperament as rated by a tester during administration of the Bayley scales does not appear to be predicted by personality characteristics of their parents.

Videotaped Observations

A modification of the IBR fashioned after the work of Matheny and Wilson (1981) was employed to rate the infants' behavior during the videotaped observations of mother–infant interactions. Table 10.8 contains the correlations between parental EASI and 16 PF measures and the factors derived from the videotaped observations. As with the CCTI measures, some relationship between parental Sociability–Extraversion and infant Affect–Extraversion can be seen in the control families at 24 months. However, this suggestion of familial influence in control families is not verified in the biological or adoptive relationships. The correlations for biological mothers are not suggestive of any genetic influence. We noted earlier that the videotape measures yielded little stability from 12 to 24 months, and this is likely to be the reason for the lack of parent–offspring resemblance.

Aggregation

As noted earlier, we combined parental ratings, tester ratings, and videotape ratings to produce aggregate measures of Affect–Extraversion, Activity, and Task Orientation. Correlations between these infant temperament scores and appropriate parental EASI and 16 PF measures are presented in Table 10.9. The results for the aggregate scores are basically an average of the results for the parental, tester, and videotape ratings. For the controls, there is some evidence for familial influence on sociability and emotionality as seen in the positive correlations between Affect–Extraversion and parental EASI Sociability and 16 PF Extraversion and the negative correlations between Affect–Extraversion and parental 16 PF Neuroticism at both 12 and 24 months. The only significant correlation for biological mothers is a negative correlation between 16 PF Neuroticism and the aggregate Affect–Extraversion factor at 24 months, which is similar to the result reported earlier for 16 PF Neuroticism and CCTI Emotionality. Also similar to previous results is the significant control father–offspring correlation for Activity at 12 and 24 months; however,

TABLE 10.8

Parent–Offspring Correlations between Parents' EASI and 16 PF Measures and Infants' Videotape Ratings

| Parent measure | Infant videotape measure | Biological | | Adoptive | | Control | |
		Mother (N = 107–126)	Father (N = 19–30)	Mother (N = 87–123)	Father (N = 97–123)	Mother (N = 98–134)	Father (N = 87–130)
12 Months							
EASI Emotionality–Fear	Affect–Extraversion	-.09	.02	-.05	.02	-.03	.02
EASI Sociability	Affect–Extraversion	-.02	-.13	.08	-.03	.02	-.06
16 PF Neuroticism	Affect–Extraversion	.03	-.01	-.03	.13	.04	.01
16 PF Extraversion	Affect–Extraversion	-.03	-.10	.10	.01	-.03	.13
EASI Activity	Activity	.02	.07	-.02	.02	.01	-.02
EASI Impulsivity	Task Orientation	-.09	.19	.11	.00	.01	-.04
24 Months							
EASI Emotionality–Fear	Affect–Extraversion	-.07	.24	.15*	.03	.10	.08
EASI Sociability	Affect–Extraversion	.02	-.16	-.10	-.06	.26*	.12
16 PF Neuroticism	Affect–Extraversion	-.08	-.15	.17	.10	.02	.01
16 PF Extraversion	Affect–Extraversion	-.09	.00	-.09	-.14	.19*	.11
EASI Activity	Activity	-.07	.25	-.04	-.02	-.06	-.07
EASI Impulsivity	Task Orientation	-.09	-.03	.08	-.06	.03	.17*

*p < .05.

210

TABLE 10.9

Parent–Offspring Correlations between Parents' EASI and 16 PF Measures and Infants' Aggregate Scores[a]

Parent measure	Infant aggregate measure	Biological		Adoptive		Control	
		Mother (N = 90–119)	Father (N = 23–30)	Mother (N = 83–117)	Father (N = 91–117)	Mother (N = 93–123)	Father (N = 81–121)
12 Months							
EASI Emotionality–Fear	Affect–Extraversion	-.03	.07	-.14	-.06	.00	-.05
EASI Sociability	Affect–Extraversion	.02	.13	.22*	.02	.17*	.14
16 PF Neuroticism	Affect–Extraversion	.03	.05	-.11	.06	-.27*	-.09
16 PF Extraversion	Affect–Extraversion	-.09	.00	.04	-.11	.20*	.13
EASI Activity	Activity	.12	.11	.02	.03	.06	.16*
EASI Impulsivity	Task Orientation	-.12	.24	-.07	-.09	.02	.04
24 Months							
EASI Emotionality–Fear	Affect–Extraversion	-.07	.33*	.02	.08	.16*	-.12
EASI Sociability	Affect–Extraversion	.03	-.10	.12	.05	.25*	.14
16 PF Neuroticism	Affect–Extraversion	-.16*	.00	-.01	.13	.01	-.15*
16 PF Extraversion	Affect–Extraversion	-.09	.06	-.05	-.09	.20*	.10
EASI Activity	Activity	.03	.05	.04	.02	-.04	.15*
EASI Impulsivity	Task Orientation	-.08	-.10	.05	-.14	-.04	-.01

[a]Combined parental, tester, and videotape ratings.
* $p < .05$.

as before, this evidence for paternal environmental influence on infant activity level is not replicated in the adoptive families.

Thus, in general, the data aggregated across parental, tester, and videotape ratings of the infants' temperament does not seem to paint a picture of the genetic and environmental origins of infant temperament that is any sharper than the blurry sketches provided by the separate measures.

Summary

The parent–offspring data based on adult self-report and mate ratings and infant ratings by parents, testers, and from videotaped observations—as well as aggregates of these measures—combine to suggest that parental personality has little power to predict infant temperament. Although the parental rating data provide some suggestion of family environmental influence on emotionality and sociability at 12 and 24 months and genetic influence on sociability and neuroticism–emotionality at 24 months, the tester ratings and videotape ratings do not generally support these suggestions. Of course, it is possible that the tester ratings and videotape ratings, although appealing because of their objectivity, cut a slice of life that is too thin to provide a meaningful index of infants' temperament. As paradoxical as it may sound, the environmental analyses presented in the next section provide stronger evidence for genetic as well as family environmental influence on infant temperament.

Environment–Infant Correlations

The previous analyses indicate that some family environmental factors might cause infants to resemble their parents in personality, particularly in the areas of sociability and emotionality. However, these influences are weak at best. This finding is not surprising, because behavioral-genetic studies involving older children consistently find that such shared or common environmental influences that make family members resemble one another are of negligible importance, particularly in the area of personality (Rowe & Plomin, 1981). Nonetheless, our data in infancy and behavioral-genetic studies of other developmental ages point to substantial environmental—more specifically, nongenetic—influence on personality. Thus, whatever the sources of environmental influences might be, they are not shared by members of the same family.

None of this denies the possibility of finding specific environmental factors that are related to infant personality development. Even though environmental factors apparently do not mediate similarity between parents' and infants' personality, the existence of relationships between specific environmental measures and infant personality certainly has not been disproved.

As indicated earlier, there are surprisingly few studies of possible relationships between environmental measures and infant temperament (reviewed by Buss &

Plomin, 1984). Studies of environmental correlates of infant development other than in the area of mental ability tend to focus on attachment and social competence (Wachs & Gruen, 1982). Older studies such as the Fels Longitudinal Study focused on aspects of personality, such as dependence and passivity, that are not often considered today (Kagan & Moss, 1962); moreover, few environmental correlates of infant personality were discovered by these studies.

The purpose of this section is to summarize relationships between specific measures of the environment and infant temperament in the CAP adoptive and control families. We examine relationships revealed by our use of two instruments: the observation–interview Home Observation for Measurement of the Environment (HOME), and the parental reports of the social climate of the home based on the Family Environment Scale (FES). We also organize items from these two measures and from physical descriptions of the home and neighborhood into the categories suggested by Gottfried and Gottfried (1984). These measures are described in Chapter 5. However, before we begin this presentation, we mention results for a less specific class of environmental influences, birth weight and gestational age.

Birth History

As noted in Chapter 14, birth history data indicate that the CAP infants are representative of the normal population with no detectable differences between

TABLE 10.10

Relationship of Birth Weight and Gestational Age to Infant Temperament

	Correlation			
	12 Months		24 Months	
Infant measure	Adopted $(N = 145–167)$	Control $(N = 106–127)$	Adopted $(N = 155–171)$	Control $(N = 107–130)$
Birth weight				
CCTI Emotionality	.01	.08	.04	.14
CCTI Activity	−.05	.08	.06	.16*
CCTI Sociability	.12	.11	.02	.14
CCTI Attention Span	.04	.21*	−.05	.12
IBR Affect–Extraversion	.06	.08	.15*	−.06
IBR Activity	−.08	.02	.11	−.10
IBR Task Orientation	.06	.14	−.08	.04
Gestational age				
CCTI Emotionality	.12	.01	.12	.04
CCTI Activity	.10	.01	.11	.06
CCTI Sociability	.01	−.04	.01	.04
CCTI Attention Span	−.01	.24*	−.05	.09
IBR Affect–Extraversion	.06	.10	.05	−.31*
IBR Activity	−.08	−.02	.09	−.15*
IBR Task Orientation	.07	.22*	−.03	.00

*$p < .05$.

adoptees and controls. Table 10.10 lists correlations of birth weight and clinical gestational age with the major measures of infant temperament. We expect no difference between adopted and control infants' correlations, but report them separately for the two groups for comparison purposes. In general, birth history shows few consistent relationships with infant personality across measures, samples, and ages. Only 3 of the 28 correlations are significant at each age; 1 significant correlation is expected by chance at each age. Thus, we conclude that, in a normal sample, variability in birth weight and gestational age play at most a minor role in explaining individual differences in infant temperament.

HOME

Table 10.11 presents correlations between the HOME environmental measures and 12-month-old temperament; correlations for 24-month-olds are listed in Table 10.12. The results are presented separately for adoptive and control families in order to explore the possibility of genetic influence in such ostensibly environmental relationships. As described in Chapter 5, we attempted to maximize the environmental variability captured by the HOME by using quantitative scores for each item rather than the traditional dichotomous scoring. Although the unrotated first principal component correlated highly with a total score, we used the component score as a measure of the general dimension represented by the HOME. Four scales based upon rotated factors were also employed rather than the six traditional scales: The four scales we used are Toys, Maternal Involvement, Encouraging Developmental Advance, and Restriction–Punishment, which are referred to as Factors 1 through 4 in the tables.

The results for the HOME General Factor at 12 months (see Table 10.11) suggest a positive relationship with infant CCTI Sociability, IBR Affect–Extraversion, and IBR Activity. The correlations are similar in control and adoptive homes, suggesting that these relationships do not involve genetic factors. In a study of 40 control 12-month-olds, Stevenson and Lamb (1979) also found that HOME total scores were related to initial sociability, although the HOME was not shown to be related to sociability during administration of the Bayley test. Our results at both 12 and 24 months indicate that all of these relationships are of marginal significance and thus require large samples for reliable detection. The aggregate measures of Affect–Extraversion and Activity suggest a slight positive relationship with the HOME General Factor; however, in the control families, aggregate Task Orientation at 12 months significantly related in a negative direction to the HOME General Factor, even though the relationships tend to be positive in the adoptive homes. This same pattern emerges more strongly for the first HOME factor, Toys, which correlates negatively in the control homes with CCTI Attention Span and IBR Task Orientation, suggesting that variety for infants might act as a distraction. However, the generally positive correlation for this relationship in the adoptive families is puzzling.

Other HOME factors yield some interesting relationships at 12 months that are

TABLE 10.11

Environment–Infant Correlations for the HOME At 12 Months

	HOME measure									
	Principal component		Factorially derived scales[a]							
			Factor 1		Factor 2		Factor 3		Factor 4	
Infant measure	A	C	A	C	A	C	A	C	A	C
CCTI (Midparent)										
Emotionality	.04	.02	.10	.08	−.09	−.10	.05	.11	−.05	−.04
Activity	.06	.08	.00	−.06	−.04	.02	.04	.13*	.24*	.18*
Sociability	.16	.17*	.01	.04	.01	.13*	.07	.07	−.04	.03
Attention Span	.04	−.01	.03	−.16*	−.06	.05	−.07	−.21*	.02	−.01
IBR										
Affect–Extraversion	.13*	.14*	−.05	−.08	.14*	.13*	.20*	.03	.02	−.02
Activity	.10	.15*	.21*	.12	.12	.05	.08	.18*	.17*	−.02
Task Orientation	.11	.04	.06	−.19*	.16*	.20*	.09	−.10	−.02	.17*
Video IBR										
Affect–Extraversion	.15*	.05	.09	.06	.13	.09	.15*	.05	−.13	−.11
Activity	.01	.02	.05	.06	−.20*	−.15*	−.01	−.04	.14	.06
Task Orientation	.16*	−.01	.16*	−.02	.20*	.05	.07	−.02	−.13	−.01
Aggregate										
Affect–Extraversion	.11	.08	−.02	−.04	.16*	.20*	.18*	.07	−.04	−.05
Activity	.12	.09	.10	−.01	−.08	−.01	.08	.16*	.30*	.08
Task Orientation	.11	−.17*	.12	−.22*	.14	.09	.03	−.15	.00	.08

[a]N for adopted (A) and control (C) infants, respectively, is 158–175 and 151–160 for CCTI, 175–177 and 150–158 for IBR, 124–127 and 118–123 for videotape, and 108–124 and 108–124 for the aggregates.

*$p < .05$.

TABLE 10.12

Environment–Infant Correlations for the HOME At 24 Months

	HOME measure									
	Principal component		Factorially derived scales[a]							
			Factor 1		Factor 2		Factor 3		Factor 4	
Infant measure	A	C	A	C	A	C	A	C	A	C
CCTI (Midparent)										
Emotionality	-.06	-.02	-.06	.13	-.02	-.08	-.06	-.05	.05	.17*
Activity	.02	-.18*	.06	-.12	-.01	-.11	-.01	-.20*	.22*	.12
Sociability	.07	.13	.08	.01	.03	.06	.07	.13	.08	.09
Attention Span	.16*	-.12	.09	-.12	.13	.03	.08	-.18*	-.06	.00
IBR										
Affect–Extraversion	.28*	.23*	.11	.03	.39*	.08	.21*	.25*	.03	.11
Activity	.18*	-.03	.07	-.02	-.06	.03	.15*	-.04	.24*	.20*
Task Orientation	.38*	.32*	.24*	.03	.29*	.17*	.30*	.30*	.02	.02
Video IBR										
Affect–Extraversion	.11	.19*	.06	.11	.23*	.20*	.06	.12	-.10	-.21*
Activity	.07	.05	-.01	-.05	.01	.17*	.09	.03	-.03	.17*
Task Orientation	-.04	.19*	.06	.11	.11	.20*	-.14*	.12	-.29*	-.21*
Aggregate										
Affect–Extraversion	.17*	.21*	.18*	.12	.16*	.17*	.11	.15*	.01	-.08
Activity	.15*	-.11	.07	-.10	.02	.08	.15*	-.16*	.16*	.21*
Task Orientation	.29*	.26*	.26*	.06	.31*	.27*	.14	.15*	-.28*	-.17*

[a] See footnote for Table 10.11.

*p < .05.

similar in control and adoptive homes. Maternal Involvement (HOME Factor 2) relates positively to sociability measures, including CCTI Sociability and the IBR, videotape, and aggregate measures of Affect–Extraversion. It also is related positively to IBR Task Orientation and negatively to videotape Activity. The third HOME factor, Encouraging Developmental Advance, tends to relate positively to emotionality and activity level. The fourth factor, Restriction–Punishment, is primarily related to Activity. Of course, any of these relationships are subject to questions concerning the direction of effects. For example, does parental punishment make children more active or are highly active children punished more?

Some of the HOME correlations at 24 months (see Table 10.12) are similar to the 12-month correlations: The HOME General Factor correlates positively with Affect–Extraversion, Maternal Involvement (Factor 2) relates positively to Affect–Extraversion and Task Orientation, and Restriction–Punishment (Factor 4) is related to Activity. However, the negative correlation between the HOME General Factor and Task Orientation at 12 months in control homes is now positive in both control and adoptive families. Also, Encouraging Developmental Advance (Factor 3) is related to IBR Task Orientation at 24 months but not at 12 months, and Restriction–Punishment is negatively related to videotape and aggregate Task Orientation only at 24 months.

Although it might appear that some evidence for genetic influence emerges at 24 months in significant differences between HOME-temperament relationships in adoptive and control homes, these differences—such as the significantly greater correlation between the HOME General Factor and videotape Task Orientation—generally involve positive correlations for one group and negative correlations for the other and are not replicated for analogous measures. Furthermore, IBR Task Orientation yields positive correlations with the HOME General Factor in both control and adoptive homes. For these reasons, we conclude that the results on balance show little evidence of genetic influence, which implies that the relationships discovered between the HOME and infant temperament are truly environmental in origin, although the issue of direction of effects remains in the interpretation of these relationships.

Gottfried Scales

The Gottfried scales are Variety of Experience (Factor 1), Provision for Exploration (Factor 2), and Physical Home Setting (Factor 3), as described in Chapter 5. These factors yield more significant correlations at 12 months than at 24 months (12 vs. 4), as shown in Table 10.13. Moreover, the adoptive and control correlations do not replicate, with one exception: The first Gottfried factor, Variety of Experience, is positively correlated with IBR Task Orientation in adoptive and control families and at 12 and 24 months. The first HOME factor also involves variety of experience and yields positive correlations with IBR Task Orientation at 24 months but not at 12 months (see Tables 10.11 and 10.12).

TABLE 10.13

Environment–Infant Correlations for the CAP Gottfried Scales[a]

	Gottfried scale											
	12 Months						24 Months					
	Factor 1		Factor 2		Factor 3		Factor 1		Factor 2		Factor 3	
Infant measure	A	C	A	C	A	C	A	C	A	C	A	C
CCTI (Midparent)												
Emotionality	-.01	-.11	.17*	.08	-.03	-.02	-.07	.01	.00	.10	-.10	.02
Activity	.01	-.01	.04	-.02	.13	.08	-.06	.03	-.03	-.05	-.06	-.13
Sociability	.03	.21*	-.03	-.04	.00	.00	.04	-.03	.00	.02	.00	.06
Attention Span	-.04	-.04	.04	-.13	.15*	-.06	-.04	.07	.02	-.12	.01	-.10
IBR												
Affect–Extraversion	.08	.11	-.07	-.07	.14*	.01	.12	-.08	.08	.09	-.01	.08
Activity	-.06	.07	.22*	.06	.07	.02	.02	.11	.06	-.01	.05	-.04
Task Orientation	.22*	.12	-.08	-.14*	-.02	-.02	.16*	.12	.16*	-.03	-.03	.03
Video IBR												
Affect–Extraversion	.11	.13	.01	-.07	-.08	-.12	-.10	-.13	.11	.10	-.01	-.01
Activity	-.23*	.08	.04	.15*	.08	-.01	.11	-.02	-.06	-.03	-.02	-.10
Task Orientation	.10	-.03	.05	-.05	-.01	-.14	-.11	-.13	.14	.10	-.07	-.01
Aggregate												
Affect–Extraversion	.00	.18*	-.07	-.04	-.02	-.06	.12	-.04	.10	.17*	-.01	.11
Activity	-.16	.15*	.06	.03	.12	.06	.12	.13	.00	-.07	-.02	-.11
Task Orientation	.09	.07	.03	-.17*	-.01	-.10	.04	.09	.19*	.02	-.04	-.06

[a]N for adopted (A) and control (C) infants, respectively, is 138–152 and 130–155 for CCTI and IBR, and 94–120 and 97–121 for videotape and aggregate measures.

*$p < .05$.

TABLE 10.14

Environment–Infant Correlations for the FES at 12 Months[a]

| | FES second-order factor | | | |
| | Personal Growth | | Traditional Organization | |
Infant measure	Adopted	Control	Adopted	Control
CCTI (Midparent)				
Emotionality	−.10	−.39*	−.09	−.02
Activity	.06	.18*	.00	−.01
Sociability	.16*	.34*	.12	.01
Attention Span	.10	.19*	.02	−.02
IBR				
Affect–Extraversion	−.01	.12	.01	−.03
Activity	−.01	.04	.03	−.11
Task Orientation	−.07	−.01	−.04	.04
Video IBR				
Affect–Extraversion	−.01	−.06	.13	.04
Activity	.08	.06	.00	−.11
Task Orientation	.05	−.05	.00	−.02
Aggregate				
Affect–Extraversion	.07	.31*	.15	.02
Activity	.11	.20*	−.07	−.23*
Task Orientation	.09	.11	.04	−.03

[a]N for adopted and control infants, respectively, is 159–164 and 151–158 for the CCTI and IBR and 107–118 and 112–128 for videotape and aggregate measures.

*$p < .05$.

FES

The most striking results involve the FES (see Table 10.14). The Personal Growth second-order factor is related to low Emotionality and high Activity, Sociability, and Attention Span. Not only are these midparent FES scores significantly related to all of the CCTI temperaments of control children, the correlations are higher than the corresponding correlations in the adoptive families; in the case of Emotionality and Sociability, the control family correlations are significantly higher than those in adoptive families. The significant correlation for Sociability in the adoptive families suggests some family environmental influences; however, the significantly higher control family correlations imply genetic influence in these relationships between midparent FES scores and midparent ratings of infant temperament. Although a similar pattern of results emerges for the aggregate measures that are composites of the parental ratings, tester ratings, and videotape ratings, the fact that the FES-temperament correlations do not emerge for either the tester ratings or the videotape ratings alone suggests the possibility that the relationship specifically involves parental perceptions of the family environment and parental perceptions of their infants' temperament. This does not imply that the relationship

TABLE 10.15

Correlations between HOME and FES Environmental Measures and Parental Personality[a]

Parental personality measure	12-month HOME total		24-month HOME total		FES Personal Growth	
	Mother	Father	Mother	Father	Mother	Father
EASI						
Emotionality–Fear	−.07	−.07	−.03	−.05	−.20*	−.15*
Emotionality–Anger	.01	.03	−.03	.01	−.16*	.03
Activity	.11	.06	.12*	.05	.16*	.21*
Sociability	.24*	.12*	.18*	.07	.24*	.19*
16 PF						
Extraversion	.21*	.13*	.18*	.11	.23*	.18*
Neuroticism	−.19*	−.10	−.13*	−.07	−.36*	−.18*

[a]Adoptive and control parents combined.

*$p < .05$.

is artifactual. Parental perceptions of the family's social climate and their perceptions of their children are important aspects of family dynamics, and it is interesting to speculate that genetic factors may be implicated in the relationship between these environmental and temperament measures.

If these FES–infant temperament relationships are in fact mediated genetically, there should exist parental characteristics that are genetically related to parental reports of the family's social climate and infant temperament. Although few parental personality characteristics appear to be genetically related to infant temperament, we considered parental personality as a possible genetic mediator of the relationship between FES and infant temperament. The relationship between home environment and parental personality has rarely been explored, although, in accord with our hypothesis, parental sociability has been shown to be correlated with major dimensions of childrearing (Buss & Plomin, 1984). Some aspects of parental personality are, in fact, correlated with the HOME and FES, as indicated in Table 10.15. The HOME General Factor is related positively to Sociability and Extraversion and negatively to Emotionality–Fear and Neuroticism. FES Personal Growth is more closely related to parental personality, again yielding positive correlations with Sociability and Extraversion, and negative correlations with Emotionality and Neuroticism. In addition, FES Personal Growth correlates positively with Activity. In general, personality–environment correlations are slightly higher for mothers than for fathers.

Does parental personality mediate a genetic relationship between environment and infant temperament? Table 10.16 addresses this issue by repeating the zero-order correlations between FES Personal Growth and CCTI temperament from Table 10.14 and then listing partial correlations with the appropriate parental personality traits partialed out. The partial correlations are presented separately for mothers and fathers because correlations between parental personality and the FES

TABLE 10.16

Zero-Order Correlations between FES Personal Growth and CCTI Temperament at 12 Months and Partial Correlations after Effects of Parental Personality Are Removed

Infant CCTI (midparent rating)	Zero-order correlation between midparent FES Personal Growth and CCTI		Mothers' or fathers' EASI scale partialed out	Partial correlations			
				Adoptive		Control	
	Adoptive	Control		Mother	Father	Mother	Father
Emotionality	−.10	−.39*	Emotionality–Fear	−.06	−.08	−.39*	−.38*
Emotionality	−.10	−.39*	Emotionality–Anger	−.07	−.18*	−.38*	−.38*
Activity	.06	.18*	Activity	.06	.08	.18*	.15*
Sociability	.16*	.34*	Sociability	.14	.13	.28*	.33*
Attention Span	.10	.19*	Impulsivity	.09	.07	.20*	.19*

*$p < .05$.

are somewhat higher for mothers (see Table 10.15). The first row of correlations indicates that the zero-order correlation between FES Personal Growth and infant Emotionality is $-.10$ in the adoptive families and $-.39$ in the controls, a significant difference suggesting genetic influence. When parents' Emotionality–Fear is partialed out, these correlations are scarcely affected for adoptive or control mothers or fathers. The partial correlations for the adoptive mothers and fathers ($-.06$ and $-.08$, respectively) are still significantly less than the partial correlations for the control mothers and fathers ($-.39$ and $-.38$). Also, partialing out parental IQ had little effect on the correlations.

Thus, we conclude that the genetic link between the environmental measures and infant temperament is not simply parental personality or IQ. If, for example, the relationship between FES Personal Growth and infant Emotionality were vitiated by partialing out parental Emotionality, then we would merely conclude that the relationship between FES Personal Growth and infant temperament was brought about by the fact that the FES inadvertently measures parental personality. However, as the data stand, they suggest that FES Personal Growth and, to a lesser extent, the HOME assess parental characteristics that are independent of EASI personality and IQ and that are related genetically to infant temperament.

Multiple Regressions of Infant Temperament on Parental Personality and Home Environment

Multiple regressions of infant temperament on several parental personality traits were described earlier and generally showed little predictive advantage over univariate analyses. We also conducted multiple regression analyses to explore the combined predictive power of parental personality and environmental measures.

Using CCTI midparent ratings of Sociability and Emotionality, the two variables that yielded the most relationships in control families, we conducted multiple regression analyses using mothers' Extraversion, Neuroticism, and Sociability measures and the FES second-order factor, Personal Growth. The results, shown in Table 10.17, indicate that, in the control families, parental personality and environmental measures each contributes predictive power and together account for over 10% of the variance in infant Sociability and Emotionality. Even though the FES measure is obtained only at 12 months, it continues to be related to infant temperament at 24 months. The data in Table 10.17 implicate genetic influence in that the multiple correlations in control families are larger than those in adoptive families.

Analysis of "Consistent" Infants

We explored the possibility that genetic and environmental influences can be seen more clearly for infants who are consistently rated as shy or emotional by both of their parents and by a tester. Data on adopted infants who are consistently shy, for

TABLE 10.17

Multiple Regressions of Infant CCTI Sociability and Emotionality on Measures of Parental Personality and FES Personal Growth

Regression	12 Months				24 Months			
	Adoptive		Control		Adoptive		Control	
	R	adj. R^2	R	adj. R^2	R	adj. R^2	R	adj. R^2
CCTI midparent Sociability on:								
Mothers' 16 PF Extraversion	.01		.24*		.08		.22*	
FES Personal Growth	.06	.00	.37*	.13	.16	.01	.35*	.11
CCTI midparent Sociability on:								
Mothers' EASI Sociability	.18*		.23*		.23*		.22*	
FES Personal Growth	.21	.03	.35*	.11	.27	.06	.33*	.10
CCTI midparent Emotionality on:								
Mothers' 16 PF Neuroticism	.15		.25*		.06		.10	
FES Personal Growth	.15	.00	.40*	.15	.13	.00	.25*	.05

*Significance ($p < .05$) of term added to multiple regression.

TABLE 10.18

Mother–Offspring and Environment–Offspring Correlations in Control Families for a Subsample of Infants Who Were Rated Consistently by Parents and by Testers

Infant measure	16 PF Extraversion	EASI Sociability	16 PF Neuroticism	EASI Emotionality–Fear	HOME General Factor	FES Personal Growth	FES Traditional Organization
12 Months							
CCTI Sociability	.16	.25	−.63*	−.24	−.02	.42*	.00
IBR Affect–Extraversion	.43*	.25	.02	.27	−.17	.12	−.14
Video Affect–Extraversion	.07	.16	−.36*	−.18	.10	.03	.14
Aggregate Affect–Extraversion	.25	.29	.29	−.19	−.16	.24	.22
N =	21–28	24–34	22–30	25–35	24–34	25–36	25–36
24 Months							
CCTI Sociability	.34*	.25	−.15	.00	.24		
IBR Affect–Extraversion	.05	−.08	−.03	−.07	.14		
Video Affect–Extraversion	.48*	.43*	−.14	−.10	.28*		
Aggregate Affect–Extraversion	.34*	.26	−.05	−.12	.37*		
N =	28–37	34–46	30–39	24–46	35–47		

*$p < .05$.

example, might show stronger relationships with environmental measures and with measures on their biological parents than do infants who are shy in one situation but not in another. In analyses of personality data from the Texas Adoption Project, Loehlin *et al.* (1981) came to the following conclusion: "Restriction to a subsample of well-measured children provided higher correlations and more evidence of heritability, particularly in the extraversion domain" (p. 309). They refer to the subsample as "well measured" because of their hypothesis that "only some children's personalities are being well measured in this study, whether as a result of deficiencies in the measurement techniques or because personalities in many pre-adolescent children are not yet clearly defined" (p. 321). Consistency was defined as an absolute standard score difference less than 1.0 between parental ratings on bipolar trait scales and self-report personality questionnaires.

With infants, of course, we have no self-report data. However, we do have parental ratings and tester ratings. In selecting a consistently rated subsample, a trade-off must take place between sample size and degree of consistency. Selection for consistency in parental ratings and tester ratings is particularly difficult because the correlation between parental and tester ratings is low (see Table 9.6). We chose a criterion that produced sample sizes of about 30 to 40 infants for most measures, samples that yield only 35% power ($p < .05$, one-tailed) to detect correlations of .20 and 60% power to detect correlations of .30. As a criterion, we selected infants whose midparent ratings and tester ratings were either both above the mean or both below the mean. Table 10.18 lists control mother–offspring and environment–offspring correlations for the major parental and environmental factors as they relate to Sociability and Affect–Extraversion measures of the infants. Of the 48 correlations, 10 are statistically significant. All but 2 of the significant correlations were also significant in the previous analyses of the total sample. The significant correlations in Table 10.18 are higher than the previously reported correlations, as dictated by the smaller sample size. However, 17 of the 48 comparisons were significant for the total sample as compared to 10 of 48 in Table 10.18; thus, no gain in detecting parent–offspring or environment–offspring relationships is accomplished by analysis of data on a consistently measured subsample of infants. Similar results were obtained for the biological and adoptive comparisons, as well as for analyses of Activity and Task Orientation. It appears that in the trade-off between consistency of measurement and sample size, the latter is more important.

Interactions between Temperament and Environment

In the temperament literature, the word *interaction* is frequently used and has become paramount to some theorists such as Thomas and Chess (1980), who propose an "interactionist view that behavioral attributes must at all times be considered . . . in their interaction with environmental opportunities, demands, and expectations" (p. 86). The interactionist position espoused by Thomas and

Chess emphasizes a particular type of interaction: matches and mismatches that contribute to goodness of fit between temperament and environment. Sometimes, interactionism is used to refer to the truism that both an organism and an environment are prerequisites for behavior. In order to understand individual differences, however, the important question is the extent to which individual differences in behavior can be explained by differences in temperament, by differences in environments, and by temperament–environment interactions. If individual differences in temperament are completely intertwined with the fabric of experience, then no main effects of temperament or of the environment will be observed and strong temperament-by-environment interactions should be found.

Research related to temperament–environment interactions has emanated from the goodness-of-fit model of Thomas and Chess, which states that the effect of temperament depends upon its fit to the environment. Aside from anecdotal examples (Thomas & Chess, 1977) and isolated research (e.g., Scholom, Zucker, & Stollak, 1979), the only systematic program of research on this topic has been conducted by the Lerners (J. Lerner, 1984; Lerner & Lerner, 1983; Lerner, Lerner, & Zabski, 1981). Their data suggest some temperament–environment interaction in the relationship between school performance and adjustment, although their method has been questioned by Plomin and Daniels (1984), who suggest the use of hierarchical multiple regression (Cohen & Cohen, 1975) to assess the statistical significance of temperament–environment interactions after the main effects of temperament and of environment have been removed. Plomin and Daniels also propose three categories of temperament interactions depending upon whether temperament is used as an independent variable, a dependent variable, or both an independent and a dependent variable in the interaction analysis. The first category represents the usual approach in which temperament, environment, and temperament–environment interactions are used to predict adjustment outcomes. The second category includes, for example, genotype–environment interaction; and the third category includes developmental interactions in which temperament and environment and their interaction are used to predict later temperament.

Interactions of the first type are discussed in the next chapter, which focuses on behavioral problems; analyses of interactions of the third type cannot be performed until CAP data are available for 3- and 4-year-olds. In this section, we consider interaction analyses of the second type in which temperament is treated as a dependent variable. Specifically, we focus on genotype–environment interaction, the extent to which environmental factors affect children differentially as a function of their temperamental dispositions. In previous sections, environmental measures, including adoptive parents' personality, have been related to infant temperament; similarly, genetic effects have been sought in correlations between biological parents and their adopted-away offspring. Genotype–environment interaction, as any statistical interaction, is the extent to which joint information about these environmental and genetic factors predict infant temperament once the main effects of environment and genotype have been removed (Plomin, DeFries, and Loehlin, 1977).

TABLE 10.19

Use of Genotype–Environment Interactions to Predict Infant Temperament[a]

Genetic factor	Environmental factor	Dependent CCTI infant measure	Genotype–environment interaction	
			12 Months R^2 change	24 Months R^2 change
BM Emotionality– Fear	AM Emotionality– Fear	Emotionality	.002	.007
BM Emotionality– Anger	AM Emotionality– Anger	Emotionality	.022	.011
BM Activity	AM Activity	Activity	.002	.002
BM Sociability	AM Sociability	Sociability	.014	.002
BM Extraversion	AM Extraversion	Sociability	.003	.000
BM Neuroticism	AM Neuroticism	Emotionality	.001	.025
BM Sociability	AP HOME General	Sociability	.003	.007
BM Extraversion	AP HOME General	Sociability	.000	.005
BM Sociability	AP FES Personal Growth	Sociability	.017	.001
BM Extraversion	AP FES Personal Growth	Sociability	.007	.001
BM Neuroticism	AP HOME General	Emotionality	.002	.004
BM Neuroticism	AP FES Personal Growth	Emotionality	.000	.001

[a]BM = biological mother; AM = adoptive mother; AP = adoptive midparent.

Table 10.19 presents a sampling of the results of the many possible combinations of biological parents' personality, adoptive parents' personality and home environment, and dependent temperament measures of the infants. None of the interactions is significant; the usual amount of adjusted variance explained is .00 for the analyses reported in Table 10.19. Of course, one must ask what power we had to detect such interactions if they are indeed present. Cohen and Cohen (1975, pp. 117–120) discuss the issue of power in multiple regressions and indicate that the probability of detecting a significant interaction will increase as the amount of variance explained by the interaction effect increases in relation to the total variance explained by the multiple regression, as the number of subjects increases, and as the number of variables decreases. Given our sample size and total variance explained of 10 to 20%, we have approximately 80% power to detect interactions that account for 5% of the total variance (i.e., 25–50% of the total variance explained). Thus, if such interactions between temperamental disposition and environment account for as much as 5% of the variance, we should have been able to detect them. However, if interaction effects account for as little as 1% of the variance, one would need a sample size of over 600 to detect a significant interaction with 80% power given an R^2 of 10 to 20%.

Two of the interactions are worth discussing even though they attained probability values of only .10. The two interactions appear to be other than chance phenomena for three reasons: First, they both involve infants' CCTI Emotionality, as predicted by biological and adoptive mothers' EASI Emotionality–Anger in one case and their 16 PF Neuroticism in the other. Secondly, the interaction in both cases explains more than the usual amount of variance at both 12 and 24 months, as seen in Table 10.19. Thirdly, the interactions are similar at 12 and 24 months: Genetic differences in emotionality appear only when adoptive mothers are low in emotionality. When adoptive mothers are above average in emotionality, adopted infants are emotional regardless of their genetic disposition. The interactions involving EASI Emotionality–Anger and infants' CCTI Emotionality at 12 and at 24 months are depicted as a dichotomous two-by-two analysis of variance in Figures 10.1 and 10.2 to assist in the visualization of these results.

In addition to the interactions described in Table 10.19, we conducted 68 other analyses using different combinations of biological mothers' data and home environment measures. Only 2 of these—less than a chance number—were statistically significant ($p < .05$). Again, however, we are led to believe that these may not be chance associations because they both involve CCTI Activity of the infants and activity level of the biological mothers. In one case, the environmental measure was the fourth factor of the HOME, which we labeled Restriction–Punishment, and

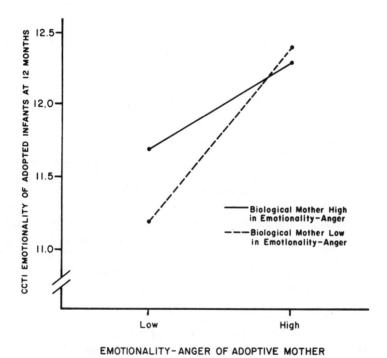

FIGURE 10.1 Midparent CCTI ratings of adopted infants' emotionality at 12 months of age as a function of biological mothers' and adoptive mothers' EASI Emotionality–Anger.

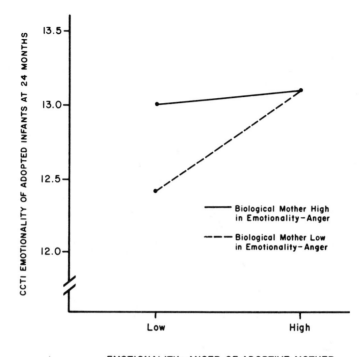

FIGURE 10.2   Midparent CCTI ratings of adopted infants' emotionality at 24 months of age as a function of biological mothers' and adoptive mothers' EASI Emotionality–Anger.

it interacted significantly with biological mothers' EASI Activity to predict 12-month-old CCTI Activity (R^2 change $= .027$, $p < .05$). In the other case, the environmental measure was the FES second-order factor that we named Traditional Organization, and it interacted significantly with biological mothers' EASI Activity to predict 24-month-old CCTI Activity (R^2 change $= .031$, $p < .05$).

At 12 months, there is a main effect of HOME Restriction–Punishment that involves a positive relationship between that environmental measure and infant activity level, inviting the interpretation that more active children elicit greater restrictiveness from their parents. As illustrated in Figure 10.3, the interaction indicates that genetic differences in activity among children are likely to be seen when parents are particularly restrictive. That is, even though there is no main effect for biological mothers' activity level on their adopted-away infants' activity, adoptees whose biological mothers are above the mean in activity level and whose adoptive parents are more restrictive than average are rated as more active than other children.

At 24 months, there is no main effect for the genetic measure (biological mothers' activity level) or for the environmental measure (FES Traditional Organization in the adoptive homes). The observed interaction, illustrated in Figure 10.4, can be

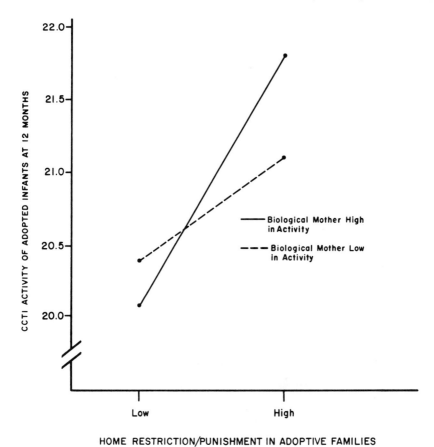

FIGURE 10.3   Midparent CCTI ratings of adopted infants' activity at 12 months of age as a function of biological mothers' EASI Activity and adoptive families' HOME Restriction–Punishment.

interpreted as indicating that children genetically predisposed to low activity level are more active given the structure of a traditionally organized family. Another way to describe the interaction is that genetic variation for activity level is manifested only in families low in traditional organization.

In summary, few significant interactions between genotype and environment emerged from the CAP temperament data. These results suggest that individual differences in temperament in infancy not only are generally unrelated to genetic and environmental indices, but also are unrelated to interactions between genotype and environment. Nonetheless, the few interactions that were observed are reasonable and interesting. They suggest the possibility that genotypic differences among children emerge more clearly in calmer and less constrained environments: Genetic differences in emotionality are seen when the rearing parents are low in emotionality, and genetic differences in activity emerge in families low on the FES Traditional Organization factor.

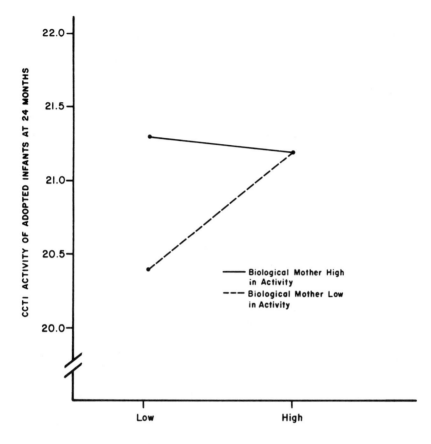

FIGURE 10.4 Midparent CCTI ratings of adopted infants' activity at 24 months of age as a function of biological mothers' EASI Activity and adoptive families' FES Traditional Organization.

Genotype–Environment Correlation

One might expect genotype–environment correlations to be particularly important in the development of temperament. Active children may experience a family life charged with energy (passive genotype–environment correlation); emotional children may be taunted by other children, exacerbating their emotional propensity (reactive genotype–environment correlation); and sociable children may go to great lengths to interact with others even in isolated environments (active genotype–environment correlation). Scarr (1981; Scarr & McCartney, 1983) has suggested a general theory of development that involves a shift from passive genotype–environment correlation in infancy to reactive and active genotype–environment correlations later in childhood. The role of children in fashioning their own temperament-related environment has also been discussed by Dunn (1980).

TABLE 10.20

Reactive Genotype–Environment Correlations: Correlations between Environmental Measures
in Adoptive Homes and Biological Mothers' Personality

	Environmental measure			
	12 Months			24 Months
Biological mothers' personality measure	HOME General Factor (N = 90–104)	FES Personal Growth (N = 138–159)	FES Traditional Organization (N = 138–159)	HOME General Factor (N = 102–108)
16 PF Extraversion	−.06	−.04	.07	−.04
Neuroticism	.12	−.20*	−.04	−.05
EASI Emotionality–Fear	.14	−.18*	−.15*	.04
Emotionality–Anger	.11	.01	.02	−.01
Activity	−.17*	−.04	.05	−.16*
Sociability	−.04	.05	.15*	−.04
Impulsivity	.01	.15*	−.05	−.07

*$p < .05$.

Genotype–environment correlation differs from genotype–environment interaction in that it literally involves correlations between genotypes and environments rather than differential effects of environment on children of different genotypes. That is, genotype–environment correlation implies that children's experiences depend upon their genetic propensities. It is important in that it affects quantitative genetic parameter estimates. For developmentalists, genotype–environment correlation holds special importance because it provides one means for answering the direction-of-effects question: When genotype–environment correlation is found, it suggests that the environment reflects rather than affects traits in children. However, we must first find a significant relationship before we can begin to worry about the direction of effects in the relationship. In the case of genotype–environment correlation, both genetic and environmental effects must be operative before a correlation can be observed. That is, genotype–environment correlation is assessed by the correlation between genetic propensities (indexed by data on biological parents) and environmental measures (indexed by measures of the adoptive parents or the adoptive homes). No genotype–environment correlation will be observed unless the genetic estimate from the biological parents affects the adopted-away child (i.e., there is genetic influence) and unless the environmental estimate also is related to the adoptees' development. Given the paucity of genetic and family environment effects in our analyses of infant temperament, we were not optimistic as we began to search for genotype–environment correlations.

Table 10.20 lists the correlations between biological mothers' personality traits and the major HOME and FES environmental measures. More significant correlations emerged than expected by chance (7 vs. 1). Only the results for the HOME General Factor are listed because the four rotated HOME factors yielded similar results. Only two significant genotype–environment correlations emerged for the HOME, although they do demonstrate replication at 12 and 24 months: Biological mothers' Activity is negatively related to the HOME General Factor, suggesting that the adoptive parents are assessed as less responsive during the HOME interview when their children are genetically predisposed towards high activity.

As usual, the FES Personal Growth factor shows the most significant relationships. In adoptive homes that are high on the Personal Growth factor, the adopted children's biological mothers are low on EASI Emotionality–Fear and 16 PF Neuroticism and high on EASI Impulsivity. This implies that adoptive parents rate the social climate of their home as higher on the Personal Growth dimension when their infants are predisposed to be less emotional and more impulsive. The FES Traditional Organization factor yields two significant correlations that suggest more organization when the infants' biological background provides a propensity toward less fearfulness and greater sociability.

In summary, there is evidence for reactive genotype–environment correlation involving activity and emotionality. This is called *reactive* because people, in this case parents, respond differently to children with different genetic propensities.

Another type of genotype–environment correlation is *passive* in that the correlation is induced by the fact that parents share both heredity and environment with their child. Thus, highly sociable parents may provide both heredity and a family

TABLE 10.21

Passive Genotype–Environment Correlations: Comparison of Standard Deviations for Adopted and Control Infants

	Standard deviation			
	12 Months		24 Months	
Infant measure	Adopted	Control	Adopted	Control
CCTI				
Emotionality	3.0	3.2	3.0	2.9
Activity	2.8	2.3	2.4	2.1
Sociability	3.7	3.7	3.7	3.3
Attention Span	2.3	2.2	2.7	2.6
IBR				
Affect–Extraversion	4.5	5.3	6.3	6.7
Activity	3.2	2.7	3.2	3.6
Task Orientation	3.3	3.3	3.1	3.1
Video				
Affect–Extraversion	1.9	1.9	1.7	2.0
Activity	1.0	1.0	0.8	0.9
Task Orientation	2.0	1.8	1.0	2.0
Aggregate				
Affect–Extraversion	0.6	0.6	0.6	0.6
Activity	0.7	0.6	0.7	0.6
Task Orientation	0.6	0.7	0.6	0.6

environment conducive to the development of sociable children. If passive gen-otype–environment correlation is important, variance among adopted children should be less than variance among control children because adopted children do not have the component of variance caused by the double-barreled effect of sharing both heredity and environment with their rearing parents. However, a competing explanation for reduced variance for adoptees is a restriction of range due to selec-tion biases. The data shown in Tables 9.12 and 9.13 belie this possibility because the variances for the three types of parents are quite comparable: Only 2 of 26 personality measures showed a significant departure from homogeneity of variance for adoptive, biological, and control parents.

Table 10.21 presents the standard deviations for the major infant temperament measures. The similarity of the standard deviations for the adoptees and controls suggests that passive genotype–environment correlation does not have an important influence upon our measures of infant temperament.

Interrelationships between Temperament and Cognition

Although both temperament and cognition are complicated enough to guarantee the need for much more research in each domain, it will eventually become impor-tant to consider their interrelationship. Developmentalists have become increasingly interested in the relationship between socioemotional and cognitive development, especially in infancy (e.g., Sroufe, 1979; Wachs & Gruen, 1982). For adolescents and adults, some relationships between personality and cognitive abilities have been reported (Turner & Horn, 1977), and one study has found cross-domain correlations between control parents and their offspring (Nagoshi et al., 1982). Some tempera-ment–cognition relationships have also been found in infancy (Bayley, 1970); two studies suggest that difficult temperament in infancy is negatively related to cog-nitive performance (Field et al., 1978; Wachs & Gandour, 1983).

In this section, we relate temperament and cognition using larger samples of adults and infants than previously reported; more importantly, we use the CAP parent–offspring design to explore the etiology of the interface between tempera-ment and cognition. One problem with research in this area is the lack of a the-oretical rationale for relating the domains of temperament and cognition and the ensuing welter of information concerning the many possible contrasts between temperament and cognition. In order to avoid huge matrices of cross-domain cor-relations, we focus on a few major traits: IQ, extraversion, and neuroticism of parents and Bayley MDI scores, sociability, and difficult temperament of infants.

For the CAP parents, the correlations between IQ and 16 PF Extraversion are .01 and .02, respectively, for 400 mothers and 280 fathers. The correlations between IQ and 16 PF Neuroticism are $-.14$ ($p < .05$) and $-.11$ for mothers and fathers, respectively. Nagoshi et al. (1982) reported similar results for Eysenck's measure of Extraversion and Neuroticism: Extraversion did not correlate significantly with

TABLE 10.22

Parent–Offspring Cross-Domain Correlations for Temperament and Cognition

		Biological mothers ($N = 152-168$)	Adoptive		Control	
			Mothers ($N = 124-170$)	Fathers ($N = 129-163$)	Mothers ($N = 129-150$)	Fathers ($N = 114-152$)
Parent measure	Infant measure					
IQ	12-mo CCTI sociability	−.03	.13	.02	.12	−.04
IQ	24-mo CCTI sociability	−.11	.11	.02	.12	.07
IQ	12-mo difficult temperament	−.12	−.17*	.00	−.13	−.20*
IQ	24-mo difficult temperament	−.09	−.18*	−.01	−.06	−.14*
16 PF Extraversion	12-mo Bayley MDI	.04	.11	.03	−.02	−.03
16 PF Extraversion	24-mo Bayley MDI	−.05	.00	.16*	.13	−.13
16 PF Neuroticism	12-mo Bayley MDI	.09	.05	−.03	−.02	−.08
16 PF Neuroticism	24-mo Bayley MDI	−.05	−.09	−.14	−.07	−.07

*$p < .05$.

adult IQ for either mothers or fathers; Neuroticism correlated significantly with IQ for mothers but not for fathers.

For the CAP infants, the correlations between Bayley MDI scores and CCTI Sociability are .10 and .00, respectively, for 179 boys and 144 girls at 12 months; at 24 months, the correlations are .28 and .07. The correlations between MDI scores and difficult temperament are .05 and .03 at 12 months; −.12 and −.01 at 24 months. The positive relationships between infant sociability and cognitive performance replicates a finding by Stevenson and Lamb (1979), and the negative relationships at 24 months between difficult temperament and cognitive performance are similar to those found by Field *et al.* (1978) and Wachs and Gandour (1983). However, the low magnitude of these temperament–cognition relationships indicates that replication of such results will be unlikely unless sample sizes are in the hundreds; to detect a correlation of .20 with 80% power ($p < .05$, two-tailed) requires a sample size of 200.

A unique analysis provided by the CAP is cross-domain correlations for infants and their biological, adoptive, and control parents. These parent–offspring correlations are listed in Table 10.22. Although the correlations are nonsignificant, an environmental relationship between parental IQ and infants' sociability is implied by the correlations of control and adoptive mothers' IQ with infants' 12- and 24-month sociability scores. The most interesting pattern of results is the generally negative relationship observed between difficult temperament for biological, adoptive, and control relationships. This finding suggests that the negative relationship observed in several studies, including ours, between infant cognitive performance and difficult temperament may originate in genetic and family environmental influences of parents' IQ on infants' difficult temperament and cognitive performance. In general, however, temperament–cognitive cross-domain relationships between parents and their infant offspring are weak.

Conclusions

Individual differences in infant temperament might reasonably be expected to show greater and more frequent relationships with parental personality and environmental measures than have been reported for mental development. It is frequently argued that development of mental abilities is highly canalized so that individual differences that are observed are unimportant. However, no one has argued that infant temperament is highly canalized. Nonetheless, the data presented in this chapter, based on the reasonably representative CAP sample with its multimethod measures of infant temperament, add substance to an emerging principle that individual differences in infancy are neither predictable from parental or environmental measures nor predictive of individual differences among children or adults. However, the exceptions to this rule are interesting, and we summarize the CAP results for infant temperament as predicted by parental personality, specific environmental influences, and combined genetic and environmental factors.

Parental Personality

In general, parental personality has little power to predict infant personality, either genetically or environmentally. Self-report data on adolescents and adults yield a median parent–offspring correlation in control families of .15; we found an average correlation of .08 for parental ratings. Aggregation improves the correlations only minimally: For midparent ratings of infant temperament, the average parent–offspring correlation is .10; aggregating parents' self-report and mate ratings and using midparent ratings of the infant yields an average parent–offspring correlation of .12. Despite the promise of an eclectic, multimethod approach, the data for tester ratings and ratings based on videotaped interactions between mothers and infants yield no systematic parent–offspring correlations—a finding that is likely to be related to the low 12- to 24-month stability for these measures.

The few available twin studies of parental ratings of infant temperament suggest heritabilities far greater than those for infant mental development. However, the pattern of twin correlations violates the twin model because the identical twin correlations are typically about .50 and fraternal twin correlations tend to be near zero, perhaps due to a contrast effect. Tester ratings on the IBR yield more reasonable patterns of twin correlations and also suggest high heritabilities in infancy: .60 for Task Orientation, .50 for Affect–Extraversion, and .30 for Activity.

The infant temperament data from the CAP and the data from twin studies of infant temperament might be compatible, however. It is important to remember that the CAP parent–offspring design has three prerequisites for isolating genetic influence: A trait must be heritable both in infancy and in adulthood, and the genetic correlation between infancy and adulthood must be substantial. If the heritabilities of infant temperament and adult temperament are both about .50 and the genetic correlation between infancy and adulthood is .25, then the expected parent–offspring correlation is approximately what we found, .06. However, the fact that a pattern of results similar to ours has been found in adoption studies involving adolescents and adults suggests that the genetic correlation between early and later stages of development increases only slightly during this time period (e.g., infancy and 30 years of age vs. adolescence and 40 years of age vs. early adulthood and 45 years of age).

In terms of specific temperaments, the CAP parental rating results hint at the possibility of genetic influence on sociability and emotionality at 24 months; results for these same traits suggest family environmental influence at both 12 and 24 months. Nonetheless, these findings do not seriously violate the general principle that individual differences in infancy are unpredictable and unpredictive because, at most, parental personality predicts less than 10% of the variance of infant temperament. However, considering the three CAP conditions for finding genetic influence—heritability both in infancy and in adulthood, and substantial genetic correlations between infancy and adulthood—the possibility of genetic influence on sociability and emotionality is exciting because it suggests some genetically mediated continuity from infancy to adulthood.

As explained in Chapter 3, we can estimate genetic continuity from infancy to adulthood if we know the correlation between biological mothers and their adopted-away offspring and if we know the heritabilities in infancy and in adulthood. The biological mother–offspring correlation for EASI Sociability and CCTI Sociability is approximately .15. Although we cannot be certain about the heritabilities of adult sociability or infant shyness, twin studies generally suggest substantial heritability in adulthood and at least moderate heritability in infancy (Buss & Plomin, 1984). Assuming a heritability of .50 for adults and .30 for infants, the genetic correlation between infancy and adulthood is .78; if the heritabilities in infancy and adulthood are both .30, the genetic correlation between infancy and adulthood is 1.0. In either case, these results suggest quite substantial genetic continuity between infant shyness and adult sociability.

Environmental Influences

The most positive results involve environmental analyses. Although correlations between adoptive parents' personality and infant temperament are meager, suggesting little shared or common familial environment, analyses of specific environmental measures such as the HOME and, especially, the FES yield some robust relationships. The importance of these findings is enhanced by the paucity of studies relating environmental measures to the development of temperament in infancy.

The HOME yields several relationships to infant temperament that are replicated in the control and adoptive homes, suggesting that the relationship is unaffected by genetic factors. At both 12 and 24 months, the HOME General Factor and the specific Maternal Involvement factor are related to sociability measures including the Affect–Extraversion factors. The Restriction–Punishment factor relates positively to infants' activity level. Relationships between HOME factors and the infant Task Orientation factors were complex at 12 months but generally in the expected direction at 24 months.

The HOME represents an environmental measure somewhere towards the objective side of a continuum from subjective to objective measures because it is an interview–observation measure completed by the experimenter. The FES, on the other hand, is much more subjective because it assesses parental perceptions of the social climate of the home. The most surprising result described in this chapter is that the FES shows the strongest relationship with infant temperament and that this relationship is substantially mediated by heredity. A second-order factor of the FES, which we derived and labeled Personal Growth, yields the most striking results. High scores on this factor occur when parents report that the family is expressive, uncontrolling, supportive, and oriented toward intellectual and cultural pursuits. Midparent scores on this factor are related to control infants' low Emotionality and high Activity, Sociability, and Attention Span.

In addition to explaining about 10% of the variance in the infant CCTI traits, these results are exciting because of the contrast they yield in control and adoptive families. For Emotionality and Sociability, the control family correlations are significantly higher than those in the adoptive families, implying that heredity mediates these relationships between midparent FES Personal Growth scores and midparent ratings of infant temperament.

Genetic influence is found only for the relationship between parental perceptions as measured by the FES and parental reports of infant temperament. We did not find similar results for the relationship between FES scores and tester ratings on the IBR or videotape ratings of infant temperament, nor did we find similar results for the HOME. This suggests that genetic influence is limited to the relationship between parents' perceptions of the home's social climate and their perceptions of their infants' temperament. The result is not completely subjective, however, because the same relationship is revealed by midparent scores on FES Personal Growth and midparent ratings of infant temperament. Far from denigrating the importance of this result, the involvement of genetic mediators between parents' perceptions of the home environment and infants' temperament, but not between more objective measures of the environment and infant temperament, adds to the plausibility of the finding. It suggests that heredity interfaces with the environment by altering perceptions of environment and experience as suggested by the work of Rowe (e.g., 1983), who consistently finds evidence for genetic influence on perceived environments.

The importance of this finding led us to explore further the genetically mediated relationship between FES Personal Growth and infant temperament. Although we found that both HOME and FES measures are related to parental personality, the relationships between these environmental measures and infant temperament are not weakened when parental personality is partialed out. Moreover, for the FES Personal Growth factor, the significantly higher correlations with infant temperament in control homes as compared to adoptive homes remain when parental personality and IQ are partialed out.

The Interface between Heredity and Environment

We also explored two concepts involving both heredity and environment: genotype–environment interactions and correlation. Analyses of genotype–environment interactions, the differential effects of environment on children of different genotypes, produced little evidence of nonlinear effects of genotype or environment on infant temperament. Nonetheless, the few interactions that emerged demand further attention because evidence for genotype–environment interaction has not been previously obtained in human behavioral-genetic analyses.

Analysis of genotype–environment correlation, the differential exposure of children to environments as a function of their genetic predispositions, were also performed. No evidence for passive genotype–environment correlation was revealed, but several reasonable examples of reactive genotype–environment correlation were isolated. Genotype–environment correlation permits causal interpretations of the direction of effects. For example, the CAP results permit us to say that children who are genetically predisposed toward high activity at both 12 and 24 months cause their parents to be less responsive as measured by the HOME. Another example is that children with a genetic propensity toward high emotionality cause parents to perceive the home environment as less supportive and expressive as measured by the FES

The focus of this chapter has been individual differences in dimensions of normal temperament. Because we recognize the interest in the extremes of these dimensions and other behavioral problems, as well as the possibility that etiologies at the extremes of a distribution can differ from etiologies of behavior within the normal range of variability, discussion of the CAP results for behavioral problems was reserved for the following chapter.

11

Behavioral Problems

Introduction

Researchers have not paid nearly as much attention to behavioral problems in infancy as they have to problems later in childhood and have seldom studied their etiology. Sleeping and eating disturbances, for example, occur so frequently that they are not viewed as problems in the usual sense of psychopathology. Furthermore, infants outgrow such difficulties, and they are not indicative of later psychopathology. Nonetheless, they can cause considerable distress for parents:

> Feeding and sleeping problems are very common in early childhood. It is still very unclear what relationship there may be between these difficulties in infancy and the preschool period, and later disturbances of feeding and sleeping. For many young children, these disturbances are probably essentially developmental problems. This does *not* mean that these difficulties should be dismissed lightly. (Dunn, 1981, p. 126)

> A baby's patterns of feeding and sleeping are of central concern to his mother from the moment that he is born. Difficulties, or deviations from the expected pattern, can cause great anxiety in the early weeks, and throughout the preschool period they remain a source of distress with real potential for damaging the relationship between mother and child. (Dunn, 1981, p. 119)

A longitudinal study of behavioral problems in London infants found that 8% of the parents of 1-year-olds and 11% of the parents of 2-year-olds worried about their infants' behavioral problems, especially those related to sleeping and eating (Jenkins, Owen, Bax, & Hart, 1984).

Problems in infancy have been emphasized during the past decade in the form of the global construct "difficult temperament," a concept developed by the New York Longitudinal Study (NYLS) research group (Thomas & Chess, 1977). Difficult temperament refers to a constellation of NYLS temperament dimensions—low rhythmicity, negative mood, low approach, low adaptability, and high intensity—although the procedures and rationale for this combination of traits have not been described in detail (Bates, 1980; Thomas & Chess, 1982). The earlier typology has given way to a continuous easy–difficult dimension. Second-order factor analyses of the nine NYLS dimensions generally find a factor that resembles an easy–difficult dimension and includes mood, approach, adaptability, and sometimes distractibility. Rhythmicity and intensity, which were included in the original conceptualization of difficult temperament, do not appear to be related to this second-order factor (Plomin, 1983a).

Although much of the initial interest in difficult temperament in infancy was aroused by its possible predictiveness of later behavioral problems, we can now conclude that difficult temperament in infancy is not related to later adjustment difficulties (Thomas & Chess, 1982). Nonetheless, infants who cry and fuss and who are fearful of and not adaptable to new situations clearly present problems for their parents. Thus, difficult temperament might be a useful variable to summarize infant behavioral problems. On the other hand, it has been suggested that it may be more profitable to consider specific behavioral problems in infancy than to focus on the global construct of difficult temperament (Daniels, Plomin, & Greenhalgh, 1984).

One way in which specific behavioral problems in infancy can be viewed is in terms of contextual categories. Infants primarily present problems in eating, sleeping, and diapering; problems in these three areas are relatively independent, which suggests the need to consider them as specific behavioral problems. Although there are surprisingly few studies relating such problems to measured aspects of the environment, it is often assumed that these contextual problems are caused by faulty parental management.

The fact that both psychoanalytic theory and learning theory have emphasized eating has led to a considerable body of research. However, most of the research focuses on the maternal behaviors related to feeding—breast versus bottle feeding, demand versus scheduled feeding, and weaning—rather than on infant eating behaviors such as reactions to new foods and regularity in eating habits. Yet there are marked individual differences in infants' eating styles that begin with the earliest sucking behavior (Dunn, 1981). Problems related to eating continue to plague parents even when their children pass infancy. For example, a study of a random sample of 3-year-olds in London showed that over 10% of the parents reported problems with their infants relating to eating, particularly finickiness over food (Richman, Stevenson, & Graham, 1975); similar results were reported earlier in the U.S. (Roberts & Schoelkpof, 1951). Furthermore, retrospective studies suggest that these later problems with eating begin in infancy (Bentovim, 1970; Brandon, 1970). A longitudinal study of over 300 children mentioned earlier found that 9% of the 12-month-olds and 29% of the 24-month-olds were reported by their parents as having some problems with their appetite (Jenkins et al., 1984).

Although sleep problems are less central to psychological theories of development, they are certainly as problematic for parents. About 20% of infants in the first 2 years of life experience regular sleep problems, primarily night waking (reviewed by Dunn, 1981). Although sleep problems have generally been attributed to anxieties about bedtime separation from parents, few studies have systematically examined the environmental correlates of these problems. Clearly there are wide individual differences among infants in how much they sleep, and these show some consistency during infancy (Jenkins *et al.*, 1984).

In addition to specific behaviors in contextual categories such as sleep disturbances and eating problems, behavioral problems in infancy can be conceptualized as the extremes of the normal dimensions of temperament discussed in Chapters 9 and 10, especially high emotionality, activity, and shyness. Because the etiology of behavior at the extremes of a normal distribution can differ from etiologies of behavior within the normal range, we decided to explore factors involved in making some infants highly emotional or very shy.

In this chapter, the CAP sample of adopted and nonadopted infants are described in terms of specific behavioral problems related to eating, sleeping, and diapering; the global construct of difficult temperament; and the extremes of the normal temperament dimensions. The etiology of these infant behavioral problems are explored by relating the infant measures to their parents' common behavioral problems including depression, hysteria, and sociopathy; normal parental personality dimensions including EASI and 16 PF measures; and assessments of the home environment including the HOME and the FES.

Descriptive Results

Chapter 4 briefly describes the CAP measures of behavioral problems in infants and their parents; replicas of the measures that are used are contained in Appendices A and C. In this section, we present the results of relevant factor analyses and descriptive information such as means, standard deviations, and intercorrelations among the infant measures and among the adult measures,

Infant Measures

Factor Structures

As mentioned earlier, the CAP includes three ways of looking at common behavioral problems in infancy. The first involves what we call contextual problems, which are sometimes referred to as functional problems. Three contexts for behavioral problems in infancy are sleeping, eating, and diapering. Items were developed to assess each of these, and the results of a factor analysis of the items are presented in Table 11.1. Other items listed in the appendices were included in the factor analyses; however, Table 11.1 includes only those items that loaded above .30 on one of the three contextual factors. The factors are similar at 12 and 24 months and

TABLE 11.1

Factor Analysis of Contextual Problems in Infancy for All Infants Combined[a]

Factor	Item descriptor	Factor loading					
		12 Months			24 Months		
		Sleep	Eat	Diapers	Sleep	Eat	Diapers
Sleep Problems	Irregular time falling asleep	.57			.68		
	Fussy–irritable time for sleep	.50			.63		
	Difficult going to sleep	.45			.59		
	Irregular time waking up				.31		
Eating Problems	Impossible to say when hungry		.40			.61	
	Impossible to say how much will eat		.71			.71	
	Dislikes new foods		.50			.38	
	Easily distracted at meal time					.43	
Diaper Problems	Much fussing about dirty diaper			.73			.90
	Cries loudly about wet diaper			.82			.74
	Very active while diapers changed			.66			.79
	Fussy while diaper changed			.57			.67

[a]$N = 330$. Only loadings greater than .30 are listed.

are quite general in nature. For example, the Sleep Problems factor includes irregularity in waking as well as difficulties in going to sleep; the Eating Problems factor involves reactions to new foods as well as regularity of eating; and the Diaper Problems factor involves reactions to wet or soiled diapers as well as responses to diaper changes. Scales are created by summing the scores for the four items on each of the three factors at 12 and at 24 months.

In addition, we explored the two Colorado Childhood Temperament Inventory (CCTI) scales neglected in the previous chapters on normal dimensions of temperament: Reaction to Foods and Soothability. The CCTI was constructed as an amalgamation of the EASI temperaments of Buss and Plomin (1975, 1984) and the nine temperament dimensions studied in the NYLS (Thomas & Chess, 1977). The Reaction to Foods and Soothability factors of the CCTI are primarily formed by NYLS items and involve specific behavioral problems to a greater extent than do the other CCTI temperament dimensions such as Emotionality, Activity, Sociability, and Attention Span. Soothability involves the ease with which a child can be calmed when fussing or crying. Reaction to Foods appears as a factor because many of the NYLS items involve infants' reactions to food, and such items form their own factor rather than loading on the intended NYLS dimensions of temperament. Interestingly, this factor, unlike the other CCTI factors, yielded no evidence of heritability in a study of young twins (Plomin & Rowe, 1977). Unlike the general contextual Eating Problems factor, the CCTI Reaction to Foods scale focuses on reactions to new foods.

The second approach is quite nearly the opposite of the approach used to study contextual problems. Rather than focusing on specific behavioral problems, we constructed a measure of the global construct of difficult temperament, which includes several types of behavioral problems. NYLS dimensions were factored to produce a general dimension of difficultness. Nine, 3-point scales similar to the parental rating "general impressions" items included the Carey NYLS instruments (Carey & McDevitt, 1978) were used. In addition, CAP parents are asked to rate the overall difficultness of their infant, an item that served as a marker variable in the factor analysis. An unrotated first principal component derived from these 10 items is obviously related to the NYLS concept of difficult temperament, as shown in Table 11.2. The highest-loading item at both 12 and 24 months is the marker variable of general difficultness, followed by mood, distractibility, and intensity of expression of feelings. Thus, this first principal component is similar to the difficult temperament factor found in other studies. Each infant is assigned a Difficult Temperament factor score on the basis of the principal component weights.

In addition to obtaining parental ratings of difficult temperament, we also attempted to construct a measure of difficult temperament based on the videotape observations of mother–infant interaction. In each of the four videotaped situations during the 12-month home visit and each of the three situations at 24 months, the following item was rated: "In general child (1) *is not difficult at all,* (2) *has rare periods of difficulty,* (3) *has occasional periods of difficulty,* (4) *is somewhat difficult,* and (5) *is extremely difficult."* The average correlation for this item across

TABLE 11.2

Factor Loadings of NYLS "General Impressions" Items on a First
Principal Component of "Difficult" Temperament

	Factor loading	
NYLS item	12 Months	24 Months
Activity level	.33	.52
Regularity	.35	.25
Response to change in routine	.55	.37
Response to new situations	.42	.23
Level of sensory threshold	.22	.04
Intensity of expression of feelings	.43	.56
Mood	.57	.53
Distractibility	.45	.53
Persistence and attention span	.35	.43
General difficultness	−.68	−.57

situations was .24 at 12 months and .35 at 24 months. The scores were summed across situations separately at each year and divided by the number of sessions to produce an average item rating. The mean at both years was 1.4, which is between the responses of *not difficult at all* and *rare periods of difficulty,* suggesting that the videotapes showed few examples of difficult behavior. This was verified by frequency analyses: Only one infant was rated as *somewhat difficult,* and no infants were rated as *extremely difficult.* Furthermore, the correlations with the parental rating of difficult temperament were only .06 and .11 at 12 and 24 months, respectively. For these reasons, we excluded the videotape measure of difficult temperament from further analysis.

Our third approach to studying behavioral problems in infancy was to select the extremes of the distributions of normal temperament described in Chapters 9 and 10. Specifically, data on the 10% of the infants who are the most active, most emotional, and most shy (low sociability) were selected for analysis, and these extremes were compared to the rest of the sample in terms of parental personality and psychopathology and environmental measures. The reason for selecting these extremes lies in the possibility that parental and environmental correlates of infant behavior at the problematic extremes of a distribution can differ from the correlates for the rest of the distribution. A more general approach to this issue involves analyses of nonlinear relationships (Vogler & DeFries, 1983); that is, if the extremes of a distribution show stronger or weaker relationships than the rest of the distribution, the relationship for the entire distribution should be curvilinear. We also conducted analyses of this type.

Means and Standard Deviations

Table 11.3 presents descriptive statistics for the contextual problems and difficult temperament measures at 12 and 24 months. The means suggest that behavioral

TABLE 11.3

Means and Standard Deviations for Infant Behavioral Problems

Measure	12 Months			24 Months		
	N	$\overline{X}$	SD	N	$\overline{X}$	SD
Sleep Problems	329	5.6	1.1	331	5.6	1.3
Eating Problems	329	6.2	1.2	330	7.2	1.4
Diaper Problems	330	7.0	1.1	317	6.4	1.3
CCTI Reaction to Foods	284	11.4	3.1	284	12.6	3.3
CCTI Soothability	284	18.6	2.3	284	17.9	2.3

problems are common in infancy, and the standard deviations imply substantial variability among infants. Only 5% of the sample was reported as generally regular within a half hour for falling asleep and waking up, generally cheerful when it is bedtime, and going to sleep right away. Only 15% of the infants would be added to this figure if a rating of *some problems* was counted for one of the four items shown in Table 11.1. Eating problems are also common: Only 1% of the sample were rated as having no problems in this domain; that is, their parents rated them as generally hungry at regular times, easy to predict how much they will eat, usually accepts new foods, and is not easily distracted at meal time. Only 3% of the sample is added if we include a rating of *some problems* for one of the four items. Concerning diaper problems, not a single infant was rated as just fussing a little about a wet or soiled diaper and as generally lying still and being happy during diaper changes.

From 12 to 24 months, sleep problems remain at the same level, eating problems increase, and diaper problems decrease. It is not appropriate to compare the levels of the three types of contextual problems because the rating scales differed for the three types. Difficult temperament was created as a standardized principal-component score separately at 12 and at 24 months; thus, the means are zero and the standard deviations are 1.0.

Variability and means were similar for adopted and control boys and girls. Cochran's C and Bartlett's Box F yielded no significant departure from homogeneity of variance for any of the behavioral problems. A multivariate test of the homogeneity of dispersion matrices for the four groups was also nonsignificant. Concerning means, a multivariate analysis of gender, adoptive–control status, and gender-by-status interactions, yielded no significant effects. At a univariate level of analysis, 2 of the 12 comparisons for gender yielded significant differences: Girls had lower means on the CCTI Reaction to Foods factor at 24 months and fewer diaper problems at 12 months. Concerning adoptive–control status, adoptees at 12 months had lower means than control infants for Eating Problems, Diaper Problems, and Difficult Temperament. The small amount of variance explained by these mean differences and the fact that the differences appeared at 12 months but not at 24 months suggest that these average differences between groups are relatively unimportant.

Intercorrelations

Intercorrelations among the six behavioral problem scores at each age are presented in Table 11.4. The pattern of correlations is similar at 12 and at 24 months. The low magnitude of most of the correlations suggests that these problems are best viewed as specific problems.

The Eating Problems scale correlates substantially with the CCTI Reaction to Foods factor: .61 at 12 months, and .56 at 24 months. However, both scales will be retained for further analysis because, as mentioned earlier, the Eating Problems scale is more general and the CCTI factor focuses on reactions to new foods.

The fact that Difficult Temperament correlates about .30 with most of the other problems is not surprising, because it is a global measure of parents' perceptions of infants' general difficultness. Thus, children rated as difficult are also rated on the average as having more problems with sleeping, eating, and diapering, as well as being more difficult to soothe. However, the correlations are of low magnitude and should not be taken as evidence for a unified syndrome of difficult temperament. Less than 10% of the variance of these specific behavioral problems is shared with the global construct of difficult temperament. Thus, it is more accurate to say that the children labeled as difficult have more sleep problems or more eating problems or are less soothable rather than to join these behavioral problems with the conjunction *and* as implied by the notion of difficult temperament as a syndrome. Although difficult temperament might be useful as a summary or composite measure of parents' perceptions of the difficulty they experience in rearing their child, these findings indicate that it is important to study specific behavioral problems regardless of their relationship to difficult temperament.

Longitudinal Stability

The behavioral problems are as stable from 12 to 24 months as are mental development and normal dimensions of temperament. The median correlation for the six behavioral problem scores listed in Table 11.5 is .49. Diaper problems are less stable than the other infant problems, perhaps because of increased attention to toilet training at 24 months of age.

TABLE 11.4

Intercorrelations among Measures of Infant Behavioral Problems[a]

Measure	Sleeping	Eating	Diapers	CCTI RF	CCTI Sooth	DT
Sleeping	—	.32	.12	.11	−.09	.36
Eating	.16	—	.07	.61	−.15	.33
Diapers	.20	.14	—	.05	−.24	.20
CCTI Reaction to Foods (RF)	.05	.56	.07	—	−.12	.28
CCTI Soothability (Sooth)	−.05	−.11	−.10	−.19	—	−.39
Difficult Temperament (DT)	.33	.37	.27	.24	−.29	—

[a]N = 316–328. 12-month data above diagonal; 24-month data below diagonal.

TABLE 11.5

Correlations from 12 to 24 Months
for Infant Behavioral Problems[a]

Measure	Correlation
Sleep Problems	.51
Eating Problems	.46
Diaper Problems	.33
CCTI Reaction to Foods	.43
CCTI Soothability	.51
Difficult Temperament	.54

[a]$N = 303–316$.

Correlations with Normal Temperament Dimensions

In an effort to explore the nature of behavioral problems in infancy, we calculated correlations of the six problem scores at each age with the temperament measures discussed in the previous chapters. The correlations, listed in Table 11.6, indicate that behavioral problems are, for the most part, independent of normal temperament dimensions. The contextual problems involving sleeping, eating, and diapering are related systematically only to CCTI Emotionality (Emo). Soothability is strongly related to CCTI Emotionality: $-.58$ at 12 months, and $-.52$ at 24 months. Difficult Temperament also relates strongly to Emotionality and moderately to CCTI Activity (Act), low Sociability (Soc), and low Attention Span (AtSp). Relationships with the tester ratings on the IBR and with videotape ratings are weaker than those with the CCTI parental ratings. The patterns of correlations are similar at 12 and 24 months, with the exception that CCTI Reactions to Foods is related to low Sociability at 24 months but not at 12 months.

Adult Measures

Factor Structures

In order to understand the etiology of these behavioral problems in infancy, we related them to parental personality and to measures of the home environment. In addition, we explored their relationship to common behavioral problems of parents. Specifically, we are interested in normal variation in parental depression, hysteria, and sociopathy. For example, the CAP adult test booklet includes the following questions concerning depression: "How would most people describe your usual mood?" "How would you describe your usual mood?" "How often do you get really 'blue' or 'depressed'?" The CAP parents answer these questions on 5-point scales. For the first two items, the 5-point rating is a dimension in which 1 means *happy,* 3 means *not happy, not sad,* and 5 means *has the blues, depressed.* The five responses for the third item indicate whether the parent is depressed once a day, week, month, 3-month period, or 6-month period, respectively.

TABLE 11.6

Correlations between Measures of Infant Behavioral Problems and Measures of Infant Temperament[a]

Behavioral problem	Temperament measure									
	CCTI				IBR			Videotape		
	Emo	Act	Soc	AtSp	AfEx	Act	TO	AfEx	Act	TO
12 Months										
Sleep Problems	.18*	.07	−.04	−.02	.04	−.01	.04	.03	−.08	.13
Eating Problems	.22*	.02	−.06	−.05	−.02	.03	.13	−.03	.02	.01
Diaper Problems	.28*	.08	−.05	−.03	−.20*	.10	−.14	−.17*	.02	−.18
CCTI Reaction to Foods	.32*	−.06	−.06	.03	−.01	−.02	.06	.00	−.02	−.05
CCTI Soothability	−.58*	.07	.37*	−.12	.19*	−.09	.01	.00	.05	.02
Difficult Temperament	.55*	.20*	−.32*	−.20*	−.17*	.05	−.02	−.10	.00	−.25*
24 Months										
Sleep Problems	.11	.10	.06	.01	.05	−.02	.10	−.01	.02	.05
Eating Problems	.23*	.00	−.07	−.19*	−.06	.00	.03	−.10	.06	−.04
Diaper Problems	.17*	.06	−.06	−.04	.02	.10	.00	−.15*	.03	−.08
CCTI Reaction to Foods	.22*	−.10	−.33*	−.12	−.15*	−.01	−.03	−.15*	−.00	−.08
CCTI Soothability	−.52*	.10	.31*	.14	.12	.03	−.01	.16*	−.10	.01
Difficult Temperament	.52*	.26*	−.01	−.31*	−.03	.04	.00	−.10	−.02	−.08

[a]N = 316–328.

*$p < .05$.

TABLE 11.7

Factor Loadings of Parental Behavioral Problems on an Unrotated First Principal
Component for Each Category of Problems[a]

	Factor loading	
Behavioral problem	Mothers	Fathers
Hysteria		
Trouble breathing	.48	.56
Pounding heart	.54	.59
Nervous spells	.55	.64
Dizziness	.54	.60
Amnesia	.50	.45
Loss of body sensation	.47	.40
Loss of appetite	.63	.61
Nausea	.60	.68
Vomiting	.42	.51
Sociopathy		
Frequent fights in school	.68	.46
Skipped school	.65	.77
Ran away from home	.69	.75
Depression		
People describe your usual mood as depressed	.88	.78
You describe your usual mood as depressed	.90	.94
How often really "blue" or depressed?	.55	.30

[a]Items are listed in their order in Appendix C. $N = 294$ for mothers and 237 for fathers
for Hysteria and Sociopathy; 486 for mothers and 352 for fathers for Depression. Only
items loading .30 or more are listed.

For hysteria and sociopathy, items were modified from the Iowa 500 project, a
35-year follow-up of about 500 probands and their 5000 relatives (Tsuang, Crowe,
Winokur, & Clancy, 1977). As indicated in Appendix C, hysteria was assessed
using 14 items that asked about various problems, such as breathing trouble and
pounding heart, that could be psychosomatic. Sociopathy was measured with 9
items involving parental alcohol problems, foster home experiences, and temper
and fighting. The sample size is lower for the hysteria and sociopathy items than for
depression because these items were not added until after half of the biological
parents had been tested.

For each of the three categories of problems, we conducted a principal-component analysis in order to extract the first unrotated component as a general factor.
Table 11.7 lists those items that loaded above .30 for both mothers and fathers on
the unrotated first principal component for each of the three sets of items. Nine
items met the criteria for hysteria, three for sociopathy, and three for depression.

Means and Standard Deviations

Scores on the items listed in Table 11.7 were summed to yield scales of Hysteria,
Sociopathy, and Depression. Means and standard deviations for these scales are

TABLE 11.8

Means and Standard Deviations for Parental Behavioral Problems

	Biological				Adoptive				Control			
	Mothers		Fathers		Mothers		Fathers		Mothers		Fathers	
Measure	$\bar{X}$	SD	$\bar{X}$	SD	$\bar{X}$	SD	$\bar{X}$	SD	$\bar{X}$	SD	$\bar{X}$	SD
Sociopathy	2.9	1.1	3.3	1.1	2.2	0.5	3.1	0.9	4.0	0.5	3.7	1.0
Depression	6.9	2.1	7.0	2.3	5.9	1.8	6.3	2.0	6.3	1.8	6.3	1.9
Hysteria	17.8	6.6	16.9	7.0	16.0	5.2	13.8	5.3	17.0	5.2	14.4	5.0
N for Depression	159		41		170		157		157		153	
N for Sociopathy and Hysteria	72		18		108		105		109		112	

listed in Table 11.8 for the three types of parents. We should emphasize that we are interested in the normal range of variation for these common problems. For example, in terms of parental depression, we do not consider our study to be related to the 13 "high-risk" depression studies currently in progress (Orvaschel, 1983). Nonetheless, depression in the normal range occurs with sufficient frequency and variation that it can be profitably analyzed in terms of continuous variation. For example, the average response to the question, "How often do you get really 'blue' or 'depressed'?," is 3.4 with a standard deviation of 1.1. This indicates that the CAP parents are depressed on the average about once every 2 months. For hysteria, only about 15% of the parents indicate that they have never had any of the nine problems listed in Table 11.7. For sociopathy, only about 20% of the parents indicate that they did not run away from home, frequently skip school, or fight at school. As expected, females had higher scores than males on hysteria and lower scores on sociopathy; however, no significant gender differences emerged for depression. The biological parents report more depression and hysteria than do other parents; however, the personality results reviewed in Chapter 9 suggest that differences between means for biological parents and means for the adoptive and control parents are likely to be due to their relative youth rather than to their status as unwed parents. Most importantly for our correlational analyses, variances for the three types of parents are similar.

Intercorrelations

The intercorrelations among parental Sociopathy, Depression, and Hysteria are shown in Table 11.9. In general, the three types of problems are relatively indepen-

TABLE 11.9

Intercorrelations among Behavioral Problems for All Parents and for Mothers and Fathers Separately

	Sociopathy	Depression	Hysteria
All Parents ($N = 477-505$)			
Sociopathy	—	.03	.00
Depression		—	.20*
Hysteria			—
Mothers ($N = 265-280$)			
Sociopathy	—	.02	.20*
Depression		—	.22*
Hysteria			—
Fathers ($N = 212-225$)			
Sociopathy	—	.06	−.01
Depression		—	.20*
Hysteria			—

*$p < .05$.

TABLE 11.10

Selective Placement Correlations for Parental Behavioral Problems

| | Correlation | | | | | | | |
| | Biological mother–adoptive mother | | Biological mother–adoptive father | | Biological father–adoptive mother | | Biological father–adoptive father | |
Measure	N	r	N	r	N	r	N	r
Sociopathy	69	−.10	66	−.19	18	.04	17	−.15
Depression	147	.06	137	.00	29	−.28	34	.19
Hysteria	71	−.17	68	.10	18	.09	17	.20

dent, although Depression and Hysteria correlate about .20. For females, Sociopathy and Hysteria also correlate .20, which is significantly different from the correlation of −.01 for males.

Selective Placement and Assortative Mating

As discussed in previous chapters, parent–child correlations in adoption studies are affected by selective placement (the correlation between characteristics of biological parents and adoptive parents) and by assortative mating (the tendency for like to mate with like). The selective placement and assortative mating correlations for parental behavioral problems are presented in Tables 11.10 and 11.11, respectively. As usual, selective placement is negligible; none of the correlations is significant, and the median correlation is .02. Assortative mating correlations are of the same low magnitude as for personality, with only one of nine correlations being significant.

TABLE 11.11

Assortative Mating Correlations for Parental Behavioral Problems

| | Correlation | | | | | |
| | Biological couples | | Adoptive couples | | Control couples | |
Measure	N	r	N	r	N	r
Sociopathy	16	.14	71	.31*	110	.07
Depression	34	.19	147	−.05	147	.09
Hysteria	18	.45	100	.16	104	.06

*$p < .05$.

Parent–Offspring Correlations

To our knowledge, there have been no previous studies of the relationship between infant behavioral problems and parental behavioral problems or personality traits other than in the area of difficult temperament. There is some evidence that maternal anxiety, depression, and extraversion may be related to difficult temperament (reviewed by Daniels *et al.*, 1984). However, no systematic investigations of this issue have been conducted—even for difficult temperament. Thomas and Chess (1977) suggest that "our most emphatic qualitative judgments, from contact with the mothers over these many years, is that we detected no significant personality attributes in those with Difficult as compared to Easy children" (p. 146).

We are also aware of no systematic behavioral-genetic studies of specific behavioral problems in infancy. The longitudinal Louisville Twin Study has obtained data on concordances for infant twins at 6 and 24 months for a number of behaviors assessed via parental interviews (Matheny, Wilson, Dolan, & Krantz, 1981; Wilson, Brown, & Matheny, 1971). These include items in areas relevant to the problems upon which we have focused: sleeping, eating, and crying. At 6 months, the concordances for 75 identical twin pairs and 45 fraternal twin pairs are .55 and .32 for a "resisting sleep" item, .70 and .53 for a "feeding problems" item, and .62 and .51 for an item concerning crying. At 24 months, the concordances are .59 and .40 for sleep, .72 and .57 for feeding, and .59 and .29 for crying. The greater concordances for identical twins as compared to fraternal twins suggest genetic influence. The only other relevant twin data come from the high school twin sample of Loehlin and Nichols (1976), who obtained retrospective reports from the twins' parents concerning the twins' behavior as infants. Only three items are pertinent: "cried a lot," "soon learned to sleep through the night and awoke only in unusual circumstances," and "was a calm and peaceful child and easy to take care of" (which appears to be related to difficult temperament). For 500 pairs of identical twins and over 200 pairs of fraternal twins, the percentage of twins whose parents reported that they were different was 5% for identical twins and 12% for fraternal twins for crying, 1% and 4% for sleeping, and 6% and 23% for the difficult temperament item. Thus, these retrospective data, like the Louisville data, suggest some genetic influence on behavioral problems in infancy.

Parental Behavioral Problems as Correlates

Parent–offspring correlations for behavioral problems are given in Table 11.12. Because there are 18 possible combinations of parental problems and infant problems at each age, we selected 7 correlations at 12 months and 3 at 24 months that yielded correlations for control mothers and fathers that were significant at a probability level less than .10. As explained in earlier chapters, we have greater power to detect correlations in control families because parents and their offspring share both

TABLE 11.12

Parent–Offspring Correlations for Parental Behavioral Problems and Behavioral Problems of Infants[a]

Infant problem	Parental problem	Biological mothers	Adoptive		Control	
			Mothers	Fathers	Mothers	Fathers
12 Months						
Sleep Problems	Hysteria	.03	.04	.02	.16*	.18*
Diaper Problems	Sociopathy	−.29*	−.15*	−.19*	−.12	−.19*
	Hysteria	−.11	.15	.05	.13	.17*
CCTI Reaction to Foods	Hysteria	.14	.05	.15*	.16*	.13
CCTI Soothability	Hysteria	.14	−.05	−.08	−.21*	−.14*
	Depression	.14*	.13	.05	−.19*	−.16*
Difficult Temperament	Hysteria	−.06	−.05	.20*	.15*	.16*
24 Months						
Sleep Problems	Hysteria	−.11	−.08	.24*	.16*	.13
Eating Problems	Hysteria	.13	.03	.05	.15*	.10
Difficult Temperament	Hysteria	.03	.00	.10	.12	.18*
N for Depression =		147	157	145	152	148
N for Hysteria and Sociopathy =		67–72	101–104	96–100	101–110	102–112

[a]Parent–offspring correlations are listed only for those comparisons for which control mother and father correlations both were significant ($p <$ .10). Biological fathers' correlations are not listed because $N = 17$.

*$p <$ .05.

heredity and family environment; thus, control parent–offspring correlations should be greater than those for the biological and adoptive relationships. The sample sizes for correlations involving parental Hysteria and Sociopathy are lower than those for Depression because these questions were not added to the adult test battery until after half of the biological parents and a third of the adoptive and control parents had been tested. Because the sample size of biological fathers was only 17, we have not presented their data. For control mothers, 19 of the 36 correlations were significant ($p < .10$) and for control fathers, 13 were significant; of these, the 10 combinations of infant and parental problems shown in Table 11.12 yielded significant correlations for both mothers and fathers. Parental Hysteria accounts for 8 of these 10 significant parent–offspring correlations.

At 12 months in the control families, parental Hysteria is positively related to infant Sleep Problems, Diaper Problems, Reaction to Foods, and Difficult Temperament and negatively related to Soothability. At 24 months, there are fewer relationships: Sleep Problems, Eating Problems, and Difficult Temperament are related to parental Hysteria.

A hint of genetic underpinnings of these familial relationships involving parental Hysteria comes from the correlations between biological mothers' Hysteria and infant problems related to eating: .14 at 12 months, and .13 at 24 months. Some possible evidence for the influence of family environment can be seen in the correlations between adoptive parents' Hysteria and adopted infants' 12-month problems related to diapering, eating, and difficult temperament and 24-month problems related to sleeping.

The two parent–offspring correlations that do not involve parental Hysteria are counterintuitive. Sociopathy of parents shows a significant negative relationship to infant Diaper Problems at 12 months for all three types of parents, suggesting both genetic and familial environmental influences. That is, parents who fought at school and ran away from home have infants who react less to wet or soiled diapers. Of course, this could be a coincidental convergence of correlations; however, it bears further study given reports that sociopaths have higher pain thresholds (Hare & Cox, 1978). The other apparent relationship between parental and infant behavioral problems, that between parental Depression and infant Soothability, is most probably due to chance because the correlation is negative in control families but positive for both biological and adoptive relationships.

Another unusual pattern of results is the reversal of correlations for the biological mothers as compared to the adoptive and control parents. This occurred for the three comparisons that involved parental Hysteria as it related to infant Diaper Problems and Soothability at 12 months and to infant Sleep Problems at 24 months. The direction of the control parent–offspring correlations in each case seems to make sense: More hysterical parents have infants who are seen as having more diapering and sleeping problems and as being less soothable. However, the correlations between biological mothers and their adopted-away infants are in the opposite direction, although the difference between the control mother correlation and biological mother correlation reached significance only for Soothability. Nonetheless, it is interesting that Loehlin, Horn, and Willerman (1982) reported a similar finding in their analyses of data from the Texas Adoption Project:

> Paradoxically . . . children of mothers with elevated Minnesota Multiphasic Personality Inventory (MMPI) scores tended to be rated as more emotionally stable than children of mothers with better adjustment on the MMPI. This latter finding was interpreted as suggesting an interaction between emotional sensitivity and the early environment. According to this hypothesis, individuals with genotypes making them vulnerable to their environments could thrive in the warm climate of the adoptive families, but turn out relatively badly in the presumably less benign families in which the unwed mothers were reared. (p. 1089).

In other words, Loehlin *et al.* (1982) speculate that what is inherited is a sensitivity to environmental influences. Typically, children with a genetic propensity towards hysteria are reared by parents who are more hysterical than average and thus might develop behavioral problems. However, adopted children with a genetic propensity towards hysteria placed randomly in adoptive homes respond favorably to the relatively placid home environment and are thus seen as having fewer problems than normal. As odd as this result might appear to be, it is interesting in that it emerged in our analysis and also in analyses of the Texas Adoption Project data.

Concerning infants' reactions to foods, we also considered the possibility that infants might show more problems related to eating simply because their parents are picky eaters. In the adult test booklet (see Appendix C), parents are asked whether they had tried and liked each of 21 foods. In order to obtain a measure of food pickiness, a score of 1 is given for each *dislike somewhat* response and a score of 2 is given for each *dislike a lot* response. On the average, parents dislike about 6 foods, and more importantly for our analyses, substantial variability exists; the standard deviations were approximately 4.0. However, parental pickiness concerning food is unrelated to the infants' reactions to foods in control families. The correlation at 12 months is $-.05$ for control mothers and .11 for control fathers; at 24 months, the correlations are $-.13$ and .18, respectively. As expected when systematic parent–offspring correlations are not observed in control families, the adoptive and biological relationships also show no systematic relationships between parental food pickiness and infants' problems related to eating.

Parental Personality Traits as Correlates

We also examined the extent to which behavioral problems of infants can be predicted from normal personality characteristics of their parents rather than parental specific behavioral problems. Table 11.13 suggests that the answer is "not much." As in the previous table, we have listed only those parent–offspring comparisons for which mother–infant and father–infant correlations were both significant ($p < .10$) in the control families. In this case, we examined comparisons involving the two second-order 16 PF factors of Extraversion and Neuroticism and the five EASI scales. Nine comparisons met the criteria at 12 months; only two comparisons met the criteria at 24 months.

TABLE 11.13

Parent–Offspring Correlations for Parental Personality Traits and Behavioral Problems of Infants[a]

		Biological		Adoptive		Control	
		Mothers	Fathers	Mothers	Fathers	Mothers	Fathers
Infant problem	Parental personality trait	(N = 38–163)	(N = 35–41)	(N = 119–164)	(N = 123–160)	(N = 128–156)	(N = 112–153)
12 Months							
Sleep Problems	EASI Emotionality–Fear	−.13	−.31*	.04	−.03	.12	.11
Eating Problems	16 PF Neuroticism	.13	−.10	.13	.12	.10	.12
	EASI Emotionality–Fear	.03	−.05	.02	.18*	.13*	.12
	EASI Emotionality–Anger	.04	.17	.00	.10	.19*	.15*
Soothability	16 PF Extraversion	−.10	−.17	−.05	−.03	.27*	.16*
	EASI Sociability	.02	−.11	.02	.13	.22*	.10
	EASI Impulsivity	−.04	−.12	.03	.05	.13*	.12
Difficult Tempera-ment	EASI Activity	.06	.11	.10	.01	−.14	−.16*
	EASI Emotionality–Anger	−.04	.16	.05	.08	.16*	.15*
24 Months							
Difficult Tempera-ment	16 PF Neuroticism	.07	−.20	.09	−.07	.22*	.12
	EASI Emotionality–Anger	.03	.02	.07	.00	.13	.14*

[a]Parent–offspring correlations are listed only for those comparisons for which control mother and father correlations both were significant ($p < .10$).
*$p < .05$.

At both 12 and 24 months, parental EASI Emotionality–Anger correlates positively with Difficult Temperament of the control infants. The other control parent–offspring correlations also are reasonable: At 12 months, parental Emotionality–Anger is positively correlated with Eating Problems, parental Extraversion and Sociability both are positively correlated with Soothability, and parental EASI Activity is negatively correlated with Difficult Temperament. At 24 months, parental Neuroticism correlates positively with Difficult Temperament.

However, these control parent–offspring correlations are not generally replicated in either the adoptive or biological relationships. Although some evidence of family environmental influence can be seen in the correlations between parental Neuroticism and Emotionality–Fear and infants' Eating Problems at 12 months, it appears that parental personality has little to do with behavioral problems of infants.

Environment–Infant Correlations

Although behavioral problems in infancy are often assumed to be environmental in origin, the specific environmental correlates of these problems have not been explored systematically. Perinatal factors appear to be related to sleeping and eating problems (Dunn, 1981) and might also be related to difficult temperament, although the evidence concerning difficult temperament is mixed (reviewed by Daniels *et al.*, 1984). Several small studies have investigated relationships between aspects of maternal behavior and difficultness in infants, although no studies that have used standard measures of mother–infant interactions or family relationships have been reported (Daniels *et al.*, 1984).

In this section, we explore the relationship between infant behavioral problems and specific measures of the infants' environment, including perinatal factors, the HOME, the Gottfried categories of environmental influence, and the FES.

Birth History

Correlations of infant behavioral problems with birth weight and gestational age are presented in Table 11.14. Although no differences were expected for the adopted and control infants because both groups are representative in terms of perinatal characteristics, the correlations for the two groups are reported separately for purposes of comparison. In general, birth weight and gestational age are only slightly related to behavioral problems in infancy. In accord with the literature, lower birth weight and gestational age tend to be related more to sleeping and eating problems in the first year, although this influence fades during the second year. At 24 months, they are related to problems involving soothability. Concerning difficult temperament, the results are mixed as is the literature on the topic: For the adoptees but not for the controls, difficult temperament at 12 months is related to lower birth weight.

TABLE 11.14

Relationship of Birth Weight and Gestational Age to Behavioral Problems[a]

	Correlation			
	12 Months		24 Months	
Infant measure	Adopted	Control	Adopted	Control
Birth weight				
Sleep Problems	−.13	−.18*	−.04	−.05
Eating Problems	−.03	−.17*	−.02	−.03
Diaper Problems	−.02	−.07	−.04	.08
CCTI Reaction to Foods	−.04	−.03	−.06	.04
CCTI Soothability	−.07	−.04	.02	−.22*
Difficult Temperament	−.15*	.05	−.09	.10
Gestational age				
Sleep Problems	−.20*	−.12	−.04	.09
Eating Problems	−.10	.00	−.06	−.07
Diaper Problems	−.02	−.03	−.06	.12
CCTI Reaction to Foods	−.02	.07	−.04	−.12
CCTI Soothability	−.18*	−.03	−.14*	−.20*
Difficult Temperament	.04	.00	−.01	.01

[a]$N = 152–166$ for adopted infants and 108–128 for controls.
*$p < .05$.

HOME

   Correlations between infant behavioral problems and the HOME factors are listed in Table 11.15. As described in Chapter 5, factor analyses of the HOME suggested the use of an unrotated first-principal-component score as a general measure of the home environment and four rotated factors—Toys (Factor 1), Maternal Involvement (Factor 2), Encouraging Developmental Advance (Factor 3), and Restriction–Punishment (Factor 4). The correlations between these HOME factors and infant behavioral problems are presented separately for the adopted and control infants in order to explore the possibility of genetic involvement in these relationships.

   At 12 months, fewer significant correlations are observed than expected by chance alone. At 24 months, however, an interesting pattern of results emerges: Only 1 of the 30 correlations is significant in adoptive families, but 11 of the 30 are significant in the control families. This pattern suggests genetic mediation of these ostensibly environmental relationships involving the HOME inventory. Most notably, the fourth HOME factor, Restriction–Punishment, is correlated with nearly all behavioral problems of infants in the control families. Greater restriction and punishment is positively related to more problems in sleeping, eating, and diapering, and it also is related to difficult temperament. Other than correlations for difficult temperament, the correlations are higher in the control families than in the adoptive families, suggesting the possibility of genetic mediation of the relationship

TABLE 11.15

Correlations between HOME Factors and Infant Behavioral Problems

	HOME Measure									
	Principal component		Factorially derived scales[a]							
			Factor 1		Factor 2		Factor 3		Factor 4	
Infant measure	A	C	A	C	A	C	A	C	A	C
12 Months										
Sleep Problems	.03	−.10	.03	−.12	−.05	−.10	.01	.03	.01	.07
Eating Problems	−.05	−.04	−.02	−.08	−.12	−.05	.04	.02	−.04	.04
Diaper Problems	.08	.08	.12	.13	−.13	−.01	.03	.07	.01	.11
CCTI Reaction to Foods	.00	−.06	.08	−.10	−.09	.03	.00	−.02	−.08	−.11
CCTI Soothability	.04	.05	.00	−.10	.11	.07	−.01	.02	−.06	−.04
Difficult Temperament	.01	−.06	.01	.06	−.05	−.10	.04	−.01	.06	.14*
24 Months										
Sleep Problems	−.11	−.02	−.13	−.02	−.05	−.03	−.05	.07	.08	.14*
Eating Problems	.05	.05	.10	.00	.05	.00	−.01	.17*	.08	.17*
Diaper Problems	.07	−.11	.03	−.06	.01	−.04	.07	−.04	.05	.18*
CCTI Reaction to Foods	.06	−.03	.12	.03	.05	−.05	−.01	.03	.08	.16*
CCTI Soothability	.03	13*	.03	−.27*	.06	.15*	.03	.20*	.09	−.10
Difficult Temperament	−.02	−.10	.06	.02	−.07	−.20*	−.01	−.03	.17*	.14*

[a]N = 165–175 for adopted (A) infants and 146–160 for control (C) infants.
*$p < .05$.

between parental restrictiveness and infant problems. Although these control–adoptive differences are of only marginal significance, this suggestion of genetic mediation of the relationship between the HOME measures and infant behavioral problems is particularly noteworthy because the HOME, unlike the FES, offers a relatively objective assessment of the home environment.

Another intriguing aspect of the HOME results involves behavioral problems related to CCTI Soothability. At 24 months in the control homes, the HOME General Factor and the first three rotated factors are significantly correlated with Soothability. Problems in soothability are related to low scores on the HOME General Factor, on Maternal Involvement, and on Encouraging Developmental Advance and, surprisingly, to high scores on the Toys factor. This latter result could be due to a relationship between a variety of experiences suggested by high Toys scores and distractions in the environment. In each case, the correlation in the control homes is greater than that in the adoptive homes, and the difference is significant in the case of the Toys factor.

Gottfried Scales

The three CAP Gottfried scales are Variety of Experience, Provision for Exploration, and Physical Home Setting as described in Chapter 5. The correlations between these environmental measures and infant behavioral problems are presented

TABLE 11.16

Correlations between CAP Gottfried Scales and Infant Behavioral Problems[a]

	Gottfried scale					
	Variety of Experience		Provision for Exploration		Physical Home Setting	
Infant measure	A	C	A	C	A	C
12 Months						
Sleep Problems	.00	−.09	−.12	−.16*	−.01	−.04
Eating Problems	−.07	−.01	−.01	−.02	−.02	−.08
Diaper Problems	.05	.03	.06	.00	.08	−.02
CCTI Reaction to Foods	−.10	.00	.14*	−.08	.00	−.15*
CCTI Soothability	.00	.16*	.05	−.20*	.05	.01
Difficult Temperament	−.04	−.15*	.09	.14	−.04	−.10
24 Months						
Sleep Problems	.01	−.10	−.13	−.01	−.07	.02
Eating Problems	.02	−.11	.03	.05	−.02	−.06
Diaper Problems	−.03	−.08	−.02	−.06	−.02	.00
CCTI Reaction to Foods	−.02	−.12	.15*	.07	−.03	−.01
CCTI Soothability	.12	−.09	−.02	−.09	.10	.06
Difficult Temperament	−.03	−.07	.01	.04	−.11	.00

[a]N = 130–168 for adopted (A) infants and 123–155 for control (C) infants.
*$p < .05$.

in Table 11.16. Unlike the HOME factors, the Gottfried scales are related to behavioral problems at 12 months, but not at 24 months. At 24 months, only 1 of 36 correlations is significant; at 12 months only 1 of 18 correlations is significant in adoptive families, but 5 of 18 are significant in control families. Again, a genetic effect on ostensibly environmental correlates of infant behavioral problems is suggested by these results.

In the analyses of the HOME, the Toys factor is related negatively to CCTI Soothability. However, the relationship bewteen Soothability and the Gottfried Variety of Experience scale is generally positive. On the other hand, the Gottfried Provision for Exploration scale generally is related negatively to Soothability. In addition, the Variety of Experience scale relates negatively to Difficult Temperament, the Provision for Exploration scale relates negatively to Sleep Problems, and the Physical Home Setting scale relates negatively to CCTI Reaction to Foods. Thus, in general, homes that provide greater variety of experience and opportunities for exploration tend to show fewer infant behavioral problems.

FES

As reported for temperament in Chapter 10, the FES Personal Growth factor again yields an interesting pattern of results (see Table 11.17). For the control infants at both 12 and 24 months, Personal Growth is negatively correlated with

TABLE 11.17

Correlations between FES Second-Order Factors at 12 Months and Infant Behavioral Problems at 12 and at 24 Months[a]

	FES second-order factor			
	Personal Growth		Traditional Organization	
Infant measure	Adoptive	Control	Adoptive	Control
12 Months				
Sleep Problems	−.04	−.10	−.11	−.19*
Eating Problems	.02	−.06	−.12	−.21*
Diaper Problems	.01	−.17*	−.02	.05
CCTI Reaction to Foods	−.06	−.06	−.10	−.04
CCTI Soothability	.06	.41*	.01	.00
Difficult Temperament	−.07	−.32*	−.05	−.02
24 Months				
Sleep Problems	−.04	−.14*	−.01	−.03
Eating Problems	−.11	−.08	−.17*	.02
Diaper Problems	.00	−.17*	−.07	−.05
CCTI Reaction to Foods	−.14*	−.07	−.04	.08
CCTI Soothability	.11	.27*	.13*	−.07
Difficult Temperament	−.14*	−.21*	−.02	.00

[a]$N = 158–163$ for adoptive families and 137–160 for controls.
*$p < .05$.

Difficult Temperament and Diaper Problems and positively correlated with CCTI Soothability. Most interestingly, all three of these relationships provide evidence of genetic influence because the correlations are larger in the control families than in the adoptive families, significantly so for Soothability and Difficult Temperament at 12 months. Overall, 2 of the 12 correlations between Personal Growth and infant behavioral problems are significant in the adoptive families, whereas 7 of the 12 are significant in control families. These results imply that some genetic factor mediates the relationship between parental perceptions of the family's social climate and infants' behavioral problems. They also represent another example of the emerging paradoxical principle that the stronger an ostensibly environmental relationship, the more likely it is to be mediated genetically.

The FES Traditional Organization factor also shows some relationships with behavioral problems, particularly with sleeping and eating problems at 12 months. Although the control family correlations are generally higher than the adoptive family correlations, the correlational differences are not large; furthermore, two correlations at 24 months—those for Eating Problems and Soothability—show significant correlations in the adoptive families and nonsignificant correlations in the control families. Of the 12 correlations, 2 are significant in each type of family.

Mediators of Genetic Influence on Ostensibly Environmental Relationships

Again, these results are similar to those for infant temperament discussed in Chapter 10: FES Personal Growth and, to a lesser extent, the HOME yielded higher correlations in control families than in adoptive families, suggesting genetic mediation of these environmental relationships. We explored variables such as parental personality traits that might conceivably underlie these findings; however, we were forced to conclude that the relationships between the environmental measures and infant temperament are independent of parental personality and IQ. Thus, the apparent genetic link between environmental measures and temperament is not simply due to inadvertent assessment of parental personality and IQ by measures that are intended to assess the infants' environment. Similar analyses partialing out parental characteristics such as personality, behavioral problems, and IQ from the relationships between environmental measures and infant behavioral problems yielded similar results. A sampling of partial correlations for the strongest environment–infant relationships is presented in Table 11.18. Clearly, some behavior or constellation of behaviors of the parents must provide the genetic link between environmental indices and infant behavioral problems; these results, however, suggest that the link is not the usual measures we obtain from parents. One possibility is that measures of the home environment assess a complex configuration of parental

TABLE 11.18

Zero-Order Correlations between Environmental Measures and Infant Behavioral Problems in Control Families and Partial Correlations after Effects of Parental Characters Are Removed

Infant measure	Environmental measure	Zero-order correlation	Parental trait partialed out	Partial correlation
12-month Soothability	12-month FES Personal Growth	.41	Mothers' 16 PF Extraversion	.37
			Fathers' 16 PF Extraversion	.39
			Mothers' 16 PF Neuroticism	.34
			Fathers' 16 PF Neuroticism	.40
			Mothers' IQ	.39
			Fathers' IQ	.40
24-month Soothability	24-month HOME Toys	−.27	Mothers' 16 PF Extraversion	−.29
			Fathers' 16 PF Extraversion	−.27
			Mothers' 16 PF Neuroticism	−.27
			Fathers' 16 PF Neuroticism	−.27
			Mothers' IQ	−.29
			Fathers' IQ	−.28
12-month Difficult Temperament	12-month FES Personal Growth	−.32	Mothers' 16 PF Extraversion	−.33
			Fathers' 16 PF Extraversion	−.30
			Mothers' Neuroticism	−.28
			Fathers' Neuroticism	−.32
			Mothers' IQ	−.31
			Fathers' IQ	−.30

TABLE 11.19

Relationship between Parental IQ and Infant Behavioral Problems

| | Correlation | | | | |
| | Biological mothers (N = 162–170) | Adoptive | | Control | |
Infant problem		Mothers (N = 164–172)	Fathers (N = 158–165)	Mothers (N = 142–153)	Fathers (N = 140–153)
12 Months					
Sleep Problems	.03	−.11	−.14*	−.01	−.08
Eating Problems	.02	−.06	−.05	−.03	.01
Diaper Problems	−.06	−.05	.10	−.18*	−.13
CCTI Reaction to Foods	−.04	−.11	−.02	−.10	.02
CCTI Soothability	−.02	.04	−.06	.22*	.05
Difficult Temperament	−.12	−.17*	.00	−.13	−.20*
24 Months					
Sleep Problems	−.15*	−.13*	−.12	−.14*	−.18*
Eating Problems	.00	−.04	−.08	−.01	.00
Diaper Problems	−.10	−.03	.06	−.20*	−.18*
CCTI Reaction to Foods	.01	−.19*	−.02	−.08	−.09
CCTI Soothability	.04	−.07	.00	.16*	.14*
Difficult Temperament	−.09	−.18*	−.01	−.06	−.14*

*$p < .05$.

behaviors in the context of the child and thus yield both higher correlations with infant behavioral problems and evidence of genetic influence. These issues and a model of genetic correlates of environmental indices are discussed by Plomin, Loehlin, and DeFries (in press).

Parental IQ

Even though we know that parental IQ is not the missing link in explaining the genetic relationship between environmental measures and the development of behavioral problems in infancy, correlations between parental IQ and infant behavioral problems are of interest in their own right. It is possible that behavioral problems of infants would be related to parental IQ if brighter parents were better able to manage their infants' behavior. We are aware of no other data reported on this topic, and, for this reason, we present correlations between parental IQ and infant behavioral problems in Table 11.19.

Several of the correlations are significant in the control families. At both 12 and 24 months, offspring of parents with higher IQ scores tend to show fewer problems related to diapering, soothability, or difficult temperament. The fact that this relationship with respect to difficult temperament is replicated in the adoptive families suggests that heredity is not involved. One possible environmental explanation is that brighter parents are better able to handle problems presented by their difficult infants.

If significant negative correlations were observed between biological parents' IQ and behavioral problems of their adopted-away infants, one could argue that brighter infants are better able to adapt to their environment. However, the only significant correlation between biological mothers' IQ and their adopted-away infants' problems occurred for Sleep Problems at 24 months. The fact that significant negative correlations between parental IQ and infant Sleep Problems were also observed for adoptive and control families suggests the more plausible environmental hypothesis involving skill in managing infant behavior.

In summary, it appears that, with the exception of problems related to eating, brighter parents tend to report fewer problems of all types in their infants. The effect of parental IQ in this case is mediated environmentally.

Multiple Regressions of Infant Behavioral Problems on Parental Characteristics and Home Environment

The combined predictive power of parental characteristics and measures of home environment was explored using multiple regression. A sampling of the multiple regressions in control families is displayed in Table 11.20. In general, as indicated by the adjusted R^2, very little of the variance for infant behavioral problems is explained. The only interesting comparison involves Difficult Temperament at 12

TABLE 11.20

Multiple Regressions of Infant Behavioral Problems on Measures of Parental Characteristics
and Home Environment for Control Families

	12 Months		24 Months	
Regression	R	adj. R^2	R	adj. R^2
Difficult Temperament on:				
Mothers' EASI Emotionality–Anger	.15		.13	
HOME Restriction–Punishment	.20	.03	.18	.02
Mothers' 16 PF Neuroticism	.21*		.26*	
FES Personal Growth	.38*	.13	.30	.07
Sleep Problems on:				
Mothers' Hysteria	.17		.14	
FES Personal Growth	.17	.01	.14	.00
Mothers' Hysteria	.17		.17	
HOME Restriction–Punishment	.17	.01	.14	.00
Eating Problems on:				
Mothers' Hysteria	.08		.15	
FES Personal Growth	.13	.00	.15	.00
Mothers' Hysteria	.08		.15	
HOME Restriction–Punishment	.12	.00	.16	.01
Diaper Problems on:				
Mothers' Hysteria	.10		.10	
FES Personal Growth	.17	.01	.17	.01
Mothers' Hysteria	.10		.10	
HOME Restriction–Punishment	.12	.00	.10	.00

*Significance ($p < .05$) of term added to multiple regression.

months of age. FES Personal Growth in control families adds significantly to the predictive power of mothers' 16 PF Neuroticism, and they combine to explain 13% of the variance of difficult temperament.

Analyses of Extremes

Another way to conceptualize behavioral problems is to view them as the extremes of normal dimensions of temperament. As mentioned earlier, it is possible that etiological factors—both genetic and environmental—that affect the extremes of a distribution differ from those that affect the rest of the distribution. Focusing on shyness and high emotionality, we explore this possibility in two ways. First, comparisons are made between parental and environmental correlates of CCTI temperament ratings of the most shy or most emotional infants and of infants from the rest of the distribution. The second approach involves the entire distribution of sociability and emotionality and asks whether the relationship between parental characteristics or home environmental measures and infant CCTI Sociability or Emotionality is linear. A nonlinear relationship implies, for example, that the

TABLE 11.21

Significant *t*-Test Comparisons of Maternal and Home Environmental Characteristics
for Shy vs. Normal (Rest of the Sample) Infants[a]

	Normal infants		Shy infants	
	$\overline{X}$	SD	$\overline{X}$	SD
Adopted infants at 12 months				
Adoptive mothers' EASI Sociability	18.9	3.3	16.4	3.3
Adopted infants at 24 months				
Adoptive FES Traditional Organization	.32	.71	−.11	.79
Control infants at 12 months				
Control mothers' 16 PF Neuroticism	54.9	16.4	68.3	12.8
Control FES Personal Growth	.16	.89	−.71	1.1
Control infants at 24 months				
Control mothers' 16 PF Neuroticism	54.9	15.5	63.2	17.4
Control mothers' EASI Sociability	17.9	3.9	15.4	4.1
Control FES Personal Growth	.14	.96	−.49	.82

[a]Significant *t*-test differences ($p < .05$) for the shy vs. normal infants are listed for three maternal traits (16 PF Extraversion, 16 PF Neuroticism, and EASI Sociability) and for three environmental measures (HOME General Factor and FES second-order factors of Personal Growth and Traditional Organization).

environment may be particularly influential at one extreme of the distribution of sociability or emotionality. Unless a nonlinear relationship can be demonstrated, it is difficult to maintain that etiologies at the extremes of a normal distribution differ from etiological factors that affect the rest of the distribution.

The first analysis required that we select the extremes of shyness and emotionality. Because developmental disorders, such as difficult temperament, typically involve 10% of the distribution, we chose the 10% most shy (lowest midparent CCTI ratings of Sociability) and 10% most emotional (highest midparent CCTI ratings on Emotionality) separately for adopted and control infants at 12 and at 24 months of age. Data on these extreme groups are not differentially influenced by rare outliers because all CAP analyses eliminate scores three standard deviations above or below the mean to ensure that the results are not biased by rare occurrences.

The extremely shy or highly emotional infants were compared to the "normal" infants in terms of maternal personality (relevant 16 PF and EASI factors) and home environment (HOME General Factor and two FES second-order factors). Significant *t*-test comparisons are listed in Table 11.21 for shyness and in Table 11.22 for emotionality. These significant differences are reasonable and generally duplicate effects that are significant for the entire distribution as reported in Chapter 10. For example, adoptive mothers of shy 12-month-olds have significantly lower scores on EASI Sociability than do the adoptive mothers of the rest of the infants; however, as seen in the previous chapter, adoptive mothers' EASI Sociability also is significantly correlated with infants' CCTI Sociability for the entire sample.

TABLE 11.22

Significant *t*-Test Comparisons of Maternal and Home Environmental Characteristics
for Emotional vs. Normal (Rest of the Sample) Infants[a]

	Normal infants		Emotional infants	
	$\overline{X}$	SD	$\overline{X}$	SD
Adopted infants at 24 months				
Adoptive mothers' EASI Emotionality–Anger	54.9	16.4	68.3	12.8
Control infants at 12 months				
Control mothers' 16 PF Neuroticism	54.4	15.9	65.8	17.1
Control FES Personal Growth	.18	.91	−.67	.94
Control infants at 24 months				
Control mothers' 16 PF Neuroticism	54.5	15.5	64.3	15.5
Control mothers' EASI Emotionality–Fear	12.8	3.3	14.5	3.1
Control mothers' EASI Emotionality–Anger	11.6	3.6	13.7	4.1
Control FES Personal Growth	.15	.95	−.38	.90

[a]Significant *t*-test differences ($p < .05$) for the emotional vs. normal infants are listed for three maternal traits (16 PF Neuroticism, EASI Emotionality–Fear, and EASI Emotionality–Anger) and for three environmental measures (HOME General Factor and FES second-order factors of Personal Growth and Traditional Organization).

The conclusion from this analysis is that the etiologies at the extremes are similar to those for the entire distribution. For the extremes as well as for the entire distribution, few relationships are observed between biological mothers' traits and temperament of their adopted-away infants, between adoptive parents and their adopted infants, or between environmental measures in the adoptive families and adopted infants. However, the observation of more relationships in control families than in adoptive families for both parental characteristics and measures of the home environment again suggests the possibility of genetic influence.

This conclusion that the etiologies at the extremes of sociability and emotionality dimensions are similar to the etiologies for the entire distribution is supported by the results of the second type of analysis in which a hierarchical multiple regression (HMR) procedure of the kind described by Vogler and DeFries (1983) was used to examine the entire distributions of infant CCTI Sociability and Emotionality. For example, infant Sociability may be regressed on an environmental measure, the square of the environmental measure, and the cube of the environmental measure. After removing the linear main effect of the environmental measure, the significance of the squared component is evaluated to determine whether the environmental measure is related to infant Sociability in a nonlinear, quadratic manner. Similarly, the third step in the hierarchical analysis assesses the possibility of a cubic relationship. Separate HMRs were conducted for adopted and control infants' Sociability at 12 and at 24 months as compared to biological, adoptive, and control mothers' EASI Sociability. Similarly, infant Emotionality was compared to mothers' EASI Emotionality–Fear and Emotionality–Anger. Finally, infant Sociability and Emotionality were compared to three environmental measures: the HOME General Factor and the two FES second-order factors.

In the 72 multiple regression analyses, only three significant nonlinear effects were detected. Although this is close to chance expectations, the novelty of this approach makes the results worth reporting. A significant quadratic effect was found for 12-month control infants' Emotionality as related to control mothers' Emotionality–Fear. Significant cubic effects emerged for 24-month control infants' Sociability as related to control mothers' Sociability and to the HOME General Factor.

The fact that nonlinear relationships did not emerge for biological mothers, adoptive mothers, or adoptive home environments indicates that genetic and home environmental effects on behavioral problems are not hidden in a web of nonlinear relationships. Of the three significant nonlinear effects for control families, one relationship (between 24-month-old Sociability and control mothers' Sociability) was identified in both the analyses of the extremes and in analyses of the entire distribution; thus, whatever, the nonlinear relationship might entail, it does not affect the basic conclusion that control mothers' EASI Sociability is related both to infants' shyness and to the entire distribution of individual differences in CCTI Sociability.

The other two significant nonlinear effects that were found in this analysis were not detected in analyses of the entire distribution. That is, no linear relationship was found between control mothers' EASI Emotionality–Fear and control infants' CCTI midparent rating of Emotionality at 12 months (Table 10.2) or between the HOME General Factor and control infants' CCTI Sociability at 24 months (Table 10.12). Because neither of these nonlinear relationships resulted in significant effects at the extremes of the Sociability or Emotionality distributions (see Tables 11.21 and 11.22), the nonlinearity either must lie elsewhere in the distribution or the isolation of these nonlinear relationships is due to chance.

Interactions between Infant Behavioral Problems and Environment

As in the analyses reported in previous chapters, we explored the possibility of genotype–environment interaction with respect to infant behavior. In Chapter 10, we mentioned three categories of interactions related to temperament. One of them, the most common, involves the use of interactions between temperament and environment to predict behavioral outcomes. In this section, we also consider interactions of this sort.

Genotype–Environment Interactions

As explained in Chapter 10, genotype–environment interaction refers to nonadditive combinations of measured genetic and environmental influences. For temperament, we found few significant interactions between genotype and environment when we examined the interaction between biological mothers' characteristics and

TABLE 11.23

Use of Genotype–Environment Interactions to Predict Difficult Temperament of Adopted Infants[a]

		Interaction	
		12 Months	24 Months
Genetic factor	Environmental factor	R^2 Change	R^2 Change
BM Depression	HOME General Factor	.016	.013
BM Depression	AP FES Personal Growth	.013	.001
BM 16 PF Neuroticism	HOME General Factor	.000	.001
BM 16 PF Neuroticism	AP FES Personal Growth	.005	.004
BM 16 PF Neuroticism	AM 16 PF Neuroticism	.016	.003
BM 16 PF Extraversion	AM 16 PF Extraversion	.001	.023
BM EASI Emotionality–Anger	AM EASI Emotionality–Anger	.020	.002
BM EASI Emotionality–Anger	HOME Restriction–Punishment	.000	.012

[a]BM = biological mothers; AM = adoptive mothers; AP = adoptive midparent.

measures of the adoptive home environment as they affect temperament of the infant adoptees. However, the few interactions that emerged are intriguing and deserving of follow-up study.

Table 11.23 presents a sampling of the genotype–environment interaction results for the many possible combinations of biological mothers' behavioral problems and personality traits with adoptive parents' behavioral problems, personality, and home environment measures as they interact to predict adoptees' difficult temperament. Although interactions are independent of main effects, we focused on those combinations of genetic and environmental measures that seemed to yield the most effects in the analyses described earlier in this chapter. The power of these analyses is discussed in Chapter 10.

The results are similar to those for temperament. None of the genotype–environment interactions in Table 11.23 is significant, and the average amount of adjusted variance explained is .00. Nonetheless, one of the interactions, explaining 2.3% of the variance, is interesting even though it is only marginally significant ($p < .10$): Biological mothers' 16 PF Extraversion interacts with adoptive mothers' Extraversion to affect infant Difficult Temperament. Figure 11.1 assists in the interpretation of the interaction by dichotomizing biological and adoptive mothers' Extraversion scores at the mean and presenting adoptees' Difficult Temperament scores in a two-by-two analysis-of-variance framework. The figure indicates that there is a main effect of adoptive mothers' Extraversion on infants' Difficult Temperament at 24 months. The interaction can be interpreted as indicating a genetic effect when the adoptive mothers have low scores on the 16 PF Extraversion factor. That is, adopted-away infants of more extraverted biological mothers are less difficult when the adoptive mothers are less extraverted. This interaction is reminiscent of the genotype–environment interaction effects reported in the previous chapter and suggest the principle that genetic differences among infants emerge under conditions of

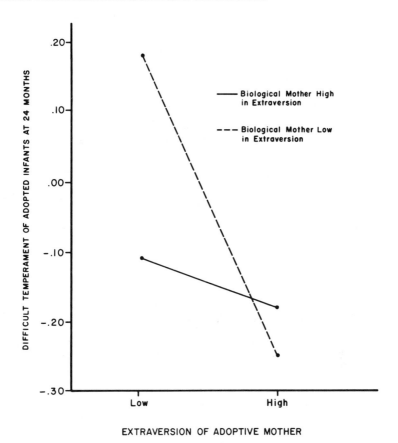

FIGURE 11.1   Midparent ratings of adopted infants' difficult temperament at 24 months of age as a function of biological mothers' and adoptive mothers' 16 PF Extraversion.

low environmental impact: in the previous analyses, permissive homes and less emotional adoptive mothers; and less extraverted adoptive mothers in the present case.

In addition to these genotype–environment interactions involving infant difficult temperament, we conducted 22 other analyses to investigate the predictability of other infant behavioral problems. Only four significant interactions emerged, and all involved biological mothers' Hysteria. This measure interacted significantly with HOME Restriction–Punishment to affect sleep problems at 12 months and to affect eating problems at 24 months. The amount of variance accounted for by the changes in the R^2 values is sizable: .074 and .093. In Figure 11.2, we plot a two-by-two representation of these interactions because they provide tests of our emerging hypothesis that genetic propensities show up more clearly in a less restrictive environment. The results provide support for the hypothesis. Infants whose biological mothers have higher scores on the Hysteria factor have more sleep and eating

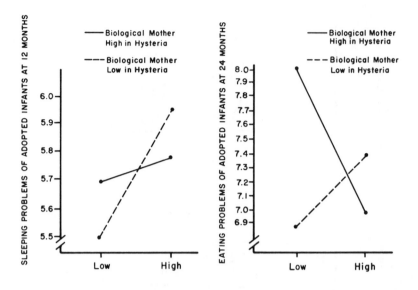

HOME RESTRICTION/PUNISHMENT IN ADOPTIVE FAMILIES

FIGURE 11.2   Midparent ratings of adopted infants' sleep problems at 12 months of age and eating problems at 24 months of age as a function of biological mothers' Hysteria and adoptive families' HOME Restriction–Punishment.

problems than do infants whose biological mothers have lower Hysteria scores only when the adoptive home is permissive. The other two significant results involved interactions of biological mothers' Hysteria with adoptive mothers' Hysteria to affect eating problems at 12 months and diaper problems at 24 months. However, plots of these interactions were not interpretable, and they appear to be irrelevant to the hypothesis that less restrictive environments allow genetic propensities to emerge.

Temperament–Environment Interactions

Another type of interaction has been mentioned more frequently in the literature than have genotype–environment interactions. These are interactions between temperament and environment as they affect behavioral problems (Plomin & Daniels, 1984). For example, emotional and unemotional children might show no difference in adjustment when reared in a stable environment; however, in an unstable environment, behavioral problems could erupt for emotional children but perhaps not for those who are unemotional. The goodness-of-fit model of Thomas and Chess (e.g., 1977) implies that interactions between temperament and environment, such

TABLE 11.24

Use of Temperament–Environment Interactions to Predict Difficult Temperament of Control Infants

		Interaction	
		12 Months	24 Months
Temperament measure	Environmental measure	R^2 Change	R^2 Change
CCTI Emotionality	HOME General Factor	.00	.04*
CCTI Activity	HOME General Factor	.00	.00
CCTI Sociability	HOME General Factor	.00	.01
CCTI Emotionality	FES Personal Growth	.01	.00
CCTI Activity	FES Personal Growth	.00	.00
CCTI Sociability	FES Personal Growth	.01	.01

*Interaction adds significantly ($p < .05$) to multiple R^2.

as matches and mismatches, affect adjustment. A systematic program of research to assess the effects of such interactions has been conducted by Lerner (1984), who has found some support for the model in studies of school-age children. Wachs and Gandour (1983) have suggested another type of temperament–environment interaction in which 6-month-old infants classified as "easy" are more sensitive to environmental influences than are "difficult" infants.

Table 11.24 presents the results of CAP analyses of temperament–environment interactions as they affect difficult temperament. The method employed was HMR, which, as in our analyses of genotype–environment interaction, removes the main effects before testing the significance of the interaction (Plomin & Daniels, 1984). The one statistically significant interaction shown in Table 11.24 suggests that CCTI Emotionality and the HOME General Factor interact to predict Difficult Temperament at 24 months. Although CCTI Emotionality and Difficult Temperament correlate .52 at 24 months (see Table 11.6), the HMR analysis removes the linear effects of CCTI Emotionality and the HOME General Factor before evaluating the significance of the interaction. The significant temperament–environment interaction accounts for 4% of the variance of Difficult Temperament and is illustrated in Figure 11.3. Unfortunately, the interaction is not particularly exciting. As expected on the basis of the correlation between Emotionality and Difficult Temperament, there is a large main effect of Emotionality on Difficult Temperament. The interaction indicates that less emotional infants are even less difficult when their homes are scored high on the HOME General Factor. The emotional infants are difficult regardless of the HOME score of their family.

Similar temperament–environment interaction analyses were performed for Sleep Problems, Eating Problems, and Diaper Problems. Altogether, we conducted 48 analyses and found 7 statistically significant interactions. However, none of the interactions was systematic across ages or measures, and their interpretations were obscure.

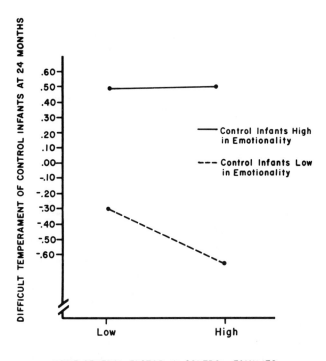

FIGURE 11.3 Midparent ratings of control infants' difficult temperament at 24 months of age as a function of infants' CCTI Emotionality and the HOME General Factor.

Genotype–Environment Correlation

Genotype–environment correlation differs from genotype–environment interaction in that it refers to the differential exposure of children to environments according to their genetic propensities. Three types of genotype–environment correlation have been identified (Plomin, DeFries, & Loehlin, 1977), as mentioned previously. The first, called passive, occurs when children are exposed to a family environment in which they share heredity as well as an environment conducive to the development of their propensities. This happens in control families in which parents share both heredity and family environment with their offspring. Passive genotype–environment correlation adds to the variance among infants. If passive genotype–environment correlation is important, the variance for adopted infants should be less than that for control infants because adopted infants are not affected by this particular component of variance; that is, they do not share both heredity and environment with their rearing parents.

Table 11.25 lists the standard deviations of behavioral-problem measures separately for adopted and control infants at 12 and at 24 months. As mentioned earlier,

TABLE 11.25

Test for Passive Genotype–Environment Correlation: Comparison of Standard Deviations for Adopted and Control Infants

	Standard deviation			
	12 Months		24 Months	
Infant measure	Adopted (N = 168–175)	Control (N = 156–160)	Adopted (N = 168–175)	Control (N = 147–155)
Sleep Problems	1.1	1.1	1.4	1.2
Eating Problems	1.3	1.2	1.4	1.3
Diaper Problems	1.2	1.0	1.4	1.2
CCTI Reaction to Foods	3.1	3.3	3.3	3.3
CCTI Soothability	2.4	2.4	2.3	2.2
Difficult Temperament	1.0	1.0	0.9	1.0

analyses of data on the adopted and control infants yielded no significant departures from homogeneity of variance; the standard deviations in Table 11.25 illustrate this point. Thus, passive genotype–environment correlation does not appear to have an important influence on the development of behavioral problems in infancy. As discussed in Chapter 10, a similar conclusion was reached concerning temperament.

Reactive genotype–environment correlation refers to the possibility that people respond differently to children with different propensities. It is important for developmentalists because it suggests environmental relationships that reflect rather than affect infant characteristics. Reactive genotype–environment correlation can be assessed by examining correlations between environmental measures in adoptive homes and characteristics of biological parents, the latter providing an estimate of the adopted infants' genetic predispositions to the extent that a character is in fact influenced genetically. That is, reactive genotype–environment correlation should be observed if the character measured in biological parents is related genetically to some behaviors or constellation of behaviors in their adopted-away infants and if these behaviors elicit environmental experiences in the adoptive homes. The behaviors of the infant that mediate the relationship between biological mothers' characteristics and measures of the adoptive home environment need not be specified. For this reason, even when measures of the adoptive home environment are not related to specific measures of infant development, it is still possible to find reactive genotype–environment correlation: Genetic propensities of the adopted infant measured by characteristics of their biological mothers might assess aspects of the infants' behavior to which adoptive parents are more likely to respond than they are to behaviors assessed by the measures of infant development used in the study.

Correlations between biological mothers' Depression, Hysteria, and Sociopathy and the major FES and HOME factors are listed in Table 11.26. In contrast to the environmental correlates of infant behavioral problems described earlier in this chapter, none of the correlations for the FES is significant nor are any of the

TABLE 11.26

Reactive Genotype–Environment Correlations: Correlations between Environmental Measures
in Adoptive Homes and Biological Mothers' Behavioral Problems

	Behavioral problem		
Environmental measure	Sociopathy $(N = 70\text{–}72)$	Depression $(N = 145\text{–}158)$	Hysteria $(N = 67\text{–}70)$
12 Months			
FES Personal Growth	−.06	−.10	−.10
FES Traditional Organization	−.02	−.10	−.09
HOME General Factor	.05	−.03	−.06
HOME Toys	−.10	−.03	−.13
HOME Maternal Involvement	.22*	.03	−.06
HOME Encouraging Developmental Advance	.20*	−.01	.03
HOME Restriction–Punishment	−.11	−.18*	−.01
24 Months			
HOME General Factor	.08	−.01	−.04
HOME Toys	−.06	−.06	−.04
HOME Maternal Involvement	.03	.01	−.07
HOME Encouraging Developmental Advance	.18	−.01	−.01
HOME Restriction–Punishment	−.06	.03	.16

*$p < .05$.

correlations with the HOME significant at 24 months. However, 3 of the 15 correlations between the HOME factors at 12 months and biological mothers' behavioral
problems are significant: Adoptive parents are less restrictive when the adoptees'
biological mothers reported frequent depression. Even more surprisingly, adoptive
parents are more involved with their infants and encouraged their developmental
advance to a greater extent when the adoptees' biological mothers had higher scores
on the Sociopathy factor. However, given the small number of significant correlations, these hints of reactive genotype–environment correlation must be viewed as
quite tentative. In general, there appears to be less evidence for reactive genotype–
environment correlation for behavioral problems than seen in Chapter 10 for
temperament.

Conclusions

Contextual problems in infancy—problems related to sleeping, eating, diapering,
and soothing—cause real difficulties for parents even though they do not portend
problems later in development. Although it is often assumed that infant behavioral
problems are brought about by faulty management on the part of parents, little is
known empirically about the etiology of these individual differences among infants.
    The global construct of difficult temperament has been studied in addition to
specific behavioral problems. Evidence that this molar level of analysis is useful as

a summary index comes from the finding that difficult temperament correlates significantly with most of the measures of specific behavioral problems at 12 and at 24 months of age. However, the need to consider specific problems is suggested by the low magnitude of their correlations with difficult temperament (correlations of about .30) and especially by the fact that different patterns of results have emerged for different specific problems.

Descriptive results of note include the finding that infant behavioral problems are as stable from 12 to 24 months as are mental ability and temperament: The median correlation is about .50. Also, difficult temperament and soothability are strongly related to parental ratings of infant emotionality. As usual, adopted and control infants are similar in terms of both means and variances, and selective placement for parental characteristics is negligible.

We have explored the etiology of individual differences in infants' sleeping, eating, diapering, and soothing problems and difficult temperament by studying their relationship to parents' personality traits, parents' behavioral problems, and major dimensions of the home environment. Our findings concerning the etiology of infant behavioral problems are discussed in terms of genetic influence, environmental correlates, and interactions between behavioral problems and the environment.

Nature

It must be emphasized that the CAP parent–offspring design will yield evidence for genetic influence (that is, significant resemblance between biological parents and their adopted-away infants) only when three conditions are met: The infant measure must be heritable, the parental measure must be heritable, and a substantial genetic correlation must exist between the infant measure and the adult measure. The stringency of these criteria makes it likely that genetic influence in infancy will remain undetected by the parent–offspring design. At the same time, when the design does yield evidence of genetic influence in infancy, these criteria make the finding even more exciting because they imply that genetic continuity exists from infancy to adulthood.

In the control families, we found a few relationships between parental personality traits and infant behavioral problems at 12 months, but these relationships are not replicated for either the biological parents or the adoptive parents. However, common behavioral problems in the parents yield more relationships with infant problems; especially noteworthy is the finding that parental hysteria is related to several infant behavioral problems at 12 months. Parents who have higher scores on the Hysteria factor also report that their infants have more problems with sleeping, eating, diapering, soothing, and difficult temperament. However, the only evidence of a genetic relationship is with regard to eating problems. Another suggestion of genetic influence occurs for the relationship between parental Sociopathy and infant problems related to diapering—this relationship is negative for both control parents and biological mothers.

The most intriguing possibility of genetic influence involves a pattern of correlations not seen previously in our analyses of the CAP infancy data. For three comparisons involving parental Hysteria, biological mothers' correlations are positive and those for the control parents and the adoptive parents are negative. Analyses of the Texas Adoption Project have yielded similar results, which led to the hypothesis that what is inherited is a sensitivity to environmental influence.

We found no evidence to support the hypothesis that infants' problems related to eating are related to parents' pickiness about food. Our analyses of the extremes of normal dimensions of temperament—the 10% most shy and most emotional infants—yielded results similar to those found for the entire distribution of temperament as reported in Chapter 10. This finding suggests that the etiologies of behavior at the extremes of dimensions of temperament are similar to the etiologies of behavior within the normal range.

Nurture

Although there are a few relationships between control parents' personality and behavioral problems of their infants, adoptive parents' personality traits are essentially unrelated to infant behavioral problems. One exception is that parental 16 PF Neuroticism and EASI Emotionality–Fear are related to infant eating problems at 12 months in adoptive families. More environmental relationships are observed for common behavioral problems of the parents. Parental Hysteria is related to eating and diapering problems and difficult temperament at 12 months and to sleeping problems at 24 months in both adoptive and control families, suggesting the impact of family environment on these infant behavioral problems. However, it is possible that these environmental relationships are caused by parental perceptions: Parents who report that they are hysterical also report more problems in their infants.

Relationships between infant behavioral problems and specific environmental factors are noteworthy. As suggested by other studies, lower birth weight and gestational age are modestly related to sleeping and eating problems in the first year, although this influence fades during the second year. Concerning the HOME factors and the FES, only a chance number of correlations with infant behavioral problems is observed in the adoptive homes, correlations that assess environmental influence unconfounded by heredity. The only suggestive evidence for environmental influence emerged for the FES Traditional Organization factor as it relates to sleeping and eating problems at 12 months and soothability and eating problems at 24 months. The observed relationships suggest that permissive parents report more problems in these areas.

Nature–Nurture Interface

Although the HOME and FES environmental measures reveal few relationships with infant behavioral problems in the adoptive homes, several relationships for both the HOME and the FES are observed in the control families. Because variances are similar in both types of families, this pattern of results suggests genetic mediation of these ostensibly environmental relationships. This intriguing possibility emerged for the HOME measures at 24 months, especially for the Restriction–Punishment factor, which is correlated with nearly all behavioral problems in the control families, and for the FES Personal Growth factor, which is related to fewer problems with diapering, soothability, and difficult temperament at both 12 and 24 months in the control families. We explored parental characteristics—such as personality traits, behavioral problems, and IQ—that might provide a genetic link between these environmental measures and infant behavioral problems, but no link was found.

As in the previous chapter, we also explored the interface between nature and nurture by searching for genotype–environment interactions and correlations. As usual, few examples of genotype–environment interaction emerged; however, the hints of interaction support the hypothesis that less constrained environments allow genetic differences among infants to emerge more clearly. As expected from the indications that ostensibly environmental relationships with infant behavioral problems tend to be mediated genetically, we found a few instances of genotype–environment correlation of the reactive type. However, analyses related to behavioral problems showed fewer genotype–environment correlations than did those for temperament.

In summary, infant behavioral problems provide no major exceptions to the rule that individual differences in infancy are generally unpredictable by parental or environmental variables. However, the positive relationships with parental Hysteria, the negative relationships with parental Sociopathy, and the reversed correlations for biological mothers are intriguing and certainly worthy of further exploration. More exciting are the results for the environmental measures that yield little evidence for environmental influence in adoptive families, but strong relationships in control families. This pattern of results—higher correlations in control families than in adoptive families—suggests that ostensibly environmental relationships in the sphere of infant behavioral problems are, at least in part, mediated genetically.

12

Physical Growth, Health, Motor Development, Handedness, and Interests

In this chapter, we briefly describe CAP results in five domains that have received little attention from previous research on individual differences in infancy. This extension of CAP analyses to previously unexplored areas provides a test of the generalizability of the conclusions that emerged from analyses of data on cognition and temperament discussed in previous chapters.

Height and Weight

Data for height and weight are useful as anchor points for comparison to behavioral data. Unlike the relatively low long-term stability of measures of cognition and temperament from infancy to adulthood, individual differences in physical growth in infancy are predictive of adult size. For height, the correlation between infancy and adulthood is .67 at 12 months and .75 at 24 months (Tanner, 1978); for weight, the correlations are .42 and .48 (Tanner, Healy, Lockhart, Mackenzie, & Whitehouse, 1956). It is noteworthy that individual differences in physical growth during infancy are predictive of adult size even though rapid developmental change occurs: From infancy to adulthood, individuals double their height and more than quadruple their weight on the average.

The CAP averages for height are 29.8 inches (75.7 cm) at 12 months and 34.1 inches (86.6 cm) at 24 months, with standard deviations of 1.4 and 1.6, respectively. The mean weights are 20.7 and 26.5 pounds (9.4 and 12.0 kg) at 12 and 24

TABLE 12.1

Parent–Offspring Correlations for Height and Weight

Infant measure	Biological		Adoptive		Control	
	Mother (N = 156–163)	Father (N = 34–39)	Mother (N = 155–162)	Father (N = 153–158)	Mother (N = 129–147)	Father (N = 130–147)
Height						
12 months	.32*	−.08	.04	.03	.33*	.30*
24 months	.32*	.14	.07	−.02	.27*	.21*
Weight						
12 months	.03	.19	−.03	−.04	.25*	.25*
24 months	.27*	.04	.00	−.02	.26*	.21*

*$p < .05$.

months, respectively, with standard deviations of 2.4 and 3.4. These results are similar to national averages (Eichorn, 1979; Tanner, 1978). Adopted and control infants do not differ for height or weight; however, boys are slightly taller than girls at both 12 months (correlation of $-.16$ with gender) and 24 months ($r = -.11$) and are also heavier than girls ($r = -.25$ and $-.20$ at 12 and 24 months, respectively). Controlling for gender, the longitudinal correlation from 12 to 24 months is .53 for height and .71 for weight. Given that height in infancy correlates about .70 with height in adulthood raises the interesting possibility that individual differences at 12 months might predict adult individual differences better than they predict individual differences at 24 months.

Parent–offspring correlations for the three types of CAP relationships are presented in Table 12.1. For both height and weight, correlations between control parents and their offspring at 12 and at 24 months are significant. None of the adoptive parent–adoptee correlations is significant; the mean correlations are .04 for height and $-.03$ for weight. With the exception of weight at 12 months, correlations between the biological mothers and their adopted-away offspring are nearly the same as the control parent–offspring correlations. The small number of biological fathers precludes the reliable detection of parent–offspring correlations of this magnitude; if the true correlation is about .25, the sample size for biological fathers allows less than a 50% chance of detecting it.

Thus, the CAP results point to substantial genetic influence on height at 12 and 24 months, and for weight at 24 months. Moreover, the correlations for the biological mothers and their adopted-away infants imply genetic continuity from infancy to adulthood. As explained in earlier chapters (see especially Chapter 6), we can estimate the genetic correlation between infancy and adulthood from biological parent–adopted child data if we know the heritabilities in infancy and in adulthood. For height, assuming heritabilities of .70 in infancy and .90 in adulthood (Plomin & DeFries, 1981), the biological mother–adoptee correlations lead to the conclusion that the genetic correlation between infancy and adulthood is about .80. In other words, the genes that affect individual differences in height in infancy continue to affect individual differences in adult height to a substantial extent. For weight at 24 months, assuming a heritability of .68 in infancy (Wilson, 1976) and .80 in adulthood (Stunkard, Foch, & Hrubec, 1984), the genetic correlation with adult weight is .73. These results are comparable to those for behavioral data reviewed in previous chapters.

Illness

Possible relationship between biomedical factors other than perinatal complications and individual differences in infant development have rarely been studied. However, there is increasing interest in such associations:

> Acute minor illness is defined here as ordinary, brief health problems, such as the common respiratory and gastrointestinal infections and the familiar instances of physical trauma experi-

enced by all children. These are the usual minor complaints that account for almost all the visits to primary health care clinicians because of illness. These illnesses and their management have not generally been considered to be significant factors in the child's development and behavior. However, there is reason to believe that this assumption of their unimportance is incorrect and is attributable to insufficient attention and research. (Carey, 1983, p. 447).

Carey describes some of the illness-induced stresses on the child and parent and their interaction, and he suggests that it is unlikely that such stresses would have no effect on development. On the other hand, in an excellent review of child illness, Starfield and Pless (1980) include a brief section entitled "Emotional Health Problems in Children with Physical Health Problems," which concludes: "Most illnesses experienced by children are relatively minor. They are usually self-limited and produce no sequelae" (p. 308).

In any case, there are very few data on the effects of common illnesses in infancy on psychological development. Research on the relationship between physical health and psychological development has considered only chronic disorders and major acute disorders. For example, data from the British study of the 1946 cohort (Douglas, 1975) show a relationship between hospitalization during the first 5 years of life and later problems such as reading disability, delinquency, and job instability. Although the results of such research support the hypothesis of biobehavioral relationships in development, it does not speak to the issue of the effect of common illnesses in infancy. For adults, however, it is generally recognized that minor illnesses can lead to psychological impairment. In their report on a cross-sectional study of 863 adults, Andrews, Schonell, and Tennant (1977) concluded that "prior physical illnesses, both major and minor, have been shown to be among the most significant of life events which predate psychological illness" (p. 328).

Surprisingly, one of the few studies with follow-up data on infant illness found that frequency of illnesses is related to positive development outcomes (Littman & Parmelee, 1978). Although this counterintuitive result might be specific to the sample, which consisted of premature infants, it has been argued that mothers of sick babies tend to be more attentive to their infants and thereby promote development (Parmalee, Beckwith, Cohen, & Sigman, 1983). The CAP data provide an opportunity to study the relationship between common illnesses in infancy and psychological development in a representative sample of infants. Furthermore, if such relationships are found, the CAP design permits the separation of genetic and environmental etiologies of the biobehavioral relationships.

In addition to studying infant illness as a covariate of psychological development, we are also interested in exploring infant illness as a dependent variable in its own right. Although much has been published concerning clinical manifestations and treatment of common illnesses in infancy, little is known about their etiology (Starfield & Pless, 1980). Longitudinal studies such as the Harvard Studies of Child Health and Development in which a 1930 cohort was studied from birth to 18 years of age (Valadian, Stuart, & Reed, 1959) and the U.S. Health Examination Survey of 1963–1965 and 1976–1977, which studied 2000 children in middle childhood and again at adolescence (Cornoni-Huntley; described in Starfield and Pless, 1980), indicate that stable individual differences exist for the frequency of contracting the common cold. The studies also show some familiality, although no attempt to separate genetic and environmental sources of familiality has been reported (Starfield & Pless, 1980).

We present CAP data, including parent–offspring correlations, for common illnesses and then consider the relationship between common illnesses in infancy and psychological development.

Description of Common Illnesses in Infancy

The CAP home visit at each age begins with a 10-min interview concerning the infant's health. Of the items listed in Appendix A, 15 involve the same variables at 12 and 24 months and yield at least 10% variability. The items and their loadings on an unrotated first principal component are shown in Table 12.2. At 12 and 24 months, this general illness factor accounts for 12% and 25% of the variance, respectively, and is marked primarily by a general health rating, number of bottles of prescribed medicine, number of different drugs prescribed, and frequency of ear infections. Although most infant illnesses involve viral and bacterial infections of the respiratory tract that sometimes lead to ear infections, this general illness factor has only moderate loadings on frequencies of colds and bronchitis. Therefore, the factor score obtained at each age is referred to as a general illness score, and we

TABLE 12.2

Factor Loadings of the Infant Illness Items on an Unrotated First Principal Component of General Illness

	Factor loading	
Illness item	12 Months ($N = 229$)	24 Months ($N = 252$)
Allergies (yes/no)	.21	.14
Frequency of colds	.43	.51
Frequency of flu	.17	.26
Frequency of ear infections	.76	.75
Frequency of bronchitis	.39	.25
Frequency of fevers	.29	.55
Frequency of severe diarrhea	.18	.16
Frequency of other illnesses	.24	.25
Number of routine checkups	.02	.14
General health rating (1 = excellent; 5 = poor)	.78	.86
Height	−.07	−.10
Weight	.06	−.16
Aspirin use (1 = never; 5 = daily)	.34	.58
Number of prescription drugs	.79	.75
Number of prescription bottles	.80	.85

TABLE 12.3

Means and Standard Deviations for Infants' Colds and Ear Infections

	12 Months			24 Months		
	N	$\overline{X}$	SD	N	$\overline{X}$	SD
Common colds	346	2.5	2.0	345	2.9	2.0
Ear infections	346	0.9	1.4	345	1.2	1.7

examine the frequency of common colds separately in order to explore differential relationships for the general illness factor and the common colds item.

Colds and ear infections in infancy are indeed common and individually variable as indicated in Table 12.3. During the first year of life, parents report that their children experience an average of two and a half colds; during the second year, the average is nearly three. About one ear infection occurs per year. The standard deviations indicate the variability of infants' illnesses. For example, no colds are reported for 15% of the infants during the first year and 6% during the second year; however, at each year about 2% of the infants have colds nearly once a month. For ear infections, about 50% (53% during the first year and 47% during the second year) have none; about 1% of the infants have nine or more per year. As suggested by the literature, some stability for illness is seen from 12 to 24 months of age. The correlation between the general illness factor scores at 12 and at 24 months is .35 for the adopted infants and .46 for the control infants.

Parent–Offspring Correlations

We used the CAP design to explore the etiology of common illnesses in infancy. Although the CAP includes no general physical examination of the parents, they are asked several health-related questions, including one about the frequency of colds. On the average, parents report two colds per year with a standard deviation of about three. Again, variability is impressive, with about 2% of the sample reporting one cold per month and 10% of the sample reporting fewer than one per year.

Parent–offspring correlations of parental cold frequency with the infants' general illness factor score, frequency of colds, and a single-item rating of general health are listed in Table 12.4. There is no evidence for a genetic relationship between parental frequency of colds and infant general illness or colds; the correlations between biological parents and their adopted-away offspring are generally negative. However, the influence of the family environment can be seen for general illness during the first year. The parent–offspring correlations average about .15 for both control and adoptive families. It is noteworthy that the common family environment effect shows up more clearly for the general illness factor and the general illness rating than for frequency of colds per se, suggesting that the effect is not specific to colds.

TABLE 12.4

Parent–Offspring Correlations for Parental Frequency of Colds and Infant Illness

	Biological		Adoptive		Control	
Infant illness	Mothers (N = 167–175)	Fathers (N = 39–43)	Mothers (N = 160–177)	Fathers (N = 156–173)	Mothers (N = 152–162)	Fathers (N = 151–161)
12 months						
General illness factor	-.11	-.04	.19*	.15*	.14*	.09
General illness rating	-.11	-.03	.14*	.17*	.17*	.24*
Frequency of colds	.02	.17	.05	.09	.12	.13*
24 months						
General illness factor	-.09	-.19	.08	.13*	.08	.04
General illness rating	-.17*	-.16	.10	.08	.04	-.01
Frequency of colds	-.09	-.09	.09	-.07	.09	.05

*p < .05.

TABLE 12.5

Correlations between the Infant General Illness Factor and Bayley Mental and Motor Scores of Adopted and Control Infants

	Correlation	
	Adopted	Control
Measure	(N = 162–178)	(N = 156–161)
12 months		
Bayley Mental Development Index	.06	.08
Bayley Psychomotor Development Index	.03	.06
24 months		
Bayley Mental Development Index	.07	.25*
Bayley Psychomotor Development Index	−.03	.02

*$p < .05$.

Relationship between Infant Illnesses and Psychological Development

To what extent is illness in infancy related to individual differences in development? Table 12.5 lists correlations between general illness factor scores and Bayley mental and motor development scores at 12 and at 24 months for adopted and control infants. For motor development, the correlations are negligible. Although only one of the four correlations for mental development is significant, the fact that all are positive suggests a possible relationship between higher Bayley mental scores and more illnesses. As noted earlier, a positive relationship would be predicted by Parmelee *et al.* (1983). We explored the possibility that the effect is due to biased reporting; perhaps more intelligent parents notice and report more illnesses in their children. However, only 1 of 12 correlations between parental IQ and infant illness at 12 and 24 months was significant, and the median correlation was −.04. Thus, although the relationship is weak, the CAP provides some support for the hypothesis of Parmelee *et al.* that infant illness is positively related to cognitive development.

Summary

Illness in infancy deserves more attention from developmentalists. The CAP data suggest moderately stable individual differences in the frequency of illness during the first 2 years of life. Common family environment, not heredity, is implicated by the significant parent–offspring correlations for both control parents and adoptive parents. Also, a counterintuitive relationship, but one predicted by Parmelee *et al.* (1983), is seen in the positive association between common illnesses in infancy and mental development.

Motor Development

Although developmentalists in the 1920s and 1930s were quite interested in motor development (see review by Dewey, 1935), researchers since then have scarcely considered the topic. Attention turned to the study of infant mental development in the hope of finding early precursors of IQ. One reason for the decline in interest in motor development was Gesell's emphasis on maturational aspects of motor development in the 1940s (Gesell, 1946) that clashed with the widespread environmentalist orientation that prevailed when developmental research in infancy resumed after the second world war. However, no one would disagree with Bayley's (1969) summary of the importance of motor development in infancy:

> Motor abilities play important roles in the development of the child's orientation toward his environment, and they influence the quality of his interactions with the environment. Locomotion and control of the body serve to enlarge the potential sphere for new and varied experiences and for individual choices in seeking or avoiding different kinds of experience. The development of manipulatory skills, which is seen most clearly in infancy, facilitates the development and employment of the various basic mental processes. (p. 3)

Bayley's test includes a scale that consists of motor development items derived largely from the work of Gesell: "The Motor Scale is designed to provide a measure of the degree of control of the body, coordination of the large muscles and finer manipulatory skills of the hands and fingers" (p. 3). Bayley items passed on average from 11 to 14 months include: stands alone, walks alone (at least 3 steps without support), gets up from lying on back, throws ball, walks sideways, and walks backward. Items passed on average from 22 to 24 months include: stands on left foot alone, jumps off floor with both feet, stands on right foot alone, walks on line, stands with both feet on walking board, and jumps from step.

In general, motor development has been studied from a universals perspective, even though this normative research did lead to tests of individual differences such as Gesell's and Bayley's. The primary questions asked were the age at which certain motor milestones are achieved and whether there are, on average, gender differences (Cromwell, 1967). Few gender differences have been reported, however, and the CAP provides no exception: Neither means nor variances on the Bayley Psychomotor Development Index (PDI) differ for boys and girls at 12 or at 24 months. A significant but slight difference (less than one-fourth of a standard deviation) exists between adopted and control infants at 24 months, although they do not differ at 12 months. The PDI means for the CAP sample are 93.0 at 12 months and 101.1 at 24 months; standard deviations are 14.7 and 13.0, respectively. These data again indicate the representativeness of the CAP sample in terms of both means and variances—the Bayley PDI was standardized for a mean of 100 and a standard deviation of 15.

We explored the etiology of individual differences in infant motor development through analyses of parent–offspring and environment–infant correlations. Even though motor development in infancy has been thought to be bereft of sequelae later in life, the CAP parents are asked to complete questions concerning athletic ability,

TABLE 12.6

Parent–Offspring Correlations for Parental Athletic Ability and Infant Motor Development

| | | Biological | | Adoptive | | Control | |
		Mothers (N = 156–159)	Fathers (N = 38–41)	Mothers (N = 159–156)	Fathers (N = 157–164)	Mothers (N = 147–158)	Fathers (N = 140–154)
Parent measure	Infant measure						
Group sports	12-month PDI	.02	.09	.12	.03	.06	.10
Individual sports		.17*	.04	.18*	.06	.15*	.15*
Group sports	24-month PDI	−.07	.14	.05	.07	.15*	.17*
Individual sports		.00	.00	.10	.21*	.19*	.19*

*$p < .05$.

TABLE 12.7

Correlations between Environmental Measures and Motor Development of Adopted
and Control Infants[a]

	Correlation			
	12 Months		24 Months	
Environmental measure	Adopted	Control	Adopted	Control
HOME General Factor	.20*	−.02	.28*	.17*
HOME Toys	.18*	.05	.23*	.14*
HOME Maternal Involvement	.11	.02	.23*	.07
HOME Encouraging Developmental Advance	.20*	.03	.20*	.09
HOME Restriction–Punishment	.09	.12	.07	.01
FES Personal Growth[b]	.09	−.06	—	—
FES Traditional Organization[b]	−.03	−.02	—	—
Gottfried Variety of Experience	−.02	−.12	−.01	−.01
Gottfried Provision for Exploration	.16*	−.02	.19*	.11
Gottfried Physical Home Setting	.04	−.10	−.01	−.06

[a]N for adoptees and controls: 174–179 and 156–164 for HOME; 167 and 160 for FES; and 136–165
and 126–152 for Gottfried scales.

[b]The FES was administered at 12 months only.

*$p < .05$.

and we explored the possibility that individual differences in infant motor development are related to the athletic abilities of their parents. As described later in this
chapter, scale scores for self reported ability in group sports and in individual sports
are obtained for CAP parents. Table 12.6 lists parent–offspring correlations of these
two scales with infant Bayley PDI scores at 12 and at 24 months. The results are
most interesting: For both control mothers and fathers, parental athletic ability is
significantly related to infant motor development at 12 and at 24 months. It is
noteworthy that these significant correlations are based on an examiner's testing of
the infant's motoric skills and parents' self-report of athletic ability. At 12 months,
both genetic and family environmental influences are suggested by the significant
correlations for biological mothers and adoptive mothers. The absence of significant
biological mother–adopted infant correlations at 24 months could be due to a real
developmental change in that the major transition to bipedalism at 12 months could
be predictive of adult athletic ability, whereas the developmental changes at 24
months might not predict athletic ability in adulthood. Nonetheless, at 24 months,
the fact that parent–offspring correlations in the control families are greater on
average than those in the adoptive families suggests some genetic influence even
though the biological parent correlations are negligible.

We also explored the relationship between the major CAP environmental measures and motor development of the adopted and control infants. The correlations
are presented in Table 12.7. Although the FES factors are not related to motor
development, the HOME measures and the Gottfried Provision for Exploration

scale show modest but generally significant correlations. However, the pattern of the correlations is odd in that they are somewhat higher—but not significantly so—for adopted than for control infants. What little relationship exists between the HOME and motor development appears to be general in that correlations emerge for most of the HOME measures as well as for the HOME General Factor.

Hand Preference

The development of hand preference is interesting in itself, and special significance could accrue if handedness proves to be an index of the development of brain specialization. The purpose of this section is to present CAP data on the development of hand preference, its etiology, and its relationships to cognitive abilities.

Considerable interest in the development of hand preference in the 1930s led to the general conclusion that hand preference begins in the second half of the first year and stabilizes at about 3 years of age (Hildreth, 1949a, 1949b). Infant hand preference has received renewed attention with some studies suggesting that the development of hand preference begins as early as 3 months of age (Caplan & Kinsbourne, 1976; Cernacek & Podivinsky, 1971) and with other studies making it clear that individual differences in the development of hand preference extend through childhood (Gottfried & Bathurst, 1983; Ramsay, Campos, & Fenson, 1979).

Next to nothing is known about the etiology of individual differences in the emergence of hand preference in infancy. Twin and family studies of fully developed hand preference have been reported, but no clear picture of the etiology of hand preference has emerged (Springer & Deutsch, 1981). Two studies involving stepparents (Hicks & Kinsbourne, 1976; Longstreth, 1980) and one study comparing control and adoptive families (Carter-Saltzman, 1980) have been reported; however, there has been no full adoption study of hand preference that includes data on biological parents.

Development of Hand Preference

Direction and strength of lateralization of the CAP adopted and control infants have been assessed from videotapes of mother–infant interaction as reported by Rice, Plomin, and DeFries (1984a). Infants' left-, right-, and both-hand responses are recorded each time an infant manipulates an object. Hand preference laterality quotients (LQ) are computed by subtracting left responses from right responses and dividing by the total responses. Multiplying by 100 yields a score that can vary from -100 (indicating all left-hand responses) to a score of $+100$ (indicating all right-hand responses). Thus, the LQ considers both strength and direction of preference, which we refer to as "relative" preference. The absolute value of the LQ assesses strength of preference without regard to direction. Median inter-rater correlations are .75 and .90 for relative hand preference at 12 and 24 months, respectively.

TABLE 12.8

Relative and Absolute Strength of Hand Preference in Adopted
and Control Infants[a]

Hand preference measure	Adopted ($N = 99$)		Control ($N = 87$)	
	$\overline{X}$	SD	$\overline{X}$	SD
12 months				
Relative strength	14.5	32.8	18.9	33.2
Absolute strength	20.0	20.0	31.2	22.0
24 months				
Relative strength	35.8	31.5	39.6	26.3
Absolute strength	41.9	22.7	47.5	25.0

[a]From Rice et al., 1984.

Means and standard deviations for relative and absolute strength of hand preference are reported in Table 12.8. Most notable is an age effect in that 24-month-olds,
on the average, show greater lateralization than do 12-month-olds. Using an LQ
score of 60 or greater as an arbitrary criterion for lateralization, 8% of the 12-
month-olds and 30% of the 24-month-olds are lateralized. This cannot be strictly
compared to lateralization rates in excess of 95% in adults because the CAP measure of handedness is based on naturalistic observations of object manipulation;
many objects can be manipulated equally well with either hand, even for strongly
lateralized individuals. Nonetheless, these results suggest that hand preferences
develop rapidly during infancy. A few infants begin to develop hand preferences
before 12 months of age, but most do not exhibit laterality until after they are 24
months of age.

Parent–Offspring Correlations

As reported by Rice et al. (1984a), parent–offspring correlations for both relative
and absolute hand preference have been computed for the entire sample as well as
for a subgroup of infants who were lateralized by 24 months of age. The number of
significant positive parent–offspring correlations is nearly chance; moreover, correlations for control parents are not replicated for biological or adoptive parents.
This inconsistent and generally nonsignificant pattern of parent–offspring correlations may be due to the fact that so few infants are lateralized at either 12 or 24
months of age.

Relationship to Cognitive Abilities

In 1938, Nelson and Richards reported that hand preference is among the 6-
month Gesell items that best predict IQ at 2 and 3 years of age. Because the widely

TABLE 12.9

Parent–Offspring Correlations for Parental Cognitive Abilities and Infants' Absolute Hand Preference

Parent measure	Infant measure	Biological mother (N = 116–125)	Adoptive		Control	
			Mother (N = 114–124)	Father (N = 115–122)	Mother (N = 95–101)	Father (N = 96–101)
IQ	12-mo handedness	−.01	−.02	−.13	.02	.03
Spatial		.03	.01	.00	.05	.04
Verbal		−.11	−.01	−.14	.01	.00
Speed		−.04	−.02	−.03	−.10	−.10
Memory		.15*	−.06	−.13	.11	.18*
IQ	24-mo handedness	−.15*	−.01	−.04	.32*	.20*
Spatial		−.14	−.16*	−.03	.25*	.13
Verbal		.01	−.03	−.01	.10	.05
Speed		−.09	.15*	−.04	.14	.02
Memory		−.10	.07	.01	.08	.21*

*$p < .05$.

used Bayley test does not include assessments of hand preference, researchers have not followed up on Nelson and Richards' finding. However, Gottfried and Bathurst (1983) found that consistent hand preference in drawing tasks shown by children from 18 to 42 months of age is related to IQ for girls. Ramsay (1984) found that onset of hand preference is correlated with advances in language acquisition. Results such as these suggest that faster rates of development of hand preference might be related to IQ via the development of brain specialization.

In the CAP, absolute hand preference at 12 months is essentially unrelated to Bayley MDI scores ($r = .03$); however, at 24 months, hand preference and Bayley MDI scores are slightly but significantly associated ($r = .14$). The CAP parent–offspring design provides the opportunity to compare rates of development of hand preference in infancy with adult cognitive abilities in order to explore the possibility of continuity from infancy to adulthood. Parent–offspring correlations for the CAP relationships are listed in Table 12.9. At 24 months, strength of infant hand preference is related to parental IQ and spatial ability in the control families. However, these relationships are not replicated for either the biological mother or the adoptive parents. Gottfried and Bathurst (1983) suggest that a relationship between IQ and consistency of hand preference from 18 to 42 months of age occurs only for girls; however, when we analyzed the CAP data separately by gender, only 5 of the 50 correlations in Table 12.9 were significantly different for girls and boys; of the 5 significant differences, only 3 involved greater positive correlations for the girls. Thus, we conclude that absolute hand preference as we have measured it at 12 and 24 months is not predictive of adult cognitive abilities, although the significance of the correlations with control parents' IQ merits further attention.

Interests

Some infants express particular interest in music, some spend most of their time playing with toys that involve large muscles, and others seem to prefer playing with cuddly toys. During each year's home visit, the CAP tester conducts a 10-min interview with the mother concerning her infant's interest in toys of different types and in books and music, trying to evaluate interest as independently as possible from availability. As indicated in Chapter 4 and described in Appendix A, the infant's relative interest in five categories is assessed. We also attempted to evaluate the infant's interests in artistic enterprises such as coloring and colors, but this item proved difficult to rate. The means and standard deviations for the five rating scales at 12 and at 24 months are presented in Table 12.10. No important gender differences or differences between adopted and control infants emerged. The mean changes from 12 to 24 months are reasonable: Infants at 24 months become more interested in fine motor toys, cuddly toys, and books.

Intercorrelations among the five scales at 12 and at 24 months and longitudinal correlations between 12 and 24 months are shown in Table 12.11. The patterns of intercorrelations are similar at 12 and at 24 months: interests in cuddly toys, books, and music tend to be positively intercorrelated. Longitudinal correlations from 12 to 24 months are significant but modest.

In the test booklet completed by all CAP parents, 19 questions assess parents' artistic, athletic, domestic, and mechanical interests; the same 19 questions are employed to assess parental abilities in each domain. Factor analyses of data on interests and abilities for the entire sample of 848 CAP parents indicated a reasonable factor structure that consists of five factors: Artistic (music, writing, visual arts, and drama–dance), Group Sports (baseball, basketball, football, and soccer), Individual Sports (racquet sports, running, skiing, swimming), Domestic Interests (cooking, sewing, gardening), and Mechanical Interests (carpentry and mechanics). Therefore, items were summed to form interest and ability scales that yield a median alpha internal consistency of .66 for interests and .57 for abilities for the six groups of CAP parents. The only substantial correlation for either interests or abilities is that between group sports and individual sports, which correlate .45 for

TABLE 12.10

Means and Standard Deviations for Infants' Interests

Measure	12 Months			24 Months		
	N	$\bar{X}$	SD	N	$\bar{X}$	SD
Fine muscle toys	336	3.0	0.9	343	3.4	0.9
Large muscle toys	336	3.3	0.9	343	3.0	0.9
Cuddly toys	338	2.3	0.9	339	3.0	1.0
Books	326	2.8	1.0	343	3.3	0.9
Music	331	2.8	0.9	337	2.6	0.8

TABLE 12.11

Intercorrelations among Measures of Infant Interests and Longitudinal Stability from 12
to 24 Months[a]

	Fine muscle	Large muscle	Cuddly	Books	Music	Stability from 12 to 24 months
Fine muscle toys	—	.00	.02	.02	.18*	.21*
Large muscle toys	.08	—	.05	.06	.08	.20*
Cuddly toys	−.16	−.04	—	.21*	.28*	.18*
Books	.13	.18*	.18*	—	.15*	.29*
Music	.22*	.15*	.14*	.21*	—	.13*

[a]N = 317–343. 12-month data above diagonal; 24-month data below diagonal.
*$p < .05$.

interest and .49 for ability. However, interests and abilities are highly correlated: .60, .70, .71, .70, and .74 for the five scales, respectively.

One reason for including measures of interests of parents and infants in the CAP
is that no behavioral-genetic studies of interests other than vocational interests have
been reported. However, the CAP parent–offspring results are disappointing: No
significant pattern of correlations emerged for any of the parent–offspring relationships. Of the 100 parent–offspring correlations in the control families (five
measures of interests for mothers and for fathers, and five measures for infants at 12
and at 24 months), 12 are significant ($p < .05$), more than twice as many as
expected by chance alone. However, the correlations show no systematic pattern.
Moreover, significant control parent–offspring correlations are not replicated for
the adoptive or the biological relationships. For the adoptive parents, 8 of 100
correlations are significant; for biological parents, 11 of 100 correlations are
significant.

Thus, this first attempt to study parent–offspring resemblance for interests finds
no familial resemblance, either genetic or environmental.

Summary

We have explored five neglected areas of infant development. Measures of physical growth (height and weight) show the greatest parent–offspring correlations
observed in the CAP. The correlations for biological mothers and their adopted-
away offspring are nearly the same as those for control parents and their children,
suggesting substantial genetic influence.

An area of increasing interest to pediatricians is the occurrence of common
illnesses in infancy and its relationship to psychological development. An unrotated
first principal component of general illness was identified and shows reasonable
stability from 12 to 24 months. No evidence of genetic influence is found in

correlations between biological parents and their adopted-away offspring; however, family environmental influence is suggested by the correlations between adoptive parents and their adopted children and those between control parents and their children especially at 12 months of age. Although the relationships are weak, there is a suggestion of a positive relationship between frequency of common illnesses and scores on the Bayley Mental Development Index.

With regard to motor development, both genetic and family environmental influences are suggested for the Bayley Psychomotor Development Index at 12 and at 24 months of age as indicated by significant correlations with parents' self-reported athletic ability. Modest correlations with the HOME measures also emerge.

A surprisingly understudied area is the development of hand preference in infancy. Few studies have been conducted since the 1930s, even though the early studies suggest that some infants exhibit laterality as early as the first year of life. Naturalistic observations from the CAP videotapes reveal a sharp increase in lateralization from 12 to 24 months, although the majority of children are not lateralized until after they are 24 months old. However, the pattern of parent–offspring correlations is inconsistent and generally nonsignificant at both 12 and 24 months, suggesting that parental hand preference relates neither genetically nor through family environment to the hand preference of infants. An intriguing possibility is that rates of development of hand preference are related to cognitive development. At 24 months, absolute hand preference correlates slightly but significantly with Bayley MDI scores; moreover, strength of hand preference is significantly correlated with parental IQ and spatial ability in the control families. This suggests a possible link between the development of hand preference and of cognitive abilities mediated by the development of brain specialization.

Finally, we have explored the domain of interests; for example, why some infants prefer cuddly toys and others prefer large muscle toys. Parent–offspring correlations between parental interests (including artistic, athletic, domestic, and mechanical) and five areas of infant interests generally yield nonsignificant and inconsistent results.

Thus, these five areas of infant development run the gamut of possible results. Physical growth shows substantial genetic influence and no influence of the family environment. Common illnesses of infancy are influenced by family environment, but not by heredity. Motor development shows both genetic and family environmental influences, as well as correlations with specific measures of the home environment. Our measures of the development of hand preference and of infant interests reveal neither genetic nor family environmental influences. The point of emphasizing this diversity of results is that we cannot make general statements about the etiology of individual differences in infancy.

13

Gender Differences

Introduction

In the analyses described in previous chapters, data for boys and girls were combined in order to increase the power of the analyses of individual differences. We have noted that means and variances for boys and girls are generally similar, although we deferred a discussion of specific findings related to gender for this chapter.

In Chapter 1, we hinted at our view that average differences between groups rarely account for much of the total variance. For example, one of the largest and most consistent cognitive differences between girls and boys involves verbal ability; girls score higher on verbal tests. Nonetheless, this average difference between boys and girls accounts for less than 1% of the variance in verbal ability (Plomin & Foch, 1981). Another way to express this finding is to say that the overlap in distributions for boys and girls is nearly 90%: If all we know about a child is gender, we know very little about the child's verbal ability. The authors of the best-known book on gender differences (Maccoby & Jacklin, 1974) now tend to emphasize the similarity of boys and girls: "The most important point is that there is very little to explain. Recent publications concentrate not on whether a sex difference exists but on how large a difference really exists" (Jacklin & Maccoby, 1983, p. 183). It has been our suspicion that gender differences in infancy account for even less variance. For this reason, even though we analyzed mean differences between boys and girls, we were not optimistic about finding important differences.

More interesting than mean gender differences is the possibility that correlations for boys and girls differ, especially parent–offspring and environment–offspring correlations, which yield information about the etiology of individual differences in infancy. There is reason to expect that such differences might be found. There have been sporadic reports in the developmental literature that boys are more susceptible than girls to environmental influences. The most frequently cited example is Bayley and Schaefer's (1964) analysis of data from the Berkeley Growth Study in which stronger relationships between maternal measures and children's development were revealed for boys than for girls. Bayley and Schaefer made explicit the hypothesis that boys are more influenced by the environment and added that girls are more influenced genetically. Another frequently cited example is a study of 29 female and 24 male 10-year-olds whose maternal environment had been assessed when they were infants (Yarrow et al., 1973). The authors found that:

> Though a number of dimensions of maternal behavior are related significantly to personal-social characteristics for the total group, a breakdown by sex shows significant correlations only for the boys . . . there are no significant relationships between the infancy environment and social characteristics of girls at ten. (pp. 1277–1278)

However, in a subsequent longitudinal study of 21 boys and 20 girls, Yarrow et al. (1973) found "many more significant relationships between the environmental variables and infant functioning for females than for males" (p. 70) and concluded that "we do not think it is prudent to emphasize a sex-specific theory of environmental influences until we have a firmer data base" (p. 116).

Nonadoptive families are not ideal for testing the hypothesis that boys are more susceptible than girls to environmental variation. A recurrent finding in the CAP is that heredity mediates relationships between environmental measures and infant development. It follows that environment–infant correlations in nonadoptive families could be of the same magnitude for boys and girls even if the boys' correlations were mediated environmentally and the girls' correlations were mediated genetically. Similarly, parent–offspring correlations in nonadoptive families might be mediated environmentally for boys and genetically for girls.

The CAP adoption design is particularly useful for testing the hypothesis that boys are more influenced by environmental factors because adopted infants share heredity with their biological parents and family environment with their adoptive parents. Thus, the hypothesis predicts that adopted boys will show higher correlations with characteristics of their adoptive parents and measures of their adoptive home environments than do girls. The second part of Bayley and Schaefer's hypothesis predicts that adopted girls should be more similar to their biological parents than are adopted boys.

Before we launch our presentation of gender differences in CAP means and correlations, statistical power should be considered. Analyses of mean gender differences are quite powerful, which is the reason why so many slight but significant average differences between the genders have been reported. For example, with our CAP sample of 156 girls and 191 boys, we have 80% power ($p < .05$, two-tailed) to detect mean differences that account for as little as 2% of the variance (Cohen, 1977). Power to detect differences in correlations is substantially less. With the same sample size, we have 80% power to detect correlational differences between boys and girls only if the z-transformed correlations differ by .30 or more—for example, correlations as different as .00 and .29 or .20 and .46. Moreover, our analyses of correlational differences will focus on the 100 adopted boys and 82 adopted girls; we have 80% power to detect correlational differences between the adopted boys and girls only if the z-transformed correlational difference exceeds .44.

Thus, it is difficult to detect different correlations for boys and girls, and replication will seldom occur unless sample sizes are enormous. A specific implication for interpretation of the CAP analyses is that the hypothesis of differential environmental relationships for boys and girls can be tested only at a gross level; that is, only if the correlational differences are large. The only positive aspect to the problem of lack of power is that significant correlational differences that emerge from the analyses will necessarily account for substantial amounts of variance.

For our analyses of gender differences in CAP means and correlations, we focus on general cognitive ability (Chapter 6), specific cognitive abilities (Chapter 7), temperament (Chapters 9 and 10), and behavioral problems (Chapter 11) using the major measures in each domain: The Bayley Mental Development Index (MDI), the Lewis–Enright scales of Bayley items, midparent ratings of temperament using the Colorado Childhood Temperament Inventory (CCTI), and midparent ratings of behavioral problems. Analyses of environmental measures focus on the HOME General Factor, the four HOME rotated factors, and two second-order FES factors.

For the correlational comparisons between boys and girls, we repeat, separately by gender, parent–offspring and environment–infant analyses reported in previous chapters for genders combined. Our goal in examining correlations separately by gender is to test the hypothesis that correlations with characteristics of adoptive parents and with measures of adoptive home environments are higher for adopted boys than for adopted girls, and that correlations between adopted girls and their biological parents are higher than are those for adopted boys. Thus, correlational differences between boys and girls are discussed only for the adoptees, their adoptive parents and biological mothers, and their adoptive home environment. The small sample size of biological fathers precludes any meaningful test of differing parent–offspring correlations for boys and girls, so these correlational data are disregarded. For gender comparisons of means and correlations, we present results only for significant gender differences and emphasize the amount of variance explained by gender and whether the number of significant differences exceeds that expected on the basis of chance alone.

Mean Differences

In our presentation of significant mean differences between boys and girls for the major infant measures, as well as for the CAP environmental measures, we refer to tables from previous chapters that list all of the comparisons conducted within each domain. The text that accompanies the tables describes the measures and analyses in detail.

TABLE 13.1

Gender Comparisons that Revealed Significant Differences between Girls and Boys
for Lewis–Enright Scales Based on Bayley Items[a]

Scale	Girls			Boys		
	N	$\overline{X}$	SD	N	$\overline{X}$	SD
12 months						
Imitation	155	1.99	1.59	190	2.41	1.65
Verbal Skill	156	1.87	1.15	191	1.62	1.10
24 months						
Lexical	154	9.04	2.56	191	8.42	3.10
Verbal (symbolic)	154	8.41	1.41	191	7.86	1.72

[a]The total number of comparisons is seven.

Cognitive Abilities

The manual for the Bayley Scales of Infant Development (Bayley, 1969) does not
report gender differences; when we presented the CAP means in Table 6.1, we
noted that there are no significant differences between boys and girls. The means for
boys ($N = 191$) and girls ($N = 156$), respectively, are 108.7 and 107.7 at 12 months
and 107.5 and 110.2 at 24 months, with standard deviations of approximately 15.
However, the Lewis–Enright scales based on factor analyses of the Bayley items
yield different results. As described in Chapter 7, three scales were constructed at
12 months and four at 24 months. Four of the seven gender comparisons (see Table
7.11 for reference) are significant as indicated in Table 13.1. Girls score higher than
boys on the Verbal Skill scale at 12 months and on the Lexical and Verbal (symbolic) scales at 24 months, indicating that gender differences in verbal ability
observed in childhood have their roots in infancy. The CAP also provides some
evidence that girls lateralize their hand preference earlier in development than do
boys (Rice *et al.*, 1984a), which might be relevant to this observed gender difference in verbal measures in infancy. Studies of older children have found differences in verbal ability to be related to lateralization differences between boys and
girls (e.g., Springer & Deutsch, 1981). The fact that boys score higher than girls on
the Imitation scale at 12 months serves to mask the effect of gender on the total
Bayley MDI score.

The gender difference for verbal ability in the CAP infants is similar to the adult
difference not only in its direction—females scoring higher than males—but also in
its low magnitude: Gender accounts for 1.2% of the variance of the 12-month
Verbal Skill scale, 1.2% of the variance of the 24-month Lexical scale, and 3.5% of
the 24-month Verbal (symbolic) scale variance. Gender also accounts for only 1.7%
of the variance of the 12-month Imitation scale.

Temperament

Of the eight comparisons for midparent ratings of CCTI Emotionality, Activity,
Sociability, and Impulsivity at 12 and 24 months, none is significantly different for

boys and girls (see Table 9.5 for reference). As mentioned earlier, the CAP sample size is large enough to detect gender differences that account for as little as 2% of the variance; thus, we can conclude that gender differences in infant temperament as measured by CCTI parental reports are negligible.

Behavioral Problems

Means and standard deviations for six behavioral problems at 12 and at 24 months of age are reported in Table 11.3. Of the 12 scores, 2 yield significant differences between boys and girls: Boys have more diaper problems than girls at 12 months (7.2 vs. 6.8, with standard deviations of 1.1 and 1.2, respectively for boys and girls) and stronger reactions to food at 24 months (13.0 vs. 12.2, with standard deviations of 3.2 and 3.4, respectively). These differences account for 2.9% and 1.4% of the variance, respectively.

Environmental Measures

We also examined the possibility that boys and girls are treated differently on the average. We were not optimistic about finding such differences because Maccoby and Jacklin's (1975) review of the large number of studies comparing parental treatment of boys and girls concluded: "Our survey of data has revealed a remarkable degree of uniformity in the socialization of the two sexes" (p. 348). For example, they found that boys and girls are treated quite similarly in terms of parental warmth, verbal interaction, restrictiveness, dependency reactions, and achievement pressure.

We examined differences for the HOME and FES environmental measures for homes of boys as compared to homes of girls. Of the 12 comparisons (5 HOME factors at 12 and at 24 months and 2 FES factors at 12 months), none yields a significant gender difference. On the basis of these results and the extant literature, we can conclude that boys and girls are treated quite similarly on the average.

Summary of Means Comparisons

Mean gender differences for temperament and behavioral problems are negligible in infancy, although girls are slightly advanced in verbal development. The CAP environmental measures yield similar means for families of boys and those of girls. We now turn to etiological comparisons in order to determine whether parent–offspring correlations or environment–infant correlations differ for boys and girls.

Parent–Offspring Correlations

As discussed earlier in this chapter, we used the CAP data set to test the hypothesis that boys are more sensitive than girls to environmental variation. In this section we discuss significant differences in parent–offspring correlations for adopted boys and girls. The hypothesis predicts that measures for the boys will be more highly correlated with those for their adoptive parents and home environments than will measures for the girls, and that girls will be more similar to their biological mothers than will boys. Control families are not useful in testing the hypothesis because control parent–offspring correlations are a function of both heredity and shared environmental influences.

Cognitive Abilities

Parent–offspring correlations for parents' IQ and infants Bayley MDI are presented in Table 6.4; none of the six correlations (biological mother, adoptive mother, adoptive father with adopted infant at 12 and at 24 months) is significantly different for boys and girls. The fact that the biological mother–adopted-away daughter correlation is not greater than the correlation for adopted-away sons does not support the hypothesis; neither does the similarity of the adoptive parent–adopted son and adoptive parent–adopted daughter correlations.

Table 7.5 contains parent–offspring correlations of infants' Bayley MDI at 12 and at 24 months with parents' scores on four rotated cognitive ability factors, as well as with the parents' 13 specific cognitive test scores. As shown in Table 13.2, of the 34 correlations for the biological mothers and the 34 correlations each for adoptive mothers and fathers, significant gender differences occur for only 5 comparisons—the number that would be expected by chance. For the four factor scores, only 1 of 8 correlations for biological mothers shows a significant difference for boys and girls; similarly, only 1 of 8 correlations shows a gender difference for adoptive mothers, and none yields a gender difference for adoptive fathers. For the 13 specific test scores of the parents, only 1 of 26 correlations involving biological mothers, 1 of 26 involving adoptive mothers, and 1 of 26 involving adoptive fathers differ significantly for boys and girls.

All five of the gender differences in parent–offspring correlations shown in Table 13.2 are positive for boys and negative for girls. For the three correlations involving adoptive parents, this lends some slight support to the hypothesis that boys are more susceptible to environmental influence if we assume that the environmental effect of parents' cognitive abilities on their children is positive in direction. However, the fact that the correlations between adopted boys and their biological mothers are higher than those for adopted girls speaks against the hypothesis.

Tables 7.13 and 7.14 extend the search for the etiology of specific cognitive abilities by considering parent–offspring correlations at 12 and at 24 months for the Lewis–Enright Bayley scales and parental general and specific cognitive abilities. Significant gender differences in parent–offspring correlations are shown in Table 13.3. For 12-month-olds, only 1 of the 15 biological mother–adopted offspring correlations yields a significant difference for boys and girls; none of the 30 adoptive parent–adopted offspring correlations differs for boys and girls. At 24 months,

TABLE 13.2

Significant Gender Differences in Parent–Offspring Correlations for Parental Abilities and Adopted Infant Bayley MDI Scores[a]

		Girls		Boys	
Parent measure	Infant measure	N	r	N	r
Biological mothers' Memory factor	12-month MDI	79	−.10	99	.26
Biological mothers' Names and Faces	12-month MDI	79	−.11	99	.21
Adoptive mothers' Memory factor	24-month MDI	79	−.20	98	.21
Adoptive mothers' Picture Memory	24-month MDI	79	−.17	98	.13
Adoptive fathers' Card Rotations	24-month MDI	77	−.20	97	.29

[a] See Table 7.5 for reference. The total number of parent–offspring comparisons examined for gender differences is 34 for each type of parent (biological mothers, adoptive mothers, and adoptive fathers). Correlations were computed between infant scores on the MDI at 12 and at 24 months and parental scores on four rotated factors and 13 cognitive tests. Correlations with parental IQ, presented in Table 6.4, showed no significant differences.

only 1 of 20 biological mother–adoptee correlations yields a significant gender difference. However, 7 of 40 correlations for adoptive parents differ significantly for boys and girls. The pattern of gender differences does not support the hypothesis, because adopted sons are more similar to their biological mothers than are adopted daughters; moreover, of the 7 significant gender differences for adoptive parent–adoptee correlations, 4 involve higher positive correlations for boys and 3 are higher for girls. Other features of the results make these gender differences appear to be unsystematic. For example, adoptive fathers' IQ yields 2 significant gender differences; however, adoptive fathers' IQ correlates positively with their adopted sons' Spatial score and negatively with their sons' Imitation score. Also, the pattern of results differs for adoptive mothers and fathers.

In summary, the CAP results provide little evidence supporting the hypothesis that infant boys and girls differ in parent–offspring correlations for cognitive abilities.

Temperament

Table 10.4 presents parent–offspring correlations between parental EASI temperaments and adopted infant CCTI midparent ratings at 12 and at 24 months; Table 10.6 shows parent–offspring correlations between 16 PF Extraversion and Neuroticism and CCTI Sociability and Emotionality of 12- and 24-month-old adopted

TABLE 13.3

Significant Gender Differences in Parent–Offspring Correlations for Parental Cognitive Abilities and Adopted Infant Lewis–Enright Bayley Scale Scores[a]

		Girls		Boys	
Parent measure	Infant measure	N	r	N	r
Biological mothers' Memory	12-mo Means-End	78	−.07	99	.34
Biological mothers' Memory	24-mo Verbal (symbolic)	78	−.20	98	.18
Adoptive mothers' Memory	24-mo Lexical	79	−.13	98	.20
Adoptive mothers' Memory	24-mo Verbal (symbolic)	79	−.15	97	.28
Adoptive fathers' IQ	24-mo Spatial	75	−.17	94	.31
Adoptive fathers' IQ	24-mo Imitation	75	.22	94	−.23
Adoptive fathers' Spatial	24-mo Spatial	76	−.19	95	.28
Adoptive fathers' Perceptual Speed	24-mo Imitation	76	.24	95	−.10
Adoptive fathers' Memory	24-mo Imitation	76	.14	95	−.30

[a]See Tables 7.13 and 7.14 for references. The total number of parent–offspring comparisons examined for gender differences is 35 for each type of parent (biological mothers, adoptive mothers, and adoptive fathers). Correlations were computed between infant scores on the seven Lewis–Enright Bayley scales (three at 12 months and four at 24 months) and parental IQ and scores on four rotated specific cognitive ability factors.

infants. In Table 13.4 we list parent–offspring comparisons that show significant gender differences. Of 12 correlations between biological mothers and their adopted-away infants, 3 are significantly different for boys and girls. In all 3 cases, adopted boys show higher correlations with their biological mothers than do adopted girls, which is contrary to the hypothesis that girls' development is more influenced genetically. For adoptive parents, none of 24 parent–offspring correlations differs significantly for boys and girls. The fact that the measures for the boys do not correlate more highly with those for their adoptive parents is also contrary to the hypothesis.

Behavioral Problems

Correlations with infant behavioral problems are presented in Tables 11.12 and 11.13 for parental behavioral problems and for parental personality. The parent–offspring correlations that yield significant gender differences are listed in Table 13.5. For biological mothers, 2 of 21 correlations differ significantly for boys and girls; significant gender differences also occur for 1 of 21 comparisons for adoptive mothers and for 2 of 21 comparisons for adoptive fathers. Although the 2 significant gender differences involving biological mothers could be due to chance, both in-

TABLE 13.4

Significant Gender Differences in Parent–Adopted Infant Correlations for Temperament[a]

		Girls		Boys	
Parent measure	Infant measure	N	r	N	r
Biological mothers' EASI Emotionality–Fear	24-mo CCTI Emotionality	70	−.22	88	.20
Biological mothers' EASI Sociability	24-mo CCTI Sociability	75	−.08	90	.36
Biological mothers' 16 PF Extraversion	24-mo CCTI Sociability	63	−.36	82	.31

[a]See Tables 10.19 and 10.21 for reference and accompanying text for details of analyses and measures. The total number of parent–offspring comparisons examined for gender differences is 12 for each type of parent (biological mothers, adoptive mothers, and adoptive fathers).

volve higher positive correlations for boys than girls. This finding is similar to the results for temperament and contradictory to the hypothesis that girls more strongly resemble their biological mothers. Boys' behavioral problems are associated positively with their adoptive parents' behavioral problems and personality measures for 2 of the 3 significant gender differences.

Summary of Parent–Offspring Correlations

We have reviewed gender differences for 104 correlations between biological mothers and their adopted-away offspring, 104 between adoptive mothers and their adopted children, and 104 between adoptive fathers and their adopted children.

TABLE 13.5

Significant Gender Differences in Parent–Adopted Infant Correlations for Behavioral Problems[a]

		Girls		Boys	
Parent measure	Infant measure	N	r	N	r
Adoptive mothers' Socio-pathy	12-mo Diaper Problems	49	−.33	55	.05
Adoptive fathers' Hysteria	12-mo CCTI Reaction to Foods	48	.04	53	.38
Adoptive fathers' EASI Emotionality–Anger	24-mo Difficult Temperament	72	.18	88	−.12
Biological mothers' 16 PF Extraversion	12-mo CCTI Soothability	65	−.23	81	.14
Biological mothers' EASI Emotionality–Fear	12-mo Eating Problems	70	−.17	88	.16

[a]See Tables 11.12 and 11.13 for reference and accompanying text for details of analyses and measures. The total number of parent–offspring comparisons examined for gender differences is 21 for each type of parent (biological mothers, adoptive mothers, and adoptive fathers).

These comparisons include general and specific cognitive abilities, temperament, and behavioral problems, and thus represent a wide sampling of development in infancy. The most obvious conclusion to be drawn from these analyses is that gender has little effect on parent–offspring correlations. Of the 104 parent–offspring correlations for each type of parent, the number of significant gender differences is 9 for biological mothers, 5 for adoptive mothers, and 8 for adoptive fathers. Given an alpha level of .05, about 5 significant gender differences would be expected by chance for each type of parent. Thus, the observed significant gender differences in parent–offspring correlations may merely represent chance occurrences.

The major reason for examining gender differences in parent–offspring correlations was to test the hypothesis that boys are more susceptible to environmental influences and girls are more influenced genetically. The near chance number of significant gender differences speaks against this hypothesis; however, examination of the significant gender differences is even more damaging. For each of the 9 significant gender differences that involve biological mothers, the correlation for the adopted boys is higher than that for girls. The only partial support for the hypothesis comes from the adoptive parent–adoptee correlations: Of the 13 significant gender differences, 9 involve higher correlations for boys than for girls. Nonetheless, our interpretation of these results is that gender has little to do with parent–offspring correlations.

Environment–Infant Correlations

The most direct test of the hypothesis that boys are more sensitive to environmental variation comes from the comparison of correlations between environmental measures and infant development for boys and girls. As mentioned earlier, adoptive families provide particularly valuable information because heredity cannot contribute to environmental relationships as it can in control families. Even though few mean differences have been observed in the CAP for environmental measures in homes of boys as compared to homes of girls, it is nonetheless possible that correlations between environmental measures and developmental measures may reveal gender differences.

We limit our discussion of environment–infant correlations to the general factor (unrotated principal component) of the HOME, four scales based on rotated factors of the HOME, and the two second-order factors of the FES as they relate to cognitive abilities, temperament, and behavioral problems of the adopted infants.

Cognitive Abilities

Correlations of the HOME and FES factors with Bayley MDI scores at 12 and at 24 months are presented in Table 6.9; environmental correlations with the Lewis–

TABLE 13.6

Significant Gender Differences in Environment–Adopted Infant Correlations for Temperament[a]

		Girls		Boys	
Environmental measure	Infant measure	N	r	N	r
HOME Toys	12-mo CCTI Activity	76	−.21	89	.15
HOME Restriction–Punishment	12-mo CCTI Emotionality	77	−.21	90	.10
HOME Toys	24-mo CCTI Activity	77	−.15	93	.18
HOME Toys	24-mo CCTI Attention Span	73	−.08	94	.24

[a]See Tables 10.11, 10.12, and 10.14 for reference. The total number of environment–infant comparisons examined for gender differences is 48 (five HOME factors at 12 and at 24 months and two FES second-order factors at 12 months as correlated with four CCTI temperament scales at 12 and at 24 months).

Enright scales of Bayley items are listed in Tables 7.15 and 7.16 for the infants at 12 and at 24 months of age, respectively. The five HOME factors at 12 and at 24 months and the two FES factors at 12 months are involved in 12 correlations with the Bayley MDI scores and in 41 correlations with the three Lewis–Enright scales at 12 months and the four scales at 24 months. Of these 53 correlations, significant gender differences emerged for only 2 comparisons. Although these are fewer significant differences than would be expected by chance, both involved the HOME Encouraging Developmental Advance factor at 24 months and higher correlations for boys than for girls. Correlations of this HOME factor with the Bayley MDI score are .39 for boys and .04 for girls; correlations with the Lewis–Enright Spatial factor are .25 for boys and −.10 for girls.

Temperament

Environment–infant correlations for temperament are reported in Tables 10.11, 10.12, and 10.14 for the HOME at 12 months, the HOME at 24 months, and the FES at 12 months, respectively, as they relate to the four CCTI temperament dimensions. Of the 48 HOME correlations for adopted infants, 4 yield significant gender differences and are listed in Table 13.6. None of these significant gender differences involves the HOME General Factor. The only systematic relationship occurs for the HOME Toys factor as it relates to CCTI Activity at both 12 and 24 months of age. In both cases, the correlation for boys is positive and that for girls is negative. The other 2 gender differences also yield positive correlations for boys and negative correlations for girls that are of roughly the same magnitude. Therefore, these results do not support the hypothesis that boys are more affected by environmental factors. None of the eight correlations for the FES showed a significant gender difference.

TABLE 13.7

Significant Gender Differences in Environment–Adopted Infant Correlations
for Behavioral Problems[a]

		Girls		Boys	
Environmental measure	Infant measure	N	r	N	r
HOME Maternal Involvement	12-mo CCTI Soothability	75	.31	92	−.06
HOME Maternal Involvement	24-mo CCTI Reaction to Foods	80	−.10	92	.22
HOME Restriction–Punishment	24-mo Difficult Temperament	79	.33	92	.02
FES Personal Growth	12-mo CCTI Reaction to Foods	74	.08	86	−.24
FES Personal Growth	24-mo Sleep Problems	75	.16	89	−.23

[a]See Tables 11.15 and 11.17 for references. The total number of environment–infant comparisons examined for gender differences is 84 (five HOME factors and two FES second-order factors correlated with six behavioral problem scales at 12 and at 24 months).

Behavioral Problems

Correlations of the HOME and FES environmental measures with infant behavioral problems at 12 and at 24 months are described in Tables 11.15 and 11.17. Of the 84 correlations in adoptive homes, only 5 (see Table 13.7) show significant gender differences. On the basis of chance alone, 4 significant differences are expected. The pattern of results for these few significant differences shows no systematic pattern to indicate that boys are more susceptible to environmental influences.

Summary of Environment–Infant Correlations

Of the 185 gender comparisons involving environment–infant correlations, only 11 are significant. This number of significant differences barely exceeds the number (9) that would be expected to occur by chance; moreover, the significant gender differences that do emerge do not appear to be systematic and offer no easy interpretation.

Summary

This chapter focuses on differences between boys and girls in means and in parent–offspring and environment–offspring correlations for general and specific cognitive abilities, temperament, and behavioral problems. With regard to mean differences, the CAP sample provides 80% statistical power to detect gender differences that account for as little as 2% of the variance. Nonetheless, there are few significant gender differences. For temperament and behavioral problems, only 2 of the 20 comparisons yield a significant mean difference between boys and girls; 1

significant difference is expected on the basis of chance alone. Boys and girls do not differ significantly for the Bayley MDI total; however, girls score slightly, but significantly, higher on the three Lewis–Enright scales involving verbal and lexical abilities. Mean gender differences are also examined for the major environmental measures. These analyses reveal no evidence that boys and girls are treated differently in any important way.

The CAP data set is also used to test the hypothesis that boys are more sensitive to environmental variation than are girls. Adoptive families provide a means of isolating family environmental influence unconfounded by heredity. Of the 104 adoptive mother–adopted infant correlations, only 5 show significant gender differences; chance alone should yield 5 significant differences when 100 comparisons are made. For the 104 adoptive father comparisons, there are 8 significant gender differences. Of these 13 significant gender differences in parent–offspring correlations for the adoptive parents and their adopted children, 9 involve higher correlations for boys than for girls, offering scant support for the hypothesis that boys are more affected by environmental factors. Interestingly, for the 104 biological mother–adopted infant correlations, 9 significant gender differences occur and in all 9 cases boys show higher correlations with their biological mothers than do girls. Were it not for the fact that the number of significant correlations only slightly exceeds the number expected on the basis of chance alone, this result might suggest that boys are more susceptible than girls to genetic influences.

Gender differences for environment–infant correlations are also examined. Of the 185 relationships between environmental measures and infant development that are analyzed for gender differences, only 11 are significantly different for boys and girls.

Our overall conclusion based on these analyses of gender differences in means and correlations is that gender has negligible impact upon individual differences in infant development. The number of significant gender differences in means and in parent–offspring and environment–offspring correlations borders on the number expected by chance alone. Little support is provided for the hypothesis that boys are more susceptible to environmental influences than are girls and that girls are more influenced genetically.

14

Applied Issues Relevant to Adoption

Introduction

An exciting aspect of the CAP has been the fact that its basic research question—the relative influences of heredity and environment on development—is an applied question from the point of view of social workers, adoptive and biological parents, and perhaps all parents. Beyond this general issue, the CAP data are relevant to some issues of specific interest to individuals involved in adoption. For example, are there differences between biological parents who relinquish their children for adoption and those who do not? Does selective placement affect the development of adopted infants? Do adoptive home environments differ importantly from nonadoptive homes? And, the most frequently asked question: Do developmental outcomes differ for adopted and nonadopted children?

The CAP is in a unique position to address several of these questions because of its longitudinal, prospective nature; its matching of adoptive and control families; and its extensive data bank on adopted and control infants, their adoptive, biological and control parents, and adoptive and control home environments. For example, if adopted children are found to differ from nonadopted children, the CAP design permits the examination of the possibility that the biological parents of adopted children differ from those of nonadopted children. Another application of the CAP design involves the study of selective placement and its effects. Although the issue of selective placement is frequently mentioned, there have been few previous attempts either to conceptualize or to explore the possible effects of selective placement on adopted children. We consider selective placement and its effects in the context of genotype–environment interaction and apply the CAP's adoption design to address this issue empirically. Of course, because the CAP data presented in this chapter were obtained from infants, any conclusions regarding outcome are tentative and subject to change as the children grow older.

The chapter begins with a discussion of factors—characteristics of biological parents, adoptive parents, the adoptive home environment, and birth history—that could lead to different developmental outcomes for adopted and control children. We then examine the CAP data for evidence of differences between adopted and control infants. This discussion focuses on averages for adoptive families as compared to control families. Regardless of the results of these analyses, it is reasonable to consider whether individual differences in the outcomes of adoption can be predicted using information about the adoptive parents and their home environment, as well as information about the biological parents. The next major section focuses on the prediction of such individual differences. The third major section considers selective placement, its extent, and its effect on the development of adopted children. In the last section of this chapter we discuss general issues of genetics as they pertain to social work in adoption.

Average Outcomes of Adoption

Two major strategies have been employed to evaluate adoption outcomes, and they yield quite different results. The first strategy involves studying the frequency of adoptees among clinical populations. Beginning with clinical case studies in the 1950s, overrepresentation of adoptees in clinical populations has frequently been reported. A Menninger Clinic study in 1962 raised alarm among social workers because it reported an incidence of 10.9% adoptees among children attending a clinic over a 5-year period (Toussieng, 1962). A 1982 study can be used as an example of research of this type. Particularly high frequencies of adoptees among children with diagnoses of attention deficit disorder, the DSM-III label for what used to be called hyperactivity, have been reported by Deutsch et al. (1982). This study suggests that over one-third of adopted boys are expected to be diagnosed as hyperactive; the report also contains a good discussion of the problems of this approach such as referral bias.

The general conclusion that emerges from such studies of clinical populations is that adoptees are at risk for many psychiatric disorders. However, this conclusion contrasts sharply with the results of studies of nonclinical samples of adopted and nonadopted children, which show few differences related to adopted versus nonadopted status (Mech, 1973). Even though no explanation for this discrepancy has been found, direct comparisons of adopted and control children are more convincing because they involve fewer problems of interpretation than do studies of clinical populations. One possible explanation of the discrepant results is that studies involving clinical populations do not specify the age or circumstances of adoption, whereas studies comparing adopted and nonadopted children typically involve early agency placements. For example, the paper by Deutsch et al. (1982) states only that the "prevalence of nonrelative adoption was determined" (p. 234) from the clinical records. If, as seems likely, these adoptions include late placements due to broken homes or other stressful circumstances, it would be less surprising to find that children subjected to these stresses evidence more psychopathology than do nonadopted children. Another possible source of the conflicting results is that studies of clinical populations consider extreme groups of adoptees, whereas studies comparing adopted and nonadopted children consider the entire distribution of adoptees. It is possible that results for the extreme groups truly differ from those for the rest of the distribution.

In addition to the classic studies comparing adopted and control children (e.g., Bohman, 1970; Hoopes, Sherman, Lawder, Andrews, & Lower, 1970; Lawder *et al.*, 1969; McWhinnie, 1967; Seglow *et al.*, 1972; Witmer *et al.*, 1963; Wittenborn, 1957), Hoopes (1982) supports the conclusion that adoption outcomes are generally favorable. The Delaware Family Study was a longitudinal adoption study of 260 adoptive families in which children and their families were studied 6 months after placement, when the children were 2 and 5 years old, and when they were between 8 and 12 years of age. The children were Caucasian, born between 1962 and 1968, and placed before 2 years of age. No data were reported for the biological parents of the adoptees. The control families consisted of 68 families "obtained from two private obstetricians in the Wilmington, Delaware area" who "were matched as closely as possible for similarities in ethnic background and religious affiliation" (Hoopes, 1982, p. 13). Although control fathers were more educated than adoptive fathers, both groups were upper middle class; over 70% of the fathers were in professional and corporate occupations. The primary data of the study consist of interviewer ratings and ratings based on tape-recorded interviews with the parents, although two WISC subtests and a few other measures were administered. Analyses of these data led to the following conclusion:

> The central implication to be drawn from the study findings is that adoption is a good service for the children and the families who adopt them. In general, both the children and the families were doing well at age 5 and during the subsequent study period when the children were in their early school years. (Hoopes, 1982, p. 97)

Although it seems clear that most adoptions turn out well, a sweeping conclusion that adoptees have no more problems than do nonadopted children is premature. The results of studies typically cited to support the conclusion that there are no differences between adopted and nonadopted children often contain some evidence of problems for adoptees. For example, the Bryn Mawr College follow-up study of 100 adoptees at 10 to 15 years of age (Hoopes *et al.*, 1970) is primarily known for its conclusion that "the adopted children showed no evidence of more pathology than the control children" (p. 73). However, the adopted children were rated by their teachers as significantly less well adjusted than control children (p. 44).

Furthermore, a seldom cited but excellent epidemiological study in England suggests some negative outcomes of adoption. The National Child Development Study (1958) was a longitudinal study of a cohort of 17,000 children born in 1958 from which 182 children had been adopted by people other than their biological relatives (Seglow *et al.*, 1972). Information about adjustment of these adoptees was derived from teacher ratings on the Bristol Social Adjustment Guides. Overall, there were no adjustment differences between the adopted children and the other children in the 1958 cohort; however, a higher proportion (23%) of adopted boys had adjustment problems as compared to the other boys (17%). Thus, although the difference is slight, this study suggests that adopted boys are at greater risk for behavioral problems.

Studies in France and Sweden also suggest that adoptees experience greater problems of adjustment. In the French study (Duyme, 1981), outcomes in adolescence were examined for 107 infants adopted by 2 years of age. Although scholastic success of the adoptees did not differ from French norms, 30% of the adoptees displayed behavioral problems such as antisocial behavior or emotional problems in contrast to 16% of a control group. In the Swedish study (Bohman, 1970), a follow-up study at 11 years of 160 adopted children, similar results were found: Scholastic success of adoptees was average, but behavioral problems as rated by teachers were more common for the adopted boys. However, another report indicates that these differences disappeared by age 15 (Bohman & Sigvardsson, 1978).

The possibility that adopted boys show greater antisocial problems fits with data suggesting a genetic rather than environmental etiology. In the Danish adoption studies of criminality of 1145 male adoptees from Copenhagen matched to non-adopted males, the biological fathers of adoptees were found to have criminal records nearly 3 times more often than did the adoptive fathers or control fathers (Hutchings & Mednick, 1975). In an adoption study of criminality in the U.S., Crowe (1974) found that adoptees born to women with felony records showed more antisocial personality than did a control group of adoptees.

One conclusion that can be drawn from these studies is that cognitive capabilities of adopted and nonadopted children do not differ. However, more research is needed on the topic of adjustment (Hershov, 1976). In the following sections, we examine factors that could lead to differences between adopted and nonadopted children—such factors as characteristics of the adoptive parents and adoptive homes, perinatal events, and (rarely considered) characteristics of the biological parents of the adoptees.

Parental Characteristics

If adoptive parents, biological parents of adoptees, and nonadoptive parents do not differ on the average, their characteristics are not likely to be a source of average differences between adopted and nonadopted children. Differences between adoptive and nonadoptive (control) parents would suggest a possible environmental source of differences between adoptees and controls. Differences between biological parents of adoptees and nonadoptive parents would suggest a possible genetic source of differences between adopted and nonadopted children.

In previous chapters, we have mentioned that CAP adoptive and control parents

TABLE 14.1

16 PF Norms and CAP Adoptive Parents

16 PF Scale	Adoptive mothers (N = 134–136)		16 PF norms[a] (N = 729)		Adoptive fathers (N = 134–135)		16 PF norms[a] (N = 2255)	
	$\overline{X}$	SD	$\overline{X}$	SD	$\overline{X}$	SD	$\overline{X}$	SD
A. Outgoing	10.3	(3.3)	11.3	(3.2)	7.8	(3.4)	10.2	(3.2)
B. Bright	8.1	(1.9)	7.0	(2.2)	8.6	(1.9)	7.0	(2.2)
C. Emotionally Stable	16.5	(3.6)	15.6	(4.0)	17.1	(3.7)	16.6	(4.1)
E. Assertive	11.3	(4.9)	11.3	(4.6)	14.1	(4.2)	12.9	(3.9)
F. Happy-Go-Lucky	14.4	(3.8)	13.5	(4.3)	13.2	(4.0)	14.2	(4.1)
G. Conscientious	14.0	(2.8)	12.8	(3.3)	14.0	(2.8)	13.4	(3.4)
H. Venturesome	14.6	(4.8)	12.9	(5.6)	14.1	(6.0)	14.8	(5.2)
I. Tender-Minded	14.2	(2.8)	13.4	(3.4)	8.2	(3.4)	9.0	(3.4)
L. Suspicious	6.6	(3.1)	6.2	(3.4)	7.6	(3.5)	7.4	(3.4)
M. Imaginative	12.1	(3.7)	13.1	(3.9)	13.0	(3.3)	13.0	(3.7)
N. Astute	9.2	(2.9)	10.4	(2.9)	8.3	(2.7)	9.2	(2.9)
O. Apprehensive	10.4	(4.0)	10.7	(4.0)	8.1	(3.8)	9.4	(4.2)
Q_1. Experimenting	6.3	(2.6)	7.7	(3.1)	8.8	(3.1)	9.5	(3.0)
Q_2. Self-Sufficient	11.0	(3.7)	10.2	(3.6)	11.7	(3.3)	10.3	(3.5)
Q_3. Controlled	13.5	(2.9)	12.5	(3.3)	14.0	(2.7)	13.3	(3.4)
Q_4. Tense	13.2	(4.8)	12.9	(4.8)	11.4	(5.0)	10.7	(4.7)

[a]From the *Norms for the 16 PF, Forms A and B (1967–68 Edition)*; Tables 13 and 16 for 729 females and 2255 males based on the general population aged 30 years.

are quite similar on the average for the diverse measures included in the CAP; biological parents are also similar to the other parents when their relative youth is taken into account. Although we review mean comparisons among the biological, adoptive, and control parents, most interesting are comparisons with normative data. In Chapter 3 (Tables 3.4 and 3.5), we indicate that both the biological parents and the adoptive parents in the CAP, as well as their parents, are similar in socioeconomic status to a representative sample in Denver and are less than one standard deviation above the entire U.S. white labor force as indicated by the 1970 census.

We mention in Chapter 9 that CAP data for biological and adoptive parents are similar to normative data for Cattell's 16 PF questionnaire. Tables 14.1 and 14.2 present 16 PF means and standard deviations for the CAP adoptive parents and biological parents, respectively, as compared to normative data from the 16 PF manual. Table 14.1 compares data on CAP adoptive parents to 16 PF norms for individuals 30 years of age on the average. The 16 PF norms are based on samples representative geographically and racially of the U.S. The means and standard deviations for the adoptive parents are remarkably similar to the normative data. The only scale that shows greater than half a standard deviation difference for both adoptive fathers and mothers is Scale B, which involves intelligence; in addition, adoptive fathers are less outgoing than the general population.

TABLE 14.2

16 PF Norms and CAP Biological Parents

16 PF Scale	Biological mothers (N = 162–164)		16 PF norms[a] (N = 1149)		Biological fathers (N = 37–38)		16 PF norms[a] (N = 1312)	
	$\overline{X}$	SD	$\overline{X}$	SD	$\overline{X}$	SD	$\overline{X}$	SD
A. Outgoing	9.6	(3.1)	11.2	(3.0)	7.6	(2.8)	9.0	(3.0)
B. Bright	8.0	(2.0)	7.0	(2.2)	7.8	(2.4)	7.0	(2.2)
C. Emotionally Stable	16.0	(4.0)	13.7	(3.8)	15.5	(3.5)	14.0	(3.7)
E. Assertive	11.1	(4.1)	11.0	(3.8)	14.3	(3.4)	13.1	(3.7)
F. Happy-Go-Lucky	16.4	(4.3)	16.0	(4.4)	16.1	(3.6)	15.3	(4.3)
G. Conscientious	11.8	(3.4)	12.2	(3.5)	11.6	(3.8)	11.0	(3.4)
H. Venturesome	12.7	(5.7)	12.6	(5.1)	13.8	(5.5)	12.6	(5.0)
I. Tender-Minded	13.2	(2.7)	13.5	(2.8)	9.1	(3.3)	8.9	(3.5)
L. Suspicious	8.0	(3.1)	9.2	(3.1)	10.0	(3.2)	10.0	(3.1)
M. Imaginative	11.7	(3.5)	10.6	(3.8)	11.2	(4.0)	11.0	(3.5)
N. Astute	9.5	(2.5)	10.3	(2.7)	8.8	(2.3)	9.3	(2.7)
O. Apprehensive	12.1	(3.7)	13.0	(3.6)	10.6	(4.2)	11.9	(3.8)
Q_1. Experimenting	8.3	(2.7)	8.3	(3.1)	10.5	(2.2)	9.7	(3.1)
Q_2. Self-Sufficient	10.8	(3.8)	9.0	(3.3)	11.9	(3.0)	10.1	(3.5)
Q_3. Controlled	11.7	(3.0)	11.4	(3.1)	11.7	(2.6)	11.1	(3.1)
Q_4. Tense	14.2	(4.4)	14.3	(4.3)	13.7	(4.4)	13.3	(4.1)

[a]From the *Norms for the 16 PF, Forms A and B (1967–68 Edition)*; Tables 1 and 4 for 1149 females and 1312 males based on high school juniors and seniors aged 17 years.

Table 14.2 is especially important because so few data of this type have been reported previously for biological parents. The 16 PF means and standard deviations for the CAP biological parents are compared to normative data from the 16 PF manual for individuals with an average age of 17 years. A comparison of Tables 14.1 and 14.2 shows several age changes, such as decreasing suspiciousness and apprehensiveness, which would have been interpreted as real differences between biological and adoptive parents if separate norms had not been available for 17-year-olds and 30-year-olds. The normative data for the 17-year-olds show that the CAP biological parents are quite similar to the standardization sample with respect to personality as measured by Cattell's 16 PF. The only differences that exceed half a standard deviation suggest that biological parents in the CAP are more mature than the normative sample: CAP biological mothers and fathers are more emotionally stable, more self-sufficient, and less outgoing.

These data are based only on those biological parents whose children were relinquished for adoption. However, 116 biological mothers have participated in the CAP testing program and then have chosen not to relinquish their infants for adoption. Although a comparison of women who place children for adoption and those who choose to keep their children is not directly germane to adoption outcomes, it bears tangentially on the topic. If they differ, then the characterization of biological parents would change if the proportions in the two groups change. Table

TABLE 14.3

Comparisons of Biological Mothers Who Relinquish Their Infants for Adoption and Those Who Do Not[a]

Measure	Mothers who relinquished children (N = 312–349)		Mothers who kept children (N = 104–116)	
	$\overline{X}$	SD	$\overline{X}$	SD
16 PF Personality Questionnaire				
A. Outgoing	9.8	(3.1)	9.9	(3.1)
B. Bright	7.8	(1.9)	7.5	(2.0)
C. Emotionally Stable	15.8	(3.8)	14.6	(3.9)
E. Assertive	11.5	(3.9)	11.4	(4.1)
F. Happy-Go-Lucky	16.5	(4.3)	15.6	(4.0)
G. Conscientious	11.8	(3.2)	11.3	(3.3)
H. Venturesome	13.0	(5.9)	12.6	(5.6)
I. Tender-Minded	13.1	(2.8)	13.4	(2.6)
L. Suspicious	8.0	(3.1)	8.6	(3.5)
M. Imaginative	11.4	(3.3)	10.7	(3.0)
N. Astute	9.5	(2.7)	9.7	(2.7)
O. Apprehensive	12.0	(3.7)	12.6	(4.0)
Q_1. Experimenting	8.5	(2.8)	8.3	(3.0)
Q_2. Self-Sufficient	10.5	(3.6)	10.9	(3.4)
Q_3. Controlled	11.9	(3.1)	11.8	(3.0)
Q_4. Tense	14.1	(4.7)	14.8	(5.0)
Education (years)	12.0	(1.8)	11.9	(1.8)
Mother's education (years)	13.3	(5.2)	12.5	(2.4)
Father's education (years)	14.0	(7.3)	13.9	(8.9)
IQ[b,c]	100.9	(15.0)	98.4	(15.0)

[a]Includes all biological mothers who participated in the CAP testing program; that is, in addition to biological mothers of CAP adoptees, the first column includes mothers who relinquished children for adoption but whose infants were not adopted by CAP families. Thus, means and N differ from those for the biological mothers in Table 14.2.

[b]Measures significantly different ($p < .05$) for the two groups.

[c]Standard score expressed as IQ with an overall mean of 100.

14.3 compares these two groups of mothers with respect to the 16 PF scales and education. Only 2 significant differences emerge from the 20 comparisons. Biological mothers who relinquished their children for adoption have slightly higher scores on the 13-item intelligence scale (Scale B) of the 16 PF. They also score higher on the CAP measure of IQ, an unrotated first-principal-component score derived from the 13 cognitive test scores. In terms of the CAP specific cognitive ability factor scores, mothers who placed their infants for adoption have slightly higher scores on the Verbal, Spatial, and Perceptual Speed factors, although only the latter factor yields a significant differences between the two groups of mothers. Nonetheless, the intelligence difference is slight, only one-sixth of a standard deviation. Thus, this difference between the two groups does not deter us from concluding that the biological mothers who relinquished their children for adoption do not differ importantly from those who chose to keep their children. Of course, this conclusion is limited to the biological mothers who participated in the CAP testing program; all of these women were being counseled at an adoption agency and were at one time leaning toward relinquishment, even though some eventually chose to keep their children.

No normative data exist for CAP parental measures other than the 16 PF. However, as indicated in previous chapters, the biological, adoptive, and control parents are generally similar. Table 9.12 presented means and standard deviations for the three types of parents for self-report and mate ratings on the EASI Temperament Survey. Of 10 comparisons, 5 yielded significant differences between the adoptive and control parents on the one hand and the biological parents on the other. However, the mean differences—greater emotionality and impulsivity in the biological parents—are likely to represent an age effect because the direction of the differences between the biological parents and the other parents is the same as the differences between the 17-year-old norms and the general population norms for the 16 PF.

The three types of parents were compared with respect to self-reported sociopathy, depression, and hysteria in Table 11.8. The biological parents reported more depression and hysteria than did the other parents; however, the mean differences are less than half a standard deviation, which indicates that they do not account for much variance. Although the differences could be due to worries caused by pregnancy, they could also suggest the possibility of differences between adopted and nonadopted children in affective aspects of adjustment, if the biological parents' characteristics are transmitted genetically to their adopted-away offspring.

Table 7.1 compared the three types of parents on the CAP cognitive tests. In accord with previous findings that adopted children do not differ from nonadopted children in scholastic achievement, no important differences emerged.

In summary, few differences can be detected among biological, adoptive, and nonadoptive parents. Thus, parental characteristics are not likely to lead to differences between adopted and nonadopted children in our sample.

Characteristics of Home Environments

Differences between the environments provided by adoptive and nonadoptive homes could lead to differences between adopted and nonadopted children. The Delaware Family Study (Hoopes, 1982) found few differences between childrearing practices of adoptive and nonadoptive parents, although adoptive mothers reported less irritability and fostered dependence to a greater extent than did nonadoptive mothers as indicated by a questionnaire on family life and attitudes. Ratings made from tape recordings of interviews with the parents when the probands were 2 years old suggested that adoptive parents were functioning better than nonadoptive parents in terms of parent–child relationships and the marital relationship. However, we are aware of no studies that used standard measures of the environment such as the Home Observation for Measurement of the Environment (HOME) and the Family Environment Scale (FES). In Chapter 5, the CAP adoptive and control families are compared for the HOME (Table 5.4) and the FES (Table 5.1). Although the CAP means on the HOME are higher than those reported in the HOME manual, the adoptive and control homes are similar to each other and to other middle-class samples. The 10 scales of the FES also indicate that the adoptive and control families in the CAP are similar, although adoptive families score higher on the Moral–Religious Emphasis scale, no doubt because the two adoption agencies participating in the CAP are sectarian social service agencies.

Perinatal Factors

If adopted children differ from nonadopted children with respect to perinatal factors such as gestational age and birth weight, differences between adopted and nonadopted children might be expected, especially in infancy when perinatal events have their greatest effect. The Delaware Family Study (Hoopes, 1982) found that adopted children born from 1962 to 1968 were lighter in weight than nonadopted children, although no sequelae of this difference could be detected. However, in the CAP with its 1975–1980 placements, no differences have been detected between adopted and control infants. In fact, the infants in both CAP groups are remarkably similar to national norms. The average birth weight of the CAP adoptees is 3221 g (1724–4218 g range); for the controls, the average birth weight is 3311 g (1996–4354). Birth weight below 2500 g, thought to occur for about 7% of live births, is considered to be a risk factor. Five percent of the CAP adopted infants and 3% of the control infants weighed less than 2500 g at birth. We also analyzed hospital records concerning clinical gestational age. For adoptees, the average gestational age is 39.6 weeks ($SD = 1.7$), with a range from 33 to 44 weeks. For the controls, the average is 39.7 weeks ($SD = 1.5$), and the range is from 34 to 43 weeks. Epidemiological data suggest that about 80% of all singletons are born at 40 or more weeks gestational age; in the CAP, 70% of the adoptees and 63% of the control infants are born at 40 or more weeks gestational age. Gestational ages less than 36 weeks are often considered as a risk factor and occur for about 3% of singleton births; in the CAP, gestational ages of 3% of the adoptees and 2.7% of the controls are less than 36 weeks.

In summary, the CAP data suggest that perinatal factors are not likely to be a source of different developmental outcomes for adopted and nonadopted children.

CAP Outcomes in Infancy

The findings discussed so far in this section indicate that perinatal factors, parental characteristics, and the home environments are not likely to be sources of differences between adopted and nonadopted children. We can also compare

TABLE 14.4

Comparisons of Adopted and Control Infants

Infant measure	12 Months				24 Months			
	Adopted		Control		Adopted		Control	
	$\overline{X}$	SD	$\overline{X}$	SD	$\overline{X}$	SD	$\overline{X}$	SD
Bayley Mental Development Index	107.3	(12.2)	109.1	(12.7)	107.9	(14.8)	109.5	(15.7)
Bayley Psychomotor Development Index	92.3	(15.3)	93.8	(14.1)	98.8	(12.9)	103.4	(13.4)*
CCTI Emotionality	11.8	(3.4)	12.8	(3.1)*	12.7	(2.8)	13.8	(2.9)*
CCTI Activity	21.0	(3.0)	21.3	(2.3)	21.0	(2.5)	21.2	(2.2)
CCTI Sociability	20.0	(3.4)	20.0	(3.7)	19.6	(3.6)	19.3	(3.1)
CCTI Attention Span	17.1	(2.5)	17.1	(2.3)	17.6	(2.8)	17.3	(2.5)
IBR Affect–Extraversion	36.1	(4.7)	34.8	(5.5)	35.1	(6.4)	36.0	(6.6)
IBR Activity	17.4	(2.9)	17.2	(2.6)	16.2	(2.9)	15.8	(3.1)
IBR Task Orientation	22.2	(3.0)	22.3	(3.2)	23.3	(3.2)	23.8	(3.3)
Videotape Affect–Extraversion	18.3	(1.8)	17.9	(1.9)	18.5	(1.6)	18.2	(2.2)
Videotape Activity	3.3	(1.1)	3.5	(1.0)	3.5	(0.8)	3.4	(0.9)
Videotape Task Orientation	13.0	(1.6)	12.5	(1.8)	16.6	(1.9)	16.5	(1.9)
Difficult Temperament	-0.2	(0.9)	0.1	(1.0)*	-0.1	(0.9)	0.0	(1.0)
Sleep Problems	5.5	(1.0)	5.7	(1.2)	5.5	(1.3)	5.6	(1.2)
Eating Problems	6.0	(1.2)	6.3	(1.2)*	7.1	(1.3)	7.2	(1.3)
Diaper Problems	6.9	(1.2)	7.2	(1.0)*	6.3	(1.3)	6.5	(1.2)
CCTI Reaction to Foods	11.2	(3.0)	11.7	(3.2)	12.3	(3.1)	12.7	(3.5)
CCTI Soothability	18.8	(2.1)	18.4	(2.2)	18.1	(2.4)	17.7	(2.2)

*Significant mean difference between adopted and control infants ($p < .05$).

adopted and control children directly in the CAP. Although confined to infancy data at this point, the CAP data bank is informative on the issue of outcomes of adoption because it provides a far broader picture of adoptees' development than do previous studies. In addition to standardized tests such as the Bayley Scales of Infant Development, the CAP includes parent, tester, and videotape ratings of temperament and behavioral problems.

Table 14.4 lists means and standard deviations for the CAP adopted and control infants at 12 and at 24 months of age on the major measures of mental and motor development, temperament, and behavioral problems. As mentioned in previous chapters, multivariate tests within each domain yield few significant differences between adopted and control boys and girls. The results of univariate tests of significance shown in Table 14.4 also suggest few significant differences between adopted and control infants at 12 or at 24 months of age. The data are presented for boys and girls combined because no significant gender differences or significant gender-by-adoptive-status interactions have been observed. The adopted infants have slightly lower Bayley Mental and Psychomotor Development Index scores at 12 and at 24 months, although the difference reaches significance only for motor development at 24 months. The difference for mental development at each age is trivial, less than one-sixth of a standard deviation. Temperament measures show only one significant difference between adopted and control children. The adoptees are less emotional at both 12 and at 24 months of age. The literature suggesting adjustment problems for adopted children makes the CAP data on behavioral problems particularly interesting. However, here again, there are few significant differences; moreover, the only significant differences reveal fewer problems for adopted infants than for control infants: Adopted infants had lower scores for difficult temperament, eating problems, and diaper problems at 12 months of age. Nonetheless, the small amount of variance involved in any differences between adopted and control infants leads us to emphasize the conclusion that there are no important differences between the CAP adopted and control children in infancy.

The Delaware Family Study also found few differences in infancy and in the early school years, leading to the conclusion that:

> These encouraging findings reinforce the belief within the child welfare field that adoption is the best way to provide substitute care and nurturing to the young child who cannot be reared by his or her family of origin. Only a small percentage of children were having problems of any significance, which contradicts a number of other research findings, particularly from the mental health field. (Hoopes, 1982, p. 97)

The CAP data, based on a broader battery of measures of the development of adopted and nonadopted infants, as well as on measures of characteristics of their parents and their home environments, confirm this conclusion.

Predicting Individual Adoption Outcomes

Even though adopted and nonadopted infants are similar on the average, as are their home environments and parents, some infants present more problems for their parents than do other infants. For the adopted infants, we can ask whether any specific factors such as parental measures or assessments of the home environment can predict successful individual outcomes. Hoopes (1982) notes that predicting the outcomes of adoption has been viewed as a key service offered by adoption practitioners: "Inherent in the agency practitioner's bringing together a family and a child in adoption is the assumption that there are some identifiable qualities in families and children, and factors in their situations, that may predict success or forecast problems for their lives together" (p. 3).

Few predictors have been found empirically (e.g., Lawder et al., 1969), and the Delaware Family Study, the major goal of which was "to determine factors that can be used to predict successful adoptions before placement" (Hoopes, 1982, p. 6), led to the following conclusion:

> It is not possible to predict later functioning of the family as assessed in an interview from interview data of the nature obtained by the adoption worker in this study before placement. Although this is a disappointing finding, it is not unexpected in light of the complexity of interrelationships between parents and children. (Hoopes, 1982, p. 32)

Stepping back from the specific issue of predicting outcomes of adoption, we can view this as a special case of attempting to find environmental predictors of individual differences in development. As seen in previous chapters, neither characteristics of adoptive parents nor measures of the adoptive home environment are good predictors of individual differences in development among adopted infants. Environmental predictors are few in number and of insufficient strength to be useful in a clinical context for placing infants into adoptive homes. Stronger relationships between environmental measures and infant development are found in control families; however, as explained in previous chapters, differences between correlations in adoptive and control families can be ascribed to genetic factors.

Thus, the infancy data from the CAP—which includes families already screened for suitability for adoption—support the conclusion that prediction of individual outcomes of adoption cannot be made with sufficient certainty to be useful to social workers in their attempt to predict the success of adoption placements or to forecast problems.

Age at Placement

The age at which adoptees are placed in their adoptive homes was thought to have an important effect on adoption outcomes beginning in the 1950s when Bowlby (1951) emphasized the importance of early attachment. Empirical studies have provided little support for the importance of age at placement in predicting individual outcomes of adoption. Although a study by Witmer et al. (1963) found a relationship with adjustment problems, several other studies revealed no effects of age at placement (Duyme, 1981; Hoopes, 1982; Kadushin, 1970; Menlove, 1965). In all of these studies, children were placed in their adoptive homes much later on the average than are the CAP adoptees; thus, it would seem unlikely that age at placement in the CAP, varying as it does only from 3 days to 172 days, is related to

TABLE 14.5

Relationships of Age at Placement and Time between Birth and Hospital Release
with Various Adoptee Outcome Measures

	Correlation			
	Time between birth and hospital release		Age at placement	
Measure	12 Months	24 Months	12 Months	24 Months
Bayley Mental Development Index	−.14*	−.15*	−.12	−.06
Lewis–Enright Bayley Scales				
12-month Means-End	−.18*	—	−.18*	—
12-month Imitation	−.08	—	−.04	—
12-month Verbal	−.12	—	−.07	—
24-month Lexical	—	−.08	—	−.09
24-month Spatial	—	−.22*	—	−.09
24-month Verbal (symbolic)	—	−.11	—	−.02
24-month Imitation	—	.02	—	.03
Bayley Psychomotor Development Index	−.18*	−.06	−.14*	−.12
IBR tester-rating factors				
Affect–Extraversion	−.09	−.10	−.11	−.11
Activity	.02	−.02	−.07	−.03
Task Orientation	−.12	−.05	−.04	−.08

*$p < .05$.

infant functioning. However, the extensive data on the CAP children led us to examine the relationship between age at placement and the major CAP infancy measures. Table 14.5 reports these correlations.

We were surprised to find negative correlations between age at placement and Bayley Psychomotor Development Index scores at 12 months. The timing of placement is primarily a function of legal issues rather than characteristics of the adoptees; thus, these data might be interpreted to be the effect of some postnatal environmental factor such as bonding. However, correlations between the adoptee outcome measures and the time between birth and hospital release (see Table 14.5) indicate the same pattern of results. Time until release from the hospital is primarily a matter of the infant's health status; thus, we suggest that the relationship between age at placement and adoptee outcome is not a function of placement age per se but rather is mediated by the length of time the child stays in the hospital, which is an index of health status. We examine the relationship between health status and development in Chapter 12.

We also explored the relationship of age at placement and time between birth and release from the hospital to environmental measures in the adoptive homes. The reason for examining these relationships is that parents might react differently to infants who are placed with them in the first week of life than to infants who are placed when they are several months old. However, we found no more than a chance number of significant correlations between the environmental measures and the placement and release variables.

Selective Placement

Selective placement—matching adoptive and biological parents—has traditionally been practiced by adoption agencies presumably because of the belief that a closer match between adoptive parents and their adopted children would contribute to a more successful adoption (Triseliotis, 1970). Selective placement has been reported to occur for physical characteristics, cultural background, race, religion, intelligence, and personality. Two relevant issues are the extent of selective placement and the effect of selective placement on adopted children and their parents.

The Extent of Selective Placement

In terms of the extent of selective placement, the most notable fact is a trend toward less selective placement, especially for behavioral characteristics such as intelligence, which is often estimated from information about parental education and occupational status (Hardy-Brown, Plomin, Greenhalgh, & Jax, 1980). Prior to the 1950s, adoption studies typically yielded correlations of .20 to .30 between educational attainments of adoptive and biological parents. Two large studies of children adopted in the 1960s yielded selective placement correlations of .10 to .20 for parental education (Horn et al., 1979; Scarr & Weinberg, 1978). A study of 206 "first" adoptions during 1967 to 1978 resulted in average selective placement correlations of .19 for education and .13 for occupational status (Ho, Plomin, & DeFries, 1979).

As indicated in previous chapters, selective placement in the CAP for adopted children born between 1976 and 1980 is negligible. The selective placement correlations for education are −.13 for biological mothers and adoptive mothers and .08 for biological mothers and adoptive fathers; for occupational status, the correlations are .01 and .17, respectively. One could argue that these selective placement correlations are underestimates because the biological parents are in their teenage years and their education and occupation are poor indices of their ultimate attainment. Social workers typically obtain data on the grandparents, the parents of the biological parents, which can be used to supplement educational and occupational information about the biological parents. However, as we noted in Chapter 3, selective placement correlations based on information about the grandparents are also negligible. For example, the correlations between the fathers of the biological mothers and the fathers of the adoptive mothers are .02 for education and −.17 for occupation; for the fathers of the adoptive fathers, the correlations are .12 and .01, respectively.

Direct measures of the parents' behavior also indicate that biological and adoptive parents are not matched by the two agencies participating in the CAP. As seen in previous chapters, selective placement correlations for general and specific cognitive abilities, personality, and behavioral problems are generally not significant. Although the CAP data fit the trend towards reduced selective placement, it is possible that the negligible selective placement found in the CAP is attributable to the placement practices of the two agencies participating in the study. A reminder that selective placement can differ at different agencies comes from an adoption study that departs from the general trend towards lower selective placement. A study of adopted Flemish children (Claeys, 1973) reported correlations between social–educational status for birth parents and adoptive parents for two adoption agencies. For one agency, the selective placement correlations ranged from .06 to .14. However, the correlations for the other agency, which expressly worked toward selective placement, were much higher (ranging from .33 to .66).

In addition to the trend towards reduced selective placement, another interesting issue relevant to the extent of selective placement is that characteristics of the infants themselves, such as their health, are no longer used to place children selectively. Early in the history of adoption services, infants were retained in foster homes for at least several months until their developmental status could be evaluated. Even in 1941, a Children's Bureau document stated: "Ordinarily an agency of recognized standing hesitates before placing a child under four months of age, even when his family background is favorable" (Colby, 1941, p. 125). This practice changed in the 1950s due to the influence of Bowlby (1951), who emphasized the dangers of institutionalization and the importance of early attachment. Today, agencies attempt to place infants as soon as legally possible; in the CAP, the average age of placement is 29 days. Because infants are placed so young, it is unlikely that characteristics of the infants are used to guide selective placement. Nevertheless, it is possible that perinatal factors such as maturity and birth complications are considered in placing infants selectively. However, in the study of 206 first adoptions during 1967 to 1978 (Ho et al., 1979), no significant correlations were found between perinatal factors—such as gestational age, Apgar ratings of the infants' condition at birth, time in hospital, and time in foster care—and characteristics of the adoptive parents.

The study by Ho et al. (1979) also considered selective placement for physical characteristics; namely, height, weight, skin color, hair color, and eye color. The selective placement correlations were modest, .15 on the average, with the exception of greater selective placement for height. An interesting sidelight is that the selective placement correlations, averaged for both adoptive parents, were greater in relation to the biological fathers than to the biological mothers for both height and education. These results imply a mistaken belief that fathers are more influential genetically.

The Effect of Selective Placement

The premise underlying selective placement is that matching adoptive parents and their adopted children promotes successful placements. Does selective placement affect the development of adopted children or the relationship between adopted children and their parents? The prevalence of selective placement in the past makes it surprising to find that the effect of selective placement has not been addressed previously except in one study. The question is an important one because possible dangers, such as raising adoptive parents' expectations that they will receive a child just like them, lurk in selective placement. Moreover, other than for height, more selective placement occurs for intelligence (or its educational and occupational indices) than for any other characteristic because it is assumed that children with the "best" backgrounds will flourish in the "best" adoptive homes. However, the necessary implication of this position is that children with the least promising backgrounds will necessarily be adopted by parents with less desirable characteristics. From the point of view of the children, the case could be made for the opposite position: negative selective placement. Children with the least desirable backgrounds might benefit most by placement in the best adoptive homes; children with the best backgrounds might develop well regardless of the adoptive home in which they are placed. This argument is made not to advocate negative selective placement, but to point out how little is known about the effects of placing children selectively.

We are aware of only one attempt to test the effect of selective placement. In a follow-up study of 195 adopted children, Wittenborn (1957) compared the differences between the educational attainments of biological and adoptive parents (as a measure of matching) with various interview measures of the adoptive parents and concluded:

> It has been asked "Is it important to seek a cultural and educational matching between adoptive parents and true parents?" . . . it appears that the discrepancy between the education of true parents and adoptive parents bears *no relationship* with the parent's acceptance of the adoptive child, the satisfactions the parents experience with the adoptive child, and the degree to which they are rejective in their relationships with the adoptive child. (pp. 136–137)

Difference scores, such as the difference between the educational levels of biological and adoptive parents, are problematic statistically, especially when the two variables that comprise the difference score are correlated as they are in the presence of selective placement (Cohen & Cohen, 1983). A more appropriate test of the effect of selective placement analyzes interactions between characteristics of biological and adoptive parents as they affect adoptees' development (Hardy-Brown *et al.*, 1980). For example, do children adopted into homes in which adoptive parents are matched to biological parents receive an extra boost in terms of their adjustment? Regardless of whether adoptive parents affect adoptees' adjustment on the average, it is possible that adoptees' adjustment is enhanced when adoptive and biological parents are matched. Another way of saying this is that, regardless of the main effects of adoptive parents' and biological parents' characteristics, does an interaction between the adoptive and biological parents' characteristics affect adoptees' development? Thus, if selective placement is important, its influence will be revealed by the effects of an interaction between biological parents' and adoptive parents' characteristics on adoptees' development. Because biological parents' characteristics can be used to estimate genetic influences and adoptive parents' characteristics estimate environmental influences, this interaction is precisely the interaction that we have referred to in previous chapters as genotype–environment interaction, which refers to the possibility that the effect of an environmental factor depends upon the genotype of the child (Plomin, DeFries, & Loehlin, 1977). The effect of selective placement on adoptees' development involves a nonlinear effect of biological and adoptive parents' characteristics that can be seen as genotype–environment interaction. Examples of this approach and reanalyses of data from two adoption studies that suggest no effect of selective placement on adoptees' mental development are described by Hardy-Brown et al. (1980).

Even though the extent of selective placement in the CAP is negligible, its data and design are useful for testing the effect of selective placement because some children are by chance placed in adoptive homes in which biological and adoptive parents are matched or mismatched. In the previous chapters, we presented numerous examples of genotype–environment interaction analyses that can now be viewed as tests of the effect of selective placement. The general finding that such effects are rare means that the effect of selective placement is negligible, at least in terms of the development of infants. The type of interaction that emerged on rare occasions is one in which a calmer, less constrained environment allows genetic propensities of children to emerge more clearly. For example, genetic differences in emotionality of adopted infants appear only when adoptive mothers are relatively unemotional; when adoptive mothers are above average in emotionality, adopted infants are emotional regardless of their genetic predisposition. Similarly, genetic differences in infant difficult temperament emerge when the adoptive mother is below average in extraversion. This type of interaction, the infant characteristics for which it occurred, and the small amount of variance accounted for by the interactions combine to make even these rare effects of selective placement inapplicable to adoption decision making.

In summary, our review of the literature and analyses of the CAP data indicate that the extent of selective placement is decreasing and that there is no evidence that selective placement affects the development of adopted children.

Genetics

Genetics has had an odd history in adoption work. Early on, particularly before adoption services became professional in the 1930s, knowledge about heredity was assumed to be critical in the adoption process, even though there was at that time little evidence for genetic influence, especially for mental and personality characteristics. For example, in 1940, a geneticist wrote:

> The geneticist finds . . . a surprising willingness to accept a genetic point of view in child adoption practice. The better child welfare agencies . . . have and are making every effort to inform themselves concerning the hereditary and social background of the children under their control. Not only do the better agencies stress the family background but they make every effort to check up on the child's mental rating and emotional constitution. (McKinley, 1940, p. 3)

However, by the 1950s, this attitude had changed among social workers to an environmental orientation (Kohlsaat & Johnson, 1954) that continues today. As Kadushin (1978) has noted:

> The orientation that is generally accepted by the adoption field (is), namely, that genetic–constitutional factors are of limited, clearly secondary, importance and that the interpersonal environment of the adoptive home is, by far, the primary influence on the adoptee's development. This orientation, which is congruent with the egalitarian values of the social work profession, has shaped the approach of social workers in discussions with adoptive parents and has determined the variables we social workers have selected to research in studies of adoption outcomes. In our attempts to understand more clearly why some adoptions succeed and others fail, we have focused on adoptive parent–adoptive child relationships and other factors in the adoptive home. We have not, except on some occasions, considered the child's genetic–constitutional factors. (p. 75).

An example of the extent to which an environmental orientation permeates research on adoption is that studies attempting to predict the outcomes of adoption often do not consider characteristics of the biological parents of the adoptees (e.g., Hoopes, 1982).

Nonetheless, social workers have implicitly indicated a strong belief in the importance of heredity in the widespread practice of selective placement. As described earlier, selective placement has been practiced, not just for physical characteristics such as height, but also for behavioral traits such as intelligence. If one did not believe that intelligence is influenced by heredity, biological parents' intelligence or indices of intelligence such as education and occupation would not be used to place infants selectively into adoptive homes.

The tide seems to be turning back towards a more balanced perspective that considers both genetic and environmental factors in development. In a section entitled ''Adoption and Genetics,'' Kadushin (1978) reviews adoption studies of intelligence, schizophrenia, and criminality and suggests that:

> Recent research conducted with sizable samples of adoptees and matched controls may require reconsideration of our emphasis and a more respectful consideration of the influence of genetic inheritance as a determinant of the adoptive child's development. (p. 74).

> The findings of all the studies cited tend to move in one direction. There is an impressive consensus that adopted children are predisposed to respond to influences they bring with them which derive from their genetic background. The biological parents are still very much present in the adoptive family, even though they may have been physically absent from the start. (p. 82)

Although the major theme of this book is that most individual differences in infancy cannot be attributed either to genetic or to family environmental factors, the CAP data indicate that genetic influences emerge as early as infancy and are easily as influential as the family environment in shaping development. What are the implications of genetic influence for the social worker placing children for adoption? Although explicit consideration of genetic influences on development will require a major shift in social work philosophy, this shift is not likely to have dire consequences—indeed, perhaps no discernible consequences—for the day-to-day work of adoption agencies. One reason to make the shift in philosophy is that it is obviously better to make informed decisions rather than decisions based on misinformation: There is nothing to be gained by sticking one's head in the sand and pretending that genetic influences do not exist. In fact, we suggest that there is much more danger in perpetuating the environmentalist fallacy that parents are entirely responsible for their children's development when the evidence indicates that parents have little systematic environmental effect on the developmental course of their children, at least during infancy.

One counter argument is that adoptive parents cannot cope with such information about the importance of heredity. However, the condescension implicit in such a statement—that social workers should decide what adoptive parents should and should not know—is reason enough for it to be ignored. Moreover, our experience with the CAP leads us to believe that adoptive parents, like other laypersons, recognize the importance of heredity; it seems to be academics who are most resistant to the idea that heredity influences development. Rather than deciding what information should and should not be shared with adoptive parents, we suggest that adoptive parents be fully informed and treated as a full partner in working towards the shared goal of providing the best possible environment for the adopted child. Counseling adoptive parents about possible vulnerabilities of a particular child could help both the prospective parent and the social worker decide whether the parents have the resources to meet the child's particular needs.

At the same time, it is important that we do not exaggerate a child's potential vulnerabilities. Biological parents and their children share half their genes—but only half; the other half makes them different. For example, adopted children with family histories of psychopathology are by no means predestined to be mentally ill; hereditary transmission of psychopathology simply suggests that such children are at higher risk than are other individuals in the population. For example, severe psychopathology such as schizophrenia involves a risk of about 10% for first-degree relatives. This means that first-degree relatives of schizophrenics are 10 times more likely than the rest of the population to be diagnosed as schizophrenic; on the other hand, it also means that 9 out of 10 first-degree relatives of schizophrenics will not become schizophrenic.

Another example of genetic transmission, less well studied than schizophrenia, is alcoholism, which carries a 20% risk for male relatives of alcoholics. This risk is 5 times the risk for males in the population. Still, four out of five sons of alcoholic fathers will not be alcoholic. Moreover, although there are no proven interventions for individuals at risk for alcoholism, it is clear that one cannot become alcoholic without consuming large amounts of alcohol. Therefore, if we knew that our son had an increased risk for alcoholism, we probably would discourage him from drinking.

The point is that all parents must learn to recognize and respect the genetic uniqueness of the individual who grows up in their home. The Chinese have an ancient adage meant to apply to biological offspring but which perhaps is even more applicable to adopted offspring: The child is a guest in our home.

15

ReCAP

Introduction

We now attempt to distill the diverse results of the CAP. Rather than summarizing each chapter, we abstract some general principles concerning individual differences in infancy and their origins. Because the findings are described in detail and with appropriate caveats in preceding chapters, we state our conclusions forthrightly. Our hope is that phrasing our conclusions in this manner will increase their heuristic value.

Nonetheless, it is appropriate that a general qualification be mentioned at this point: The results of the CAP depend upon its design, sample, and measures. Although this truism applies to any study, an examination of the limitations associated with each of these aspects of the CAP is in order. The design is basically a parent–offspring design in which adopted infants and nonadopted infants are studied at 12 and 24 months of age; parents are tested only once. From a genetic point of view, the parent–offspring design limits the CAP to finding genetic influence only when three conditions are met: The measure in infancy must be heritable; the measure in adulthood must be heritable; and the measure in infancy must be genetically correlated with the measure in adulthood. Thus, when evidence of genetic influence is found, it suggests not only heritable variation in infancy and in adulthood, but also genetic continuity from infancy to adulthood. Similarly, the parent–offspring design does not assess the contemporary family environment shared by siblings; it focuses on experiences that make parents and their children similar. The design is particularly useful for assessing specific family environmental factors taking into account parental characteristics and, most importantly, controlling for the effects of heredity in the search for environmental influence.

Generalizations from any study also are limited by the sample. Over 90% of the CAP biological, adoptive, and control parents are Caucasian. The sample is representative of middle-class metropolitan populations as indicated by means and variances for occupational status and education as well as for other measures of the parents, infants, and their home environments. Thus, the CAP is a study of the normal range of variation in middle-class Caucasian homes, and its results may not apply to other populations.

Finally, CAP conclusions are limited to the measures employed in the 3-hour adult test sessions and in the $2\frac{1}{2}$-hour home visits at 12 and 24 months. Our results could be specific to these measures. Our goal in selecting measures was to sample extensively and broadly rather than intensively and narrowly. With the advantage of nearly a decade's hindsight, we would exclude some measures and include others. Nonetheless, the multivariate approach of the CAP has been useful in painting a panorama of individual differences in infancy.

Although these limitations of the CAP are important, its strengths deserve mention as well. The CAP employs a full adoption design that includes biological parents (who share only heredity with their adopted-away children) and adoptive parents (who share only family environment with their adopted children). The power of the design is enhanced by the inclusion of matched control families, parents who share both heredity and family environment with their offspring. Other features add to the CAP's uniqueness: It is prospective and longitudinal; the sample is large, including 182 adoptive families and 165 control families with infants tested at both 12 and 24 months of age; the sample is reasonably representative of middle-class Caucasian homes; the adopted infants are placed in their adoptive homes at less than 30 days of age on the average; selective placement is negligible (for example, the median correlation between biological parents and adoptive parents for IQ is $-.03$); the approach is multivariate (we have summarized data for about 70 measures of the infants at each age and about 60 measures for their parents); and environmental assessment is emphasized.

Principles Concerning the Origins of Individual Differences in Infancy

On the basis of data on the CAP infants at 12 and 24 months of age, we attempt to formulate some principles concerning the origins of individual differences in infancy. In the remainder of the chapter, we discuss 12 general principles, beginning with genetic etiology, turning to the environment, and concluding with a consideration of principles that involve both heredity and environment.

The Etiology of Individual Differences in Infancy Includes Heredity

Despite the fact that the CAP parent–offspring design is limited to detecting genetic influences shared by adult parents and their infant offspring, evidence of genetic influence has been observed. Infant mental development, as assessed by the Bayley MDI total score as well as spatial items and a spatial scale derived from the Bayley items at 24 months, displays some genetic influence. Measures of language acquisition tend to show genetic influence, as do the sums of all Bayley verbal items at 12 and at 24 months; a measure of communicative development at 24 months; and, especially, a general factor of communicative competence at 12 months based on analyses of videotaped mother–infant interactions. Genetic influence for the latter measure remains even when the MDI score is partialed out. Limited genetic influence exists for certain infant temperaments, such as sociability and emotionality, and for some behavioral problems. In Chapter 12 we saw that motor development in infancy may be influenced genetically and that physical growth is substantially affected by heredity. As we discuss later, some of the strongest evidence for genetic influence comes, surprisingly, from analyses involving environmental measures.

There Is Genetic Continuity from Infancy to Adulthood

One of the most dramatic findings of the CAP is evidence of genetic continuity from infancy to adulthood. Although genetic variance is generally less important in infancy than in adulthood, characters in infancy are highly correlated genetically with adult analogs. Genetic correlations from infancy to adulthood exceed .60 for cognition, temperament, and physical characters.

This conclusion is surprising in light of the current emphasis among developmentalists on discontinuities rather than continuities in development. It is based on the fact that, from a genetic perspective, the CAP parent–offspring design provides an instant longitudinal study from infancy to adulthood. As mentioned earlier, correlations between biological parents and their adopted-away infants can be found only when the character in infancy is heritable, when the character in adulthood is heritable, and when the genetic correlation between infancy and adulthood is substantial. Thus, whenever significant correlations are found between biological parents and their adopted-away infants, genetic continuity from infancy to adulthood is implied. If the heritabilities of a character are known for infants and for adults, we can estimate the genetic correlation between infancy and adulthood. For example, the correlation between Bayley MDI scores of adopted infants and their biological parents' IQ is about .10. Twin data suggest a heritability of about .15 for infant Bayley MDI and a heritability of about .50 for adult IQ. Together these data suggest that the genetic correlation between infant Bayley MDI scores and adult IQ scores is about .75, as indicated in Chapter 6. This implies that, although heritability is low in infancy, genes affecting infant Bayley MDI scores continue to affect individual differences in adult IQ scores.

The consistent finding of substantial genetic correlations from infancy to adulthood led us to pose an amplification model of developmental behavioral genetics: Once genes come to affect a character in infancy, they continue to affect the character in adulthood. As discussed in Chapter 6, no isomorphism between cognitive processes in infancy and in adulthood is assumed. For example, genetic continuity from infant Bayley MDI scores to adult IQ might be due to different processes—"infancy genes" might affect rate of acquisition of language, whereas "adult genes" might affect symbolic reasoning. However, it is also possible that similar cognitive processes are involved, as has been argued in the case of infant novelty preference (Fagan, 1984).

GENES PRODUCE CHANGE AS WELL AS CONTINUITY IN DEVELOPMENT

To the extent that genetic correlations from infancy to adulthood are less than 1.0, genetic change from infancy to adulthood is implied. Moreover, data from twin studies suggest that heritability is less in infancy than in adulthood, especially for cognition. For example, the heritability of infant Bayley MDI scores is about .15, whereas the heritability of adult IQ scores is about .50. This increase in the relative magnitude of genetic variance between infancy and adulthood could be due to the influence of genes expressed only later in development, to the amplification of those genes expressed during infancy, or to a damping of the effects of early environmental influences (e.g., differences in gestational age).

INDIVIDUAL DIFFERENCES IN INFANCY ARE GENETICALLY RELATED TO ADULT GENERAL COGNITIVE ABILITY

A variety of CAP analyses involving the Bayley MDI total score, factors based on the Bayley items, the Bayley items themselves, and various language measures have revealed significant parent–offspring correlations for parental IQ, but not for parents' specific cognitive abilities—verbal, spatial, perceptual, and memory. For example, variability in rates of language acquisition by the infants is related to IQ of biological and control parents, not to parental verbal ability or other specific cognitive abilities. These results suggest that the nature of infant intelligence as it relates genetically to adult cognition involves *g*, general cognitive ability. Even though infants show more diversified cognitive abilities at 24 months than at 12 months, 24-month mental test items or scales do not predict adult specific cognitive abilities; they predict adult IQ alone. Given that specific cognitive abilities are heritable later in life (DeFries, Vandenberg, & McClearn, 1976), these results suggest developmental change in genetic effects upon cognition: Genes that differentially affect specific cognitive abilities are not expressed until after infancy.

ASSOCIATIONS BETWEEN
ENVIRONMENTAL MEASURES AND
INFANT DEVELOPMENT ARE OFTEN
MEDIATED GENETICALLY

Paradoxically, some of the strongest evidence for genetic influence comes from analyses of environmental measures. In adoptive homes, correlations between environmental measures and infant development assess environmental influence unconfounded by hereditary similarity between parents and their children. In control families, however, environment–infant correlations can be due at least in part to hereditary influences. If heredity has an effect upon the relationship between an environmental measure and infant development, the environment–infant correlation will be higher in control families than in adoptive families. In the CAP, such is the case for most domains of infant development.

For example, 24-month Bayley MDI scores correlate .44 with the HOME General Factor in control families; in adoptive families, the correlation is .29. Similarly, the 24-month MDI and the HOME Encouraging Developmental Advance factor correlate .44 in control families and .22 in adoptive families. For the Lewis–Enright factors derived from Bayley items, environment–infant correlations are also generally higher in control families than in adoptive families, especially for verbal factors at 24 months. For example, the correlations for the HOME General Factor in control and adoptive families, respectively, are .34 and .26 for the Lexical factor and .36 and .19 for the Verbal (symbolic) factor. The control and adoptive comparisons for the HOME Encouraging Developmental Advance factor are .36 and .23 for the Lexical factor and .37 and .14 for the Verbal (symbolic) factor. The same pattern of results is found for the Sequenced Inventory of Communication Development (SICD) measure of communicative development: The HOME General Factor correlates .50 with the SICD total score in control families and .32 in adoptive families; the correlations for the HOME Encouraging Developmental Advance factor are .50 and .27.

Higher environment–infant correlations in control than in adoptive families are not limited to mental development and language. For temperament, regression analyses of measures of infant temperament and various environmental measures (see Chapter 10) yielded a multiple correlation of .37 for control families and .14 for adoptive families at 12 months; at 24 months, the multiple correlations are .31 and .18, respectively, for the control and adoptive families. Few correlations are found between behavioral problems and environmental measures; however, when they do occur, they tend to be higher in control than in adoptive families. For example, at 24 months, correlations of sleep problems, eating problems, and diaper problems with the HOME Restriction–Punishment factor are .14 versus .08, .17 versus .08, and .18 versus .05 in the control and adoptive homes, respectively. The second-order FES Personal Growth factor also is more highly correlated with infant soothability and difficult temperament in control than in adoptive homes (.41 vs. .06 and −.32 vs. −.07, respectively).

Because means and variances are similar for adoptive and control families for both environmental and infant measures, these results lead to the conclusion that heredity mediates ostensibly environmental relationships.

A general model of this interface of nature and nurture is described elsewhere (Plomin *et al.*, in press). The model estimates the genetic and environmental components of environmental influences; for the CAP data described above, the model indicates that the genetic components of these environmental correlations are fully as large as the environmental components. One assumption is that the means and, especially, the variances must be similar for adoptive and control families for both environmental and infant measures—which they are in the CAP. A second assumption is that selective placement is minimal. If substantial selective placement occurs, then environment–infant correlations in adoptive families will contain a genetic component that will reduce the difference between environment–infant correlations in nonadoptive and adoptive families. Thus, the model will overestimate the environmental contribution to the correlation and underestimate the genetic contribution. However, selective placement is negligible in the CAP. A third assumption is that reactive and active varieties of genotype–environment correlations are minimal. However, the effect of genotype–environment correlations of this type is similar to the effect of selective placement—causing overestimation of the environmental contribution and underestimation of the genetic contribution. The fact that the CAP data suggest substantial genetic contributions to environmental influences despite the likelihood of reactive and active genotype–environment correlations strongly supports the conclusion that the CAP environmental associations are mediated genetically, at least to some extent. There are two important points related to this finding.

1. *The genetic mediation of associations between environmental measures and infant development is not to be found in traditional measures of parental characteristics.* What process could account for such a finding? It is obvious that the environment itself cannot be transmitted genetically to children. The answer must be that environmental measures are correlated with parental characteristics that are related genetically to the infant measures, a form of passive genotype–environment correlation. For example, parental IQ is an obvious candidate to explain the genetic relationship between the HOME measures and mental development. Similarly, parental personality might account for genetic relationships between environmental measures and infant temperament and behavioral problems. However, when we

partial out these parental characteristics, the same pattern of relationships remains; that is, the environment–infant correlations in control families are still higher than those in adoptive families. For example, the HOME General Factor correlates .44 with 24-month Bayley MDI scores in control families and .29 in adoptive families. When control parent IQ is partialed out, the correlation between the HOME and 24-month Bayley MDI is reduced only from .44 to .41, and the correlation in adoptive families changes only from .29 to .25. Removing the effects of parental personality from correlations between environmental measures and infant temperament also scarcely changes the pattern of significantly higher correlations in control families than in adoptive families.

Thus, we conclude that the genetic mediation of associations between environmental measures and infant measures of mental development is not simply parental IQ or personality. What, then, are the genetic links? We know that genetic mediation of the relationship between the HOME measures and Bayley scores must be due to some parental characteristics that are correlated with the HOME and are correlated genetically with infants' Bayley scores. Furthermore, these parental characteristics must be independent of IQ. Two kinds of parental characteristics could meet these requirements. The first involves cognitive factors independent of IQ that are genetically related to infant scores on the Bayley test. For example, the HOME seems to assess sensitive parenting, which could be a component of intelligence in a larger sense than is the abstract reasoning ability that is emphasized in adult IQ tests. The social intelligence involved in sensitive parenting could then be genetically related to Bayley scores independently of parental IQ. The second type of parental characteristic involves nonintellectual factors that are genetically related to a noncognitive component of the Bayley test. For example, the HOME must to some extent assess social poise of the parents, which could be related genetically to infant social competence, which, in turn, could lead to higher scores on the Bayley test. The evidence for genetic mediation of relationships between the HOME factor involving parental encouragement of developmental advance and infant development suggests another possibility. Achievement motivation is probably not related strongly to parental IQ, but could be related genetically to infant motivation to perform well on the Bayley test.

The nature of the genetic mediation of associations of environmental measures with infant temperament and behavioral problems also remains unclear. Parental characteristics indexed by the environmental measures must be related genetically to infant temperament and behavioral problems even though the parental personality characteristics that we studied are not involved.

In addition to expanding our understanding of the nature and nurture of individual differences in infancy, finding the genetic mediators of associations between environmental measures and infant development should also provide interesting information concerning adult characteristics. In the case of cognition, the genetic mediators must involve characteristics of parents that are independent of parental IQ and yet are associated genetically with infant mental development as assessed by the Bayley test. In the case of temperament, they must involve parental characteristics that are independent of traditional self-report measures of adult personality and yet are genetically related to infant measures. Because parents' personality in general is not related genetically to traits of their infants, the answer to this puzzle will reveal those parental characteristics that are predictive genetically of infant temperament.

2. *Ostensibly environmental relationships found in nonadoptive families must be viewed with caution because genetic factors may mediate the relationship.* Regardless of the process by which heredity comes to mediate the relationship between environmental measures and infant development, an important implication of these results is that correlations between ostensibly environmental measures and infant development in nonadoptive families cannot be assumed to be purely environmental. As for all correlations, variable X can cause variable Y, variable Y can cause variable X, or a third factor can account for both X and Y. In the case of correlations between environmental measures and infant development, the first two possibilities have been given considerable attention in attempting to answer the question of the direction of effects: Do environmental variables cause or reflect differences in the behavior of infants? However, we suggest that a third factor, heredity, may be responsible for the correlations: Environmental measures are related to infant development because the environmental measures are systematically associated with genetic factors shared by parents and their infants.

The possibility that heredity mediates relationships between measures of environment and measures of infant development calls into question most previous research on the topic because nearly all of this research has studied nonadoptive families in which both heredity and family environment are shared by parents and their children. If the goal is simply to predict infant development, then it is unimportant whether predictability accrues for genetic or environmental reasons. However, attempts to understand the etiology of individual differences in infant development require that genetic and environmental threads in the web of environment–infant relationships be disentangled. For example, if the relationship between the HOME measures and infant mental development is assumed to be purely environmental, intervention plans might be devised to guide parents toward childrearing styles characteristic of high scores on the HOME. However, to the extent that the relationship between the HOME and infant mental development is mediated genetically, intervention of this type will be ineffective and possibly counterproductive.

Finally, it is important to note that evidence of genetic mediation of environmental relationships is not necessarily eliminated by partialing out parental characteristics. For example, we have seen that evidence of genetic mediation of the relationship between the HOME and infant Bayley scores remains even when the effects of parental IQ are removed. We conclude that etiologies of individual differences in infancy cannot be identified by correlational studies of nonadoptive families. Confirmation that ostensibly environmental relationships are in fact environmental in origin must come from studies that use behavioral-genetic designs such as studies of adoptive families and step-families, or from studies in which environmental variables are systematically varied in randomly selected families.

Variations in Family Environment Are Related to Individual Differences in Infancy

Use of the adoption design permits study of the relationship between environmental measures and infant development by eliminating the possibility of confounding by genetic effects that is always present in studies of nonadoptive families. In CAP adoptive families, individual differences in infant mental development are related to family environmental variables as assessed by various indices including phenotypes of adoptive parents and specific measures of the environment such as the HOME and FES. For example, about 10% of the variance of infant Bayley MDI scores is associated with adoptive parents' IQ, although path analyses indicate that most of this effect is mediated by the HOME measure. As discussed in Chapter 6, regression analyses revealed that the multiple correlation between Bayley MDI scores and several environmental measures in adoptive families is .22 at 12 months and .35 at 24 months. The measures of home environment at 24 months predict Bayley MDI scores independently of socioeconomic status and parental education in adoptive homes.

Family environmental variables also are related to rates of language acquisition by adopted infants. Interestingly, however, variability in language-learning environments is unrelated to variability in developmental rates of language acquisition at 12 months of age. Environmental measures in adoptive homes that are related to verbal development as assessed by scales derived from Bayley items, as well as by a measure of communicative development, include the HOME General Factor and the HOME Encouraging Developmental Advance factor.

Although adoptive parents' personality is not related to temperament of adopted infants in the CAP, several relationships between specific environmental measures and infant temperament have been observed in the adoptive families. For example, at both 12 and 24 months, the HOME General Factor is related to parental reports of infant sociability, as well as to tester and videotape ratings of extraversion of the infants; the HOME Maternal Involvement factor is related to tester and videotape ratings of task orientation and sociability; HOME Encouraging Developmental Advance is positively correlated with tester ratings of extraversion; HOME Restriction–Punishment is positively related to infant activity; and FES Personal Growth is associated with infant sociability.

Family environment as assessed in the CAP appears to have little effect on behavioral problems, although shared family environment is a factor in common illnesses and motor development. Athletic ability of adoptive parents, as well as several HOME scales and the general factor, are associated with motor development as measured by the Bayley Psychomotor Development Index.

In addition to demonstrating the importance of family environment in the etiology of individual differences in infancy, our analyses of environmental measures yielded several unexpected results. Most exciting is the finding that environment–infant relationships are generally higher in control families than in adoptive families, which, as discussed earlier, suggests that heredity mediates some relationships between ostensibly environmental measures and infant development. Three other important environmental results should be mentioned.

1. *The effects of early environment are mediated by contemporary environmental influences.* Longitudinal relationships between 12-month environmental measures and 24-month infant scores disappear when the effects of 24-month environmental measures are removed. This suggests that early environment at 12 months has no special effect on infant development.

2. *The major environmental intervention of adoption has little effect upon infant development.* In Chapter 14, we compared adopted and control infants for the various CAP measures. No important differences have been found for mental development, temperament, or behavioral problems. The fact that the upheavals of separation from the biological mother during the first few days of life and placement in a temporary foster home for a few weeks before final placement in an adoptive home have few discernible effects suggests that seemingly traumatic experiences during the first month of life have little influence on infant development.

3. *Birth weight and gestational age are not importantly related to individual differences in infancy.* Correlations between perinatal factors and infant development are generally low and nonsignificant in the CAP sample. In the area of behavioral problems, a few modest relationships have been observed: Lower birth weight and gestational age are associated with slightly more sleeping and eating problems at 12 months and with more soothing problems at 24 months. There is a significant correlation between gestational age and 12-month Bayley MDI in control infants; however, the relationship is not replicated for adopted infants, and it disappears at 24 months. Similarly, factors derived from the Bayley items show no systematic association with perinatal factors.

The Relative Extent of Genetic and Environmental Influence Varies for Different Characters

The issue of the etiology of individual differences in infancy cannot be dismissed lightly by saying that both nature and nurture are important. For example, the data presented in Chapter 12 indicate that physical growth shows substantial genetic influence and no influence of the family environment; that infant illnesses are influenced by family environment, but not by heredity; that motor development shows both genetic and family environmental influence; and that neither genetic nor family environmental factors as we have measured them affect the development of hand preference and infant interests.

GENETIC AND ENVIRONMENTAL
INFLUENCES ON INFANT
DEVELOPMENT COACT IN AN
ADDITIVE MANNER

When individual differences among CAP infants have been found to be related to genetic or environmental factors, the relationship is additive; nonadditive interactions rarely account for a significant portion of variance.

1. *Genotype–environment interaction is rare.* Genotype–environment interaction refers to the appealing notion that the effect of environmental factors depends upon genetic differences among individuals. That is, genetic and environmental influences combine in a nonadditive manner to affect development. However, only a chance number of significant genotype–environment interactions is found when genotype is estimated by biological mothers' scores and environment is estimated by adoptive parents' scores or by specific measures of the home environment. For mental development, 15 genotype–environment interaction analyses were conducted; none was significant. For temperament, 80 genotype–environment analyses yielded only 2 significant interactions, fewer than would be expected to occur by chance. Finally, for behavioral problems, 30 genotype–environment analyses produced only 4 significant interactions. Thus, taken together, we observed precisely the number of significant interactions expected on the basis of chance.

2. *Temperament and environment do not interact in their effect on behavioral problems.* Although both temperament and environment are related to behavioral problems, the relationships are additive. Of 48 analyses of temperament–environment interactions, 7 interactions were significant but only 1 was interpretable.

We also explored other types of interactions, such as stability of infant measures from 12 to 24 months as it interacts with environmental variables, environmental stability as it interacts with parental characteristics, and various relationships as they interact with gender. Rarely were significant interactions found.

CORRELATIONS BETWEEN
ENVIRONMENTAL MEASURES AND
INFANT DEVELOPMENT ARE LINEAR

It is reasonable to expect that the environment affects children in a nonlinear manner, perhaps affecting children at one end of the distribution differently than it affects other children. For example, we might predict that bright children profit disproportionately from environmental stimulation. However, 36 analyses of relationships between environmental measures and infant mental development yielded only 2 significant curvilinear relationships, which is what would be expected on the basis of chance alone. These analyses led to the next general principle concerning etiologies of behavior at the extremes of distributions.

PARENT–OFFSPRING RELATIONSHIPS
AT THE EXTREMES OF THE NORMAL
CONTINUUM ARE SIMILAR TO THOSE
FOR BEHAVIOR WITHIN THE
NORMAL RANGE

When we examined the extremes of dimensions—for example, the 10% most shy and the 10% most emotional infants—we found no evidence that their patterns of parent–offspring or environment–offspring relationships are different from those for infants whose behavior fell within the normal range of variability. We also employed a more general approach to this issue of the normal versus abnormal by searching for the curvilinear parent–offspring relationships that would occur if infants at the extreme of the distribution were differentially affected by genetic or environmental factors. However, no more than a chance number of curvilinear relationships was observed. Thus, we conclude that genetic and environmental factors operating at the extremes of the normal distribution are not different qualitatively from those that affect the rest of the distribution. In other words, the behavior of shy children is not different etiologically from that of other children in a qualitative sense; they simply are quantitatively affected to a greater extent by both genetic and environmental factors.

This conclusion suggests that it may be profitable to study common behavioral problems of development—such as attentional and emotional disorders and learning disabilities—in the context of the normal distribution; that is, they are likely to originate from the same genetic and environmental sources that produce individual differences throughout the distribution. In terms of both symptomatology and etiology, behavioral problems may involve extremes of a multivariate normal distribution. If so, this could have many implications for both identification and intervention.

GENOTYPE–ENVIRONMENT
CORRELATIONS ACCOUNT FOR
LITTLE VARIANCE

As explained elsewhere (Plomin *et al.*, in press), genetic mediation of relationships between environmental measures and infant development implies the existence of at least some passive genotype–environment correlation. However, analyses of CAP data have revealed no evidence of passive genotype–environment correlation as assessed by the comparison of variances for adopted and control infants. Nonetheless, this may be a weak test of passive genotype–environment correlation given the standard errors of the variance estimates.

CAP analyses disclosed only slight evidence of reactive genotype–environment correlation. However, our power to assess this type of genotype–environment correlation is limited to comparisons of biological parents' scores (as estimates of genotype of the adopted infants) with environmental indices such as adoptive parents' scores or specific measures of the home environment. For cognition, only 1 of 18 possible genotype–environment correlations is significant. For behavioral problems, only 3 of 36 genotype–environment correlations are significant. For temperament, however, 7 of 28 genotype–environment correlations attained significance. For example, at both 12 and 24 months, biological mothers' activity level is negatively correlated with the HOME General Factor in adoptive families, suggesting that adoptive parents show less responsivity as assessed by the HOME when their children are genetically predisposed towards high activity.

GENDER HAS A NEGLIGIBLE IMPACT
ON INDIVIDUAL DIFFERENCES IN
INFANT DEVELOPMENT

Gender, like birth order, is an easy variable to analyze; many studies have found mean gender differences in various behaviors. However, rarely is the number of significant results evaluated in relation to the number expected by chance, and even more rarely is consideration given to the variance explained by such group differences. We conclude that gender explains a negligible amount of variance in infant development as assessed by the CAP measures.

1. *There are few mean differences between boys and girls, and these account for little variance.* Although the CAP has 80% power to detect mean gender differences that account for as little as 2% of the total variance, few significant differences have been found. Girls score higher than boys on 3 verbal scales based on Bayley items; however, even this gender difference accounts for only 2% of the total variance. For the other 26 comparisons involving cognition, temperament, and behavioral problems, there are only 3 significant mean differences, and 1 significant difference would be expected on the basis of chance alone.

2. *Boys and girls are treated similarly in infancy.* None of the 12 comparisons of means for boys and girls on environmental measures has revealed a significant gender difference.

3. *The origins of individual differences in infancy are similar for boys and girls.* For 312 comparisons of parent–offspring correlations, only 22 are significantly different for boys and girls; 16 significant differences would be expected to occur by chance. For 185 comparisons of environment–offspring correlations, only 11 significant differences emerge and 9 would be expected on the basis of chance alone. Although the CAP has adequate power to detect only large differences in correlations for boys and girls, the results do not support the hypothesis that boys are more sensitive to environmental influence than girls.

Conclusion

This distillation of the CAP results yields one last general principle: Much remains to be learned about the origins of individual differences in infancy. Genetic and environmental factors seldom account for more than 10%, and never more than 20%, of the variance in infancy. It is possible that individual differences in the rate of infant development are so tightly programmed by evolutionary canalization that variability is curtailed. However, canalization would seem to be less important for some domains (such as temperament) than for others (such as mental development), whereas the lack of predictability is pandemic.

We predict that future research will explain more of the variance. In terms of genetics, it should be remembered that the CAP parent–offspring design does not provide estimates of heritability in infancy per se, but rather identifies only that portion of genetic variance in infancy that also has an effect in adulthood. Developmentally contemporaneous behavioral-genetic designs, such as studies of adoptive siblings reared together and of nonadoptive siblings—forthcoming in the CAP as younger siblings are tested—as well as twin designs, are likely to show that heredity accounts for greater amounts of variance than is apparent in correlations between biological parents and their adopted-away offspring.

In terms of environmental influences, we are using only the first generation of measures, and surely some improvement in predictive power can be expected as newer measures of the environment become available. For example, the HOME is the first environmental measure systematically constructed to predict mental development. In other areas such as specific cognitive abilities, temperament, and behavioral problems, no attempt has as yet been made to construct environmental measures specifically designed to predict individual differences in each domain.

Individual differences in most areas of infancy other than general mental development have just begun to be explored. For example, surprisingly few studies have addressed the origins of individual differences in specific cognitive abilities, language and communication, novelty preference, temperament, and common behavioral problems. Next to nothing is known about the relationship of other important variables such as health status to individual differences in infant mental ability, motor ability, laterality, and interests.

We hope that the results of the Colorado Adoption Project that we have reported in this book will serve to stimulate and guide future research in this relatively unexplored area, the origins of individual differences in infancy.

APPENDIX A

CAP Infant Measures

An overview of the infant measures used at 12 and 24 months was presented in Chapter 4. What follows is a detailed description of all infant measures, with complete information for unpublished measures and references for those that are published. We begin with questionnaires collected from the parents during the home visit and then list the information obtained during the home visit and rated during or after the home visit.

I. Information Collected from Parents during the Home Visit

A. *Colorado Childhood Temperament Survey* (Rowe & Plomin, 1977). [Completed by mother and father before first- and second-year visits.]

B. *Behavioral Problems Questionnaire.* [Completed by mother and father before first- and second-year visits. Many of the following items are similar in content to those of the revised Infant Temperament Questionnaire (Carey & McDevitt, 1978); however, they are sufficiently different to merit listing them.]

Please answer the following items about the behavior of this child by circling the letter preceding the most appropriate alternative. Please answer honestly—there are no right or wrong answers.

Sleeping

How does the child respond to being held just before bedtime?
(a) seems to melt into parent's arms, likes to be cuddled
(b) accepts cuddling sometimes, sometimes not
(c) seems to stiffen in parent's arms, does not like being held closely

Is the child regular about the time of falling asleep?
- (a) generally regular—usually asleep or on the point of dropping off at the same time each night, give or take half an hour
- (b) sometimes regular, sometimes not
- (c) not regular at all—times may vary by one to two hours or more, impossible to say when usual time for sleeping is

What is the child's usual mood at the time of falling asleep?
- (a) generally cheerful—easily coaxed out of an unhappy mood
- (b) sometimes happy, sometimes fussy
- (c) generally fussy and irritable—often rather unhappy about going to sleep

How active is the child once in bed?
- (a) usually snuggles in immediately, lies fairly still
- (b) moves around a little, doesn't go to sleep right away
- (c) moves around a lot, goes to sleep with difficulty

Is the child regular about the time of waking up?
- (a) generally regular—usually awakes at the same time each morning, give or take half an hour
- (b) sometimes regular, sometimes not
- (c) not regular at all—impossible to say hour at which child usually awakens

What is the child's usual mood at the time of waking up?
- (a) generally cheerful—easily coaxed out of an unhappy mood
- (b) sometimes happy, sometimes fussy
- (c) generally fussy and irritable—often rather unhappy about getting up

How active is the child after rising in the morning?
- (a) immediately up and about, very active and fully awake
- (b) a little sleepy at first, takes a little while to wake up
- (c) awakens slowly, takes a lot of time to get going in the morning

Eating

How does the child show feelings of hunger?
- (a) protests actively and loudly
- (b) protests somewhat
- (c) may whimper, but does not protest loudly

Does the child seem hungry at regular times?
- (a) generally wants and takes milk, juice or food at about the same times each day
- (b) sometimes hungry at regular times, sometimes not
- (c) impossible to say when hungry times will be

Can you judge how much the child will eat at each meal?
- (a) generally takes about the same amount of food, milk, etc.—easy to predict how much the child will eat
- (b) sometimes can predict how much the child will eat, but often not
- (c) impossible to say how much the child will eat

How active is the child at meal times?
- (a) plays about, squirms, cannot stay still
- (b) settles down and gets on with eating
- (c) usually quite still, dawdles some, likes to take time over meals

How does the child react to new foods?
- (a) usually accepts new foods—swallows them quickly and without fussing
- (b) sometimes likes new foods, sometimes picky
- (c) usually dislikes new foods—may make a face, spit food out, clench jaws, etc.

At meal time, how easily distracted is the child by noises or by changes in place or routine?
  (a) easily distracted
  (b) sometimes distracted, sometimes not
  (c) usually goes right on eating in spite of distractions

Soiling and Wetting

Are the child's bowel movements regular?
  (a) generally regular—not many changes from a usual pattern
  (b) sometimes regular, sometimes not
  (c) very irregular—no real pattern
Does the child fuss when diaper is soiled with a bowel movement?
  (a) much fussing about a dirty diaper, persistent crying
  (b) sometimes fusses, but not with a lot of insistence
  (c) usually just a little whimpering, or may not complain at all
Does child fuss when diaper is wet (no bowel movement)?
  (a) usually cries loudly about a wet diaper
  (b) sometimes fusses
  (c) usually just a little whimpering, or may not complain at all
How active is the child while diapers are being changed?
  (a) squirms, wiggles, kicks a lot
  (b) moves some
  (c) generally lies still
What is the child's usual mood when diapers are being changed?
  (a) fussy and wants to be left alone, often unhappy and cranky
  (b) sometimes fusses, sometimes not
  (c) cheerful, seems to enjoy the attention, happy

Playing

How does the child play?
  (a) intensely—much activity, talking, laughing
  (b) sometimes intensely, sometimes quietly
  (c) usually plays quietly and calmly
While playing with one toy, how easily is the child distracted by another toy?
  (a) usually drops the first toy and picks up the other
  (b) sometimes distracted, sometimes not
  (c) usually continues playing with the first toy

Procedures

How does the child react to a bath?
  (a) usually smiles or laughs
  (b) accepts it
  (c) usually cries or fusses
How does the child react to *new* procedures, such as the first time nails are trimmed or hair is cut?
  (a) usually accepts it calmly
  (b) sometimes accepts it, sometimes not
  (c) usually fusses or cries

How does the child respond to discipline?

  (a) usually obeys instructions

  (b) may forget, sometimes ignores instructions

  (c) usually ignores instructions, continues to disobey

C. *Questionnaire for NYLS Difficult Temperament Rating.* [Completed by mother and father before first- and second-year visits. Although these items are quite similar to the "general impressions" of Carey and McDevitt's (1978) revised Infant Temperament Questionnaire, our wording differs somewhat.]

Activity level (amount of physical activity) of child during sleep, eating, playing, dressing, etc.

  (a) high

  (b) medium

  (c) low

Regularity of bodily functioning with respect to sleep, hunger, bowel movements, etc.

  (a) fairly regular

  (b) sometimes regular, sometimes irregular

  (c) fairly irregular

Child's response to change in routine.

  (a) generally accepts change

  (b) sometimes accepts change, sometimes not

  (c) is slow to accept change

Child's response to new situations (initial reaction to new food, people, places, toys or procedures).

  (a) usually approaches

  (b) sometimes approaches, sometimes withdraws

  (c) usually withdraws

Level of child's sensory threshold (for example, the amount of change in sound or other stimuli necessary to attract the attention of the child).

  (a) much stimulation needed

  (b) medium

  (c) little stimulation needed

Intensity of child's expression of feeling.

  (a) generally intense

  (b) sometimes intense, sometimes mild

  (c) generally mild

Mood of the child (amount of pleasant or unpleasant behavior throughout the day).

  (a) generally pleasant

  (b) sometimes pleasant, sometimes unpleasant

  (c) generally unpleasant

Child's distractibility (degree to which new sounds, toys, people, etc. interfere with ongoing behavior).

  (a) easily distractible

  (b) sometimes distracted, sometimes not

  (c) usually not distracted

Child's persistence and attention span (how long activities tend to continue with or without interference).

  (a) usually persistent

  (b) sometimes persistent, sometimes not

  (c) usually not persistent

In general, the temperament of the child is:

  (a) about average

  (b) more difficult than average

  (c) easier than average

D. *Questionnaire Answered by Family Doctor or Pediatrician.* [Collected from parents at first- and second-year visits.]

Note: Please include information pertaining only to the past twelve months, _____.
1. Name of child _____ Date _____
2. Age of the child at time of visit (in months) _____
3. Illnesses and abnormalities: (check if item has occurred)

	Has occurred within last 12 months	Comments
Hypotonia	_____	
Ataxia	_____	
Diskinesia	_____	
Nystagmus	_____	
Impaired extraocular movements	_____	
Nonfebrile seizures	_____	
Other CNS abnormalities	_____	
Abnormality of gait or posture	_____	
Delayed motor milestones	_____	
Heart problems	_____	Circle one: Mild Moderate Severe
Hypoxia with unconsciousness	_____	Length: Estimate minutes/ seconds: Cause:
Any other abnormality	_____	

4. Height _____ (inches) Weight _____

II. Information Obtained during Home Visit

A. *Ratings by Home Tester.* [first- and second-year visits; a rating of 3 represents an average score]

Global Ratings of Child's Reaction to Strangers (first 5 minutes)

Attachment to mother	1 2 3 4 5
Social responsiveness to strangers	1 2 3 4 5
Fear of strangers	1 2 3 4 5

Ratings of Child's Response to Kinesthetic Stimulation (bounced and swung by tester during Psychomotor section of Bayley)

Enjoyment of movement (parent rated)	1 2 3 4 5
Enjoyment of movement (observed)	1 2 3 4 5
How much does *mother* swing, jiggle, or bounce child? (kinesthetic stimulation)	1 2 3 4 5
Kinesthetic stimulation from father?	1 2 3 4 5
Kinesthetic stimulation from others?	1 2 3 4 5
Enjoyment of cuddling (parent rated)	1 2 3 4 5
Enjoyment of cuddling (observed)	1 2 3 4 5

B. *CAP Health Inquiry Interview.* [first- and second-year visits]

Events

Frequency	No. of times to doctor	
————	————	Allergies—if so, specify types:
————	————	Head injuries
————	————	Seizures
————	————	Strep/Staph
————	————	Unconsciousness (cessation of breathing)
————	————	Colds
————	————	Flu
————	————	Tonsillitis
————	————	Ear infections
————	————	Bronchitis
————	————	Pneumonia
————	————	Fevers (102+)
————	————	Severe diarrhea
————	————	Other illnesses or serious accidents—if so, specify:

General

1. Number of routine checkups in past year ————

2. General health (circle one)

	1	2	3	4	5
	excellent	above average	average	below average	poor

3. About how long does it take your child to recover from a cold?

	1	2	3	4	5
	1 or 2 days	3–5 days	about a week	1½ weeks	2 weeks or more

4. Is your child receiving standard immunizations?   no   yes

5. Current height ———— Current weight ————

6. Dental: # of teeth ———— Date of first tooth ————

7. Use of aspirin or aspirin substitutes

	1	2	3	4	5
	never	occasionally	moderately often	frequently	daily

8. Prescription drugs: # of kinds ————

    # of bottles ———— (count each refill separately)

C. *Bayley Scales of Infant Development* (Bayley, 1969). [first- and second-year visits]

D. *Uzgiris–Hunt Ordinal Scales of Psychological Development—Scales I, II, IIIA, IIIB* (Uzgiris & Hunt, 1975). [first-year visit only]

E. *List of True Words.* [first-year visit and 18-month telephone interview]

F. *Sequenced Inventory of Communication Development*—Expressive Scale: items 15–24, 26–34; Receptive Scale: items 9–23, 25–27 (Hedrick, Prather, & Tobin, 1975). [second-year visit only]

G. *Developmental Milestones*. [second-year visit only]

1. How much of an attempt has been made to toilet train the child?
   1—none at all
   2—slight
   3—average
   4—frequent
   5—constant
2. How has the child reacted to toilet training?
   1—objects strongly
   2—whimpers or appears unhappy
   3—accepts it but neither unhappy nor happy
   4—easy going and cooperative
   5—enjoys it, initiates attention to it
3. How effective is the toilet training for the child's urination control?
   1—not responding at all
   2—rarely responding
   3—responding once in a while
   4—responding more often than not
   5—completely trained
4. How effective is the toilet training for the child's defecation control?
   1—not responding at all
   2—rarely responding
   3—responding once in a while
   4—responding more often than not
   5—completely trained
5. How does the child usually react when asked to do something?
   1—almost always protests or fusses
   2—often protests or fusses
   3—average
   4—often goes along with the request
   5—almost always willingly goes along with the request
6. How often has the child had a temper tantrum in the last month? _____ (usually occurs when the child's being dressed or doing something he/she dislikes)
7. How many naps does the child take per day? _____
8. How long a nap does the child take on the average? _____
9. How long an evening sleep does the child have? _____
10. How messy is the child when eating?
    1—extremely messy
    2—between 1 & 3
    3—average
    4—between 3 & 5
    5—never messy
11. When did the child go to table foods? _____ (age in months)
12. When did the child use the cup rather than the bottle (breast feeding)? _____
13. How independent is the child when eating, dressing and bathing, i.e., how much does the child insist on doing things by himself?
    1—almost never
    2—occasionally
    3—average
    4—often
    5—almost always

H. *Interview With Mother Concerning Child's Interests.* [first- and second-year visits]

    1. Gross motoric objects (#26, #27 and #28 on Caldwell)
      Rating of child's liking of gross motoric objects (5 = strong liking;   1 2 3 4 5
      favorite class of objects)
    2. Fine motoric objects (#32 and #33 on Caldwell)
      Rating of child's liking   1 2 3 4 5
    3. Cuddly objects (#31 on Caldwell)
      Rating of child's liking   1 2 3 4 5
    4. Cognitive (books of child's own)
      Rating of child's liking   1 2 3 4 5
    5. Musical objects (records, toy instruments, musical toys)
      Rating of child's liking   1 2 3 4 5
    6. Artistic objects (crayons)
      Rating of child's liking   1 2 3 4 5

I. *Videotape Ratings of Temperament*—first-year situations: free play, pegboard, roughhouse, feeding; second-year situations: free play, train, dollhouse. [The following ratings were developed by Matheny and Wilson (1981) using Bayley's Infant Behavior Record as a starting point for the development of temperament ratings applicable to videotape recordings. We further modified Matheny and Wilson's ratings in order to make them more suitable to our videotape situations; for this reason, we list our items and comments to raters explicating what we sought to rate in each of 10 categories.]

Emotional Tone. Consider all factors that provide clues to emotional tone such as facial expression, vocalizations, motor excitement.

    (1) Extremely upset; cannot be soothed
    (2) Generally upset; can sometimes be soothed
    (3) Upset, but can be soothed
    (4) Little upset
    (5) Bland; undifferentiated overt emotionality
    (6) Generally *bland,* with indication of being content, happy
    (7) Contented, happy (lots of smiling)
    (8) Happy to animated; smiling & laughing
    (9) Excited or animated; lots of laughing

Look for *general* emotional tone. For example, a child can get a 7, even if one or two times he expresses displeasure, if *overall* he is happy and content; an upset child may not be upset the *entire* time, but can still receive a score of 2.

Attentiveness.

    (1) Unoccupied, nonfocused (e.g., vacant staring)
    (2) Minimal or fleeting attention (i.e., glances at objects but that is only interest shown)
    (3) Between 2 & 4
    (4) Occasional sustained interest in new toy, person, event
    (5) Moderate attention to each new toy, person, or activity; attention may shift fairly often
    (6) Attention shifts occur occasionally (may be because of mother's direction)
    (7) Focused and sustained attention
    (8) Between 7 & 9
    (9) Continued and persistent attention to the point of "being glued" or "fixed" to an event, person, or object

Attentiveness refers to the child's tendency to persist in attending to any one object, person, or activity, *aside from attaining a goal*. It is important to distinguish attentiveness and goal directedness: A child may score high on attentiveness but low on goal directedness if he/she is absorbed in manipulating an object with no apparent end, or is focusing on the mother's actions.

Vocalizing. Crying *does not* qualify as a vocalization.
  (1) Definitely quiet, no vocalizations
  (2) Occasional, rare vocalizations—very short (monosyllabic)
  (3) Few vocalizations and of short duration (can be more than one syllable)
  (4) More frequent vocalizations—occur only as part of the activity (i.e., responding to mother, attempt to obtain an object); amount of vocalizing is still somewhat constrained
  (5) Vocalizations occur readily as part of the activity
  (6) Child appears to enjoy the vocalizing aspect of an activity; begin to see vocalizing for sake of vocalizing (i.e., child seems to enjoy use of a particular word)
  (7) Child obviously enjoys vocalizing for the sake of vocalizing; vocalizing becomes a major aspect of an activity
  (8) Vocalizing becomes excessive but child still exhibits some periods of silence (i.e., while concentrating on a task)
  (9) *Excessive* vocalizations; high vocal excitement

Activity. Refers to body motion without locomotion; self-initiated movements of part of the body, except mouth movements. *Focus more on fine motor activity*. Look at amount of manipulating rather than simply holding objects.
  (1) Stays quietly in one place, with practically no self-initiated movement
  (2) Usually quiet and inactive; occasionally responds appropriately in situations calling for activity—responds hesitantly, slowly
  (3) Responds appropriately in situations calling for some fine motor activity (e.g., activity in response to mother's demands or suggestions), but doesn't often initiate activity
  (4) Child initiates activity on his/her own without waiting for mother's suggestions
  (5) Moderate activity—the child is manipulating objects much of the time but stops on occasion to gaze at objects, observe mother
  (6) Between 5 and 7
  (7) Initiates activity during much of the period of observation; child obviously enjoys activity for its own sake
  (8) Approach to being "hyperactive"; activity seems to lack direction
  (9) "Hyperactive," child never stops to observe or think about a task; often activity has no apparent end

Locomotion. Includes upper body movements (i.e., leaning whole body forward to reach something). Refers to gross body movements (i.e., rolling over, crawling, walking). May include "scooting" around.
  (1) No change in position, lies or sits in place, no gross upper body movements (i.e., reaches with hands only)
  (2) One or two changes in position (i.e., moving upper body to obtain object, bottom leaves chair)
  (3) Few changes in position; sporadic or short-lived movement in space; brief repositioning to obtain or exploit objects as part of activity. This rating may include lots of limb movement (e.g., kicking in chair)
  (4) Child more readily moves when required by the situation
  (5) Changes in position are frequent but are not an apparent end in themselves
  (6) Occasional evidence of locomotion as an end in itself
  (7) Locomotion is an interest in itself; however, the child will still exhibit quiet periods
  (8) Locomotion is pronounced; almost continuous, an end in itself, but not extreme
  (9) Child is continuously moving; may have to be restrained; will not sit still for longer than a few seconds at a time ("perpetual motion machine").

Orientation to Parent. For ratings 1–4, assure that the ratings apply to the negative reactions of the child to person rather than to the apparent activity in which the person is engaging. For example, the child may be negative to having some maintenance (nose-wipe, diaper change) but not negative to the provider of the maintenance.

It may be helpful to see this continuum as not one of emotional tone (negative–positive) but as one of avoidance–approach behaviors. A child can be quite upset and still approach or show a gesture of wanting to be picked up, held, or the like.

(1) Actively negativistic, struggling, aggressive, strongly avoiding, fleeing, or withdrawn
(2) Frowning, fussing, or low-level negativism
(3) Wary, hesitant, passively resistant, avoidant
(4) Sobered, disapproving, turning away, stilling, perfunctory negative acts
(5) Indifferent or ignoring
(6) Acceptant in a passive sense; can be bland in facial expression but compliant in interaction; spectator
(7) Positive (friendly, eager, smiling) participation; approachful, reactive
(8) Excited, eager, responsive participation
(9) Very strongly oriented, demanding; possessive of interaction (can be negative)

Cooperativeness.

(1) *Actively* resists all suggestions or requests
(2) Generally does not cooperate; complies with one or two suggestions
(3) *Actively* refuses one or two suggestions; *or* ignores suggestions about half the time
(4) Generally responsive (but there is still occasional passive resistance or ignoring)
(5) Responds to or accepts the situation in a passive way; neither cooperative nor resistant in manner
(6) Responds both passively and actively; may sometimes seem to enjoy the give-and-take with the mother
(7) In general, seems to enjoy the give-and-take with the mother throughout the session
(8) Between 7 & 9
(9) Eagerly enters into suggested activities

Goal Directedness (Purposeful Activity). Emphasis is on persistence in trying to achieve a goal (within context of task, activity, or structured situation). For example, a child may achieve a goal after only one try. If this is the only time he attempts a goal-directed effort, he will receive a low score. Another child may try throughout the entire session to accomplish one task—this can earn a high score. Consider how many opportunities for goal directedness, as well as child's actual performance during activities.

Note that a child may be involved in goal-directed behavior without necessarily exhibiting this characteristic. For example, whenever the child is engaging in nonfocused behavior, the mother actively provides direction.

Goal directedness may include a social goal (i.e., getting mother's attention) as well as object-oriented goals.

(1) No evidence of directed effort
(2) Makes an occasional attempt at a goal-directed action; does not repeat attempts—only tries once and gives up
(3) Makes a few attempts at a goal, but shows no interest in carrying to completion
(4) Between 3 & 5
(5) More persistent attempts at achieving goal; may try a number of times but will quit if unsuccessful
(6) Occasionally attempts a goal when repeated efforts are necessary
(7) *Persistent* efforts to reach goal or solve a problem (but does not always achieve goal)
(8) Sees a task through to completion most of the time
(9) Compulsive absorption with a task until it is solved

Sounds Banging.

(1) No interest in using toys or other objects for the purpose of making noise
(2) Occasional interest in banging
(3) About half the toys will be used for banging, at least once, to "try it out."
(4) Banging occurs frequently or for part of the time with every toy
(5) Noisemaking is clearly an interest in and of itself; child spends almost the entire session banging something

Difficultness. In general, child is:

(1) Very easy to deal with (not difficult at all)
(2) Rarely difficult
(3) Average (occasional periods of difficultness)
(4) Somewhat difficult
(5) Extremely difficult

APPENDIX B

CAP Environmental Measures

The environmental measures are described briefly in Chapter 4 and in more detail in Chapter 5. Two of the major measures, the Family Environment Scale (FES) and the Home Observation for Measurement of the Environment (HOME), are published and references are given. We list the items of the HOME only to indicate our revisions that permit quantitative as well as dichotomous scoring. The three sources of environmental information are parental self-report, tester observations, and combined tester observations and interviews. The environmental measures are organized accordingly in this appendix.

I. Parental Self-Report

Family Environment Scale (FES; Moos, 1974). [Prior to the first-year visit, both mothers and fathers complete Form R of the FES. We altered the true–false format to a 5-point scale: *strongly disagree, somewhat disagree, in between, somewhat agree,* and *strongly agree.*]

II. Tester Observations

Ecological Ratings. [The tester rates the following items on the basis of conditions observed during the first- and second-year visits; a rating of 3 represents an average score]

1 *Noise Levels*

   (a) External sources of noise (e.g., airports, freeways, neighbors, quiet countryside)

                                                                                             1 2 3 4 5

   (b) Internal sources of noise (e.g., voice levels, appliances, TV, radio)   1 2 3 4 5

   (c) Acoustical quality of rooms (due to ceiling height, carpeting, insulated draperies, acoustical ceiling)   1 2 3 4 5

2 *Global Ratings of Home Environment*

   (a) Visual–aesthetic rating   1 2 3 4 5

   (b) Imageability (weak vs. strong images in home; presence of objects that differentiate this home from others)   1 2 3 4 5

   (c) Coloring   1 2 3 4 5

       Number of Colors   1 2 3 4 5

   (d) Spatial arrangement of furniture   1 2 3 4 5

   (e) Cleanliness   1 2 3 4 5

   (f) Vegetation inside house   1 2 3 4 5

   (g) Outdoor space available to child (e.g., backyard)   1 2 3 4 5

   (h) Brightness/darkness of house from artificial lighting (note number of "hidden" fixtures, etc.)

                                                                                             1 2 3 4 5

   (i) Amount of sunlight (note number of windows, how densely house is placed, sky lights, etc.)

                                                                                       1 2 3 4 5

   (j) Precious objects, or easily destroyed objects, within child's reach (e.g., plants, precious china, valuable books)   1 2 3 4 5

   (k) Dangerous objects within child's reach (e.g., electrical outlets, pesticides under the sink, drugs)

                                                                                  1 2 3 4 5

3 *Global Ratings of Neighborhood*

   (a) Public contact   1 2 3 4 5

   (b) Smog, pollution in neighborhood   1 2 3 4 5

   (c) Density of neighborhood—neighborhood crowding (people per residential acre) 1 2 3 4 5

4 *Humidity*

   (a) Humidity level   1 2 3 4 5

   (b) Source of humidity (circle one):

       1. With hot air; pan inside duct
       2. Humidifier separate from heating system
       3. Vaporizer or aquariums
       4. None

5 *Heating* (circle one in each group)
   (a) Type of heating:
       1. Central
       2. Floor furnace
       3. Space heaters
   (b) Type of heating:
       1. Hot air with ducts
       2. Hot water with radiators (or convectors)
       3. Steam (old houses only)
   (c) Type of fuel:
       1. Gas
       2. Oil
       3. Coal
       4. Electric
       5. Solar
   (d) Air conditioning:
       1. Yes
       2. No
   (e) Temperature: 1   2   3   4   5
                                                                       Cold   Hot

III. Tester Observations–Interviews

A. *Home Observation for Measurement of the Environment* (HOME; Caldwell
   & Bradley, 1978). [At both the first- and second-year visits, we modified the
   HOME in such a way as to permit us to score it in the traditional dichotomous
   manner as well as in a quantitative manner that we hoped would capture more
   of the variability in middle-class homes. Because this involves changing the
   wording of the HOME items, the modified items are listed below. Incidents
   are counted whenever possible, and ratings are made on a 5-point scale in
   which a score of 0 represents *rarely or never* and a score of 4 represents *very
   often.*]

I. Emotional and Verbal Responsivity of Mother

1. Mother spontaneously vocalizes to child during visit (exclude scolding).
   (Count)   _____
2. Mother responds to child's vocalizations with a vocal or verbal response.
   (Count)   _____
3. Mother tells child the names of objects during visit or says name of
   person or object in a "teaching" style. (Count)   _____
4. Mother's speech is distinct, clear, and audible to interviewer.   Yes   No
5. Mother initiates verbal interchanges with observer—asks questions,
   makes spontaneous comments. (Rate)   0   1   2   3   4
6. Mother expresses ideas freely and easily and uses statements of
   appropriate length for conversation (e.g., gives more than brief answers).   Yes   No

**7. Mother permits child to engage in "messy" types of play. (Rate: Score of 2 = occasionally)   0 1 2 3 4

  8. Mother spontaneously praises child's qualities or behavior during visit. (Count)   _____

  9. When speaking of or to child, mother's voice conveys positive feeling. (Rate)   0 1 2 3 4

 10. Mother caresses or kisses child during visit. (Count)   _____

 11. Mother shows positive emotional responses to praise of child offered by visitor. (Rate)   0 1 2 3 4

II. Avoidance of Restriction and Punishment

 12. Mother shouts at child during visit. (Count)   _____
 13. Mother expresses overt annoyance with or hostility toward child. (Count)   _____
 14. Mother slaps or spanks child during visit. (Count)   _____
**15. Mother reports that physical punishment occurred during the past week. (Count)   _____
 16. Mother scolds or derogates child during visit. (Count)   _____
 17. Mother interferes with child's actions or restricts child's movements during visit. (Count)   _____
 *18. Books present and visible. (Count)   _____
 *19. Family has pets. (Score 1 for unresponsive pets—e.g., goldfish; 2 for at least one cuddly pet.)   0 1 2 3 4

III. Organization of Physical and Temporal Environment

**20. When mother is away, care is provided by how many different substitutes. (Count)   _____
**21. Someone takes child into grocery store at least once a week on the average.   Yes No
**22. Child gets out of house how many times a week? (Count)   _____
**23. How often is child taken to doctor's office or clinic for checkups and preventive health care? (Count)   _____
**24. Child has a special place in which to keep his toys and "treasures."   Yes No
 25. Child's play environment appears safe and free of hazards.   Yes No

IV. Provision of Appropriate Play Materials

 *26. How many muscle activity toys or pieces of equipment. (Count)   _____
 *27. How many push or pull toys. (Count)   _____
 *28. Child has stroller or walker, kiddie car, scooter, or tricycle. (Count)   _____
 29. Mother provides toys or interesting activities for child during the interview. (Rate)   0 1 2 3 4
 *30. Provides learning equipment appropriate to age—mobile, table and chairs, high chair, play pen. (Count)   _____
 *31. Provides learning equipment appropriate to age—cuddly toy or role-playing toy. (Count)   _____
 *32. Provides eye–hand coordination toys—items to go in and out of receptacle, fit-together toys, beads. (Count)   _____

*33. Provides eye–hand coordination toys that permit combinations—stacking or nesting toys, blocks or building toys. (Count) _____

*34. Provides toys for literature and music (books, records, toy musical instruments, jack-in-box). (Count) _____

V. Maternal Involvement with Child

35. Mother tends to keep child within visual range and to look at child. (Rate)   0 1 2 3 4

**36. Mother "talks" to child while doing her work. (Rate)   0 1 2 3 4

*37. Mother consciously encourages developmental advance. (Rate)   0 1 2 3 4

*38. Mother invests "maturing" toys with value via her attention. (Rate)   0 1 2 3 4

**39. Mother structures child's play periods. (Rate)   0 1 2 3 4

*40. Mother provides toys that challenge child to develop new skills. (Count) _____

VI. Opportunities for Variety in Daily Stimulation

**41. How much caregiving does father provide?

0	1	2	3	4
once a week or less	every other day	once a day (less than an hour)	1–2 hours a day	more than 2 hours per day

**42. How many times per week does mother spend time with child with books?

0	1	2	3	4
less than once a week	at least once a week	every other day	every day	more than once a day

**43. How many meals does child eat with mother and father per day? _____

**44. How many times a month do relatives (or close friends) visit or do they visit relatives or friends? (Count) _____

**45. How many books of his own does child have? (Count) _____

*May require an interview probe unless can be observed.

**Will require interview probe unless mother mentions spontaneously.

B. *Variety of Objects* [interview with mother during first- and second-year visits]

1. Gross motoric objects (count) _____
2. Fine motoric objects (count) _____
3. Cuddly objects (count) _____
4. Cognitive (count child's own books) _____
5. Musical objects—records, toy instruments, musical toys (count) _____
6. Artistic objects—e.g., crayons (count) _____

C. *Restriction* [count during first- and second-year visits]

1. Restricted by mother from approaching or interacting with experimenter _____
2. Restricted from "messy" play (esp. food) _____
3. Restricted from dangerous situations (e.g., electrical outlets) _____
4. Restricted from precious objects _____
5. Restricted from rooms in house _____
6. Restricted by physical holding against child's will _____

D. *Complexity and Responsiveness of Objects* [based on objects the infant is observed to touch during the first-year visit only].

Complexity: A rating of 3 represents an average score.

1. Tactile variety   1 2 3 4 5
2. Variety in colors   1 2 3 4 5

Responsiveness (object's capacity to respond contingently to the infant's manipulation; includes household objects and toys): Count objects . . .

1. with moving parts (inner or outer)   _____
2. with reflected image   _____
3. that change shape and contour (by bending, crumpling, squashing, etc.)   _____
4. that make noise (i.e., noises inherent in object)   _____

E. *Social Contact* [count based on interview with mother]

First- and second-year visits:

1. Number of people living in home   _____
2. Number of children same age as proband in neighborhood   _____
3. Number of hours mother works outside of home   _____

Second-year visit only:

4. Total number of babysitters proband has seen   _____
5. Times per month parent has babysitters   _____
6. Number of neighborhood children proband plays with   _____
7. Number of children played with all together   _____
8. Number of regular playmates (at least once a month)   _____
9. Number of people including child with whom proband eats breakfast, lunch, and dinner _____

APPENDIX C

CAP Adult Measures

As described in Chapter 4, all CAP adults—biological parents, adoptive parents, and nonadoptive (control) parents—complete the same 3-hour test booklet. For archival purposes, this appendix contains the unpublished parts of the booklet. Tests are listed in order of their administration. For the cognitive tests, we provide only the instructions and examples of the items because the 96 pages of tests would be too expensive to reproduce and because most of the tests are copyrighted.

The following preliminary instructions appear on the front cover of the test booklet:

PLEASE DO NOT OPEN THE BOOKLET YET. Timing is critical for many of the tests, so it is important that everyone begins at the same time.

Most instructions will be given through use of a tape recording. This phase will begin shortly.

BREAKS. There will be two breaks—one approximately every 45 minutes—with refreshments. Please let us know if there is anything we can do to make you more comfortable.

IF YOU NEED HELP, or if you have a question, please let the test administrator know. We can help with clarifying instructions but, of course, cannot help with specific test items.

MANY TIME LIMITS ARE SHORT. You are not expected to finish all items on a test. Just work at your most efficient rate, and don't worry about unfinished items.

The instructions given on the first page of the booklet are as follows:

Please work only on those pages numbered with an "S." The "S" pages are concerned with describing yourself, your environment and your experiences in the past as well as the present. Please consider each question and answer honestly. Time is limited, however, so do not spend too much time on any single question. If you have a problem understanding or answering any question, please let the examiner know.

PLEASE BE ASSURED THAT ALL INFORMATION IS FOR RESEARCH PURPOSES ONLY AND IS REQUIRED BY LAW TO BE KEPT CONFIDENTIAL.

Following these instructions are "S" pages 2 through 33, which are printed on blue paper to distinguish this section of the test booklet from the section that contains the cognitive tests.

Handedness (S-2)

Circle one

1. Which hand are you using to write with right now?   left   right
2. Which hand do you eat with?   left   right   either
3. Which hand do you use to throw a ball at a target?   left   right   either
4. Which hand do you hold scissors in to cut paper or cloth?   left   right   either
5. If you lit a match, which hand would you hold the match in?   left   right   either
6. Which hand would you hold a tennis or badminton racquet in?   left   right   either
7. If you thread a needle, which hand would hold the thread?   left   right   either
8. Which hand do you use to brush your teeth?   left   right   either
9. If you hammered a nail, which hand would hold the hammer?   left   right   either
10. When you remove a lid from a jar, which hand holds the lid?   left   right   either
11. Indicate if any of the following individuals are (or were) *left-handed*:

    The other parent of the child: Yes _____   No _____   Don't know _____
    Your father: Yes _____   No _____   Don't know _____
    Your mother: Yes _____   No _____   Don't know _____

    Your brothers: How many left-
                   handed?   _____
                   How many right-
                   handed?   _____
                   Don't know   _____
    Your sisters: How many left-
                   handed?   _____
                   How many right-
                   handed?   _____
                   Don't know   _____

Smoking (S-3)

With respect to smoking, are you an ex-smoker, a smoker, or a non-smoker? Please select Box A, Box B, or Box C, and answer the questions in that box.

BOX A
Ex-smoker

_____ I am an ex-   I used to smoke: (check one or more)
smoker.   _____ cigarettes _____ pipes _____ cigars
(Please read   Ex-smokers: *Please skip to page S-4.*
Box A.)

BOX B
Smoker

_____ I am a   I presently smoke: (check one or more)
smoker.   _____ cigarettes _____ pipes _____ cigars
(Please read   Smokers: *Please skip to page S-5.*
Box B.)

BOX C
Non-smoker (check one only)

_____ I am a non-   1. _____ I have never smoked cigarettes, pipes or cigars.
smoker.   2. _____ I have tried these a few times but never continued.
(Please read   3. _____ I smoke no more than once or twice a month.
Box C.)   Non-smokers: *Please skip to page S-6.*

This Page is for Ex-Smokers Only (S-4)

1. At what age did you start smoking tobacco?

	5–10 yrs.	11–15 yrs.	16–20 yrs.	21–25 yrs.	over 26 yrs.
cigarettes	_____	_____	_____	_____	_____
cigars	_____	_____	_____	_____	_____
pipes	_____	_____	_____	_____	_____

2. How much did you smoke in a day?
   cigarettes (for example, ½ pack a day): _____
   cigars (for example, 3 cigars a day):   _____
   pipes (for example, 3 pipefuls a day):   _____
3. How long did you smoke?

	0–1 yr.	1–5 yrs.	6–10 yrs.	11–20 yrs.	over 20 yrs.
cigarettes	_____	_____	_____	_____	_____
cigars	_____	_____	_____	_____	_____
pipes	_____	_____	_____	_____	_____

4. Check the appropriate box which describes what and how you smoked:
   cigarettes: _____ mentholated   _____ nonmentholated
               _____ filtered   _____ nonfiltered
               _____ smoke inhaled   _____ smoke not inhaled
   cigars: _____ smoke inhaled   _____ smoke not inhaled
   pipes: _____ smoke inhaled   _____ smoke not inhaled
5. How long has it been since you smoked or used tobacco?

	0–1 yr.	1–5 yrs.	6–10 yrs.	11–20 yrs.	over 20 yrs.
cigarettes:	_____	_____	_____	_____	_____
cigars:	_____	_____	_____	_____	_____
pipes:	_____	_____	_____	_____	_____

6. Why did you stop smoking? _____

Ex-smokers: Please go on to page S-6

This Page is for Smokers Only (S-5)

1. At what age did you start smoking tobacco?

	5–10 yrs.	11–15 yrs.	16–20 yrs.	21–25 yrs.	over 26 yrs.
cigarettes	_____	_____	_____	_____	_____
cigars	_____	_____	_____	_____	_____
pipes	_____	_____	_____	_____	_____

2. How much do you presently smoke per day?
   cigarettes (for example, ½ pack a day): _____
   cigars (for example, 3 cigars a day): _____
   pipes (for example, 3 pipefuls a day): _____
3. How long have you been smoking tobacco?

	0–1 yr.	1–5 yrs.	6–10 yrs.	11–20 yrs.	over 20 yrs.
cigarettes	___	___	___	___	___
cigars	___	___	___	___	___
pipes	___	___	___	___	___

4. Check the appropriate box which describes what and how you smoke *now*:
   cigarettes: ___ mentholated   ___ nonmentholated
               ___ filtered   ___ nonfiltered
               ___ smoke inhaled   ___ smoke not inhaled
   cigars: ___ smoke inhaled   ___ smoke not inhaled
   pipes: ___ smoke inhaled   ___ smoke not inhaled
5. Check the appropriate box which describes what and how you smoked *in the past*:
   cigarettes: ___ mentholated   ___ nonmentholated
               ___ filtered   ___ nonfiltered
               ___ smoke inhaled   ___ smoke not inhaled
   cigars: ___ smoke inhaled   ___ smoke not inhaled
   pipes: ___ smoke inhaled   ___ smoke not inhaled

Smokers: Please go on to page S-6

16 PF (1967–68 Edition)—Form A (S-6 through 15)

[Two pages of examples and instructions are followed by 187 16 PF items with 3-point rating scales.]

Musical Interest (S–16)

Do you sing or play a musical instrument? If yes, please answer the following questions. If no, please go on to the next page.

1. Which instrument or instruments do you play? Or do you sing? _____
2. How long have you played each instrument? Or sung? _____
3. How often do you play or sing (for example, once a day)? _____
4. Do you take lessons or are you self taught? _____
5. Do you usually read music or do you play or sing "by ear"? _____
6. How well do you play or sing? ___ very much of an amateur
                                 ___ an amateur, but have some talent
                                 ___ medium level; not good enough to do it for money, but not bad for an amateur
                                 ___ could sing or play in a professional capacity
7. Do you have "perfect pitch"? ___ yes
                                 ___ no
                                 ___ don't know

Interests and Talents (S–17)

Instructions

For each of the following activities, please rate how interested you are (that is, how much you like to do it) and how talented you are (that is, how well you can do it). A rating of "1" means that you are not at all interested or talented; a rating of "5" means that you are very interested or talented. Circle your rating.

	How interested are you?					How talented are you?				
	not at all				very much	not at all				very much
Artistic										
Music	1	2	3	4	5	1	2	3	4	5
Writing	1	2	3	4	5	1	2	3	4	5
Drawing, painting, sculpture, etc.	1	2	3	4	5	1	2	3	4	5
Acting, drama, ballet, etc.	1	2	3	4	5	1	2	3	4	5
Other (specify): _____	1	2	3	4	5	1	2	3	4	5
Physical Activity										
Baseball	1	2	3	4	5	1	2	3	4	5
Basketball	1	2	3	4	5	1	2	3	4	5
Football	1	2	3	4	5	1	2	3	4	5
Soccer	1	2	3	4	5	1	2	3	4	5
Racquet games (tennis, etc.)	1	2	3	4	5	1	2	3	4	5
Running	1	2	3	4	5	1	2	3	4	5
Skiing	1	2	3	4	5	1	2	3	4	5
Swimming	1	2	3	4	5	1	2	3	4	5
Other (specify): _____	1	2	3	4	5	1	2	3	4	5
Domestic and Mechanical Arts										
Cooking, baking, etc.	1	2	3	4	5	1	2	3	4	5
Sewing, knitting, embroidery, etc.	1	2	3	4	5	1	2	3	4	5
Gardening	1	2	3	4	5	1	2	3	4	5
Carpentry, metalwork, etc.	1	2	3	4	5	1	2	3	4	5
Mechanical, automotive, etc.	1	2	3	4	5	1	2	3	4	5
Other (specify): _____	1	2	3	4	5	1	2	3	4	5
Other Interests (please specify)										
_____	1	2	3	4	5	1	2	3	4	5
_____	1	2	3	4	5	1	2	3	4	5
_____	1	2	3	4	5	1	2	3	4	5
_____	1	2	3	4	5	1	2	3	4	5

Television and Reading (S–19)

1. How many magazines do you read each month? (circle one)
   none   1–2   3–6   7–10   over 10
2. How many books do you read each month? (circle one)
   none   1–2   3–6   7–10   over 10
3. Estimate how many books you presently have in your home: (circle one)
   0–50   51–100   101–200   201–500   over 500

4. About how many hours a week do you usually watch television? (circle one)

never	1–5	5–10	10–20	over 20
watch	hours	hours	hours	hours

5. Below are listed different kinds of shows that are presented on television. Please indicate about how often you watch each kind by putting a number next to it. Rate *each* one as:

$$1 = almost\ always$$
$$2 = frequently$$
$$3 = occasionally$$
$$4 = rarely$$
$$5 = never$$

____ Daytime serials   ____ Movies
____ Quiz and game shows   ____ Comedy series
____ Cartoons   ____ Drama or adventure series
____ Newscasts   ____ Variety–entertainment shows
____ Talk shows   ____ Documentary (such as National Geographic specials)
____ Sports

Miscellaneous (S-20 and 21)

1. How many brothers and sisters do you have? ____ brothers
   ____ sisters

2. During most of your childhood, to age 15 years old, where did you live?
   ____ rural farm or town, population under 2500
   ____ small city (population under 50,000)
   ____ metropolitan area (population 50,000 to 500,000)
   ____ large metropolitan area (population over 500,000)

3. With whom did you live most of the time up to age 15 years?
   ____ both mother and father
   ____ mother only
   ____ father only
   ____ other (please specify) _____

4. Who made most of the decisions until you were age 15 years?
   ____ mother
   ____ father
   ____ both equally

5. From what ethnic group are your parents?

	Caucasian	Afro-American	Oriental	Mexican-American	Other (specify)
Mother:					
Father:					

6. From what ethnic group is the other parent of your child?
   ____ Caucasian   ____ Afro-American
   ____ Mexican-American   ____ Oriental
   ____ Other (please specify) _____

7. How many hours of sleep do you average per night (average number of hours)? ____

8. How many cups of coffee (with caffeine) do you usually drink per day (average number of cups)? ____

9. How much alcohol do you consume on the average?

	4 or more per day	2–3 per day	1 per day	1 per week	less than 1 per week
Beer (number of cans or bottles)	_____	_____	_____	_____	_____
Wine (number of glasses)	_____	_____	_____	_____	_____
"Hard" liquor (number of shots)	_____	_____	_____	_____	_____

10. When was the last time you drank . . . (for example: about *one day* ago) . . .

        beer?   about _____ ago

        wine?   about _____ ago

    "hard" liquor? about _____ ago

11. What is your birthdate? _____

                          month   day   year

12. What is your height? ____ feet ____ inches

13. What is your weight? ____ pounds

14. How long does it usually take you to get to sleep?

less than 5 minutes	5–15 minutes	15–30 minutes	30–60 minutes	over an hour
_____	_____	_____	_____	_____

15. How well do you usually sleep?

    _____ very soundly, never wake up

    _____ soundly, wake up only once

    _____ "light" sleeper, wake up several times

    _____ very "light" sleeper, sleep fitfully, wake up often

16. How often do you usually catch colds? (for example: once a month) _____

Survey of *Your* Personality (S-22)

Please rate your behavior by circling one of the numbers following each item. No item will apply to you in every situation, but try to consider your usual behavior. Please answer quickly and honestly—there are no right or wrong answers.

	strongly disagree				strongly agree
I make friends very quickly.	1	2	3	4	5
I like to keep busy all the time.	1	2	3	4	5
I like to plan things way ahead of time.	1	2	3	4	5
I often feel insecure.	1	2	3	4	5
I have trouble controlling my impulses.	1	2	3	4	5
It takes a lot to get me mad.	1	2	3	4	5
I usually prefer to do things alone.	1	2	3	4	5
I often feel as if I'm bursting with energy.	1	2	3	4	5
I often feel like crying.	1	2	3	4	5
I always like to see things through to the end.	1	2	3	4	5
I am known as hot-blooded and quick-tempered.	1	2	3	4	5
I am very sociable.	1	2	3	4	5
I like to wear myself out with exertion.	1	2	3	4	5
I am easily frightened.	1	2	3	4	5
There are many things that annoy me.	1	2	3	4	5

I have many friends.	1	2	3	4	5
I'll try anything once.	1	2	3	4	5
When I do things, I do them vigorously.	1	2	3	4	5
When displeased, I let people know it right away.	1	2	3	4	5
When I get scared, I panic.	1	2	3	4	5
I usually seem to be in a hurry.	1	2	3	4	5
I yell and scream more than most people my age.	1	2	3	4	5
I tend to be impulsive.	1	2	3	4	5
I tend to be a loner.	1	2	3	4	5
I am almost always calm—nothing ever bothers me.	1	2	3	4	5

Occupations (S–23)

1. Please describe *only* the occupation or occupations that you have *right now* and indicate the number of years that you have worked full-time or part-time at each occupation. Please list the type of business (for example, restaurant, insurance, department store) and your specific job (for example, manager, salesperson, clerk, homemaker).
   Present occupation(s):

	Type of Business	Your Specific Job	Full-time Years	Part-time Years
A.	_____	_____	_____	_____
B.	_____	_____	_____	_____
C.	_____	_____	_____	_____

2. Please list as many of the occupations that you have had in the past that you can remember, and the approximate number of years that you have worked at these occupations. Begin at "A" with your most recent previous occupation not counting those listed above.
   Past occupation(s):

	Type of Business	Your Specific Job	Number of Years
A.	_____	_____	_____
B.	_____	_____	_____
C.	_____	_____	_____
D.	_____	_____	_____

3. Do you expect to change your present occupation within the next 4 years? ____ NO ____ YES ____ MAYBE
   If YES or MAYBE, please indicate the occupation or the exact type of work you expect to do:
   _____ type of business
   _____ specific job
4. What is your father's occupation?
   _____ type of business
   _____ specific job

Survey of *the Other Parent's* Personality (S-24)

Please rate the behavior of *the other parent* by circling one of the numbers following each item. No item will apply in every situation, but try to consider the other parent's usual behavior. Please answer quickly and honestly—there are no right or wrong answers.

In the blanks, please say *the other parent's* name when reading the item.

	strongly disagree			strongly agree	
_____ makes friends very quickly.	1	2	3	4	5
_____ likes to keep busy all the time.	1	2	3	4	5
_____ likes to plan things way ahead of time.	1	2	3	4	5
_____ often feels insecure.	1	2	3	4	5
_____ has trouble controlling impulses.	1	2	3	4	5
It takes a lot to make _____ mad.	1	2	3	4	5
_____ usually prefers to do things alone.	1	2	3	4	5
_____ often seems to be bursting with energy.	1	2	3	4	5
_____ often cries.	1	2	3	4	5
_____ always likes to see things through to the end.	1	2	3	4	5
_____ is known as hot-blooded and quick-tempered.	1	2	3	4	5
_____ is very sociable.	1	2	3	4	5
_____ likes to get worn out with exertion.	1	2	3	4	5
_____ is easily frightened.	1	2	3	4	5
There are many things that annoy _____.	1	2	3	4	5
_____ has many friends.	1	2	3	4	5
_____ will try anything once.	1	2	3	4	5
When doing things, _____ does them vigorously.	1	2	3	4	5
When displeased, _____ lets people know it right away.	1	2	3	4	5
When scared, _____ panics.	1	2	3	4	5
_____ usually seems to be in a hurry.	1	2	3	4	5
_____ yells and screams more than most people that age.	1	2	3	4	5
_____ tends to be impulsive.	1	2	3	4	5
_____ tends to be a loner.	1	2	3	4	5
_____ is almost always calm—nothing seems to bother _____.	1	2	3	4	5

Education (S-25)

1. What is the highest grade of regular school completed (for example, 3 years of high school) . . .
   _____ by the other parent?
   _____ by you?
   _____ by your mother?
   _____ by your father?
2. Are you currently attending school? ____ yes ____ no
   If *yes*, how much school do you expect to complete? _____
   If *no*, do you have plans to return to school? ____ yes ____ no

Religion (S-25)

1. What religion were you raised in? (Do not enter "Christian," "Protestant," etc. Be more specific.) _____
2. What religion do you presently practice? (If none, enter "none.") _____

3. How often did you attend religious service in the past year?

_____ every week

_____ at least once a month

_____ less than once a month

_____ not at all in the past year

Headaches (S-26 and 27)

Please answer the following questions about headaches for yourself, your mother and your father by checking the appropriate answers.

	you	mother	father
Frequently get headaches? yes	_____	_____	_____
no	_____	_____	_____
don't know	_____	_____	_____

If you, your mother, or your father frequently get headaches, please answer the following questions *for that person only.*

	you	mother	father
How often? every day	_____	_____	_____
twice a week	_____	_____	_____
once a week	_____	_____	_____
once a month	_____	_____	_____
don't know	_____	_____	_____
How troublesome are they when they hit?			
noticeable, but no bother	_____	_____	_____
can't do some things	_____	_____	_____
can't do much	_____	_____	_____
incapacitated, can't do anything	_____	_____	_____
don't know	_____	_____	_____
Where do they hurt?			
whole head	_____	_____	_____
eyes and nose mostly	_____	_____	_____
right side of head	_____	_____	_____
left side of head	_____	_____	_____
don't know	_____	_____	_____
Do eyes water and nose run when the headaches strike?			
yes	_____	_____	_____
no	_____	_____	_____
don't know	_____	_____	_____
Does the head throb as if something is squeezing it again and again?			
yes	_____	_____	_____
no	_____	_____	_____
don't know	_____	_____	_____
Do the eyes have problems like blurred vision, focusing problems, or seeing "shooting stars?"			
yes	_____	_____	_____
no	_____	_____	_____
don't know	_____	_____	_____
What time of day do the headaches usually hit?			
morning	_____	_____	_____
afternoon	_____	_____	_____
evening	_____	_____	_____
night	_____	_____	_____

How long do they usually last?
  1 hour   _____ _____ _____
  2–3 hours   _____ _____ _____
  half a day   _____ _____ _____
  1 day   _____ _____ _____
  2–3 days   _____ _____ _____
  a week   _____ _____ _____
How old when headaches started?
  age   __yrs. __yrs. __yrs.
  don't know   _____ _____ _____
Had them in the last six months?
  yes   _____ _____ _____
  no   _____ _____ _____
  don't know   _____ _____ _____
Has medicine (other than aspirin) been prescribed for the headaches?
  yes   _____ _____ _____
  no   _____ _____ _____
  don't know   _____ _____ _____

Food Preference (S-27)

People vary a lot in their likes and dislikes for particular foods. Please indicate what you think of the following types of food by rating the following foods. Please use the following key for your ratings:

KEY: Don't know (haven't tasted this food):   0
      I like it very much: 1
      I like it a little: 2
      No preference, I can take it or leave it: 3
      I dislike it a little: 4
      I strongly dislike it, never eat it: 5

Fried eggs: _____	Radishes (raw): _____	Watermelon: _____
Grapefruit: _____	Cooked cabbage: _____	Beef steak: _____
Bean soup: _____	Cottage cheese: _____	Veal chops: _____
Chili: _____	Swiss cheese: _____	Liver: _____
Chicken: _____	Canned salmon: _____	Chocolate: _____
Tea: _____	Lamb or mutton: _____	Buttermilk: _____
Cucumber: _____	Raw tomatoes: _____	Raw onion: _____

Fears & Foibles (S-28 and 29)

1. Nearly everyone does some silly things that make no sense. Please answer the following questions as honestly as possible.

  Can you walk in crowds without feeling   _____ no   _____ yes
  nervous?

    If no, how afraid of crowds are you?   _____ very much, can't go in them
                                          _____ quite a bit, avoid them if possible
                                          _____ a bit, but I don't mind them

  Can you go in elevators without feeling   _____ yes   _____ no
  nervous?

If no, how afraid are you?   _____ very much, can't go in them
                                           _____ quite a bit, avoid them if possible
                                           _____ a bit, but I don't mind them

Can you fly in airplanes without feeling   _____ yes   _____ no
nervous?
If no, how afraid are you?   _____ very much, can't go in them
                                           _____ quite a bit, avoid them if possible
                                           _____ a bit, but I don't mind it

Comments about your fear of crowds or elevators or airplanes:

_____

_____

_____

2. We often do some things over and over, even though we know it doesn't make sense, but we feel nervous if we don't do it—for example, checking gas or lights in the house over and over, or washing hands even if they're not dirty.
   Do you do any little things like this? _____ yes _____ no
   Comments (please include when it started): _____

   _____

   Does your mother or father do anything like this: _____ yes _____ no
   Comments: _____

   _____

3. Have you, your mother, or your father ever had something like epilepsy (convulsive seizures)?
   _____ yes _____ no
   If yes, please describe:_____

   Who? _____ you _____ mother _____ father
   When started? _____ years old.
   Lose consciousness? _____ yes _____ no
   On medication? _____ yes _____ no
      If yes, kind of medication: _____
   Do you know what caused seizures? _____ yes _____ no
      If yes, please describe: _____

Would you be willing to participate in future research of this type? _____ yes _____ no
Comments: _____

_____

	Happy		Not happy, not sad		"Has the blues," depressed
How would most people describe your usual mood?	1	2	3	4	5
How would you describe your usual mood?	1	2	3	4	5
How would you describe your mother's usual mood?	1	2	3	4	5
How would you describe your father's usual mood?	1	2	3	4	5
How often do you get really "blue" or "depressed?"	_____ once a day _____ week _____ month _____ 3 mo. _____ ½ yr.				

What do you do when you get very depressed? _____
_____
_____

Motion-Sickness (S-29)

Some people become sick to their stomach while traveling in a car, boat, or airplane. This is called "motion-sickness." Little is known about the reasons why some persons are easily affected while others are not.

1. Have you ever been carsick? _____ yes _____ no
   If yes, how often? _____ long rides only _____ short rides
   _____ every time I ride in cars
   do you still get carsick? _____ yes _____ no
2. Have you ever taken a boat ride longer than an hour?
   _____ yes _____ no
   If yes, did you get seasick? _____ yes _____ no
3. Have you ever made a trip on a commercial air line?
   _____ yes _____ no
   If yes, were you sick during the trip? _____ yes _____ no
4. Would you get sick if you rode on some of the rides at fairgrounds or amusement parks? Check your answers below:

	Yes	No	Don't know	Never rode on one
Would you get sick. . .				
. . . on a merry-go-round?	___	___	___	___
. . . on a ferris wheel?	___	___	___	___
. . . on a roller coaster?	___	___	___	___
. . . swinging on a swing?	___	___	___	___

Questions Related to Speech Problems (S-30 and 31)
(Please answer by circling "yes" or "no")

1. Do you have a history of a stuttering or stammering problem?	Yes	No
2. Do/did you have a definite problem with any of the following:		
a. Saying certain sounds or words?	Yes	No
(Such as your name, or "Hello")		
b. Talking to people in authority?	Yes	No
(A teacher or boss)		
c. Getting words out or getting started speaking?	Yes	No
d. Catching your breath while speaking?	Yes	No
3. Have you ever been considered a "fast talker"?	Yes	No
4. Has there ever been a problem with gaps or hesitancy in your speech?	Yes	No

B. Family History
   1. Have any of your brothers ever stuttered?   Yes No
      If yes, how many stutter? _____
   2. Have any of your sisters ever stuttered?   Yes No
      If yes, how many stutter? _____
   3. Did either of your parents ever stutter?   Yes No
      If yes, who? _____
   4. As far as you know, is there anyone else (uncle, cousin, nephew, etc.) in your   Yes No

C. Speech History

If you have answered "yes" to any of the preceding questions, please answer all the following questions.

	Relation					
	Self	Brother(s)	Sister(s)	Father	Mother	Other relative (please specify): _____
1. At what age did the speech problem begin?	_____	_____	_____	_____	_____	_____
2. Was there any accident, illness or family disruption at the time the speech problem started? Include disorders such as cerebral palsy, epilepsy, brain injury, etc. If yes, describe: _____	_____	_____	_____	_____	_____	_____
3. Was a speech therapist ever seen for an evaluation or therapy?	_____	_____	_____	_____	_____	_____
If no, was any formal diagnosis of stuttering ever done?	_____	_____	_____	_____	_____	_____
4. Is the speech problem still present?	_____	_____	_____	_____	_____	_____
If no, what was the age of improvement?	_____	_____	_____	_____	_____	_____

Medical and Developmental History (S-32 and 33)

	Never	Less than once a year	About once a year	About once a month	Once a week	Daily
1. How often do you experience. . .						
Trouble breathing?	_____	_____	_____	_____	_____	_____
Rapid or pounding heartbeat?	_____	_____	_____	_____	_____	_____
Spells of nervousness?	_____	_____	_____	_____	_____	_____
Dizziness?	_____	_____	_____	_____	_____	_____

Loss of memory (amnesia)?	___	___	___	___	___	___
Loss of feeling or sensation in a part of the body?	___	___	___	___	___	___
Loss of vision or blurred vision?	___	___	___	___	___	___
Loss of hearing?	___	___	___	___	___	___
Loss of appetite?	___	___	___	___	___	___
Large changes in weight?	___	___	___	___	___	___
Nausea or stomach pains?	___	___	___	___	___	___
Vomiting?	___	___	___	___	___	___
Miss school or work because of illness?	___	___	___	___	___	___
Take medicine for nervous or emotional problems?	___	___	___	___	___	___

For Women	Never	Less than once a year	About once a year	Several times each year
Have you had any difficulty with your menstrual periods?	___	___	___	___
Menstrual cramping?	___	___	___	___
Irregular periods?	___	___	___	___
Excessive bleeding?	___	___	___	___
Several months without a period?	___	___	___	___

2. Does it seem to you that you are sick a lot more than most people? ___ yes ___ no
3. While you were living at home, did your parents spend time in the hospital because of physical illness?
   father: ___ no ___ yes—how long? _____
   mother: ___ no ___ yes—how long? _____
4. Has either of your parents been hospitalized or taken medicine for nervous or emotional problems?
   father: ___ no ___ yes—describe: _____
   mother: ___ no ___ yes—describe: _____
5. Has either of your parents ever had problems related to excessive use of alcohol?
   father: ___ no ___ yes—describe: _____
   mother: ___ no ___ yes—describe: _____
6. Did you ever live in a foster home? ___ no ___ yes
7. Do you have trouble controlling your temper? ___ no ___ yes
8. Were you ever in a fight during your junior high or high school years? How many times?
   ___ yes ___ once or twice ___ 5–10 times
   ___ more than 10 times ___ no
9. Did you frequently skip school? ___ no ___ yes
10. Did you ever run away from home overnight or longer? ___ no ___ yes
11. How strong is your desire to "keep on the move," or to move from place to place without settling down?
    ___ not at all ___ sometimes ___ most of the time

STOP HERE. PLEASE DO NOT WORK ON ANY PAGES OTHER THAN THE BLUE ONES IN
THE FRONT OF THIS TEST BOOKLET.

Cognitive Tests

As mentioned earlier, we cannot reproduce the cognitive tests because they are too lengthy (96 pages) and most are copyrighted. However, in order to provide a clearer picture of the content of the tests, the instructions and a sample item for each test are presented here.

PMA Vocabulary

In each row, circle the word which means the same or nearly the same as the underlined word. There is *only one* correct choice in each line.

1. <u>moist</u>   curt   humane   damp   moderate

HFSC Picture Memory—Immediate Recognition

In this test you are asked to look *for 45 seconds* at 40 objects pictured on the following two pages. Then, on a signal from the test administrator, you will be asked to turn the page and to show how many objects you can remember. Only circle those objects that are *exactly the same* as the ones shown before, because wrong answers will be subtracted from your score. If you make a mistake, don't bother to erase, just cross out the picture that should not be circled and continue with the test.

ETS Things Categories

This is a test to see how many things you can think of that are alike in some way. In the test you will be given a *new topic* for each of the two parts and you will have 3 minutes for each.

The category is "round." Go ahead and write all the *things that are often round*.

ETS Card Rotations

Each problem in this test consists of a figure on the left of a line and 8 figures on the right. You are to decide whether each of the 8 cards on the right shows the same side of the figure or the opposite side. Put a plus (+) on each figure that shows the same side and a minus (−) if it shows the opposite side. You will have 3 minutes for each of the 2 pages of this test.

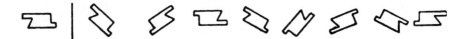

ETS Subtraction and Multiplication

This is a test to see how quickly and accurately you can subtract and multiply. Your score on this test will be the number of problems solved correctly. You will have *2 minutes* for each of the two parts of this test.

Subtract:

89	52	60	51	85	18	49	83	42	68
-60	-48	-39	-28	-23	-11	-37	-57	-23	-47

Multiply:

73	41	69	29	16	63	60	52	85	36
x 8	x 5	x 3	x 9	x 8	x 8	x 4	x 4	x 6	x 7

ETS Word Beginnings and Endings

This is a test of your ability to think of as many words as you can that begin with one letter and end with another. For the two parts of the test you will be given *different* first and last letters. You will have *3 minutes* for each part.

Write as many words as you can that *start with S* and *end with P*.

HFSC Picture Memory—Delayed Recognition

A little while ago you were asked to memorize two pages of pictured objects. On the following two pages, some of those pictures appear again. When the test administrator tells you to turn the page, please *circle* those pictures you remember seeing before.

PMA Pedigrees

Look at the chart for the answers to the questions below.

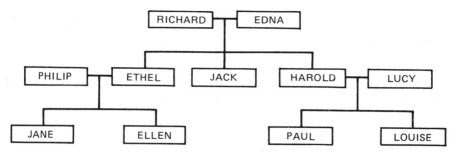

Now answer these questions by looking at the chart, and *circling* the right answer.

1. How many nephews has Harold?

0   1   2   3   4

ETS Hidden Patterns

How quickly can you recognize a figure that is hidden among other lines? This test contains many rows of patterns. In each pattern you are to look for the figure shown below:

The figure must always be in this position, not on its side or upside down. Your task is to *circle* each pattern in which the figure appears. Your score on this test will be the number circled correctly minus the number circled incorrectly. Work as quickly as you can without sacrificing accuracy. You will have 2 minutes for each of the two parts of this test.

Minnesota Paper Form Board

In this test you are asked to draw a line, or lines, showing where the figure on the left should be cut to form the pieces on the right. Sometimes you have to be careful to do this without flipping any of the pieces over. Please don't spend too much time on any item. If you don't find the correct answer after a reasonable time, move on to the next item.

Raven's Progressive Matrices

On every page in this test there is a pattern with a piece missing. Each time you have to decide which of the pieces below is the correct piece to complete the pattern. When you have found the right one, circle its number with your pencil.

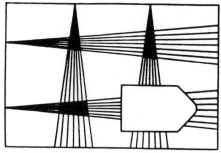

Remember, there is only <u>one</u> best answer

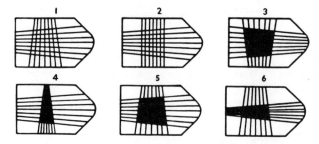

Names and Faces—Immediate Recall

In this test you are asked to look for *one minute* at 16 people with their first names. Try to remember the names of the people. On a signal from the test administrator, you will be asked to turn the page where you will see the people in a different order *without* their names. You will be asked to remember their names and write them under the photo.

Beth

Rose

Tom

Kay

ETS Vocabulary

This is a test of your knowledge of word meanings. In each row, circle the word which means the same or nearly the same as the underlined word. There is *only one* correct choice in each line.

<u>salubrious</u>   mirthful   indecent   salty   mournful   healthful

ETS Identical Pictures

How fast can you match a given object? This is a test of your ability to pick the correct object quickly. At the left of each row is an object. To the right are five test objects one of which matches the object at the left. Your score on this test will be the number of objects circled correctly minus a fraction of the number circled incorrectly. Work as quickly as you can without sacrificing accuracy. You will have *1½ minutes* for each of the two parts of this test.

Colorado Perceptual Speed Test

This is a test to see how quickly you can find matching groups of letters and numbers. You see below several lines of letter and number groups. Look at the group on the left of the colon (:). Now, find the exact copy of that group in the four choices on the other side. *Circle the exact copy.* You will have one minute for each of the two parts.

rckl: lrkc   rckl   rkcl   klcr

Names and Faces—Delayed Recall

A little while ago you were asked to memorize the names of 16 people. On the following page, the people appear again. When the test administrator tells you to turn the page, please write their names under their photos.

References

Adler, J. (1976). The sensing of chemicals by bacteria. *Scientific American, 234*, 40–47.

Allport, G. W. (1937). *Personality: A psychological interpretation*. New York: Holt.

Anastasi, A. (1961). *Psychological testing*. New York: Macmillan.

Anderson, L. D. (1939). The predictive value of infancy tests in relation to intelligence at five years. *Child Development, 10*, 203–212.

Andrews, G., Schonell, M., & Tennant, C. (1977). The relationship between physical, psychological, and social morbidity in a suburban community. *American Journal of Epidemiology, 105*, 324–329.

Baker, L. A. (1983). *Bivariate path analysis of verbal and nonverbal abilities in the Colorado Adoption Project*. Unpublished doctoral dissertation, University of Colorado, Boulder.

Baker, L. A., DeFries, J. C., & Fulker, D. W. (1983). Longitudinal stability of cognitive ability in the Colorado Adoption Project. *Child Development, 54*, 290–297.

Bates, J. E. (1980). The concept of difficult temperament. *Merrill-Palmer Quarterly, 26*, 299–319.

Bayley, N. (1949). Consistency and variability in the growth of intelligence from birth to eighteen years. *Journal of Genetic Psychology, 75*, 165–196.

Bayley, N. (1955). On the growth of intelligence. *American Psychologist, 10*, 805–818.

Bayley, N. (1969). *Manual for the Bayley Scales of Infant Development*. New York: Psychological Corporation.

Bayley, N. (1970). Development of mental abilities. In P. H. Mussen (Ed.), *Carmichael's manual of child psychology* (3rd ed., Vol. I). New York: Wiley.

Bayley, N., & Schaefer, E. S. (1964). Correlations of maternal and child behaviors with the development of mental abilities: Data from the Berkeley Growth Study. *Monographs of the Society for Research in Child Development, 29*(6, Serial No. 97).

Beckwith, L. (1971). Relationships between attributes of mothers and their infants' IQ scores. *Child Development, 42*, 1083–1097.

Bell, R. Q. (1968). A reinterpretation of the direction of effects in socialization. *Psychological Review, 75*, 81–95.

Bentovim, A. (1970). The clinical approach to feeding disorders of childhood. *Journal of Psychosomatic Medicine, 14*, 267–276.

Bloom, B. S. (1964). *Stability and change in human characteristics*. New York: Wiley.

Bohman, M. (1970). *Adopted children and their families*. Stockholm: Proprius.

Bohman, M., & Sigvardsson, S. (1978). An 18-year, prospective, longitudinal study of adopted boys. In J. Anthony, C. Koupernick, & C. Chiland (Eds.), *The child in his family: Vulnerable children*. London: Wiley.

Bouchard, T. J. (1983, June). *Traits and the concepts of convergence and divergence in the development of human personality*. Paper presented at the Fourth International Congress on Twin Studies, London, England.

Bowlby, J. (1951). *Maternal care and mental health*. Geneva: World Health Organization.

Bradley, R. H., & Caldwell, B. M. (1980). The relation of home environment, cognitive competence, and IQ among males and females. *Child Development, 51*, 1140–1148.

Bradley, R. H., Caldwell, B. M., & Elardo, R. (1979). Home environment and cognitive development in the first 2 years: A cross-lagged panel analysis. *Developmental Psychology, 15*, 246–250.

Brandon, S. (1970). An epidemiological study of eating disturbances. *Journal of Psychosomatic Medicine, 14*, 253–257.

Brooks, J., & Weintraub, M. (1976). A history of infant intelligence testing. In M. Lewis (Ed.), *Origins of intelligence: Infancy and early childhood*. New York: Plenum.

Burks, B. (1928). The relative influence of nature and nurture upon mental development: A comparative study of foster parent-foster child resemblance and true parent-true child resemblance. *Twenty-Seventh Yearbook of the National Society for the Study of Education*, Part 1, 219–316.

Burt, C. L. (1949). The structure of the mind: A review of the results of factor analysis. *British Journal of Educational Psychology, 19*, 100–111, 176–199.

Buss, A. H., & Plomin, R. (1975). *A temperament theory of personality development*. New York: Wiley-Interscience.

Buss, A. H., & Plomin, R. (1984). *Temperament: Early developing personality traits*. Hillsdale, NJ: Erlbaum.

Caldwell, B. M., & Bradley, R. H. (1978). *Home Observation for Measurement of the Environment*. Little Rock: University of Arkansas.

Caldwell, B. M., & Herscher, L. (1964). Mother-infant interaction during the first year of life. *Merrill-Palmer Quarterly, 10*, 119–128.

Cameron, J., Livson, N., & Bayley, N. (1967). Infant vocalizations and their relationship to mature intelligence. *Science, 157*, 331–333.

Caplan, B., & Kinsbourne, M. (1976). Baby drops the rattle: Asymmetry of duration of grasp by infants. *Child Development, 47*, 532–534.

Carey, W. B. (1983). The effect of general medical illness and its treatment on development and behavior: Acute minor illness. In M. D. Levine, W. B. Carey, A. C. Crocker, & R. T. Gross (Eds.), *Developmental behavioral pediatrics*. Philadelphia: Saunders.

Carey, W. B., & McDevitt, S. C. (1978). Revision of the Infant Temperament Questionnaire. *Pediatrics, 61*, 735–739.

Carter-Saltzman, L. (1980). Biological and sociocultural effects on handedness: Comparison between biological and adoptive families. *Science, 209*, 1263–1265.

Casler, L. (1976). Maternal intelligence and institutionalized children's developmental quotients: A correlational study. *Developmental Psychology, 12*, 64–67.

Cattell, P. (1960). *The measurement of intelligence of infants and young children*. New York: Psychological Corporation.

Cattell, R. B., Eber, H. W., & Tatsuoka, M. M. (1970). *Handbook for the Sixteen Personality Factor Questionnaire (16 PF)*. Champaign, IL: Institute for Personality and Ability Testing.

Cavalli-Sforza, L. L. (1975). Quantitative genetic perspectives: Implications for human development. In K. W. Schaie, V. E. Anderson, G. E. McClearn, & J. Money (Eds.), *Developmental human behavior genetics*. Lexington, MA: Lexington Books.

Cernacek, J., & Podivinsky, F. (1971). Ontogenesis of handedness and somatosensory cortical response. *Neuropsychologia, 9*, 219–231.

Chomsky, N. (1957). *Syntactic structures*. The Hague, The Netherlands: Mouton.

Chomsky, N. (1980). Rules and regulations. *Behavioral and Brain Sciences, 3,* 1–15.

Claeys, W. (1973). Primary abilities and field-independence of adopted children. *Behavior Genetics, 3,* 323–338.

Clarke, A. M., & Clarke, A. D. B. (1976). *Early experience: Myth and evidence.* New York: The Free Press.

Cloninger, C. R., Rice, J., & Reich, T. (1979). Multifactorial inheritance with cultural transmission and assortative mating. III. Family structure and analysis of separation experiments. *American Journal of Human Genetics, 31,* 366–388.

Cohen, J. (1977). *Statistical power analysis for the behavioral sciences.* New York: Academic Press.

Cohen, J., & Cohen, P. (1975). *Applied multiple regression/correlation analysis for the behavioral sciences.* New York: Halstead Press.

Cohen, J., & Cohen, P. (1983). *Applied multiple regression/correlation analysis for the behavioral sciences* (rev. ed.). New York: Halstead Press.

Colby, M. R. (1941). *Problems and procedures in adoption* (Children's Bureau Publication No. 262). Washington, DC: U.S. Government Printing Office.

Coll, C. G., Kagan, J., & Reznick, J. S. (1984). Behavioral inhibition in young children. *Child Development, 55,* 1005–1019.

Corley, R. P., DeFries, J. C., Kuse, A. R., & Vandenberg, S. G. (1980). Familial resemblance for the Identical Blocks Test of spatial ability: No evidence for X linkage. *Behavior Genetics, 10,* 211–215.

Crowe, R. (1974). An adoption study of antisocial personality. *Archives of General Psychiatry, 31,* 785–791.

Crowell, D. H. (1967). Infant motor development. In Y. Brackbill (Ed.), *Infancy and early childhood.* New York: Free Press.

Crumpacker, D. W., Cederlöf, G., Friberg, L., Kimberling, W. J., Sörensen, S., Vandenberg, S. G., Williams, J. C., McClearn, G. E., Grevér, B., Iyer, H., Krier, M. J., Pedersen, N. L., Price, R. A., & Roulette, I. (1979). A twin methodology for the study of genetic and environmental control of variation in human smoking behavior. *Acta Geneticae Medicae et Gemellogiae, 28,* 173–195.

Daniels, D., Plomin, R., & Greenhalgh, J. (1984). Correlates of difficult temperament in infancy. *Child Development, 55,* 1184–1194.

DeFries, J. C. (1975). Commentary on "Quantitive genetic prespectives: Implications for human development," by L. L. Cavalli-Sforza. In K. W. Schaie, V. E. Anderson, G. E. McClearn, & J. Money (Eds.), *Developmental human behavior genetics.* Lexington, MA: Lexington Books.

DeFries, J. C., Ashton, G. C., Johnson, R. C., Kuse, A. R., McClearn, G. E., Rashad, M. N., Vandenberg, S. G., & Wilson, J. R. (1976). Parent–offspring resemblance for specific cognitive abilities in two ethnic groups. *Nature, 261,* 131–133.

DeFries, J. C., Gervais, M. C., & Thomas, E. A. (1978). Response to 30 generations of selection for open-field activity in laboratory mice. *Behavior Genetics, 8,* 3–13.

DeFries, J. C., Hegmann, J. P., & Weir, M. W. (1966). Open-field behavior in mice: Evidence for a major gene effect mediated by the visual system. *Science, 154,* 1577–1579.

DeFries, J. C., Johnson, R. C., Kuse, A. R., McClearn, G. E., Polovina, J., Vandenberg, S. G., & Wilson, J. R. (1979). Familial resemblance for specific cognitive abilities. *Behavior Genetics, 9,* 23–43.

DeFries, J. C., Kuse, A. R., & Vandenberg, S. G. (1979). Genetic correlations, environmental correlations, and behavior. In J. R. Royce & L. P. Mos (Eds.), *Theoretical advances in behavior genetics.* Alphen aan den Rijn, The Netherlands: Sijthoff & Noordhoff.

DeFries, J. C., & Plomin, R. (1978). Behavioral genetics. *Annual Review of Psychology, 29,* 473–515.

DeFries, J. C., Plomin, R., Vandenberg, S. G., & Kuse, A. R. (1981). Parent–offspring resemblance for cognitive abilities in the Colorado Adoption Project: Biological, adoptive, and control parents and one-year-old children. *Intelligence, 5,* 245–277.

DeFries, J. C., Vandenberg, S. G., & McClearn, G. E. (1976). The genetics of specific cognitive abilities. *Annual Review of Genetics, 10,* 179–207.

DeFries, J. C., Vandenberg, S. G., McClearn, G. E., Kuse, A. R., Wilson, J. R., Ashton, G. C., & Johnson, R. C. (1974). Near identity of cognitive structure in two ethnic groups. *Science, 183,* 338–339.

Deutsch, C. K., Swanson, J. M., Bruell, J. H., Cantwell, D. P., Weinberg, F., & Baren, M. (1982). Overrepresentation of adoptees in children with the attention deficit disorder. *Behavior Genetics, 12,* 231–238.

Dewey, R. (1935). *Behavior developments in infants; a survey of the literature on prenatal and postnatal activity, 1920–1934.* New York: Columbia University Press.

Dixon, L. K., & Johnson, R. C. (1980). *The roots of individuality: A survey of human behavior genetics.* Belmont, CA: Wadsworth.

Douglas, J. W. B. (1975). Early hospital admissions and later disturbances of behavior and learning. *Developmental Medicine and Child Neurology, 17,* 456–480.

Dunn, J. (1980). Individual differences in temperament. In M. Rutter (Ed.), *The scientific foundation of developmental psychiatry.* London: William Heinemann Medical Books.

Dunn, J. (1981). Feeding and sleeping. In M. Rutter (Ed.), *Scientific foundations of developmental psychiatry.* Baltimore: University Park Press.

Dunn, J., & Kendrick, C. (1982). *Siblings.* Cambridge: Harvard University Press.

Duyme, M. (1981). Les enfants abandonnes: Role des familles adoptives et des assistantes maternelles (*Monographies Francaises de Psychologie, No. 56*). Paris: Centre National de la Recherche Scientifique.

Eaves, L. J., Last, K. A., Young, P. A., & Martin, N. G. (1978). Model-fitting approaches to the analysis of human behavior. *Heredity, 41,* 249–320.

Eichorn, D. H. (1969, September). *Developmental parallels in the growth of parents and their children.* Presidential address (Division 7) presented at the meeting of the American Psychological Association, Washington, DC.

Eichorn, D. H. (1979). Physical development: Current foci of research. In J. D. Osofsky (Ed.), *Handbook of infant development.* New York: Wiley.

Elardo, R., & Bradley, R. H. (1981a). The Home Observation for Measurement of the Environment (HOME) scale: A review of research. *Developmental Review, 1,* 113–145.

Elardo, R., & Bradley, R. H. (1981b). The Home Observation for Measurement of the Environment: A comment on Zimmerman's critique. *Developmental Review, 1,* 314–321.

Emerson, R. A., & East, E. M. (1913). The inheritance of quantitative characters in maize. *University of Nebraska Research Bulletin, 2,* 5–120.

Epstein, S. (1980). The stability of behavior. II. Implications for psychological research. *American Psychologist, 35,* 790–806.

Epstein, S. (1983). Aggregation and beyond: Some basic issues in the prediction of behavior. *Journal of Personality, 51,* 360–392.

Eysenck, H. J. (1947). *Dimensions of personality.* London: Kegan, Paul, Trench, Trubner & Co.

Eysenck, H. J. (1967). *The biological basis of personality.* Springfield, IL: Thomas.

Eysenck, H. J. (1983). A biometrical–genetical analysis of impulsive and sensation seeking behavior. In M. Zuckerman (Ed.), *Biological bases of sensation seeking, impulsivity, and anxiety.* Hillsdale, NJ: Erlbaum.

Fagan, J. F. III (1973). Infants' delayed recognition memory and forgetting. *Journal of Experimental Child Psychology, 16,* 424–450.

Fagan, J. F. III (1974). Infant recognition memory: The effects of length of familiarization and type of discrimination task. *Child Development, 45,* 351–356.

Fagan, J. F. III (1982). A visual recognition test of infant intelligence. *Infant Behavior and Development, 5,* 75.

Fagan, J. F. III (in press). A new look at infant intelligence. In D. K. Detterman (Ed.), *Current topics in human intelligence.* Norwood, NJ: Ablex.

Fagan, J. F. III & Singer, L. T. (1983). Infant recognition memory as a measure of intelligence. In L. P. Lipsett (Ed.), *Advances in infancy research* (Vol. 2). Norwood, NJ: Ablex.

Falconer, D. S. (1981). *Introduction to quantitative genetics* (2nd ed.). London: Longman.

Fantz, R. L. (1964). Visual experience in infants: Decreased attention to familiar patterns relative to novel ones. *Science, 146,* 668–670.

Fantz, R. L., & Nevis, S. (1967). The predictive value of changes in visual preference in early infancy. In J. Hellmuth (Ed.), *The exceptional infant* (Vol. 1). Seattle: Special Child Publications.

Feldman, M. W., & Lewontin, R. C. (1975). The heritability hang-up. *Science, 190,* 1163–1168.

Field, T., & Greenberg, R. (1982). Temperament ratings by parents and teachers of infants, toddlers, and preschool children. *Child Development, 53,* 160–163.

Field, T., Hallock, N., Ting, G., Dempsey, J., Dabiri, C., & Shuman, H. (1978). A first-year follow-up of high risk infants: Formulating a cumulative risk index. *Child Development, 49,* 119–131.

Fillmore, E. A. (1936). Iowa tests for young children. *University of Iowa Studies in Child Welfare, 11,* 1–58.

Fisch, R. O., Bilek, M. K., Deinard, A. S., & Chang, P. N. (1976). Growth, behavioral, and psychologic measurements of adopted children: The influences of genetic and socioeconomic factors in a prospective study. *Behavioral Pediatrics, 89,* 494–500.

Freeman, D. (1983). *Margaret Mead and Samoa: The making and unmaking of an anthropological myth.* Cambridge, MA: Harvard University Press.

Freeman, F. N., Holzinger, K. J., & Mitchell, B. C. (1928). The influence of environment on the intelligence, school achievement, and conduct of foster children. *Twenty-Seventh Yearbook of the National Society for the Study of Education,* Part 1, 103–217.

Freud, S. (1949). *An outline of psycho-analysis* (J. Strachey, Trans.). London: Hogarth Press.

Fulker, D. W., & DeFries, J. C. (1983). Genetic and environmental transmission in the Colorado Adoption Project: Path analysis. *British Journal of Mathematical and Statistical Psychology, 36,* 175–188.

Fullard, W., McDevitt, S. C., & Carey, W. B. (1978). *Toddler Temperament Scale.* Unpublished manuscript, Temple University, Philadelphia.

Fuller, J. L., & Thompson, W. R. (1978). *Foundations of behavior genetics.* St. Louis, MO: C. V. Mosby.

Galton, F. (1875). The history of twins as a criterion of the relative powers of nature and nurture. *Journal of the Anthropological Institute, 6,* 391–406.

Garfinkle-Claussner, A. S. (1979). *Genetic and environmental influences on the development of Piagetian logico-mathematical concepts and other specific cognitive abilities: A twin study.* Unpublished doctoral dissertation, University of Colorado, Boulder.

Gesell, A. L. (1946). The ontogenesis of behavior. In. L. Carmichael (Ed.), *Manual of child psychology.* New York: Wiley.

Gesell, A. L. (1954). The ontogenesis of infant behavior. In L. Carmichael (Ed.), *Manual of child psychology.* New York: Wiley.

Golden, M. & Birns, B. (1975). Social class and infant intelligence. In M. Lewis (Ed.), *Origins of intelligence: Infancy and early childhood.* New York: Plenum.

Goldsmith, H. H. (1983). Genetic influences on personality from infancy to adulthood. *Child Development, 54,* 331–355.

Goldsmith, H. H., & Campos, J. J. (1982). Toward a theory of infant temperament. In R. N. Emde & R. Harman (Eds.), *The development of attachment and affiliative systems.* New York: Plenum.

Gottfried, A. W. (1984). *Measures of socioeconomic status in child development research: Data and recommendations.* Manuscript submitted for publication.

Gottfried, A. W., & Bathurst, K. (1983). Hand preference across time is related to intelligence in young girls, not boys. *Science, 221,* 1074–1076.

Gottfried, A. W., & Brody, N. (1975). Interrelationships between and correlates of psychometric and Piagetian scales of sensorimotor intelligence. *Developmental Psychology, 11,* 379–387.

Gottfried, A. E., & Gottfried, A. W. (1984). Home environment and mental development in middle-class children in the first three years. In A. W. Gottfried (Ed.), *Home environment and early cognitive development: Longitudinal research.* New York: Academic Press.

Griffiths, R. (1954). *The abilities of babies: A study in mental measurement*. New York: McGraw-Hill.

Guilford, J. P., & Fruchter, B. (1973). *Fundamental statistics in psychology and education* (5th ed.). New York: McGraw-Hill.

Hardy-Brown, K. (1981). An analysis of environmental and genetic influence on individual differences in the communicative development of fifty adopted one-year-old children. *Dissertation Abstracts International, 41*, 3025B. (University Microfilms No. 81–03, 074).

Hardy-Brown, K. (1982, June). *Communicative development in the first year of life: Genetic and environmental influences*. Paper presented at the meeting of the Behavior Genetics Association, Fort Collins, CO.

Hardy-Brown, K. (1983). Universals in individual differences: Disentangling two approaches to the study of language acquisition. *Developmental Psychology, 19*, 610–624.

Hardy-Brown, K., Plomin, R., & DeFries, J. C. (1981). Genetic and environmental influences on rate of communicative development in the first year of life. *Developmental Psychology, 17*, 704–717.

Hardy-Brown, K., Plomin, R., Greenhalgh, J., & Jax, K. (1980). Selective placement of adopted children: Prevalence and effects. *Journal of Child Psychology and Psychiatry, 21*, 143–152.

Hare, R. D., & Cox, D. N. (1978). Psychophysiological research on psychopathy. In W. H. Reid (Ed.), *The psychopath*. New York: Brunner/Mazel.

Harlow, H. F., & Harlow, M. K. (1962). Social deprivation in monkeys. *Scientific American, 207*, 136–146.

Harris, P. L. (1983). Infant cognition. In P. H. Mussen (Ed.), *Handbook of child psychology (4th ed.): Vol. II. Infancy and developmental psychobiology*. New York: Wiley.

Hauser, R. M., & Featherman, D. L. (1977). *The process of stratification: Trends and analysis*. New York: Academic Press.

Hedrick, D. L., Prather, E. M., & Tobin, A. R. (1975). *Sequenced inventory of communication development*. Seattle: University of Washington Press.

Hegvik, R. L., McDevitt, S. C., & Carey, W. B. (1982). The Middle Childhood Temperament Questionnaire. *Developmental and Behavioral Pediatrics, 3*, 197–200.

Herrnstein, R. J. (1982, August). IQ testing and the media. *The Atlantic Monthly*, pp. 68–74.

Hershov, L. (1976). Adoption. In M. Rutter & L. Hershov (Eds.), *Child psychiatry: Modern approaches*. Oxford: Blackwell Scientific Publications.

Hess, R., & Shipman, V. C. (1965). Early experience and the socialization of cognitive modes in children. *Child Development, 36*, 869–886.

Hicks, R. E., & Kinsbourne, M. (1976). Human handedness: A partial cross-fostering study. *Science, 192*, 908–910.

Hildreth, G. (1949a). The development and training of hand dominance: II. Developmental tendencies in handedness. *Journal of Genetic Psychology, 75*, 221–254.

Hildreth, G. (1949b). The development and training of hand dominance: III. Origins of handedness and lateral dominance. *Journal of Genetic Psychology, 75*, 255–275.

Ho, H-Z., Foch, T. T., & Plomin, R. (1980). Developmental stability of the relative influence of genes and environment on specific cognitive abilities during childhood. *Developmental Psychology, 16*, 340–346.

Ho, H-Z., Plomin, R., & DeFries, J. C. (1979). Selective placement in adoption. *Social Biology, 26*, 1–6.

Hollenbeck, A. R. (1978). Early infant home environments: Validation of the Home Observation for Measurement of the Environment Inventory. *Developmental Psychology, 14*, 416–418.

Hollingshead, A. B. (1975). *Four-factor index of social status*. Unpublished manuscript, Yale University, New Haven, CT.

Honzik, M. P., MacFarlane, J. W., & Allen, L. (1948). Stability of mental test performance between 2 and 18 years. *Journal of Experimental Education, 17*, 309–322.

Hoopes, J. L. (1982). *Prediction in child development: A longitudinal study of adoptive and nonadoptive families*. New York: Child Welfare League of America.

Hoopes, J. L., Sherman, E. A., Lawder, E. A., Andrews, R. G., & Lower, K. D. (1970). *A followup study of adoptions, Volume II: Post-placement functioning of adopted children*. New York: Child Welfare League of America.

Horn, J. M., Loehlin, J. C., & Willerman, L. (1979). Intellectual resemblance among adoptive and biological relatives. *Behavior Genetics, 9,* 177–207.

Housman, D., & Gusella, J. (1980). Use of recombinant DNA techniques for linkage studies in genetically based neurological disorders. In E. S. Gershon, S. Matthysse, X. O. Breakefield, & R. D. Ciaranello (Eds.), *Genetic research strategies for psychobiology and psychiatry.* Pacific Grove, CA: Boxwood Press.

Hunt, J. McV. (1961). *Intelligence and experience.* New York: Ronald Press.

Hunt, J. McV. (1979). Psychological development: Early experience. *Annual Review of Psychology, 30,* 103–143.

Hutchings, B., & Mednick, S. A. (1975). Registered criminality in the adoptive and biological parents of registered male criminal adoptees. In R. R. Fieve, H. Brill, & D. Rosenthal (Eds.), *Genetic research in psychiatry.* Baltimore, MD: Johns Hopkins Press.

Hylton, L. (1965). Trends in adoption, 1958–1962. *Child Welfare, 44,* 377–386.

Jacklin, C. N., & Maccoby, E. E. (1983). Issues of gender differentiation. In M. D. Levine, W. B. Carey, A. C. Crocker, & R. T. Gross (Eds.), *Developmental behavioral pediatrics.* Philadelphia: Saunders.

Jencks, C. (1972). *Inequality.* New York: Basic Books.

Jenkins, S., Owen, C., Bax, M., & Hart, H. (1984). Continuities of common behavior problems in preschool children. *Jounral of Child Psychology and Psychiatry, 25,* 75–89.

Jöreskog, K. G., & Sörbom, D. (1976). *LISREL III: Estimation of linear structural equation systems by maximum likelihood methods.* Chicago: International Educational Services.

Kadushin, A. (1970). *Adopting older children.* New York: Columbia University Press.

Kadushin, A. (1978). Children in adoptive homes. In H. S. Maas (ed.), *Social service research: Reviews of studies.* New York: National Association of Social Workers.

Kagan, J., & Moss, H. (1962). *Birth to maturity: A study in psychological development.* New York: Wiley.

Kaiser, H. F., Hunka, S., & Bianchini, J. C. (1971). Relating factors between studies based upon different individuals. *Multivariate Behavioral Research, 6,* 409–422.

Kamin, L. J. (1974). *The science and politics of IQ.* Potomac, MD: Erlbaum.

Kamin, L. (1981). Studies of adopted children. In H. J. Eysenck & L. Kamin (Eds.), *The intelligence controversy.* New York: Wiley-Interscience.

Kenny, D. A. (1979). *Correlation and causality.* New York: Wiley-Interscience.

Keogh, B. K. (1982). Children's temperament and teachers' decisions. In R. Porter & G. M. Collins (Eds.), *Temperamental differences in infants and young children* (Ciba Foundation Symposium 89). London: Pitman.

Klackenberg-Larsson, I., & Stensson, J. (1968). Data on the mental development during the first five years. *Acta Paediatrica Scandinavica, 4*(Suppl. 187).

Kohen-Raz, R. (1967). Scalogram analysis of some developmental sequences of infant behavior as measured by the Bayley infant scale of mental development. *Genetic Psychology Monographs, 76,* 3–21.

Kohlsaat, B., & Johnson, A. M. (1954). Some suggestions for practice in infant adoptions. *Social Casework, 35,* 91–99.

Krietzberg, V. S. (1978, April). *The development of mental abilities: A multidimensional model of intelligence in infancy.* Paper presented at the meeting of the Eastern Psychological Association, Washington, DC.

Kuse, A. R. (1977). *Familial resemblances for cognitive abilities estimated from two test batteries in Hawaii.* Unpublished doctoral dissertation, University of Colorado, Boulder.

Langinvainio, H., Kaprio, J., Koskenvuo, M., & Lonnqvist, J. (1983, June). *Finnish twins reared apart: II. Personality factors.* Paper presented at the Fourth International Congress on Twin Studies, London, England.

Lawder, E., Lower, K., Andrews, R. G., Sherman, E. A., & Hill, J. G. (1969). *A followup study of adoptions: Vol. 1. Post-placement functioning of adoption families.* New York: Child Welfare League of America.

Lawrence, E. M. (1931). An investigation into the relation between intelligence and inheritance. *British Journal of Psychology Monograph Supplements, 16,* 1–80.

Leahy, A. M. (1935). Nature–nurture and intelligence. *Genetic Psychology Monographs, 17,* 236–308.

Lerner, J. V. (1984). Temperament interaction. *Merrill-Palmer Quarterly, 30,* 177–188.

Lerner, J. V., & Lerner, R. M. (1983). Temperament and adaptation across life: Theoretical and empirical issues. In P. B. Baltes & O. G. Brim (Eds.), *Life span development and behavior* (Vol. 5). New York: Academic Press.

Lerner, J. V., Lerner, R. M., & Zabski, S. (in press). Temperament and elementary school children's actual and rated academic abilities: A test of a "goodness of fit" model. *Journal of Child Psychology and Psychiatry.*

Levine, M. D., Carey, W. B., Crocker, A. C., & Gross, R. T. (1983). *Developmental-behavioral pediatrics.* Philadelphia: Saunders.

Lewis, M. (1983). On the nature of intelligence: Science or bias? In M. Lewis (Ed.), *Origins of intelligence: Infancy and early childhood.* New York: Plenum.

Lewis, M., & Enright, M. K. (1983). *The development of mental abilities: A multidimensional model of intelligence in infancy.* Unpublished manuscript.

Lewontin, R. C. (1975). Genetic aspects of intelligence. *Annual Review of Genetics, 9,* 387–405.

Li, C. C. (1975). *Path analysis: A primer.* Pacific Grove, CA: Boxwood Press.

Littman, B. L., & Parmelee, A. H. (1978). Medical correlates of infant development. *Pediatrics, 61,* 470–474.

Locke, J. (1823). *The works of John Locke.* London: Thomas Tegg.

Loehlin, J. C. (1979). Combining data from different groups in human behavior genetics. In J. R. Royce & L. P. Mos (Eds.), *Theoretical advances in behavior genetics.* Alphen aan den Rijn, The Netherlands: Sijthoff and Noordhoff.

Loehlin, J. C. (1982). Are personality traits differentially heritable? *Behavior Genetics, 12,* 417–428.

Loehlin, J. C. (1983). John Locke and behavior genetics. *Behavior Genetics, 13,* 117–121.

Loehlin, J. C., Horn, J. M., & Willerman, L. (1981). Personality resemblance in adoptive families. *Behavior Genetics, 11,* 309–330.

Loehlin, J. C., Horn, J. M., & Willerman, L. (1982). Personality resemblance between unwed mothers and their adopted-away offspring. *Journal of Personality and Social Psychology, 42,* 1089–1099.

Loehlin, J. C., & Nichols, R. C. (1976). *Heredity, environment and personality.* Austin, TX: University of Texas Press.

Longstreth, L. E. (1980). Human handedness: More evidence for genetic involvement. *Journal of Genetic Psychology, 137,* 276–283.

Longstreth, L. E., Davis, B., Carter, L., Flint, D., Owen, J., Rickert, M., & Taylor, E. (1981). Separation of home intellectual environment and maternal IQ as determinants of child IQ. *Developmental Psychology, 17,* 532–541.

Lyon, M. E., & Plomin, R. (1981). The measurement of temperament using parental ratings. *Journal of Child Psychology and Psychiatry, 22,* 47–53.

Lytton, H., Martin, N. G., & Eaves, L. (1977). Environmental and genetical causes of variation in ethological aspects of behavior in two-year-old boys. *Social Biology, 24,* 200–211.

Maccoby, E. E., & Jacklin, C. N. (1974). *The psychology of sex differences.* Stanford: Stanford University Press.

Magnusson, D., & Endler, N. S. (Eds.). (1977). *Personality at the crossroads: Current issues in interactional psychology.* Hillsdale, NJ: Erlbaum.

Mangan, G. (1982). *The biology of human conduct: East–West models of temperament and personality.* Oxford: Pergamon Press.

Matheny, A. P. (1980). Bayley's Infant Behavior Record: Behavioral components and twin analyses. *Child Development, 51,* 1157–1167.

Matheny, A. P., & Wilson, R. S. (1981). Developmental tasks and rating scales for the laboratory assessment of infant temperament. *JSAS: Catalog of Selected Documents in Psychology, 11*, 81–82. (Ms. No. 2367)

Matheny, A. P., Wilson, R. S., Dolan, A. B., & Krantz, J. Z. (1981). Behavioral contrasts in twinships: Stability and patterns of differences in childhood. *Child Development, 52*, 579–588.

McCall, R. B. (1972). Similarity in developmental profile among related pairs of human infants. *Science, 178*, 1004–1005.

McCall, R. B. (1977). Challenges to a science of developmental psychology. *Child Development, 48*, 333–344.

McCall, R. B. (1979). The development of intellectual functioning in infancy and the prediction of later IQ. In J. D. Osofsky (Ed.), *Handbook of infant development*. New York: Wiley.

McCall, R. B. (1981). Nature–nurture and the two realms of development: A proposed integration with respect to mental development. *Child Development, 52*, 1–12.

McCall, R. B., Applebaum, M. I., & Hogarty, P. S. (1973). Developmental changes in mental performance. *Monographs of the Society for Research in Child Development, 38*(3, Serial No. 150).

McCall, R. B., Eichorn, D. H., & Hogarty, P. S. (1977). Transitions in early mental development. *Monographs of the Society for Research in Child Development, 42*(3, Serial No. 171).

McCall, R. B., Hogarty, P. S., & Hurlburt, N. (1972). Transitions in infant sensorimotor development and the prediction of childhood IQ. *American Psychologist, 27*, 728–748.

McDevitt, S. C., & Carey, W. B. (1981). Stability of ratings vs. perceptions of temperament from early infancy to 1–3 years. *American Journal of Orthopsychiatry, 51*, 342–345.

McKinley, G. M. (1940). Genetics in child adoption practice. *Child Welfare League of America Bulletin, 19*(No. 3).

McKusick, V. A. (1981). *Mendelian inheritance in man* (6th ed.). Baltimore: Johns Hopkins University Press.

McWhinnie, A. M. (1967). *Adopted children: How they grow up*. New York: Humanities Press.

Mead, M. (1928). *Coming of age in Samoa*. New York: William Morrow.

Mech, E. V. (1973). Adoption: A policy perspective. In B. M. Caldwell & H. N. Ricciuti (Eds.), *Reviews of child development research: Vol III. Child development and social policy*. Chicago: University of Chicago Press.

Menlove, F. L. (1965). Aggressive symptoms in emotionally disturbed adopted children. *Child Development, 36*, 519–532.

Metzl, M. N. (1980). Teaching parents a strategy for enhancing infant development. *Child Development, 51*, 583–586.

Mischel, W. (1968). *Personality and assessment*. New York: Wiley.

Moore, T. (1967). Language and intelligence: A longitudinal study of the first eight years. Part I. Patterns of development in boys and girls. *Human Development, 10*, 88–106.

Moos, R. H. (1974). *Preliminary manual for Family Environment Scale, Work Environment Scale, and Group Environment Scale*. Palo Alto, CA: Consulting Psychologists Press.

Moos, R. H., & Moos, B. S. (1981). *Family Environment Scale manual*. Palo Alto, CA: Consulting Psychologists Press.

Moss, H. A., & Jones, S. J. (1977). Relation between maternal attitudes and maternal behavior as a function of social class. In P. H. Leiderman, S. R. Tulkin, & A. Rosenfeld (Eds.), *Culture and infancy: Variations in human experience*. New York: Academic Press.

Mueller, C. W., & Parcel, T. L. (1981). Measures of socioeconomic status: Alternatives and recommendations. *Child Development, 52*, 13–30.

Munsinger, H. (1975). Children's resemblance to their biological and adopting parents in two ethnic groups. *Behavior Genetics, 5*, 239–254.

Nagoshi, C. T., Johnson, R. C., Ahern, F. M., Danko, G. P., Wilson, J. R., Yamamoto, L. S., Samet-Driver, J., & Vandenberg, S. G. (1982). Correlations of measures of personality and cognitive abilities within and across generations. *Behavior Genetics, 12*, 327–342.

Nelson, K. (1981). Individual differences in language development: Implications for development and language. *Developmental Psychology, 17*, 170–187.

Nelson, V. L., & Richards, T. W. (1939). Studies in mental development: III. Performance of twelve-month-old children on the Gesell schedule, and its predictive value for mental status at two and three years. *Journal of Genetic Psychology, 54,* 181–191.

Newman, J., Freeman, F., & Holzinger, K. (1937). *Twins: A study of heredity and environment.* Chicago: University of Chicago Press.

Nichols, P. L., & Broman, S. H. (1974). Familial resemblance in infant mental development. *Developmental Psychology, 10,* 442–446.

Nilsson-Ehle, H. (1908). Einige ergebnisse von Kruezungen bei Hafer und Weisen. *Botanische Notiser, 4257, 4294.*

Orvaschel, H. (1983). Maternal depression and child dysfunction: Children at risk. In B. B. Lahey & A. E. Kazdin (Eds.), *Advances in clinical child psychology* (Vol. 6). New York: Plenum.

Parkinson, J. S. (1977). Behavioral genetics in bacteria. *Annual Review of Genetics, 11,* 397–414.

Parmelee, A. H., Beckwith, L., Cohen, S. E., & Sigman, M. (1983). In J. D. Call, E. Galenson, & R. L. Tyson (Eds.), *Frontiers of infant psychiatry.* New York: Basic Books.

Pedersen, N. L., Friberg, L., Floderus-Myrhed, B., McClearn, G. E., & Plomin, R. (1983, June). *Swedish early separated twins: Identification and characterization.* Paper presented at the Fourth International Congress on Twin Studies, London, England.

Plomin, R. (1974). *A temperament theory of personality development: Parent–child interactions.* Unpublished doctoral dissertation, University of Texas, Austin.

Plomin, R. (1981). Heredity and temperament: A comparison of twin data for self-report questionnaires, parental ratings, and objectively assessed behavior. In L. Gedda, P. Parisi, & W. E. Nance (Eds.), *Progress in clinical and biological research Vol. 69B, Twin research 3, Part B. Intelligence, personality, and development.* New York: Alan R. Liss.

Plomin, R. (1982). Behavioral genetics and temperament. In R. Porter & G. M. Collins (Eds.), *Temperamental differences in infants and young children* (Ciba Foundation Symposium 89). London: Pitman.

Plomin, R. (1983a). Childhood temperament. In B. Leahy & A. Kazdin (Eds.), *Advances in clinical child psychology* (Vol. 6). New York: Plenum.

Plomin, R. (1983b). Developmental behavioral genetics. *Child Development, 54,* 253–259.

Plomin, R., & Daniels, D. (1984). The interaction between temperament and environment: Methodological considerations. *Merrill-Palmer Quarterly, 30,* 149–162.

Plomin, R., & DeFries, J. C. (1979). Multivariate behavioral genetic analysis of twin data on scholastic abilities. *Behavior Genetics, 9,* 505–517.

Plomin, R., & DeFries, J. C. (1980). Genetics and intelligence: Recent data. *Intelligence, 4,* 15–24.

Plomin, R., & DeFries, J. C. (1981). Multivariate behavioral genetics and development: Twin studies. In L. Gedda, P. Parisi, & W. E. Nance (Eds.), *Progress in clinical and biological research, Vol. 69B, Twin research 3, Part B. Intelligence, personality, and development.* New York: Alan R. Liss.

Plomin, R., & DeFries, J. C. (1983). The Colorado Adoption Project. *Child Development, 54,* 276–289.

Plomin, R., DeFries, J. C., & Loehlin, J. C. (1977). Genotype–environment interaction and correlation in the analysis of human behavior. *Psychological Bulletin, 84,* 309–322.

Plomin, R., DeFries, J. C., & McClearn, G. E. (1980). *Behavioral genetics: A primer.* San Francisco: Freeman.

Plomin, R., DeFries, J. C., & Roberts, M. K. (1977). Assortative mating by unwed biological parents of adopted children. *Science, 196,* 449–450.

Plomin, R., & Foch, T. T. (1981). Sex differences and individual differences. *Child Development, 52,* 383–385.

Plomin, R., & Kuse, A. R. (1979). Genetic differences between humans and chimps and among humans. *American Psychologist, 43,* 188–190.

Plomin, R., Loehlin, J. C., & DeFries, J. C. (in press). Genetic and environmental components of "environmental" influences. *Developmental Psychology.*

Plomin, R., & Rowe, D. C. (1977). A twin study of temperament in young children. *Journal of Psychology, 97,* 107–113.

Plomin, R., & Rowe, D. C. (1979). Genetic and environmental etiology of social behavior in infancy. *Developmental Psychology, 15,* 62–72.

Ramey, C. R., Mills, P., Campbell, F. A., & O'Brien, C. (1975). Infants's home environments: A comparison of high-risk families and families from the general population. *American Journal of Mental Deficiency, 80,* 40–42.

Ramsay, D. S. (1984). Onset of duplicated syllable babbling and unimanual handedness in infancy: Evidence for developmental change in hemispheric specialization? *Developmental Psychology, 20,* 64–71.

Ramsay, D. S., Campos, J. J., & Fenson, L. (1979). Onset of bimanual handedness in infants. *Infant Behavior and Development, 2,* 69–76.

Rao, D., Morton, N., & Yee, S. (1974). Analysis of family resemblance. II. A linear model of familial correlation. *American Journal of Human Genetics, 26,* 331–359.

Reiss, A. J. (1961). *Occupations and social status.* New York: Free Press.

Rice, T., Plomin, R., & DeFries, J. C. (1984a). Development of hand preference in the Colorado Adoption Project. *Perceptual and Motor Skills, 58,* 683–689.

Rice, T., Plomin, R., & DeFries, J. C. (1984b). *Infant precursors of adult cognitive abilities.* Unpublished manuscript.

Richman, N., Stevenson, J., & Graham, P. (1975). Prevalence of behaviour problems in 3-year-old children: An epidemiological study in a London borough. *Journal of Child Psychology and Psychiatry, 16,* 272–287.

Roberts, K. E., & Schoelkopf, J. A. (1951). Eating, sleeping, and elimination practices in a group of 2½-year-old children. *American Journal of Diseases of Childhood, 82,* 121.

Rogosa, D. (1980). A critique of cross-lagged correlation. *Psychological Bulletin, 88,* 245–258.

Rothbart, M. K., & Derryberry, D. (1981). Development of individual differences in temperament. In M. E. Lamb & A. L. Brown (Eds.), *Advances in developmental psychology* (Vol. 1). Hillsdale, NJ: Erlbaum.

Rowe, D. C. (1981). Environmental and genetic influences on dimensions of perceived parenting: A twin study. *Developmental Psychology, 17,* 203–208.

Rowe, D. C. (1983). A biometrical analysis of perceptions of family environment: A study of twin and singleton sibling kinships. *Child Development, 54,* 416–423.

Rowe, D. C., & Plomin, R. (1977). Temperament in early childhood. *Journal of Personality Assessment, 41,* 150–156.

Rowe, D. C., & Plomin, R. (1981). The importance of nonshared (E_1) environmental influences in behavioral development. *Developmental Psychology, 17,* 517–531.

Royce, J. R. (1973). The conceptual framework for a multi-factor theory of individuality. In J. R. Royce (Ed.), *Multivariate analysis and psychological theory.* New York: Academic Press.

Rushton, J. P., Brainerd, C. J., & Pressley, M. (1983). Behavioral development and construct validity: The principle of aggregation. *Psychological Bulletin, 94,* 18–38.

Sanchez, O., & Yunis, J. J. (1977). New chromosome techniques and their medical applications. In J. J. Yunis (Ed.), *New chromosomal syndromes.* New York: Academic Press.

Scarr, S. (1975). An evolutionary perspective on infant intelligence: Species patterns and individual variations. In M. Lewis (Ed.), *Origins of intelligence.* New York: Plenum.

Scarr, S. (1981, April). On the development of competence and the indeterminant boundaries between cognition and motivation: A genotype–environment correlation theory. Paper presented at the meeting of the Eastern Psychological Association, New York.

Scarr, S., & McCartney, K. (1983). How people make their own environments: A theory of genotype environment correlations. *Child Development, 54,* 424–435.

Scarr, S., Webber, P. L., Weinberg, R. A., & Wittig, M. A. (1981). Personality resemblance among adolescents and their parents in biologically related and adoptive families. *Journal of Personality and Social Psychology, 40,* 885–898.

Scarr, S., & Weinberg, R. A. (1977). Intellectual similarities within families of both adopted and biological children. *Intelligence, 1,* 170–191.

Scarr, S., & Weinberg, R. A. (1978). The influence of "family background" on intellectual attainment. *American Sociological Review, 43,* 674–692.

Schiff, M., Duyme, M., Dumaret, A., Stewart, J., Tomkiewicz, S., & Feingold, J. (1978). Intellectual status of working-class children adopted early into upper-middle-class families. *Science, 200,* 1503–1504.

Scholom, A., Zucker, R. A., & Stollak, G. E. (1979). Relating early child adjustment to infant and parent temperament. *Journal of Abnormal Child Psychology, 7,* 297–308.

Seglow, J., Pringle, M. L., Kellmer, P., & Wedge, P. (1972). *Growing up adopted.* Windsor: NFER.

Shields, J. (1962). *Monozygotic twins brought up together and apart.* Oxford, England: Oxford University Press.

Shirley, M. M. (1933). *The first two years: A study of twenty-five babies. Vol. III: Personality manifestations.* Minneapolis: University of Minnesota Press.

Siegel, L. S. (1979). Infant perceptual, cognitive, and motor behaviours as predictors of subsequent cognitive and language development. *Canadian Journal of Psychology, 33,* 382–395.

Sklar, J., & Berkov, B. (1974). Abortion, illegitimacy, and the American birth rate. *Science, 185,* 909–915.

Skodak, M. (1939). *Children in foster homes: A study of mental development.* Iowa City: University of Iowa Press.

Skodak, M., & Skeels, H. M. (1949). A final follow-up on one hundred adopted children. *Journal of Genetic Psychology, 75,* 85–125.

Snygg, D. (1938). The relation between the intelligence of mothers and of their children living in foster homes. *Journal of Genetic Psychology, 52,* 401–406.

Spearman, C. (1904). "General intelligence" objectively determined and measured. *American Journal of Psychology, 15,* 201–292.

Spearman, C. E. (1927). *The abilities of man.* London: Macmillan.

Springer, S. P., & Deutsch, G. (1981). *Left brain, right brain.* San Francisco: Freeman.

Sroufe, L. A. (1979). Socioemotional development. In J. D. Osofsky (Ed.), *Handbook of infant development.* New York: Wiley.

Stafford, R. W. (1961). Sex differences in spatial visualization as evidence of sex-linked inheritance. *Perceptual and Motor Skills, 13,* 428.

Starfield, B., & Pless, I. B. (1980). Physical health. In O. G. Brim & J. Kagan (Eds.), *Constancy and change in human development.* Cambridge, MA: Harvard University Press.

Stevenson, M. B., & Lamb, M. E. (1979). Effects of infant sociability and the caretaking environment on infant cognitive performance. *Child Development, 50,* 340–349.

Stott, L. H., & Ball, R. S. (1965). Evaluation of infant and preschool mental tests. *Monographs of the Society for Research in Child Development, 30*(3, Serial No. 101).

Stunkard, A. J., Foch, T. T., & Hrubec, Z. (1984). *The heritability of human obesity. I. Twin studies.* Manuscript submitted for publication.

Tanner, J. M. (1978). *Fetus into man: Physical growth from conception to maturity.* Cambridge, MA: Harvard University Press.

Tanner, J. M., Healy, M. J. R., Lockhart, R. D., Mackenzie, J. D., & Whitehouse, R. H. (1956). The prediction of adult body measurements from measurements taken each year from birth to 5 years. *Archives of Diseases in Childhood, 31,* 372–381.

Theis, S. V. S. (1924). *How foster children turn out.* New York: State Charities Aid Association. (Publ. No. 165).

Thomas, A., & Chess, S. (1977). *Temperament and development.* New York: Brunner/Mazel.

Thomas, A., & Chess, S. (1980). *The dynamics of psychological development.* New York: Brunner/Mazel.

Thomas, A., & Chess, S. (1982). Temperament and follow-up to adulthood. In R. Porter & G. M. Collins (Eds.), *Temperamental differences in infants and young children* (Ciba Foundation Symposium 89). London: Pitman.

Thompson, L. A., & Fagan, J. F. (1983, July). *A family study of infant recognition memory.* Paper presented at the meeting of the Behavior Genetics Association, London, England.

Thompson, L. A., Plomin, R., & DeFries, J. C. (in press). Parent–infant resemblance for general and specific cognitive abilities in the Colorado Adoption Project. *Intelligence*.

Thorndike, E. L. (1905). Measurement of twins. *Archives of Philosophy, Pyschology, and Scientific Methods, 1*, 1–64.

Thorndike, R. L. (1940). Constancy of the IQ. *Psychological Bulletin, 37*, 167–187.

Thurstone, L. L. (1938). Primary mental abilities. *Psychometric Monographs, 1*.

Toussieng, P. W. (1962). Thoughts regarding the aetiology of psychological difficulties in adopted children. *Child Welfare, 41*, 59–65.

Triseliotis, J. (1970). *Evaluation of adoption policy and practice*. Edinburgh: University of Edinburgh.

Tsuang, M. T., Crowe, R. R., Winokur, G., & Clancy, J. (1977). Relatives of schizophrenics, manics, depressives and controls. In *Proceedings of the Second International Conference on Schizophrenia*. New York: Wiley.

Turner, G., & Optiz, J. M. (1980). Editorial comment: X-linked mental retardation. *American Journal of Medical Genetics, 7*, 407–415.

Turner, R. G., & Horn, J. M. (1977). Personality scale and item correlates of WAIS abilities. *Intelligence, 1*, 281–297.

Uzgiris, I. C., & Hunt, J. McV. (1975). *Assessment in infancy*. Urbana: University of Illinois Press.

Valadian, I., Stuart, H., & Reed, R. (1959). Patterns of illness experiences. *Pediatrics, 24*, 941–971.

Vale, J. R. (1980). *Genes, environment and behavior: An interactionist approach*. New York: Harper & Row.

Van Alstyne, D. (1929). *The environment of three-year-old children: Factors related to intelligence and vocabulary tests*. New York: Columbia University, Bureau of Publications.

Vogler, G. P., & DeFries, J. C. (1983). Linearity of offspring–parent regression for general cognitive ability. *Behavior Genetics, 13*, 355–360.

Wachs, T. D. (1979). Proximal experience and early cognitive–intellectual development: The physical environment. *Merrill-Palmer Quarterly, 25*, 3–41.

Wachs, T. D. (1983). The use and abuse of environment in behavior–genetic research. *Child Development, 54*, 416–423.

Wachs, T. D., & Gandour, M. J. (1983). Temperament, environment, and six-month cognitive–intellectual development: A test of the organismic specificity hypothesis. *International Journal of Behavioral Development, 6*, 135–152.

Wachs, T., & Gruen, G. (1982). *Early experience and human development*. New York: Plenum.

Wachs, T. D., Uzgiris, I. C., & Hunt, J. McV. (1971). Cognitive development in infants of different age levels and from different environmental backgrounds: An exploratory investigation. *Merrill-Palmer Quarterly, 17*, 283–317.

Watson, J. B. (1928). *Psychological care of infant and child*. New York: Norton.

Werner, E. E., & Bayley, N. (1966). The reliability of Bayley's revised scale of mental and motor development during the first year of life. *Child Development, 37*, 39–50.

White, B., & Watts, J. C. (1973). *Experience and environment: Major influences on the development of the young child* (Vol. 1). Englewood Cliffs, NJ: Prentice-Hall.

Whittier Social Case History Manual. (1921). California Bureau of Juvenile Research, Bulletin No. 10.

Willerman, L. (1973). Activity level and hyperactivity in twins. *Child Development, 44*, 288–293.

Wilson, J. R., DeFries, J. C., McClearn, G. E., Vandenberg, S. C., Johnson, R. C., & Rashad, M. N. (1975). Cognitive abilities: Use of family data as a control to assess sex and age differences in two ethnic groups. *International Journal of Aging and Human Development, 6*, 261–276.

Wilson, R. S. (1976). Concordance in physical growth for monozygotic and dizygotic twins. *Annals of Human Biology, 3*, 1–10.

Wilson, R. S. (1977a). Sensory–motor and cognitive development. In F. Minifie & L. Lloyd (Eds.), *Communicative and cognitive abilities: Early behavioral assessment*. Baltimore: University Park Press.

Wilson, R. S. (1977b). Twins and siblings: Concordance for school-age mental development. *Child Development, 48*, 211–223.

Wilson, R. S. (1983). The Louisville Twin Study: Developmental synchronies in behavior. *Child Development, 54,* 298–316.

Wilson, R. S., Brown, A. M., & Matheny, A. P. (1971). Emergence and persistence of behavioral differences in twins. *Child Development, 42,* 1381–1398.

Wilson, R. S., & Matheny, A. P. (1983a). Assessment of temperament in infant twins. *Developmental Psychology, 19,* 172–183.

Wilson, R. S., & Matheny, A. P. (1983b). Mental development: Family environment and genetic influences. *Intelligence, 7,* 195–216.

Witmer, H. L., Herzog, E., Weinstein, E. A., & Sullivan, M. E. (1963). *Independent adoptions: A followup study.* New York: Russell Sage Foundation.

Wittenborn, J. R. (1957). *The placement of adoptive children.* Springfield, IL: Charles C. Thomas.

Wright, S. (1931). Statistical methods in biology. *Journal of the American Statistical Association, 26*(Suppl.), 155–163.

Yarrow, L. J. (1963). Research in dimensions of early maternal care. *Merrill-Palmer Quarterly, 9,* 101–114.

Yarrow, L. J., Goodwin, M. S., Manheimer, H., & Milowe, I. D. (1973). Infancy experiences and cognitive and personality development at ten years. In S. Stone, H. T. Smith, & L. B. Murphy (Eds.), *The competent infant: Research and commentary.* New York: Basic Books.

Yarrow, L. J., & Pedersen, F. A. (1975). The interplay between cognition and motivation in infancy. In M. Lewis (Ed.), *Origins of intelligence: Infancy and early childhood.* New York: Plenum.

Yarrow, L. J., Rubenstein, J., & Pedersen, F. (1975). *Infant and environment: Early cognitive and motivational development.* New York: Wiley.

Yates, A. (1977). *Multivariate exploratory data analysis: True exploratory factor analysis.* Unpublished manuscript.

Zimmerman, M. (1981a). The Home Observation for Measurement of the Environment: A comment on Elardo and Bradley's review. *Developmental Review, 1,* 301–313.

Zimmerman, M. (1981b). The Home Observation for Measurement of the Environment: A rejoinder to Elardo and Bradley's comment. *Developmental Review, 1,* 322–329.

Author Index

Subject Index

DEVELOPMENTAL PSYCHOLOGY SERIES

continued from page ii

MARSHA B. LISS. (Editor). *Social and Cognitive Skills: Sex Roles and Children's Play*

DAVID F. LANCY. *Cross-Cultural Studies in Cognition and Mathematics*

HERBERT P. GINSBURG. (Editor). *The Development of Mathematical Thinking*

MICHAEL POTEGAL. (Editor). *Spatial Abilities: Development and Physiological Foundations*

NANCY EISENBERG. (Editor). *The Development of Prosocial Behavior*

WILLIAM J. FRIEDMAN. (Editor). *The Developmental Psychology of Time*

SIDNEY STRAUSS. (Editor). *U-Shaped Behavioral Growth*

GEORGE E. FORMAN. (Editor). *Action and Thought: From Sensorimotor Schemes to Symbolic Operations*

EUGENE S. GOLLIN. (Editor). *Developmental Plasticity: Behavioral and Biological Aspects of Variations in Development*

W. PATRICK DICKSON. (Editor). *Children's Oral Communication Skills*

LYNN S. LIBEN, ARTHUR H. PATTERSON, AND NORA NEWCOMBE. (Editors). *Spatial Representation and Behavior across the Life Span: Theory and Application*

SARAH L. FRIEDMAN AND MARIAN SIGMAN. (Editors). *Preterm Birth and Psychological Development*

HARBEN BOUTOURLINE YOUNG AND LUCY RAU FERGUSON. *Puberty to Manhood in Italy and America*

RAINER H. KLUWE AND HANS SPADA. (Editors). *Developmental Models of Thinking*

ROBERT L. SELMAN. *The Growth of Interpersonal Understanding: Developmental and Clinical Analyses*

BARRY GHOLSON. *The Cognitive-Developmental Basis of Human Learning: Studies in Hypothesis Testing*

TIFFANY MARTINI FIELD, SUSAN GOLDBERG, DANIEL STERN, AND ANITA MILLER SOSTEK. (Editors). *High-Risk Infants and Children: Adult and Peer Interactions*

DEVELOPMENTAL PSYCHOLOGY SERIES